The COLLECTED WORKS of
Catherine
MARSHALL

The COLLECTED WORKS *of*
Catherine
MARSHALL

Two Bestselling Works Complete in One Volume

To Live Again

Beyond Our Selves

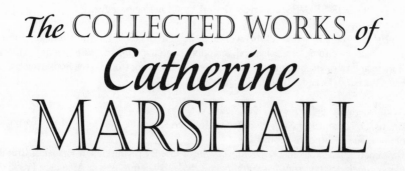

Inspirational Press • New York

Previously published in two separate volumes:

TO LIVE AGAIN, copyright © 1957 by Catherine Marshall;
renewed 1985 by Leonard E. LeSourd.
BEYOND OUR SELVES, copyright © 1961 by Catherine Marshall.

Acknowledgments for *Beyond Our Selves:*
Cairns, D.S., from *The Faith That Rebels.* Richard R. Smith, New York, N.Y., 1930. By
permission of Harper & Brothers.
Davenport, Russell, from *The Dignity of Man,* 1955. By permission of Harper & Brothers.
Gossip, Arthur John, from *The Interpreter's Bible.* By permission of Abingdon Press.
Jung, C.G. from *Modern Man in Search of a Soul.* By permission of Harcourt, Brace and
World, Inc., and Routledge and Kegan Paul, Ltd., London, England.
Kunkel, Fritz and Kickerson, Roy E., from *How Character Develops.* By permission of
Charles Scribner's Sons.
Lewis, C.S., from *Beyond Personality.* By permission of The Macmillan Company and
Geoffrey Bles, Ltd.
Moffatt, James, from *The Bible: A New Translation,* 1922, 1935, and 1950. By permission of
Harper & Brothers.
Montague, Margaret Prescott, from "Twenty Minutes of Reality," 1916, by the Atlantic
Monthly Company, Boston, Massachusetts.
Oursler, Fulton, from *Why I Know There Is a God,* 1950. Reprinted by permission of
Doubleday & Company, Inc. and Mrs. April Armstrong.
Phillips, J.B., from *The Gospels Translated into Modern English.* By permission of The
Macmillan Company and Geoffrey Bles, Ltd.
Simpson, A.B., from *The Gospel of Healing,* 1935. By permission of Christian Publications,
Inc., Harrisburg, Pennsylvania.

First Inspirational Press edition published in 1997.

Inspirational Press
A division of BBS Publishing Corporation
386 Park Avenue South
New York, NY 10016

Inspirational Press is a registered trademark of BBS Publishing Corporation.

Published by arrangement with Baker Book House.

Library of Congress Catalog Card Number: 97-73423

ISBN: 0-88486-176-7

Printed in the United States of America.

Contents

TO LIVE AGAIN

Acknowledgments

I WISH TO express my deep appreciation to Frances Jane Munsey, my efficient secretary, whose never-failing patience and good humor have constantly lightened my task; to Harlow Hoskins for his help in typing the manuscript; to Dr. Raymond I. Lindquist for the stimulus of his vigorous and able criticism; to Ruth Welty for her fine editorial suggestions; to my sister, Emma Lynn Hoskins, for her culinary help in the chapter on Evergreen Farm; to John R. Munsey for preparing the drawing of the William Penn house plan; to Samuel G. Engel and Eleanore Griffin for their suggestions on the movie chapters; and to Peter John, who continues to be my senior editor.

I am also grateful to the Fleming H. Revell Company, New York, for permission to quote from *Mr. Jones, Meet the Master* by Peter Marshall; and to Alfred A. Knopf, Inc., and the Society of Authors as the Literary Representative of the late Miss Katherine Mansfield, for permission to quote from *The Journal of Katherine Mansfield*, edited by John Middleton Murry. Finally, I should like to express my appreciation to the many friends who have graciously granted me permission to quote from their letters to me and to tell their stories.

Contents

One
Crisis

ON THE GRAY morning of January 25, 1949, my world caved in. At 8:15 A.M. my husband's tired and damaged heart stopped beating. Five minutes later the doctor called. The measured words coming through the telephone receiver were like physical blows from which I instinctively recoiled. . . . "Oh no! Not *that!*" And then a deep breath, like that of a drowning person gulping for air. . . . "How? Why? Please tell me what happened?"

The controlled voice on the other end of the phone went on with maddening deliberation, "Dr. Marshall seemed to stand the ambulance trip to the hospital quite well. Sedation soon reduced the pain in his chest and arms. There was no immediate need for oxygen. The night nurse on the floor went by his room shortly before eight o'clock this morning. Dr. Marshall seemed to be comfortable—was, in fact, sleeping. So the nurse didn't disturb him.

"Meanwhile, I telephoned one of the nurses on his case during his first attack, and she had agreed to come. Shortly after eight she came on duty. It was she who found him. . . . Dr. Marshall died in his sleep—very peacefully."

I found myself unable to speak. I was hanging on to the telephone receiver as if that small black instrument could hold me up.

"Mrs. Marshall, do you want to come down to the hospital?" the doctor asked. "What order shall I give?"

5

When I found my voice again, it sounded hollow, alien. . . . "Please—yes, I'll be right down. Don't let them move him until I get there—please."

"I assure you nothing at all will be disturbed. Mrs. Marshall, may I say—I'm *sorry*."

How can real life seem more like a dream than any dream? What is reality? Life? Death? Who can tell? A whirling head, a furiously beating heart, unseeing eyes, unsteady legs must somehow walk on into the dream, to be enveloped by it, to feel its clamminess, to protest it. . . . One must pick up life again, even though one feels as dead on the inside as a wound-up tin soldier—mechanically—setting one foot—in front of the other.

At the moment when the telephone had rung, Peter John, our nine-year-old son, had been getting ready to leave for school. He had been standing nearby and had overheard my half of the conversation with the doctor. I had replaced the telephone on its cradle, had stood there for a moment as in a daze. Then suddenly I became aware of a small blond boy there in the hall, looking at me with uncomprehending blue eyes.

Almost instantly, two thoughts surged through me—an intimation of what the news I had just heard meant for this little boy's future, and my own need to feel close to him. I knelt and impulsively pulled him into my arms.

"Peter, the doctor told me that Daddy just died." There were no tears in my voice; I was still too stunned. But Peter John burst into a flood of little-boy tears.

I knelt there holding him close, feeling the warmth of his body pressed against mine. He was quivering. Only once since babyhood had I ever seen Peter John tremble like that.

The incident came back to me so vividly. . . . As an eight-year-old, Peter John had been away to summer camp for the first time. His father and I had received a letter from him written on ruled paper in his big, round, scrawly hand:

Dear Mummy and Daddy,
I am still very homesick. Could you come and take me home before Sunday? I would like it very much. If you can't would you please come and take me home Monday.

Love,
Peter

We had kept in touch with the counselors by telephone. "Don't come," they had advised. "Write your son, but stay away from him. This often happens. He'll get over it."

But he hadn't. The homesickness had gotten worse and worse. Then he had come down with a summer cold and had landed in sick bay.

"We'll go to see how he is," his father had conceded. "But Catherine, we've got to be firm with Peter—no soft stuff now. He's got to grow up."

As soon as Peter John had seen his father in the infirmary door, he had leaped into his arms. The little figure in crumpled summer pajamas had clung around his father's neck, his legs wound around him, the blond head buried in the broad shoulder. Sobbing and quivering—even as he was now in my arms—he had said, "If—if you—love me—you'll—take—me home."

Love him? Who could have doubted it, watching that scene? The rugged-looking Scotsman, his curly hair a bit unruly . . . his blue-gray eyes moist . . . stroking the blond head with his big mechanic's hand . . . his carefully-mustered sternness melting like ice in the sun. . . .

"All right, Peter," he had said softly, the burr of his accent softened by emotion. "I understand. We'll take you home. But you are to stop crying."

"And now," I thought, as I held that same little boy in my arms, "you will never again hear that voice or feel that hand."

As I knelt there, the front door opened. It was my brother Bob and his wife Mary. I sat on the davenport in the living room beside Bob and repeated all that the doctor had said. Still there were no tears. The whole thing seemed utterly unreal. Peter dead! How could Peter be dead? Surely, God would somehow, someway, still intervene. . . .

He was not to intervene in the way I hoped, but in quite another way—equally miraculous. Just how miraculous I was not to realize until much later. I was to be led by that Power outside myself into areas beyond my knowledge, along the path that leads through and out of the Valley of the Shadow of Death. There would be rocky ledges, steep slopes, slippery places, many a fork in the road where a clear-cut decision would be required. I knew none of the trails: the Valley was untrodden country. Yet by sure steps I would be led through it. I was to discover the Lord as my Shepherd—quite literally and in many practical ways.

As soon as I could get ready, Bob and Mary drove me to the hospital. At my request, they let me go alone to Peter's room, but a young interne insisted on going up with me in the elevator. As the elevator ascended we were silent. Then as we walked up to the closed door, the interne—his eyes searching my face—asked, "Mrs. Marshall, are you really all right? Are you quite sure that you want to go in there alone?"

I nodded. He opened the door and stepped aside. "Then I'll wait for you here in the hall," he said. "Call if you need me."

I was young, had looked on death only twice before. Yet one glance at the still form on the bed and I knew that the man I loved was not there.

But the little hospital room was not empty; I was not alone. For a while there was a transcendent glory. Though I did not understand it then and cannot explain it now, I knew that Peter was near me. And beside him, another Presence, the Lord he had served through long years—years stretching back to boyhood experiences on the moors of Scotland.

"There are some things," Peter had been fond of saying from his pulpit, "that can never be proven by argument, by logic, or by reason; things that are matters of perception—not of proof. There are some things that can never be poured into the cold molds of human speech." This was exactly the case with what happened to me during that hour in the hospital room.

I was not the only one who witnessed it. As I sat by the bed, there came a soft tap on the door. Slowly it was pushed ajar, and I saw my closest friend, Alma Deane Fuller, framed in the doorway. She stood there hesitantly, wanting to be with me, yet fearful of intruding. What she saw can best be told in her own words, as she described it to me in a letter the following week:

> I don't think you have any idea how transformed you were in that hour. I have never seen you look so beautiful. The smile that was on your face was my first glimpse of the heavenly glory which surrounded every part of Peter's going. I know you well enough to know when something has been added to you, and you were unquestionably filled by a newness and a differentness, and all the love in the world was in your eyes.
>
> That little hospital room was filled with the same power that was in you. It was charged with it. I shall never be able to thank you enough for asking me to come in. It was in those moments that I learned what Christ's power over death is. Glory filled that room. . . .

Having actually experienced that glory, I thought at that moment that I would never again doubt the fact of immortality. In a deep and intuitive way, beyond argument or intellectual process, deeper than tears, transcending words—was the knowledge that human life does not end in six feet of earth.

I was also, minute by minute, learning something else . . . that our God can handle even the worst that can happen to us as finite human beings. Since Christ is beside us, no troubles that life can bring need cast us adrift. This is a knowledge which can release us from lifelong bondage to fear. So I found it.

Yet my realization of the splendor was not to last. At a precise moment, the two vivid presences withdrew. Suddenly I saw Death stripped bare, in all its ugliness. With very human eyes I saw it . . . the face of the man I loved. . . . *There's nothing pretty about death. Those who sentimentalize it, lie.* . . . Carbon dioxide escaping from the sagging jaw . . . the limp hands . . . the coldness and pallor of the flesh. . . . *No wonder they call us the white race. I never knew that skin could be that white* . . . the finality of it . . . the pathos.

Sometimes when one is walking through moments of high drama, there is a curious detachment. It is as if the mind separates itself from the emotions and stands off to observe. Was it the numbing effect of my grief that for a time gave me an aloofness that enabled me to think, *Every detail of this moment will be forever stamped on your mind—the sight of it—the sound of it. This is the raw stuff of which life—and death— are made. Now you know.*

Yet of this part of the experience I was not to speak—not for a long, long time. In reply to those who would say, "What a lovely, peaceful expression he had on his face," I could only smile and say nothing. What would have been the point of replying, "But you never saw the expression on his face. That lovely, peaceful look must have been contrived by—" No, no, I couldn't say that. . . .

Or how could one explain that, when we see death starkly, stripped of all our techniques for camouflaging it, when one knows that the beloved person has left the pathetic shell empty, then the shell becomes— well—almost repugnant?

Shivering, I rose to leave the room. I knew that this would be the last time on this earth I would look on my husband's face. An instinct stronger than reasoning, sounder than custom or convention, told me that the inner spirit had taken all the shock it could stand for a while, was standing dangerously close to an emotional precipice. So there in the hospital room, I said my last *au revoir*.

Now there was nothing to do but to walk out. My legs would obey my will and carry me out of the hospital room. I was sure they would. Had they not always obeyed me before?

I sensed that out beyond the door, out beyond the chilly hospital corridor, a new life awaited me. That was the last thing in the world I wanted. But then Peter had not wanted a new life either—not yet anyway—not at forty-six. And already he was embarked on that other adventure.

My heels tapped out a sharp rhythm on the floor. The door clicked shut behind me. Flooding my heart, pounding at my brain, were the whirling thoughts—Now you are all alone, all on your own. What does the new life hold? You are not ready to live without him. You are not trained to earn a living. How are you going to get along?

But part of the whirling thoughts were mistaken. I was not alone, not altogether on my own. It only seemed to be that way. For this was fear, natural enough under the circumstances. But deeper than fear was the sure knowledge that from the moment of Peter's death, God had taken over Peter John and me in a new way.

That this was so became quite apparent during the next few days. A Power outside myself lifted my spirit up and carried me steadily and surely through the necessary mechanics always connected with death.

Many bereaved people have experienced this. Some of them account for it simply as one result of the numbness that follows shock; others say that it is a refusal to accept reality. All of this is true. But there is more to it than that. Even emotional torpor and an inability to understand are nature's gracious gifts for the crucial moments of bereavement. They are like an anesthesia that enables one to bear the cruel wound that the spirit has sustained.

Looking back, I know that what I experienced was much more than just being stunned. God gave me added capacities. The first was the ability to think of other people and their needs. I found myself especially concerned about the void left in the congregation which Peter and I had served. Such flinging off of egocentricity was unlike me. It was something added. I was not really that mature a person.

Then there was the gift of a series of detailed instructions straight from God. It was not even necessary to ask for them. Like a child, I was taken over and managed. It was as if, at the time of Peter's death, I literally stepped into the radiant Kingdom of God on earth.

I longed to have certain friends near me. It was not necessary to wire or to telephone them. Even as I wished for them, they were on their way to Washington. There was no straining over the planning of the funeral service; all details were as clear as if they were set in type.

It was a service that included our entire congregation, Peter's friends and mine, in a way that few funerals ever do. I was aware that many of those who would be there needed to be ministered to as much as I did. Their minds were full of their loss. . . . "How are we going to get along without his leadership?" Their faith was shaken. The spiritual crisis would not have been so poignant had not Peter, through his preaching and ministering in Atlanta and then in Washington, succeeded so well in making Christ real to thousands of people, in helping them to see Him walking beside them in the hurly-burly of everyday life. "And now," they wondered; "how does Dr. Marshall's early death jibe with all that he himself believed and preached? Does his death somehow cancel everything?"

The service was at eleven o'clock on Thursday morning at the New York Avenue Presbyterian Church where Peter had served for over eleven years. I sat in my usual place—the pastor's pew—with my family around me, Peter John beside me.

My first inclination after Peter's death had been to shield Peter John as completely as possible. How much could a nine-year-old stand? Perhaps he should be sent away to a friend's or neighbor's until the services were over. Might not exposing him to this time of upheaval leave permanent scars?

Somehow I was saved from this false reasoning. Shunting him off at this time would have left far worse scars than including him. After all, child or not, he was a person in his own right, a member of our family. It was my husband who had died, but it was also Peter John's father. Our son too had emotional needs. One of them was to be loved, to know that he belonged. He needed to feel, along with the rest of us, the tenderness at the center of heartbreak and the warmth of the Christian community. That was why Peter John was sitting beside me now, solemn but dry-eyed.

The old church had never been so crowded except on an Easter Sunday morning. Downstairs in the lecture room several hundred people listened over loud-speakers. Hundreds were turned away for lack of space. Outside on the sidewalks, hundreds more stood silent and bareheaded, refusing to leave.

Government workers, Senators, Senate pageboys, the Vice President, judges, clerks, typists, secretaries, housewives, the Negro janitors of the church, the boys from the parking garage who, still in their uniforms, had slipped across the street—they were all there, fused into a unity and sweetness of spirit through which unmistakable spiritual power pulsated. In the air was a vibrancy, as of the dynamo of the Spirit of God. Yet there was nothing mawkish about it—little weeping.

That vast congregation rose and sang together as one voice. The choir, 110 young people, sang the anthem that Peter had loved best— part of Mendelssohn's "Elijah":

> O, Rest in the Lord,
> Wait patiently for Him,
> And He shall give thee
> Thy heart's desire. . . .

Several of Peter's close friends in the ministry spoke quietly—with humor here and there. How could anyone think of Peter Marshall without seeing in his mind's eye Peter's flashing smile and hearing his infectious laughter?

One of them, Ed Pruden, the pastor of Washington's First Baptist Church, later told me that the tone of the entire service was changed for him by an incident that had happened just before the service began.

Those who were to take part in the service had gathered in Peter's church study. As the hands of the clock in the bell tower moved toward eleven o'clock, Mr. Bridge, the associate minister of our church, asked the seven men to line up preparatory to their filing onto the rostrum.

He consulted a paper in his hand, "Let me see now . . . Dr. Pruden, will you go to the head of the line, please?"

There was a moment's silence. Then as Dr. Pruden moved to the front of the line, he smiled broadly. As if at a signal, several of the other ministers began to laugh.

A puzzled look crossed Mr. Bridge's face. Obviously, he could see nothing funny about what he had said. Under the circumstances, the levity seemed strangely out of place.

But as the little procession moved down the stairs and out toward the church sanctuary, Dr. Pruden hastened to explain to Mr. Bridge, "You know, once a week, if we could possibly manage it, five or six of us ministers used to have lunch together at the cafeteria just down the street. After we would get in line, pick up our trays and silverware, inevitably the same thing would happen. The group would be so engrossed in conversation that the cafeteria line would move off and leave us. Somehow, I always seemed to be the first one to see the gap in the line. Then, as unobtrusively as possible, I would rush up ahead of the others to help keep the line moving.

"But always Peter would spot me. Then his hearty laughter would ring out, 'There goes Ed to the head of the line, gang. Always afraid the food's going to run out.'

"It was just that when you said, 'Dr. Pruden, you go to the head of the line,' each of us could hear Peter's laughter. It was almost as if it were his way of saying to us, 'I see you made it again, Ed. Don't you dare go in there to my people and lead them in any service of mourning over me. I'm still very much alive, still with you—still one of the gang—and don't forget it.'"

Later in the service, Mr. Bridge said the same thing in a different way. The words he spoke were to gather significance for me in the years ahead:

> Let me say in a few words, and in very simple words, try to express what we are trying to do this morning. We are endeavoring to establish a new relationship. We have known Peter Marshall in the flesh. From now on we are to endeavor to know him in the spirit, and to know him in the spirit just as really as we have known him in the flesh. . . .
>
> Peter Marshall is still, and will continue to be one of the ministers of this church, though no longer visible to us. The fellowship we have with him will remain unbroken, and may God give us wisdom, grace and strength to join hands with him. . . .

Throughout the service I was conscious of Peter John beside me. I kept wondering what all this could possibly mean to a nine-year-old, what thoughts were going through his mind. . . . Was he perhaps remembering his birthday party less than a week before? At that time, his father had helped with an elaborate treasure hunt.

Each small guest had gone to our garage to find the beginning of the string that was to lead him to his treasure. In preparing this game, the two Peters and I had had great fun taking the strings up the stairs to the first floor, the second, under beds, behind bureaus, into the most unlikely places. In the end, we three had gotten hilarious watching one another all tangled up in string.

The party had been on January 21; four days later Peter was dead. And now—each year when Peter John's birthday came around, he and I would be thinking of that other anniversary. I reached out for his small hand. . . .

Then the service was over. The family and I walked down the long center aisle of the church behind the casket. While I was intensely aware of certain details of the scene evolving around me—in particular of the love on the faces of certain close friends as I passed—in another way I was moving as in a dream. Part of my mind and my emotions were still numb, still blocked off.

Of course, the numbness—the dream—could not last. For we, still in the flesh, are clay with feet of clay. And clay belongs to earth. By the following Friday, eight days after the funeral, I had come back to earth with a thud. Peter's death was real—final. There would be no reprieve from the cruel fact. With this realization, the long pull of the healing of a desolated heart had begun.

On that Friday, it was my mother who caught the first fury of my rebellion. She and Dad were still with us; they had planned to stay for ten days.

With my descent to earth had come physical exhaustion. Mother insisted that I go to bed. But there was no need to leave me alone because I could not sleep. So Mother sat in the little needle-point rocker near my bed and wisely let me pour out my torrent of thoughts and the surging emotions that all but engulfed me.

First, I sought to blame myself. Had I done everything possible to save Peter? Had it really been God's will that Peter die? Or was this just another failure on my part? Had I, for example, somehow failed to fulfill the conditions of answered prayer?

Then I remembered that I had been annoyed with my husband for a time and childishly petulant on the last Sunday of his life.

On the way home from church, we had the radio on. Just as Peter had brought the car to a halt before our front door, a radio announcer had mentioned the approaching St. Valentine's Day.

Peter had reached across for my hand. . . . "Will you be my valentine, Catherine?" he had asked gaily.

And I had withdrawn my hand and ruthlessly crushed his small moment of gaiety by replying sarcastically, "Oh, sure! I'll be your valentine, having a gay time all by myself here in Washington while you're in Des Moines. I hear you decided to accept that invitation, too."

For a passing moment a look of pain had crossed his face. The remembrance of that look stung and hurt me now.

Between sobs I told Mother of the episode and verbally whipped myself, "How could I have been like that? What on earth got into me? I'm supposed to be a woman—not a child. How could I have been so immature, so disgustingly petty?"

Other people too were caught up in my rebellion. Grief fanned into flame my resentment against all those who had known of Peter's heart condition and yet had persisted in heaping demands on him. These demands had snowballed from 1947 on, after he had become Chaplain of the Senate.

"How often I've stood by," I said to Mother, "and heard someone say to Peter in one moment, 'Dr. Marshall, please don't overdo. You just must take care of yourself. We need you so . . .' And then in the very next moment, plead with him to speak to their pet group. Their organization was always different; their group should always be the exception. How selfish can human beings be?"

Then having struck out at people, I lashed out again at God. "Why? Why did it have to end this way?" I asked bitterly. "Have Peter and I been duped? Has everything that Peter preached been pious nonsense? If God is a God of love and has the power to help us, why didn't He do something about Peter's heart?"

Sorely troubled, Mother watched me and groped for words that might help. Yet she knew her words would make little difference at the moment. It was enough that she was there to listen. She knew that every bitter thought—against myself and other people and God—needed to come up and out.

She understood my need for an answer to my agonizing question . . . where is the God of love who cares about the individual in what has happened? She knew that if this question were not faced and answered, there could be no healing of my bruised heart; that without an answer, I would then be forced either to flee life or to live it on a busy-busy level, dragging an anesthetized spirit after me. She knew that my great need was still to be oriented to God, centered in Him, so that my life would have an anchor. But she also knew that this could not be forced.

"In God's own time," she told me quietly, "you will get God's answers."

I was a particularly ill-equipped widow. Death had never before invaded my immediate family circle. Moreover, I had consistently evaded it as a fact of human experience. Even as a minister's wife, I had exhibited an ingenuity approaching genius about side-stepping funerals.

It had begun back in childhood. One of my remarks on this subject had become something of a classic in our family.

When I was six, I had an uncle who was killed one December 22 in a tragic automobile accident. Uncle John was to be buried on Christmas afternoon. The noon meal just before the funeral, at which quite a number of relatives were gathered, was anything but gay.

I am told that after I listened for some time to the solemn grown-up talk about funeral plans, suddenly—during a lull in the conversation— I announced in a clear, firm voice, "Well, I'm not going. I never have been able to get anything out of funerals." That immediately broke up the solemnity.

While this was a silly childish remark, it nevertheless revealed the emotional coloration that everything connected with death had for me even then. It was an attitude that I carried over into adult life.

Peter saw this in me. Once during his first convalescence, he had insisted on telling me about his business affairs. I remembered the scene all too well.

"Get a pencil and a piece of paper, Catherine," he had ordered. "There are some facts you must have down for ready reference in case anything should happen to me."

I had been almost defiant. "I'll put this stuff down to humor you. But I can't stand to hear you talk that way. Nothing is going to happen to you. Don't be foolish. . . ."

My husband's blue-gray eyes had crinkled at the corners with amusement. "You act, Catherine, as if death can be avoided by willing it away. After all, it does come to all life on this planet."

And I had sat there thinking, How can any man with a serious heart condition be this objective, get outside himself that much?

The voice with the burr went on, gently teasing, "In this area, you're like a little girl. One of these days, Catherine, you're going to have to come to terms with the fact of death. But that will have to be in your own way and your own time. I can't do this for you. . . . Now take this down. . . . My lock box at the bank is 731. All important papers are there. The key is with the others on my key ring. First, I'll summarize the insurance program for you. . . ."

In many ways, I was still a little girl. I had adored and leaned on my husband. Like many a sheltered woman who has married young, I had never once figured out an income tax blank, had a car inspected, consulted a lawyer, or tried to read an insurance policy. Railroad timetables and plane schedules were enigmas to me. My household checking account rarely balanced. I had never invested any money; I had been driving a car for only three months. I would never even have considered braving a trip alone to New York.

Now I was faced with all of these practical matters, plus many, many more.

There was some insurance, but not enough. I had no idea where Peter John and I would live after we left the Manse. I was not trained to earn a living. I had married when my college diploma was warm from the dean's hand, before I had even earned a teacher's certificate. . . . The adjustment that faced me, therefore, posed a challenge in every way in which a woman can be challenged.

Two
To Comfort
All That Mourn

MOST PEOPLE ACCEPT intellectually a belief in some kind of life after death. But usually it remains a theoretical belief until death invades one's immediate family circle.

Then at the time of the funeral, we are handed the victory. The working through of the specific problems that sorrow brings must come later.

Many know that initial victory. As with all God's gifts, we do nothing to earn or to deserve it. Undoubtedly a loving Father knows that without this kind of help, many of us could never withstand the emotional shock, would never even be able to get through the funeral.

At that time, the first need of the bereaved person is for comfort—just plain comfort. In sorrow, we are all like little children, hurt children who yearn to creep into a mother's arms and rest there; have her stroke our foreheads and speak softly to us as she used to do. But, of course, that is impossible; we are grown men and women. Yet the need for comfort remains.

Our God has promised precisely that. . . . "Comfort ye, comfort ye my people, saith your God. . . ." "For thus saith the Lord. . . . As one whom his mother comforteth, so will I comfort you. . . ."

Strangely in my case I was given the beginning of that experience of comfort a few hours prior to my husband's death. That morning Peter

18

had wakened about three-thirty with severe pains in his arms and chest. The doctor had come as quickly as he could. He had insisted that Dr. Marshall be taken immediately to the hospital.

As we had waited for the ambulance, Peter had looked up at me through his pain and said, "Catherine, don't try to come with me. We mustn't leave Wee Peter alone in this big house. You can come to the hospital in the morning."

Reluctantly I had agreed. I knew that he was right, though I wanted so much to be with him.

After the ambulance had come and gone, I went back upstairs and sank to my knees beside the bed. There was the need for prayer, for this was an emergency indeed. It could mean only one thing—another massive heart attack. But how was I to pray? Swirling emotions had plunged my mind into utter confusion.

Suddenly the unexpected happened. Over the turbulent emotions there crept a strange all-pervading peace. And through and around me flowed love as I had never before experienced it. It was as if body and spirit were floating on a cloud, resting—as if Someone who loved me very much were wrapping me round and round with His love.

I knelt there marveling at what was happening. I had done nothing, said nothing, to bring it about. Through my mind trooped a quick procession of thoughts . . . *the Three Persons of the Godhead . . . Father, Son, and Holy Spirit. . . . Sometimes I've known the Spirit within as a nudge, as direction, or reminder, or conscience. . . . Once especially I knew the Son—in that wonderful incident that was the turning point in my long illness. . . . But this is different . . . this must be the Father. . . . Maybe this is what the Bible means by that lovely statement—"underneath are the everlasting arms." That describes exactly what I'm feeling. . . .*

But what did this mean in relation to Peter, his ailing heart, and the emergency that threatened us? I thought it meant that everything was going to be all right, that Peter would be healed. There seemed to be nothing for which to ask God. Surely there was no need of asking for His Presence; that Presence was all around me. So my prayer took the form simply of thanking Him for the miracle that His love could be such a personal love; for His tender care of Peter and Wee Peter and me.

At 8:15 that same morning, Peter had stepped across the boundary that divides this life from the next. Then I knew that the experience of the night before had meant something far different. I had been granted it so that when the blow fell, I might have the certainty that a loving Father had not deserted me.

Several years later I heard of someone else who had had a similar experience—Rufus Jones, the Quaker. In July, 1903, Dr. Jones was on the high seas en route to Birmingham, England, to lecture. He had left his only son, Lowell, whose mother had died some years previously, at a grandmother's home in New York State.

On the night before landing in Liverpool, Dr. Jones awakened about two in the morning. In his stateroom there was a strange air of sadness. He lay there wondering what it meant. Suddenly he was all but overwhelmed with a feeling of the Presence of God. Tender, illimitable love filled the room and seemed to hold Rufus Jones in warm embrace. Finally toward daybreak, he fell asleep, still not knowing the significance of what had happened.

At Liverpool a cable awaited him. Lowell had been stricken with an undiagnosed paralysis. Both breathing and speech had been affected.

But just before the end, the eleven-year-old boy had raised his arms and said with wonder in his voice, "Oh, Mother!" Then he had slipped away.

Afterwards Dr. Jones said, in describing that night before Lowell's death, "It was the most extraordinary experience I have ever had."[*] Just as I had, he had felt the full power of God's consoling love even before he was aware that tragedy had struck.

After comfort, the next need of the bereaved is for the ability to distinguish between body and spirit. In this age of materialism most of us have had little practice with it.

One friend, whose husband had died six weeks before, expressed this perfectly. "My biggest need," she told me, "is to believe that Bill is not in that grave. If I could be sure of that, I could stand the personal hurt."

I understood her difficulty. The moment I had stepped into Peter's hospital room after his death, I had known that the man I loved was no longer in the body on the bed. That was a patent, indisputable fact. I had

---

[*]Jones, Rufus, *The Luminous Trail*, 162–164, The Macmillan Company, New York, 1947.

thought I would be able to hold on to that conviction. Yet less than two weeks later, I was having difficulty with it.

One morning about that time I was awakened early by the chirping of birds in the ivy outside my bedroom window. Somewhere in that twilight zone between sleeping and waking it seemed that Peter spoke to me. "Catherine," he said clearly, "don't think of me as dead."

How could he possibly have known, I wondered, that since the brief committal service I had been unable to think of him except as dead? In imagination I saw his body lying in the receiving vault. This was a temporary arrangement until a final decision about burial could be made.

Was this really Peter speaking to me, or was it some sort of a subconscious suggestion? I did not know. I wanted to believe that my husband was still alive. But my descent to earth after the funeral had been so abrupt that doubts had come crowding in. At any rate, wherever the brief message came from, it was the precise word I needed at the moment. I could neither forget nor ignore it.

In subsequent days I found myself pondering Peter's statement. If he were still alive, then where was he? What was he doing? With no idea of the answers to those questions, how could I visualize him or think of him as alive?

That brought me to a question my every emotion cried out to have answered . . . what is my relationship to my husband now?

In marriage I had found my identity, my answer to the question, "Who am I?" As a woman, much of my orientation in life had been centered in my relationship to one man. It is this way with most women.

Then when death cleaves the marriage partnership, the woman left alone feels that her whole basis for living has been washed out. She must begin all over again. . . . "Who am I now?"

Words that Mr. Bridge, the associate minister of our church, had spoken at Peter Marshall's funeral service, kept coming back to me. . . .

This morning . . . we are endeavoring to establish a new relationship. We have known Peter Marshall in the flesh. From now on we are to endeavor to know him in the spirit. . . . The fellowship with him will remain unbroken. . . .

Those had been sincere though lofty words. Were they true? For me, the fellowship had certainly been broken.

"Till death do us part," Peter and I had vowed on our wedding day. The fact was that death had now suddenly and ruthlessly parted us. Across that chasm, Mr. Bridge had said that we were to build a bridge to Peter Marshall's spirit.

I could not even imagine how to begin. Thus, I found my prayers taking a new turn. In a childlike way I began pleading with God for some glimpse of Peter, for some knowledge of his new setting, of what he was doing.

The response came in a vivid dream. It was a dream with a self-authenticating quality. Now, years later, every detail is still clear. Of no other single dream in my life can I say that. I also learned from it some of the details of the life we are to lead after death that have rung true with the testing of time.

In the dream I was allowed to visit Peter in his new setting. First I searched for him in a large rambling house with many rooms and airy porches. There were crowds of people about but Peter was not among them.

Then I sought him in the yard. Finally, at some distance, I saw him. "I'd recognize that characteristic gesture—that certain toss of the head any time," I thought, as I began running toward him. I found myself able to run with a freedom I had not known since childhood. My body was light; my feet were sure. As I drew nearer I saw that Peter was working in a rose garden. He saw me coming and stood leaning on his spade, waiting for me.

I rushed into his arms. Laughing, he pulled me close and rubbed his nose on mine.

"I knew it was you," I said breathlessly, "by the way you tossed your head. I've come home to you."

Then, resting there in his arms, I felt something strange. Mixed with the tenderness of Peter's love was a certain restraint. He was not holding me as a lover.

My impression was that Peter was bewildered at what had happened, still surprised at his own death. 1 wondered if the large many-roomed house, the yard, and the rose garden comprised some small part of what the Scriptures call "heaven." I had always thought that people in heaven would be extremely happy. Peter's attitude did not quite fit that pattern.

Then I awakened. The feeling of Peter's strong arms around me lingered, and my cheeks were wet with tears.

Days later I was still pondering this strange dream. Then it began to come clear. Peter had not expected his life to end so suddenly on that gloomy Tuesday morning. He, like me, had confidently anticipated a different outcome to the problem of his damaged heart.

Five minutes after death he was essentially the same person that he had been before death. There had been no dramatic change except that he had shed his physical body as one would take off an overcoat. But the spiritual body in which he found himself—if that's what one could call it—gave him the same appearance as before.

He was being left alone to work in the rose garden to give him time to recover from his bewilderment, to find himself again. It seemed an especially thoughtful and loving touch that in the meantime he had been given work of a kind he had especially loved on earth—cultivating roses.

But it was that touch of restraint toward me in Peter's attitude about which I thought most. I asked God to tell me what that meant.

When the reply came, it was to have considerable significance for my future. A long time was to pass before I would have the courage to share this bit of insight with other widows, especially when their grief was new. For the dead are so terribly silent. The one whose sorrow is fresh longs for nothing so much as the touch of a vanished hand, the sound of a beloved voice. One in whom the wound of grief is still unhealed yearns for the assurance that, if immortality means anything at all, it means that one's love will be untampered with, will be just as it was here on earth.

Yet will the relationship between husband and wife be the same? From Christ's own lips—as recorded in the Gospel of Matthew—we are given quite another thought about this. He spoke in answer to a sardonic question put to him by a group of Sadducees, who did not believe in the resurrection of the body. They posed a case about a woman who in this life had had seven husbands, and then asked the pointedly ridiculous question: "Therefore, in the resurrection, whose wife shall she be of the seven, for they all had her?"

And Jesus answered in part:

> ... in the resurrection they neither marry nor are
> given in marriage, but are as the angels in heaven.
> (MATTHEW 22:30)

In other words, Christ seemed to be saying that after death the woman would not be "a wife" to any one of her former husbands. That is, there is no marriage in heaven; one's relationship even to the person one has loved on earth is different then.

Precisely what the new relationship was to be I did not then understand. I did not know what being "like the angels in heaven" would be like, and I was not at all sure I wanted to know. On the whole, I thought it a revolting idea.

Yet I guessed that part of what this meant was that the one who has stepped over into the next life still remembers every tender moment on earth, still cares what happens to those left behind, still wants to help them, still considers this as part of his continuing mission—but that the emotion of his love is intensified and purified. With this purification, as in a refiner's fire, all selfishness and self-seeking, the usual possessiveness that comes with love, and the fire and excitement of physical love—all this is consumed, gone forever.

I remembered how often Peter had said from his pulpit, "Death has no scissors with which to cut the cords of love." Of course he had been right. Yet it is difficult for us to imagine love without possessiveness, just as it is hard for us to imagine anything more wonderful than physical love.

And yet we have the Apostle Paul, in his famous love poem (I Corinthians 13) setting love at the summit of all spiritual gifts, describing for us in gladsome detail what it will be like someday. It was on this conception of a new kind of love, on a different kind of relationship with Peter, that I had to fix my mind.

In the days following my dream, it was as if God were saying to me, "Because I want you to get this matter straight from the beginning, I am trusting you now with part of this truth. Some of it you will not understand; some of it will be hard for you to take. But I shall never give you more than you can bear. You must not only trust in the truth of any-thing that comes directly from My Hand, but you can know that what I give will be good."

You are not really trusting God until you are trusting Him for the ultimates of life. . . . So the thought had come to me in a moment of prayer several years before. And what are the ultimates of life? Life and death, health, economic necessities, the need to find one's own place in the world, to love and to be loved.

When life has tumbled in and we sit in the wreckage—stripped, dazed, with all of life's values askew—our hearts are full of questions about these ultimates. We question ourselves. We question life. We question God. We even have moments of doubting the existence of God. . . . How could a loving God have allowed this to happen to me? How am I to get my questions answered, my values straight again?

Like every bereaved person, I too was full of questions—momen-tous urgent questions. . . . If there is life after death, will we know our-selves to be ourselves . . . ? Will we remember all that has happened in this earthbound life . . . ? Will we recognize one another then . . . ? But how can there be recognition unless we have bodies of some kind . . . ? Do those in the next life know what we are doing here on earth . . . ? How can heaven be happy if those who still love us can see our earthly heartaches and tragedies?

Prior to Peter's death, I had never seriously considered such ques-tions. Now they were important. I wanted authoritative answers. If I asked other people or even read books on the subject, I would at best merely be getting other people's opinions.

Therefore, I went directly to the most authoritative source I knew—the Scriptures. And I discovered what I should have known before—that when you and I go to the Bible out of great need to learn what it has to say to us, it is then that we get real help.

My first discovery was that reading what the Bible has to say about death and immortality immediately bathes the subject in the sunlight of normalcy, lifts it out of the realm of the dark and sinister unknown. What a grave injustice we do ourselves when we fail to take advantage of this help and go on through life fearing and wondering!

Then I found out, by both direct word and by inference, that the New Testament reassures us that the next life is not only a fully conscious one with every intellectual and spiritual faculty intact, but that these faculties are heightened. . . .

> For now we see through a glass darkly;
> but then face to face: now I know in part;
> but then shall I know even as also I am
> known. (1 CORINTHIANS 13:12)

We shall be able to remember, to think, to will, to love, to worship, and to understand so much more on the other side of the barrier of death. Our new life will be no sleeping, nonconscious, or unfeeling existence.

There are many suggestions of this in Scripture. For example, before His crucifixion, Jesus told His apostles, "But after that I am risen, I will go before you into Galilee," and He did. He met them on the shores of the Sea of Galilee (John 21:1), and on the Mount of Transfiguration in Galilee to which He had directed them (Matthew 28:16).

After His resurrection He kept saying to His disciples, "Lo, I have told you" thus and so, referring to conversations He had had with them before His death.

In the same way, in Christ's parable of the rich man and Lazarus, He pictures both men as having a fully conscious life after death, of recollecting earthly life with no break in memory

Then there are Christ's words from the Cross. . . .

> And he [one of the thieves who was being
> crucified] said unto Jesus, "Lord, remember
> me when thou comest into thy kingdom."
>
> And Jesus said unto him, "Verily, I say unto
> thee, today shalt thou be with me in paradise."
>   (LUKE 23:42–43)

Christ's words to the dying thief would have been nonsense had He not meant that after death on that very day, both He and the thief would know themselves to be themselves, would remember that they had suffered together, would recognize each other.

The Scriptures say that we shall have a spiritual body. . . .

> There is a natural body, and there is
> a spiritual body. (1 CORINTHIANS 15:44)

This spiritual body will give us much the same appearance that we have had on earth, except that if imperfect or deformed or diseased, all will be made perfect. . . .

> It [the body] is sown in corruption; it is
> raised in incorruption:
> It is sown in dishonor; it is raised in
> glory: it is sown in weakness; it is
> raised in power. . . . (1 CORINTHIANS 15:42–44)

Christ's resurrection body gives us some idea of the characteristics of the new body we shall have. For one thing, we shall transcend time and space barriers. . . .

> On the evening of that same day—the
> first day of the week—though the disciples
> had gathered within closed doors for fear of
> the Jews, Jesus entered and stood among them
> saying, "Peace be with you!"
>
> So saying he showed them his hands and his
> side; and when the disciples saw the Lord,
> they rejoiced. . . . (JOHN 20:19–20)

There were appearances and reappearances. . . .

> After that he was seen of above five hundred
> brethren at once; of whom the greater part
> remain unto this present, but some are fallen
> asleep. . . . (1 CORINTHIANS 15:5–6)

As to my question about how much those in the next life know of what is going on in this one, a passage like Hebrews 12:1 would seem to be conclusive. It speaks of a long list of the heroes of the faith—Abraham,

Joseph, Moses, Gideon, Samson, David, all men who had long ago passed
off the stage of history. Then the passage goes on. . . .

> Therefore, with all this host of witnesses
> encircling us . . . we must run our appointed
> course with steadiness . . . (HEBREWS 12:1)*

But we have been taught that life with Christ is a happy life. Could
it be happy if earthly sorrows are known in heaven? The Bible seems to
be silent on this point, perhaps because we mortals have no basis on
which to understand.

But several thoughts came to me. Perhaps those on the other side
see the end from the beginning, and that makes all the difference. Moreover, we know that the higher we rise spiritually, the more unselfish
we become; the more we are concerned about others, the more we long
to minister to them. Therefore, is it reasonable to suppose that those in
the next life would be more preoccupied with their own ease and happiness and less concerned about those they love and have left behind than
we are? I don't think so. In fact, happiness—especially in the next life—
could scarcely come from oblivion, inactivity, lack of knowledge, or
selfishness.

Lastly, I found that the Bible does not ignore sorrow as a fact of
human experience. Some of the loveliest words of Scripture are for the
sore of heart. . . .

> I will not leave you comfortless. . . . (JOHN 14:18)

> . . . he hath sent me to bind up the broken-
> hearted . . . to appoint unto them that mourn
> in Zion, to give unto them beauty for
> ashes, the oil of joy for mourning, the
> garment of praise for the spirit of
> heaviness. . . . (ISAIAH 61:1, 3)

I was surprised to find that a great number of promises in the Bible
are directed specifically to widows and to children who have had to part
with one or both parents.

---

*Moffatt, James, *The Bible: A New Translation*, Harper & Brothers, New York, 1935.

Yet here is an odd thing—the word "widower" does not occur any-where in the Bible. Perhaps this means that the patriarchs and others who had lost a wife did not stay unmarried long enough even to get the word "widower" in the concordance! Or is this just another example of the realism of the Bible? The status of women during those centuries made their widowhood a precarious existence. Surely they needed God's help. . . .

> The Lord will destroy the house of the
> proud; but he will establish the border
> of the widow. (Proverbs 15:25)

> Yet leave to me your orphans, I will
> save them; let your widows trust me.
> (MOFFATT; JEREMIAH 49:11)

> . . . thou art the helper of the fatherless.
> (THE BOOK OF COMMON PRAYERS; PSALM 10:18)

And this, the most beautiful promise of all. . . .

> Fear not . . . thou shalt not remember the
> reproach of thy widowhood any more for the
> Lord hath called thee as a woman forsaken
> and grieved in spirit . . . with great mercies
> will I gather thee. . . .

> And all thy children shall be taught of the
> Lord; and great shall be the peace of thy
> children. . . . (ISAIAH 54:4, 6, 7, 13)

The help for the bereaved to be found in the Scriptures is indeed limitless.

It is not part of God's plan that the sorrowing should languish in self-pity. I had learned this long before in an entirely different connection.

During the years when I was in bed with tuberculosis, a good friend came one day to the Manse to call. Anita was a tall, stately woman, always exquisitely dressed, who was married to one of Washington's wealthiest men. She was also a spirited woman with the gift of a rare discernment.

On this particular afternoon, Anita did not walk into my bedroom— she marched in. She did not even bother to sit down.

Standing in the middle of the big room, she cleared her throat as for a speech. Her eyes were sparking as much light as the star sapphire on her right hand. . . . "Catherine, you've been on my mind for days. I've been tempted to feel sorry for you. I'll be damned if I'll feel sorry for you. Forgive the language, but I feel just that vehemently about it.

"Pity wouldn't help you a bit. Besides, why should I pity you? You have all you need—the strength and the guidance of God—"

Her words were flung at me like ice water striking my face. I might have resented them, but I didn't. In fact, when I had recovered from the first shock of the ice water, I felt exhilarated, even as Anita had hoped I would.

My thoughts raced . . . All right, don't pity me, then. . . . See if I care! I'll show you! Enough of this weakness and secluded life. . . . I'm going to get out of here. And courage mounted in me like mercury rising in a thermometer in the sun.

From that visit I learned something important about comfort. During those years, I had hundreds of sickroom calls. Yet that one of Anita's towers like a mountain top above the others.

Just so, God's way of comforting us towers over man's usual methods. In our attempts to console one another, softness and sympathy loom large. If we think of comfort in terms of a word picture, it would be that of soothing and placating a hurt child: "There now, don't cry." It is true that these qualities, particularly in the very beginning, are present in God's help for his hurt and bereaved children, because He is a God of love. Indeed it was that kind of comfort that I had received from Him in those early morning hours before Peter's death.

Yet now I found the other side of God's comfort. Anita had been close to the truth. God's comfort doesn't walk on tiptoe as in a sickroom; it marches. There is steel at its backbone. It is a bugle call for reinforcements. It makes us remember that the word "comfort" is derived from the word *fortis*—which means strong.

God comforts us with strength by adding resources. His way is not to whittle down the problem but to build up the resources.

I opened my New Testament and found there exactly that concept of comfort. . . .

Discipline always seems for the time to be
a thing of pain, not of joy; but those who
are trained by it reap the fruit of it
afterwards. . . .

So up with your listless hands! Strengthen
your weak knees! And make straight paths for
your feet to walk in. . . . (MOFFATT; HEBREWS 12:11–12)

This made me remember a recurring note in Peter Marshall's preaching, a note that at the time I had resented, had secretly refused to accept. . . .

There are in our day some philosophies growing
in popularity that teach the attractive idea
that God always reveals His love by removing the
distasteful and the unpleasant from our lives.

But where in the Bible do you find support
for this attractive and alluring concept?
Certainly not from the lips of Jesus.

On the contrary you are startled to discover how
plainly and bluntly Christ told His disciples to
expect trouble.

"In the world ye shall have tribulation.
  But be of good cheer." That is His message.
"Be of good cheer . . . I have overcome the world."

No . . . Christians are not spared. . . .
The calamities of life knock on their door
        with the same startling swiftness . . .
and the rain falls on the just
        as well as the unjust.

There is no hint or intimation anywhere in the Gospel
that they who follow Him shall never hunger
                    or be out of work
                    or be left alone.

No, there is no hint of such immunity. . . .
But there is the promise of something far better . . .
    the promise of deliverance . . .
not from these things . . . but in these things.

There is an air of reality about the Gospel. . . .
It is not a fairy tale in which Cinderella's rags
    are changed into the robes of a queen . . .
but rather a promise in which Cinderella in her rags
    becomes more queenly.

And now in my own dark hour, I found in God's dealing with me exactly that note of stringent reality about which Peter had so often preached. God was asking me to grow up, to take a new step toward maturity.

This element of stringency, a firmness which the New Testament calls "God's discipline" or "chastening," was a big factor in the next lesson God provided in my progress out of grief. I needed a grip on my relationship with God Himself, a new understanding based not on sentimentality but on bedrock truth, and just as important, on trust. This was a necessity, because only as my relationship with God was made clear-cut would other relationships, including the new one with Peter, fall into place. And without this kind of clarity, God would not have been able to take me along those rocky paths that lead from the Valley of the Shadow.

On the second of February, nine days after Peter's new life had begun, I had awakened early and was propped up in bed reading. Out of the early morning quietness a voice from beyond my own thoughts seemed to speak. It had about it the quiet authority, the take-it-or-leave-it unforgettable quality that in my experience the voice of God in the depths of the spirit always has.

"Apparently," the message went, "you did not really mean what you said to Me."

I knew perfectly well what the statement meant. It referred to a specific promise I had made to God one anxious afternoon of the previous September.

At that time, four months before my husband's death, I had known that only a miracle could save Peter. The first attack of coronary thrombosis had come out of the blue to an ostensibly healthy and vigorous man of forty-three. This had been a severe attack, necessitating a five-month convalescence.

For the first few months after his return to an active ministry, Peter had been cautious. But he was a man in whom there was an incalculable zest for life. Writing sermons, preaching, pastoral calling, his Senate duties, playing games with small groups of friends, stamp collecting, all that went into being an avid baseball fan, fishing, gardening—no day held enough hours for all he wanted to include in it.

In the year following his heart attack, I tried reasoning with my husband in an effort to change some of those habits. Our talks together were always calm and rational. Peter did not mean to be unreasonable. He had no desire to flirt with death, and he well knew the danger of overactivity. It was just that in the end his zest for life submerged all caution. Nothing ever really changed as a result of our talks.

Many of Peter's friends also entered into a loving conspiracy with me to try to get him to take more time off from his church and Senate duties. Often even these efforts boomeranged; he was all too inclined to take too strenuously what was meant to be relaxation.

In late June of 1947 one of the church officers, George Hildebrand, prevailed on Peter to join a group going on a deep-sea fishing trip to the Chesapeake. He not only went, but took Peter John along. It was an all-male party.

The day was warm and the sunshine on the blue waters of the Bay inviting. What's more, the fish just weren't biting.

"That water sure looks good," Mr. Hildebrand commented, grinning. Then he walked to the bow of the boat, stripped, and dived in.

"Man overboard!" someone yelled. The rest of the party promptly stripped and dived overboard too.

Peter, in the water at 200 yards from the boat, was vigorously waving his arms and shouting exuberantly to the others, "Look at the invalid!"

The skipper was vastly amused by the turn the fishing party had taken. He cupped his hands to his mouth and shouted at Peter, "Boy, if only folks at the church could see their minister now!"

I remember that Mr. Hildebrand, in telling me of this day with Peter, had added, "What on earth are you going to do with a man like that?"

The truth was that none of us knew what to do with a man like that.

Peter's attitude toward his own condition had not been improved by the fact that, after recovery from his first attack, there had apparently been no further difficulty. He had not been bothered with any shortness of breath, dizziness, swelling ankles, or arm pains. Some mild symptoms might actually have been a blessing, since he would then have been warned of the true situation. Without any symptoms, he was undertaking more and more.

As out-of-town speaking engagements piled up, I battled my increasing fear for Peter. The second year after his attack, he had made ten such trips; the next year, it had been twenty. And these had been sandwiched in between a constant round of in-town duties, talks, and appearances.

Peter knew full well what my conviction was: that it was only out of the framework of a keen sense of stewardship of his body that we could ask God to take care of his heart. I was not at all convinced that all the speaking engagements came from God.

But all my human efforts had failed to curb my husband's whirlwind pace. I therefore concluded that either Peter's heart would have to be healed so completely that there would be no need of curtailing activities, or his temperament and whole approach to life would have to be changed. Only God could do either.

Nothing seemed left for me but a complete relinquishment of the man I loved to his Lord. It was with this that I wrestled on that September afternoon in Washington, fear and trust struggling for mastery. Then thoughts began flowing to me. It was as if God were speaking in a quiet inner voice in my heart. I wrote down the thoughts:

> Trust Me—that's all. Are you really willing to put your future into My hands? Are you willing to tell Me to manage it as I please? Let yourself trust Peter to Me. It's like trusting yourself to the water. . . . It seems dangerous to you to trust him to Me in that way, because you will feel that if anything is done, you must do it. Do you really think that you can do more than the Lord of the Universe? You have scarcely realized your presumption. . . .

Trust—trust—trust—the word had been used over and over. It was indeed like trusting myself to the water. My feeling was like that of a child poised and teetering on the end of a high diving board.

At that time out of the depths of my fear I had made an act of giving Peter's future and mine to God for Him to do with as He pleased. The relinquishment had been as complete as I was able to make it. It had been made in my will, even as my every human emotion had cried out against it.

Practically speaking, this meant that my attitude hereafter would be "hands off." I would stop battling Peter's out-of-town speaking engagements, his ever-increasing Washington commitments. A few days later I told Peter about this decision, and he had been pleased. He was happy to have an end to the conflict between us.

But now, months later, God was saying, "Apparently you did not really mean that relinquishment that day. . . ." The clear implication seemed to be that God had taken the transaction between us, made in my will, at face value, as a covenant, as He always does a promise made to Him by one of His children. I was now being challenged. My bluff was being called. Did I really believe in the existence of God enough to believe that when I spoke to Him, He heard; when I made Him a promise, He accepted it and held me to it?

Had not God promised us that "He healeth the broken in heart, and bindeth up their wounds?" (Psalm 147:3) This was the God of love speaking. But God's sternness in dealing with me did not seem quite like love. Yet I thought of the many times when it had taken far more love for me to hold my son to what I knew was right than to indulge him. This is the kind of firmness that is even a proof of love. The Bible tells us this too.

> For the Lord disciplines the man he loves. . . .
> It is for discipline that you have to endure.
> God is treating you as sons; for where is the
> son who is not disciplined by his father.
> (MOFFATT; HEBREWS 12:6–7)

Now that I understood how God regarded a promise, I remembered a technique that Peter had often used. It was the method of finding a specific promise in the Bible that applied to one's need and then claiming it as a definite transaction between an individual and his Lord. A favorite quotation had often been on Peter's lips at such a time of claiming. He had written it on the flyleaf of his Bible. It was a statement of David Livingstone, the Scottish missionary and explorer of Africa. . . . "It is a word of a Gentleman of the most sacred and strictest honor, and there is an end on't."

In precisely that spirit I claimed for myself and the son whom Peter and I had brought into the world, this promise:

> And we know that all things [the things we under-
> stand and those we do not; the joyous things and the
> tragic] work together for good to them that love God,
> to them that are the called according to his purpose.
>
> (ROMANS 8:28)

I did not yet know where the comfort of God's strength was leading me or what I was to do with it. Yet during those days, God was steadily asking me not to fear where Truth would lead. Truth may be painful, but it makes us free. God is not interested in coddling us, but in liberating us for further creativity, for the new life that we are forced to make.

Much of this was hard to swallow, but in its stringency lay its self-authentication. Though my private world had tumbled in, God was still in His Universe.

Did I actually think that the God who had led Peter Marshall from Scotland to the United States, from the Tube Mill to the seminary, who had provided for all his needs when he had no money, who had saved his life on several occasions when it could so easily have been lost— would that God have deserted Peter in death and me in life? Even through the veil of occasional doubt, I knew better.

Three
Turn Around
and Face Today

AT THE MANSE out on Cathedral Avenue, papers covered with columns of figures were spread all over the dining-room table. Three men had come to spend an evening with me to talk about business matters. One of them, a young insurance agent, had everything neatly worked out in a series of graph columns.

"It's by far the wisest course to spread Dr. Marshall's insurance over a reasonably long period of time. After all, it will be eight years before Peter John goes to college." He was using a well-sharpened pencil as a pointer to the skyscraper-looking graphs.

"Doing it that way, how much income will we have each month?" I asked.

"One hundred and seventy-one dollars a month for the first eight years. That includes Dr. Marshall's pension from the Presbyterian Ministers' Fund. Then the monthly income will take a drop."

One of the other men, an engineer, said, frowning, "You're really going to have to be realistic about this, Catherine. That won't be enough to include keeping the car. You should probably sell it."

"And you're scarcely strong enough to hold down a real job," the other friend added. "By the way, what could you do job-wise?"

I began to have a suffocating feeling. "I—I don't quite know. I married right out of college—have only a bachelor of arts degree—not even teacher training. I couldn't be a secretary. I don't know shorthand and I use only my own brand of hunt and peck on the typewriter."

The three men were troubled. They had all been Peter's close friends and were genuinely fond of me. As a bread-earning widow, they looked on me as an especially poor risk . . . no vocational training and twelve years in which Peter had sheltered me from business affairs.

"I don't think you realize how desperate your situation is," one friend insisted. "One hundred and seventy-one dollars a month in Washington just won't do it, won't even cover the bare necessities. You're going to have to cut living expenses to the bone."

"And I do think you are going to have to sell the Cape Cod cottage quickly," another added.

The three men left that night the more distressed because they realized that they had failed to convince me that I was now in actual financial straits. They were right. There was in me a stubborn refusal to accept their gloomy forecasts—financial or otherwise.

Yet I had not argued with them, because facts and figures had substantiated all they had said. There the facts were, down on paper in neat columns. How could figures lie? Yet somehow I felt that they did lie.

Alone in my room I stared out the window into the moonlight shining on swaying treetops. Suddenly I was back in a crowded little tearoom on Connecticut Avenue. It had been a Sunday just after church. My husband, Wee Peter, and I had been having dinner together with Alma Deane Fuller, whom we always called "A. D." She was the friend who, during my illness in 1944, had given up a job on Capitol Hill to keep house for us.

Over our main course, we three adults had been discussing life insurance. A. D. and I had been taking a very lofty ivory-towerlike attitude. Peter had seemed amused at us and a trifle annoyed. But partly he had only himself to blame, because we were still in the clouds where the high-flying phrases of his Sunday morning sermon had tossed us.

"We say we trust God. But then most people go right out and buy as much life insurance as they can afford," I remembered A. D. had said. "Their actions belie their words."

Peter's knife had been poised over a slice of lamb. "But don't you think God wants us to have a sense of responsibility about our families? Surely business common sense and thrift are right!"

I knew well that this had been a fair representation of my husband's point of view. After all he was a Scotsman! But throughout our married life I had always resented our going without so many things in order to buy insurance.

"Think of George Müller, the founder of the British orphanage system in the last century," I said in a hopelessly stuffy fashion. "The way he sold all his household goods and trusted God for all resources for himself and his hundreds of orphans. Don't you really think, Peter, that if a husband were to die, God could be trusted to supply what a widow needs?"

"I'm not George Müller," Peter had said gloomily.

If a husband were to die. . . . The words were echoing in my mind now. It had happened. How could I have been so glib about it? How had I managed to go through life acting as if I and those I loved were somehow immune to the universal experience of death?

I didn't know. But I recognize how grateful I was now for the love and caring behind Peter's insurance, inadequate though it might be. At least it gave me some feeling of security, something on which to fall back.

And yet, I thought, A. D. and I were right too. There's something missing from the somber picture the men painted tonight.

The moonlight was almost white. One brilliant star above the tree-tops winked like a solitaire. Suddenly, standing there at the window, I knew what the missing factor was. My three friends who had meant to be so kind, had reckoned without God.

So now I was up against one of those poignant ultimates of life— the economic one. Immediately I decided on my course. I would refuse to be destitute. I would simply not give in to poverty.

When soon after Peter's death I had claimed that promise that "all things," even those that appeared to be stark tragedy, would "work together for good," I had not expected the good to be limited to spiritual blessing. Working together for good, I had reasoned, would surely be good as we human beings understand it. It must also include the money for rent and clothes and food. A sense of adventure had crept in; it would be exciting to see how God would help me to work out my problems.

But how did one go about trusting God for money? It was to take weeks—indeed years—to get the full answer to that question. But when His grand design for me was revealed in its entirety, it answered so much more than my bare economic needs; indeed, it led me to a new career, a new life.

How He managed it seems like a fairy tale. In my wildest dreams I could never have anticipated what happened. God's plans for His children are always so much more bountiful than our best-laid plans for ourselves. To put this in the classic language of the Apostle Paul, I found for myself that God is still

> ... able to do exceeding abundantly,
> above all that we ask or think. ...
> (EPHESIANS 3:20)

In the meantime, however, I was having to work through the practical problems that always follow a death in the family. For these, I was not presented with any celestial road map of the way out for the lacerated of heart. Road maps are not God's usual way. I had to learn the path step by step, incident by incident, as I lived it out.

As I look back, certain principles applicable to any bereaved person emerge from those experiences. For one thing, no major decisions should be made in the weeks immediately following a death in the family. One has experienced deep shock. There must be a recovery from this condition before it is possible to have a firm basis for making proper decisions.

For example, I was fortunate in not having to make any immediate decision as to where my son and I were going to live when we moved out of the Manse, the house that the church provides for its minister and his family. This was a spacious ten-room brick house in Washington's Cleveland Park area.

Six days after their minister's death, I received an official letter from the board of trustees of the church:

Dear Catherine:

We want you to know that the Manse is available to you until such time as it is required by the church. ... Your continuing there will help maintain ties that were so sadly broken these past few days. ... We hope that you will be agreeable to this suggestion.

We do not know of course when the church will again require the Manse, but we will notify you at least three months in advance or sooner if possible. ...

God bless you and keep you—and little Peter.

Very sincerely,
s/ Charles A. Stott
Secretary, Board of Trustees

This generosity on the part of the officers of the church proved important to me in several ways. Familiar, beloved, and once-shared possessions helped to soothe a sore and wounded spirit. All five seascapes on the walls of the bedroom that Peter and I had shared together; the well-worn games in the game closet; the same familiar few blocks in which to walk our cocker Jeff—somehow, this was for me balm rather than added hurt. It gave a sense of continuity to life.

Sometimes one's friends are inclined to feel that a swift change of setting will hasten the healing process. For most people, and for me in particular, this would have been running away. Changing my setting, even removing all physical reminders of my old life, would have left me still the same person.

Next I found that the mechanics connected with death are actually helpful, though they may seem hard. In the very beginning one may feel that these practical activities are an intrusion into grief. The bereaved person looks out on the world with new eyes, marveling that other people on the streets and in the shops are going on about their business as if nothing has happened, as if everything were just the same.

For a time, during busy hours, one can forget the pain. Then a tiny thing—anything—brings it flooding back. Opening a drawer and coming across a small Christmas card written in a well-known hand; the sight of a distant figure walking down the street, wearing the same kind of slouch hat . . . and suddenly the old stabbing pain is back.

How is it possible, one wonders at such a time, to force oneself to sort out dresser and desk drawers; to dispose of clothes that a loved person will never need again; to listen attentively to the reading of a will; to write checks; to put one's mind to business and insurance details; to acknowledge somehow the dozens of telephone calls and personal messages, the loving offerings of food brought to one's home, the funeral flowers, the notes of sympathy?

The truth is that the empty heart needs work for the hands to do. I learned that there is a certain therapy in these necessary mechanics, as on the day when I had to go down to the church to clean out Peter's office, so that his successor might have the use of it.

I remember shutting the door and sitting down at his big desk. The flavor of Peter's personality was all around me. Two walls of the room were covered with his theological books. On one wall was a group of etchings—all seascapes—and in their midst was one fine lithograph of the American flag.

From the top of one of the bookcases a bust of Sir Walter Scott stared down at me. Beside the bust was a carefully detailed model of John Knox's house in Edinburgh. . . . Once Peter and I had walked hand in hand up those narrow steps into that queer little medieval house.

I pulled out drawer after drawer of the desk, preparatory to emptying their contents into cartons. Each drawer was in meticulous order. On the desk before me was Peter's date book. Oddly enough, stuck in the front of it was a newspaper clipping entitled, "Would You Live a Longer Life If You Could?"

The book was open to the week of January 23. It was to have been a busy week. Peter's neat, very British handwriting informed me that on Tuesday, January 25, he was to have had lunch with his friend, Harold Folk. That night he was to have presided over the St. Andrews Society Burns's Night Dinner at the Mayflower Hotel. Instead, that evening someone else had given a eulogy for Peter Marshall. How rudely death had interrupted every plan!

I sat there, half believing that at any moment I would hear Peter's firm step on the stone stairs, see him appear in the doorway, hear him asking me, "What in t'thunder are you doing at my desk . . . ?"

Yet it was fortunate that there was not time for me to sit there and turn my dreams into mourning. Work was waiting. The books had to be taken off the shelves, packed into boxes; a decision made about what was to be done with them. The etchings had to be taken down and packed, the desk drawers emptied. As my hands worked that day, there was a strange sweet easing of my pain.

A third lesson I learned was not to try to hide or steel the emotions. Trying to force oneself to be brave will not heal the heart. This is hard for men—especially American men—who are trained to believe that tears are the sign of weakness. But it is forever true that when the storms of life are savage, it is the tree that bends with the wind that survives. Tensing up, walling up the heart, damming up the tears, will inevitably mean trouble later on, perhaps years later. There is emotional release in letting the tears flow.

This principle I discovered for myself on the Sunday following Peter's death. The question was . . . would I attend church as usual, sit in my customary spot at the New York Avenue Presbyterian Church? The church was of all places most uniquely connected with Peter Marshall. I knew that my absence on that particular Sunday would be completely understood, indeed expected. Yet an instinct told me to take heed on the business of facing up to life.

That Sunday, as I sat in the pastor's pew, someone else stood in Peter's pulpit. Peter had been there preaching powerfully and poignantly seven days before; he would never be there again. Through the entire service, tears overflowed swiftly and silently. I was as embarrassed as anyone would have been, but I was powerless to stop them. I saturated handkerchief after handkerchief.

Sitting beside me was a Chinese woman. In that silent communion that lies at the heart of the Christian fellowship, her compassionate and understanding spirit reached out to enfold me. Words were not necessary. I did not know who she was, I had never seen her before; yet I knew that she understood. The silent message of her love got through to me.

Going to the church that Sunday was one of the hardest things I had ever done, but postponing it would only have made it harder.

Subsequently, I had to follow this same pattern in returning to our Cape Cod cottage and to other places where Peter and I had been happy together. But each step forward I found a little easier than the step before.

I was learning, as I lived it out, still another step in the healing of the brokenhearted. That was the therapy to be found in keeping one's heart wide open to other people.

When a deep injury to the spirit has been sustained, the tendency of the sorrowing is to shut the heart and bar the door lest hurt be heaped upon hurt. Yet isolation is not the way toward mental health. Of course, the newly bereaved person needs periods of stabilizing solitude both for physical rest and to gain perspective. But in between times, he needs to accept as fully as he can the love that flows from friends and family.

The truth is that this spontaneous sympathy from other human beings is only a small token, a pale reflection of the great heart of a compassionate and understanding Father. And God's love is always a healing love. The one who—almost involuntarily—shuts his heart against his friends and lets bitterness creep in is, in a tragic way, insulating himself against that reenergizing love of God.

When my own private crisis came, I certainly knew nothing about the way out of grief. I had never heard that psychologists and psychiatrists consider the matter of establishing new patterns of interaction with other human beings one of the most important laws for recovery. Conversely, they feel that to turn inwards upon oneself at such a time places the bereaved person in danger of emotional suicide.

Part of the miracle of God's direction was the fact that I was enabled immediately after my husband's death to open my heart wider than ever before. For the temperament with which I was born was that of a deep reserve; I was not naturally endowed with the gregariousness and outgoingness of my husband.

Yet on that fateful January 25, within an hour after I had returned home from the hospital, friends began dropping in. One couple who had been particularly fond of Peter, sought me out in my bedroom. I remember that the young wife, her cheeks wet with tears, threw her arms around my neck. "Darling," she cried, "I love you so. We're going to have to stick awfully close together now."

My split-second choice at that moment was made by instinct—not in my conscious mind at all. It was a choice of whether or not I would merely politely tolerate such an overflowing exuberance of love—or really accept it. In yielding to it, I found a oneness with all human beings, a kinship with all suffering in the world—an authentic glimpse of the Kingdom of God actually at work in a given community.

And so I opened wide the door of the Manse. People came with warm handclasps and tear-filled eyes. They brought what they knew best how to make—soup, chicken salad, baked ham, angel food cake, custard, chess pie. And somehow, they found in our home an atmosphere that dried their eyes, that made them loath to leave. The gap of Peter's absence was sorely felt. But the love that flowed like a great tidal wave through the Christian community that was our church family, blessed us all.

The telegrams and notes piled up. They were not only from people of our own faith or nationality. There was, for example, a card saying that money had been given to the Jewish National Fund for a tree to be planted in memory of Peter Marshall; a letter from a friend in the British House of Commons; an official letter of sympathy from the Sisterhood of Adas Israel. Where love is, God is. And He was definitely there in this overflowing human compassion.

Yet it is God alone who can finally heal the brokenhearted. Grief is a real wound, a mutilation, a gaping hole in the human spirit. After all, the ties that bind parents to children, brothers to sisters, and husbands to wives are the deepest of bonds, as real as love is real. Some beloved person has been wrested, torn bodily from one's life. The hurt is none the less real because the family physician cannot probe it; Christ alone is physician to the spirit.

Because we no longer have Christ's physical presence with us, our connection with Him must be through prayer. "Ye have not because ye ask not," our Bible tells us in a shaft of pinpointed sunlight on the question of prayer. Yet there have been times in my life when I have been unable to ask for myself in an effective way. At such times I have been filled with fear or undue emotional stress. I was in just that condition in the weeks immediately following Peter's death.

That was why I sought out a friend, Rebecca Beard, and asked her to claim for me through prayer the help I needed. Rebecca was a physician who, several years before, had given up her practice to experiment with techniques of spiritual therapy. She was to be in Washington only briefly visiting friends, but had agreed to see me.

On the afternoon of my appointment, she received me in a small upstairs room in the home where she was a guest. Dr. Beard was a big, gray-haired woman whose outstanding characteristic was motherliness.

Soon I was pouring out my heart to her—all the hurt of it, the ineptness and the fear I felt about facing the future alone. As during the church service on the Sunday following Peter's death, the tears flowed copiously.

My friend just let me talk. She said little. She attempted no pat explanation of Peter's death; offered no advice for the future. Sometimes there were tears in her own eyes as she watched me.

Then finally, when the well of my emotion was dry, she said quietly, "As a doctor, I have only one remedy to offer for what ails you. Let's talk to Christ about it."

Her prayer was a simple heartfelt claiming of Christ's promise to bind up the brokenhearted. Then when she had finished, without another word she gathered me into her ample arms. That afternoon it was as if a gentle Hand were laid on my heart.

From that moment the healing began somewhere in the depths of my being. As a wound that heals from the inside out, so the restoration was to come, gently, almost imperceptibly.

I know now that this specific asking for the touch of the Great Physician for my torn emotions was an invaluable step. I also do not believe that this prayer would have had the same effectiveness had it not been made in my presence. Nor can it be as effective if it is a casual prayer, a sort of overflow of good will on the part of one's friends. The prayer for the healing of the brokenhearted must be an appointed prayer act—at a definite time and in a definite place. This is a responsibility that clergymen and Christian friends need to undertake for the sorrowing; they fail us if they do not.

Since death had invaded our family circle, God had been working in me at the level of the spirit. I might have anticipated that. But now, for me as for everyone who is called to walk this trail, God's hand became wonderfully apparent in the world of practical men and external affairs.

Four
Work for
the Hands to Do

PETER MARSHALL HAD done a lot of preaching in his lifetime about a practical God who cares about us human beings as individuals, who "knows folks' names," who is quite as capable of guiding us in the market place as in the cathedral.

I had thought this a fine thesis and had accepted it as true. But now came the acid test; an economic imperative stared me in the face. Already I had claimed God's promise that He would bring "good" for my son and me out of the seeming tragedy of Peter's early death. I had assumed that this would have to include economic good, else it would be for the angels—not for widows on this earth. But the next question haunted me . . . what was the right job? I did not know. After all, I had had no experience with any work outside my own home. How could I start all over?

Actually the answer to my prayer was already on the way. A design was in the process of being woven, though I was still too close to the warp and the woof to see the pattern.

Only seven days after Peter had begun his new life a friend had written to me:

. . . the following matter is on my heart and a like sentiment has come my way from various people in the congregation. Please forgive me for

*bringing it up so soon. I, along with thousands, earnestly hope that you
will see to it that Peter's sermons, his prayers in the Senate and from his
pulpit, will be published. . . . Spiritual insight pungently expressed is necessary food. I'm certain you understand that. Old clichés no longer mean
much. Ours is a virile faith needing virile expression. Peter was blessed
with such an ability. . . .*

A few days later I wrote a former professor of mine at Agnes Scott
College, the head of the English department:

*Dear Dr. Hayes:
Thank you so much for your wonderful letter written the day after
Peter died. . . .
I have no idea now what the future holds or what it is God wants me to
do. I just hope that I can take this great crisis in my life in the spirit of an
adventure, or as Peter expressed it once in a sermon to young people—as
going out "under sealed orders."
In the immediate future there is the task of answering between five and
six hundred letters, and all through them there runs a request for the publication of some of Peter's sermons. Already I have had overtures from
two of the smaller publishing houses. Editing the sermons would probably be of real help to me, in that the work would give me something constructive to think about in the days ahead. I do also have a deep conviction that they should be given to the world. . . .*

That conviction grew with each day that passed. It was buttressed
by a groundswell of requests from friends, parishioners, and people whom
I did not even know. It almost seemed as if everyone who had heard Peter
from the pulpit and had been stirred by his preaching now wanted a book
of his sermons so that his words would not be lost to them.

About this time, one of our friends who was similarly enthusiastic
was in New York on business. One morning as he was walking down
Fifth Avenue he noticed a glass door with the words on it:

THE FLEMING H. REVELL COMPANY
BOOK PUBLISHERS SINCE 1870
NEW YORK, LONDON, GLASGOW

On an impulse he walked in and asked to see the president of the
company. The ensuing conversation was soon reflected in a letter to me

from that official, William Barbour. He suggested that he or his chief editor, Frank Mead, come to Washington to confer with me about publishing a book of Dr. Marshall's sermons. He came himself on February 27 and took back with him to New York some of the sermon manuscripts. Enthusiastic comments from his editor followed quickly in the mail and then an offer to publish.

Putting the Revell Company's definite proposition alongside the two that had already come to me, I had to decide between placing the sermon manuscripts in the hands of a church denominational publisher or letting the New York house handle them. The decision was not difficult. Though I had great respect for the work of the church publishers, I knew that their distribution was necessarily limited, indeed all but confined to church groups. I believed that Peter's work had a wider appeal.

I could not forget all those messages of sympathy and heartfelt letters that had come to me after Peter's death from people of a great variety of religious denominations, Jewish and Catholic as well as Protestant.

And I reasoned, had not one of my husband's favorite texts been the words of Christ: "I came not to call the pious, but the irreligious"? It was the average man or woman beset with problems who stood on the fringe of the church, or altogether outside it, whom Peter had always yearned to reach. His sermons had so often been slanted toward the average man. So the decision was made; I turned my face to New York.

The notation on my little green date book for Tuesday evening, March 8, read: "Work on sermons." Peter had left some six hundred sermon manuscripts filed in three worn, black-and-white cardboard boxes. The proposed book could include at the most only twenty to twenty-five. The problem was . . . on what basis should I go about trying to choose from the six hundred?

It appeared that my immediate task was to sort the sermon manuscripts into types—Biblical word pictures; those that dealt with modern problems: worry, tension, fear, sex, divorce, health, death; special-occasion sermons; those Peter had preached during World War II; those with a national or patriotic flavor. Some of my contemporaries at the church had offered to help with the reading and sorting.

On that March evening, six of us were sitting around the dining-room table at the Manse surrounded by a sea of papers. The manuscripts were spread in little piles on the table, even on the floor. We found it hard to make progress with the sorting, because first one and then another of us would keep intruding on the silent reading.

"Just listen to this," someone would say. "You've got to hear this!"

It is the same old brass of willful
disobedience coated with the chromium
of the twentieth century.

"And this. . . ."

Christianity began as good news. . . .
We have permitted it to be diluted
into good advice.

"Oh—but listen to this. . . ."

In Mathematics, one-half plus one-half
equals one. . . .
But this formula does not hold in the
Church.
We cannot add two half Christians to
make one effective Christian.

We could not even be sad about our task, because Peter's humor and exuberance for life kept flashing out at us from the typed pages. Suddenly, someone would begin chuckling. . . .

Modern politics appear to be related to the
art of conjuring. . . .
The skeletons in the nation's cupboards are
replaced by the rabbits that come out of the
politicians' hats.

Then another would interrupt, "Do you remember this statement that Peter made during the war years?"

Evil may be triumphant for a moment.
But it is always deprived of the results
of its triumph.

> The conquests of their armies to date are
> hollow victories. . . .
> The flies have conquered the flypaper.

And another one:

> There are some good people who feel that they
> are the custodians of the public morals, the kind
> of person who will come to you—in love, of
> course—and say, "I want to tell you some
> things for your own good."

Yes, I remembered. How often Peter had said to me, "If there's anything I can't *stand*, it's people seeking me out to tell me something 'for my own good.'"

Along with the cardboard boxes of sermon manuscripts was a long, slim wooden box filled with Peter's sermons which had been printed locally in pamphlet form. Soon after we had come to Washington the project had been initiated by a group of the church women. The pamphlets had sold for ten cents. During all the war years, they had been distributed free to any serviceman or woman who had asked to be on the mailing list. Consequently, the distribution had been global.

Tom Wharton, a packaging engineer and a deacon in our church, was one of those present that night to help us sort sermons. He seemed to be in a quiet and thoughtful mood. I noticed that he kept pulling printed sermons out of the wooden box and comparing them with typed manuscripts.

All at once he said, "Catherine, would you come here a minute? I want you to see something."

I crossed to the other side of the table, and Tom patted the chair beside him. "Sit down here and look at these two passages side by side."

The pamphlet sermons had been printed in the usual way prose is set in type. . . .

> There is a silent uplifting impartation from the Absolute. It does us good
> to look up and see Orion driving his hunting dogs across the Zenith, or
> Andromeda shaking out her tresses over limitless space.

It enlarges the self to have studied great architecture; to know great art—
the red of Titian, the sunsets of Turner, the seas of Winslow Homer; to
have felt the spell of epic heroisms; to have swung to the rhythmic pulse
of Homer; to have known the tenderness of Francis of Assisi . . . to have
heard the whirring of angels' wings in Milton's "Paradise Lost"; to have
been swept away on the streams of Beethoven's music; to engrave the pro-
logue to the Gospel of John on the heart; and to march with the majestic
affirmations of the Nicean Creed.

It does something inside a man. It stretches him mentally, stirs him mor-
ally, inspires him spiritually. . . .

But the typed sermons looked different, more alive, almost like poetry . . .

> There is a silent uplifting impartation from the Absolute.
> It does us good to look up and see
> Orion driving his hunting dogs across the Zenith . . .
>   or Andromeda shaking out her tresses over limitless space.
> It enlarges the self to have studied great architecture . . .
> to know great art—the reds of Titian . . .
>   the sunsets of Turner . . .
>   the seas of Winslow Homer . . .
> To have felt the spell of epic heroisms . . .
>   to have swung to the rhythmic pulse of Homer . . .
>   to have known the tenderness of Francis of Assisi . . .
>
> To have heard the whirring of angels' wings in Milton's "Paradise
>   Lost" . . .
> to have been swept away on the streams of Beethoven's music . . .
>
> To engrave the prologue to the Gospel of John on the heart . . .
>   to march with the majestic affirmations of the Nicene Creed.
>
> It does something inside a man.
> It stretches him mentally . . .
>   stirs him morally . . .
>   inspires him spiritually . . .

Years before, as a young minister, Peter had been intrigued by the
sermon manuscripts of Dr. Trevor Mordecai of Birmingham, Alabama,
a Welshman whose preaching he had much admired. Dr. Mordecai had

devised a way of typing his sermons that had assisted him in delivery. Peter had found the idea useful and had adapted it to suit his own needs, carefully teaching each succeeding secretary exactly how he wanted his sermons typed.

The device had two chief characteristics: all lists or series of nouns, adjectives, phrases, or even descriptive clauses were typed in stair-step fashion; and every new sentence was typed flush with the left-hand margin rather than being indented.

"The typewritten copies are certainly much easier to read than the printed ones," I had to admit.

"Exactly! Catherine, I feel sure that the book should be printed just as Peter had his sermons typed. In fact, I'd even go so far as to say that doing them any other way would be unfair to Peter."

Such an idea had never once occurred to me. "Let me have time to think it over," I told Tom. "If you're right about this—well—I'll have to come to it in my own way, slowly."

This would, I felt sure, have been just as new an idea to Peter. His stair-step device had been solely for his own use in delivering the sermons orally. Certainly he had never thought of having the pamphlets printed in anything but the time-tested manner. In fact, the publication of the individual sermons was as far as he had ever been willing to go. Steadily, he had resisted the thought of any book publication. "I'm a preacher," had been his viewpoint, "not an author or an editor."

Over the next few days I made more comparisons of passages set up in the two ways and had to acknowledge that in the typed format the words seemed to come alive on the page. The reader caught the emphasis of word or clause that the speaker's voice had supplied in oral delivery. The extra amount of white space made reading a pleasure. And the phrases and clauses fell readily into the rhythms implicit in their meanings. In comparison, the printed pamphlet sermons seemed dry reading.

But how, I wondered, would an old and conservative publishing house receive the suggestion of such a novel typography for the proposed book.

I need not have feared; the event was not in my hands. During this period I was haunted by the feeling that I was treading a path that had been planned for me; that I was acting out a role the script for which I had not written; that I was walking through doors that another Hand opened for me. I know now that this was no idle imagining. Time after time circumstances and events proved it so.

For one thing, just the right persons began to appear on my horizon at the precise moment they were needed. This was to prove such a stimulating adventure in the matter of human relationships that I had little time to be lonely or to do any nursing of my grief.

On Sunday, March 20, for instance, while I was still mulling over Tom's idea, I had dinner at the apartment of two career girls. One of them, Sara Leslie, a tall, willowy brunette who had come to Washington from Tennessee, had had full apprenticeship training as a printer. I was amazed to learn that this attractive and very feminine girl had successfully invaded such a predominately masculine field. In addition, she had a great love for all that goes into the making of books.

After dinner that day, the conversation turned to the possibility of printing Dr. Marshall's sermons in the unusual format. Miss Leslie was intrigued, eager to help. Through her interest I was brought into contact with a specialist in the field, a man in the publications division of the State Department. He, in turn, introduced me to one of Washington's top-flight designers of fine books, Warren Ferris, then chief typographer at the Government Printing Office.

I soon learned that the Government Printing Office does far more than print Congressmen's speeches and turn out agricultural pamphlets. There, in his office, Mr. Ferris showed me several of the beautiful special editions he had designed. He even set out to introduce me to some of the mysteries of the art of bookmaking. He analyzed books for me, discussing the matter of type faces, the quality, weight, and rag content of the paper, the leading, and the margins. I found all of this exciting. And my excitement increased when, as soon as Mr. Ferris had seen a sampling of Peter's sermon manuscripts, he had endorsed Tom's idea as an inspired one.

Meanwhile, day by day my astonishment grew at what was happening to me. What had I done to deserve such adventure? But then I realized that no one of us ever deserves God's blessings. This realization was, in turn, the soil out of which my gratitude could grow. And gratitude is a sure cure for self-pity—that special illness at the heart of all grief.

Soon, at the fitting moment, there came the next right person on my horizon. I had a visit from our Cape Cod neighbors, the Robert Ingrahams. Earlier in his life, Bob Ingraham had been associated with a publishing business. He now volunteered to assemble for me some opinions of New York professionals in the printing field. That, Bob felt, would give me some expert backing for the coming interview with my publisher.

There was still another link in the chain that was being forged. My conference with Frank Mead, of the Revell Company, was to be on April 21. On the evening of April 20, I had a surprise visit from Glenn Clark, an author, teacher, and old friend who had given me much spiritual inspiration in the past. Dr. Clark appeared at my door with a timing so precise that only God could have engineered it.

He was a short, stocky man with a fringe of gray hair around a shiny bald spot. His face wore such a benign expression that it gave him a somewhat beatific air.

Since I had had a few hours' notice of his visit, I had prepared several parallel passages from Peter's sermons for him—some in the stair-step manner, some with the usual paragraphing.

My guest sat on the davenport, leaning over the typed sheets and sermon manuscripts spread out on the coffee table. Curled up in a red leather chair nearby, I was fascinated watching his plump, expressive hands as they hovered over the papers.

Finally he straightened up, leaned back in an attitude of complete relaxation.

"You've made the right decision all right."

"But will Dr. Mead think so? He comes tomorrow, you know."

Dr. Clark leaned back even further, became more contemplative. He put the tips of his forefingers together in a precise gesture, as we used to as children when we playfully made a church, the steeple, and the people with our hands. . . . "Here's one thing—I'm sure of it. These parallel passages you've typed out are too short. I didn't get the full impact of how readable Peter's stuff is until I looked at some full sermons. Don't show Dr. Mead fragments tomorrow. Show him complete sermons—typed ones, and the same ones printed in the pamphlets."

Somehow Glenn Clark's visit supplied me with the one thing I had most needed—the conviction that the book project about to be undertaken was God's venture—not mine. Only on the solid foundation of that conviction could my house of faith for the success of the project be built. After that a sense of destiny about what I was doing never deserted me.

Before Dr. Clark left that night, he and I had eased the task ahead with prayer. As a result, what happened the next day shamed my small faith. What I had anticipated as being arduous—convincing the publisher to try a radical experiment in design—did not turn out to be difficult at all. The interference had already been run; the work already done.

Dr. Mead listened carefully. He was in a reflective mood, seemed to be absorbed in what I was saying.

"I'll have to check all this with my associates," he said upon leaving. "I can promise you, however, that we shall give the whole matter careful consideration. I'll let you know in a few days."

With more than a little trepidation, I awaited the verdict. Within the week it came. The Revell Company would be willing to publish the book of sermons in Dr. Marshall's unusual typography. This proved to be an important decision—more so than it may seem. It was to play a large part in the success of the book of sermons.

On June 9, I wrote to Mr. Barbour: "If we can handle this book right, I believe that it is going to hit the country like a ton of bricks. . . ."

What Mr. Barbour did not know was that I intended personally to see to it that the book was handled right. Like many a sheltered woman making her initial sally into professional life, I went at it hammer and tongs. Certain masculine traits I had not known I possessed came trooping to the forefront to take command. They submerged moderation, balance, and perspective.

I thought that I should keep my fingers on every decision, large and small. Thereafter, until the book was off the presses, someone at the Revell Company received a letter or a phone call from me almost every day. Having acquired a smattering of knowledge from Mr. Ferris and Miss Leslie, I worked it overtime.

The type face for the book . . . what would they think of setting it in Granjon or Baskerville? Would they please set up sample pages in both type faces and submit them to me?

And what about the size of the book? They had suggested $5\frac{3}{8} \times 8$. I would prefer 6×9.

As if this weren't enough, I then went into the matter of the quality of paper to be used. Would they agree to Crocker Burbank "Saturn," wove or laid, 50 pound or its equivalent?

I even suggested a special color for the binding, for all the world as if this were a room I was decorating.

In retrospect, I know that I went to unbelievable lengths. . . . I had a bright idea concerning the breaks in the chapters. Why not use a tiny stylized thistle design? It would be unusual and appropriate, would give an added fillip—like a bunch of artificial carrots on a woman's hat. Promptly, I had an artist friend submit a sample drawing to my defenseless publisher.

I would stop at nothing. I believed in the book, and everything in connection with it had to be perfect. I developed some ideas about advertising copy and wrote some samples. Would the men at the Revell Company like to see them?

Undoubtedly they would not! Yet they bit their tongues, summoned all their patience and diplomacy, and replied that, of course they would. Perhaps they sensed something unusual about the situation. Or perhaps a bit of my enthusiasm and sense of destiny about the book was catching.

They even let me do the proofreading. I insisted on it! Nor would I do it in less than the best professional manner.

For this task the help of five friends was enlisted. One evening they came to the Manse, and we paired off into three couples—one pair in the living room, one in the sun parlor, one upstairs.

Then two sets of the galley proofs were divided into thirds. Each couple was given two copies of their third. One read aloud while the other person held a set of galleys and followed it silently, watching for printing errors. We found a few. But now I know that the proofreader at the Revell Company would undoubtedly have found them anyway!

There remained one big question . . . who was to write the introduction to *Mr. Jones, Meet the Master?* This gave me my chance to exercise a little diplomacy. The publisher felt that some prominent friend of Peter's, like Senator Kenneth Wherry or Senator Arthur Vandenberg, should be invited to write it. I refused to believe that Peter's material needed "a name" to launch it. Anyway, I wanted to write it myself.

I knew full well that the men of the Revell Company looked on me as a fond wife without either writing talent or experience who was bitten with somewhat grandiose ideas. They had a point. I had given them a hard time indeed!

"Would you be willing," I cautiously asked Dr. Mead, "to let me put on paper the introduction I have in mind? Then if you like it—fine. If you don't—then you can go ahead with other plans. That way you can't lose."

Probably out of weariness, Dr. Mead agreed. One night, sitting propped up in bed, the bed and floor awash with papers, I wrote a seven-page sketch of Peter Marshall, the man, *as* I had known him. I called it "Here Is Peter Marshall" and sent it off to New York.

Two days later Mr. Barbour telephoned me. There was undisguised surprise in his voice. "Three of us here have read your introduction. We didn't think you—that is, well, I mean, it couldn't be more perfect. Of course we want to use it."

Those seven pages of original writing turned out to be my foot in the door of the publishing world.

Meanwhile as the editing work on the sermons progressed, I began to experience the deep satisfaction and inner contentment known only to those who have found the right vocational spot for them. It was not that my adjustment to bereavement was complete. In fact, it had scarcely begun. The great void was still there. Half of my personality was still missing.

But in spite of that, it was as if I had come home to my own element. The work of editing, the virility of the sermon material itself, the intuitive knowledge that people near and far would find these messages food for hunger of the spirit, the flashing facets of Peter's personality that shone from the typewritten pages, the feel of paper and pencil in my hands—every bit of it was pure joy. I knew then that many things in the years gone by had been meant as preparation for this task.

During the long quiet days of work on the editing of the manuscripts while Peter John was in school, many a scene out of the past came to my mind all unbidden. . . . My minister father's book-lined study, always the heart of our home, with our friends, the books, lining the walls floor to ceiling on two sides. It was here that our family always gathered in the evening. While mother darned or mended, and father read, we three children did our lessons. I could still see us sprawling full length on the floor; or sitting at one of the pull-out leaves of father's roll-top desk; or in the old leather Morris chair within arm's reach of the *Book of Knowledge*, Stoddard's *Lectures*, the *Harvard Classics*, and McLaren's *Commentaries on the Scriptures*.

Our parents never insisted that we go off by ourselves to our up-stairs bedrooms in order to concentrate on our homework. We did our reading and writing right there in father's study, and the warmth and happiness of the room became a part of the studying itself. Father and mother always near . . . the typewriter on its homemade stand . . . the ferns . . . the bird cage with a singing canary . . . mother's rolls raising on the hot-air register . . . the shades drawn against the winter night. It was here that I started several novels in notebooks that I bought for two for five cents. None progressed beyond the second or third chapters— but my dreams did.

It was in that room that a love for books, for reading them, handling them, collecting them, even the dream of someday writing them, be-came part of my life.

A romanticist to the core, I delighted in *Just David*, the Gene Stratton Porter books, and every one of the fourteen volumes of the *Little Colonel* series. On the other hand, I tried the *Elsie Dinsmore* books and found them abhorrent. Perhaps I discovered Elsie when I was too old for her. At any rate, I remember finding her brand of sticky piety offensive.

I remembered other moments of childhood. I saw myself standing at my bedroom window looking out, but not seeing the mountain just across the valley. For at that instant a dream was being planted in my heart. I had just finished a very girlish book, *Emily of New Moon*. The heroine wanted to be a writer; I had just discovered that I did, too. The words I had read haunted me. . . .

"Emily why do you want to write? Give me your reason."

"I just love to write."

"A better reason—but not enough—not enough. Tell me this—if you knew that you would be poor as a church mouse all your life—If you knew you'd never have a line published—would you still go on writing—would you?"

"Of course I would," said Emily disdainfully. "Why, I have to write—I can't help it. . . . I've just got to."

"Oh—then, I'd waste my breath giving advice at all. If it's in you to climb you must—there are those who must lift their eyes to the hills—they can't breathe properly in the valleys. . . . Go on-climb! . . ."

At sunset Emily sat in the lookout room. It was flooded with soft splendor. Outside in sky and trees, were delicate tintings and aerial sounds. . . .*

Outside my window was only my mountain. But Emily had left her mark.

Soon after that came college and the assignment of my first freshman term paper. The English teacher had given us a choice of several writers to study. I had chosen the English girl, Katherine Mansfield—had chosen better than I knew. After reading several volumes of her short stories, I came upon her *Journal.* Every line of it had spoken to something buried deep in me and had awakened a response. The way Katherine Mansfield had fingered life, rolled it on her tongue, so that not one, but a dozen taste buds tasted it. . . . She had been as a little girl with guileless round eyes, saying, "See! New shoes!"

The term paper had become incidental. Preparing for it was not work, it was the breath of life. I had discovered pure gold and I reveled in it. Into a notebook I copied lines from the *Journal* that I especially liked:

She was the same through and through. You could go on cutting slice after slice and you knew you would never light upon a plum or a cherry or even a piece of peel. . . .

Throttling, strangling by the throat a helpless, exhausted little black beach bag. . . .

I keep walking and walking round the letter, treading on my toes and with my tail in the air; I don't know where to settle. There's so much to say. . . .

The sun has gone in; it's beginning to thunder. There's a little bird on a tree outside this window not so much singing as sharpening a note. He's getting a very fine point on it. . . .*

*Montgomery, L. M., *Emily of New Moon*, Frederick A. Stokes Company, New York, 1923. Used by permission.
*Murry, J. Middleton (ed.), *Journal of Katherine Mansfield*, pp. 60, 82, 157, 178, Alfred A. Knopf. Inc., New York, 1927. Used by permission.

Immediately I had decided that I too would keep a journal—only I would tell no one about it. It would be no mere girlhood diary of daily happenings. In it I would try to put down as accurately and memorably as I could my deepest feelings and reactions to life. A great earnestness about this had carried me through four years and several volumes.

Later on in college I had heard Edna St. Vincent Millay spend an evening reading her own poetry, and with her "had looked on beauty bare." Thereafter, for the remainder of my college days I had concentrated on writing poetry; mostly sonnets and sonnet sequences. The poetry club had taken me under its wing. My English teachers had been patiently helpful in criticizing what I had written, though they were continually urging me not to take myself quite so seriously.

Graduation and marriage had followed. Peter and I had taken a delayed honeymoon trip to his home in Scotland. The next Christmas I had presented him with a neatly typed *Journal of a Trip to Scotland*, bound in a handsome leather notebook. The writing had been a labor of love and was for his eyes alone. Like Emily of New Moon, I had to keep on writing.

Three years after our son was born, the doctors had discovered that I had an early case of tuberculosis. The treatment was enforced bed rest twenty-four hours a day. My immediate physical world narrowed to the big front bedroom of the Manse. It was a pleasant airy room with five windows, some of them framed with ivy, and the pale yellow wallpaper made it seem always sun-drenched. There was the mahogany Chippendale furniture on which Peter and I had splurged, the deep-blue rugs, the seascapes on the walls—some original watercolors and two Turner reproductions.

Soon I had worked out a daily schedule—mealtimes on a tray; hours of absolute rest in morning and afternoon; time set aside for reading; periods of playing quiet bedside games with Peter John. I asked that a little bookcase be moved close to my bed so that writing materials would be near. Propped up in bed again, I took pencil in hand and was soon filling notebook after notebook.

This period turned into a time of soul searching, of repeated attempts to evaluate the meaning of human life in general and mine in particular.

One of the books which had helped me at that time had spoken of the value of probing to find one's precise dreams, one's positive longings—"the soul's sincere desires." The author had suggested that the uncovering of these real hungers—not those superficially laid on by society, but the ones God Himself has planted within each of us—could then become the foundation for prayers sure to be answered. The reasoning behind this had been explained in a simple but impressive analogy—that when God plants the pattern of an oak tree in an acorn, it is certainly His will that the acorn become an oak.

I had understood the value of such an urge toward self-discovery. Among other "soul's sincere desires" set down in my notebook at that time had been this one:

> To become a writer who will make real contribution to my generation
> and to the world.

Into the notebook also went my attempt to analyze and sift my motives in order to find out whether or not this desire to be a writer was truly a God-given dream:

> If I *thought* I wanted to be a writer, but what I really wanted was fame
> or money, or even that my name would not die after me, then this would
> be false desire. But such I do not believe to be the case.
>
> The writer dream must be part of my pattern because I've had it since I
> was a little girl, when my dreams must still have been pretty fresh, as from
> the hand of God.
>
> I have always loved ideas. I enjoy trying to express them in as accurate
> and beautiful a way as possible. It gives me real soul satisfaction. . . .

After pondering all this for many days, necessarily long quiet days, I had felt that this dream passed the most honest tests I could devise. And just about that time two verses in the New Testament had leaped up at me as though written in fire:

> And this is the confidence that we have in
> Him—that if we ask anything according to His
> will He heareth us:
>
> And if we know that He hear us, whatsoever
> we ask, we know that we have the petitions that
> we desired of Him. (1 JOHN 5:14, 15)

If then the wish to be a writer was God's will for me, He would hear me when I asked for the help I needed; and, if He heard, then this wish would some day be granted. So I had sent that particular dream wafting back toward heaven with the confident awareness that He had already heard.

To it, I had added a petition equally important. It was that God would thereafter send into my life the right persons at the right time for the implementation of these dreams. Never before had I thought to ask for this blessing of the right friends.

But it had finally dawned on me that life in our day is no longer possible on a lone-wolf basis; that one can succeed in any field only as he is a success with the people in that field. I had reasoned that, in order for God's will to be done in the lives of men and women in our time, there would have to be a coming together—a juxtaposition of ideas, persons, and events at the propitious moment.

Having tossed these two dreams heavenward, I had then climbed out of my sickbed, walked off, and left them. Always thereafter, the wish for their fulfillment had been in me somewhere just under the surface. Yet I had not consciously thought of them again for more than four years.

Yes, it had all been preparation—unplanned on my part. Thinking back on this, I was to discover a thread running through my life, never quite disappearing, never quite grasped until the present moment. But now strange events had placed the pencil back in my hands. Not only that, but since Peter's death I had watched unfolding before my wondering eyes that very juxtaposition of ideas, persons, and events about which I had prayed four years before.

Consequently, there was in me a profound gratitude to God and to other people. To God, because I was keenly aware of His firm hand on the life situation of one widow. To other human beings, because their warmth and outgoing generosity had enabled them to be the channels for some of God's will for me—whether they were aware of being channels or not.

Through this series of events, which I could never have engineered myself, I learned several unforgettable lessons.

I learned that money is really only ideas that have been converted into a form usable in the exchange markets of earth. The corollary is that these ideas must be of a kind that will be of some help to other people. Then the way to pray for economic resources is to ask God for new and creative ideas that will make a contribution—no matter how small—to lighten the tasks or illumine the lives of one's contemporaries.

Thus I learned something of what the Kingdom of God (or the "Kingdom of Right Relationships") really means. ". . . for we are members one of another," the Scriptures tell us. Certainly we are! I discovered for myself the interrelatedness of all human life; how dependent we are on others for success in any line of work; what an unpayable debt we owe to other men—living and dead.

Five

Open the Hands

IT IS AMAZING how a word can have definite emotional tone. Thus, for a long time after Peter's death, the word "widow" was despicable to me—as loathsome as had been the word "tuberculosis" in the early days of my bout with that disease.

To such ridiculous lengths did I carry this reaction that I even disliked to open an envelope addressed to "Mrs. Catherine Marshall." To my emotion-saturated reasoning, the writer of the letter might just as well have printed WIDOW in large capital letters after the name. And how I hated to see the descriptive term, "The late Peter Marshall. . . ." What a silly way of putting it, I thought. Late? Late to what?

Such violent reactions were of course sure signs that I was still not facing reality. For the truth was that I was a widow, whether or not I was willing to accept and wear the various tags appended to widowhood.

My resentment about this took varying forms. One evening one of my husband's stamp-collector friends came to the Manse to call. The man had once been widowed, but had remarried. On the table was the manuscript of the introduction to the book of sermons on which I had been working. My guest was interested in it and was soon picking up some of the typewritten pages to scan them. . . .

Our home reflected Peter's taste. . . . The boy who had grown up near the Firth of Forth, and who at fourteen had run away to join the Royal Navy, never got over his passion for the sea. So we ended up with four seascapes in the living room, two large ones in the dining room, five in our bedroom and a few others scattered throughout the house.

His taste in color was just as decided. Blue. . . .*

Suddenly the friend put his finger on the page to keep his place and commented: "I suppose it's just as well that you are getting down details like this so soon. But you won't be talking or writing like this for long. Time not only heals, it erases practically everything. You'll be surprised how quickly your life with Peter will come to seem like a dream, or as if it happened to somebody else in another lifetime."

Then he went back to reading the manuscript while I stood there, stunned, saying nothing, feeling only revulsion for the idea he had just expressed. I certainly did not want time just to form a protective scab over a still grievously painful area. Surely, I thought, it would be far better for the wound to heal cleanly, really heal from the inside out.

And though intellectually I knew that I couldn't live in memories, still who would want Time to come with a big eraser and obliterate every tender remembrance? Doesn't the future always have to be built on the past? Wouldn't real healing mean that what had gone before—the flaws in the weaving as well as the most perfect and treasured parts of the design—would all eventually fall into proper place? In that way and that alone, I thought, could the fabric of my life be all of one piece.

There was as yet no such unity in me. There were even indications that my subconscious mind was still stubbornly refusing to accept the fact of Peter's death.

At intervals of weeks or even months I kept having one recurring dream. It had variations of detail, but always the same agonizing theme. In the dream, my husband was not dead; he and I were estranged. There would follow all the emotional torment over such a separation. Always in the dream, there would be a reaching out for Peter, an effort to contact him, to win him back. Then when the anguish was at its height, I would awaken.

The first two times a dream had followed this pattern, I had quickly dismissed it from my mind as being just a dream, of no consequence whatever. But then, when it came to be repeated over and over, like a

*Marshall, Peter, *Mr. Jones, Meet the Master*, p. 13, Fleming H. Revell Company, New York, 1949. Used by permission.

phonograph needle caught in the groove of a defective record, I began to wonder how to deal with it. I reasoned that my subconscious mind was being forced to come up with some explanation of why Peter was no longer by my side. This was apparently the explanation it had hit upon. I kept wishing that the needle would find another groove, or else get on with the next theme.

But I was not yet ready to leave that particular emotional plateau. The dream recurred often that spring. In particular I remember one afternoon. . . . I had lain down for a nap. Some little girls were playing hopscotch on the sidewalk in front of our house. There was the repeated thud of rocks being dropped by the children on the pavement outside, the sound of a window shade flapping in a lazy breeze from a half-open window. I dozed—then after a while the clatter of a rock half awakened me. My mind, struggling back to consciousness, had sent the message . . . *Something is wrong—terribly wrong.* Suddenly my heartbeat speeded up, started racing. Fear made my mouth dry. Then as I shook off sleep a little more . . . *Peter is gone.* . . . *No, he can't be. This is just a bad dream, a nightmare. It will pass.*

I forced myself back to full consciousness and wearily turned over in bed. This was a way of waking that was becoming all too familiar. The stabbing awareness, the nightmarish quality of a half-remembered fact, the pain that touches every nerve ending—all this is well known to those who have experienced shock. I lay there trying to assimilate the situation, trying to force myself to look squarely at the facts.

But what is the truth anyway? I wondered. And suddenly I thought that I recognized Truth in that intuitive way that it has flashed into the human mind since the beginning of time. . . . *Perhaps it is this life that is the dream. One of these days I shall wake up and find Peter again and know that he's not dead at all. Then I shall be what the world calls dead myself. But meantime, how am I going to force my subconscious mind to accept the fact that my husband is gone?*

Part of the answer to that question came through finding that my recovery from these emotional wounds was in direct proportion to my ability to stop steeling myself against them and begin accepting the pain inherent in my personal loss. I now know that the healing process for any of life's frustrations, disappointments, and sorrows can begin the moment we stop resisting them. Tightly closed hands are not in a position to receive anything—not even comfort. It matters little whether they are hands clenched in rebellion or just piteously trying to clutch the past.

Just as women have discovered that the pain of childbirth becomes supportable as they stop resisting it, open their total beings to it, and relax—so it is with emotional pain. The cup of grief is heavy and it holds a bitter brew. But one can at least take the cup with both hands and put it to one's lips at intervals, then, for a while, turn to something else. Somehow the cup becomes lighter, a little more bearable, its contents less bitter each time the cup is voluntarily grasped.

The voluntary part is important. That is the point at which the human will enters the picture. I cannot believe that the mere passage of time will effect a permanent and healthy repair. Time helps, but there must also be the cooperation of the will actively assenting to the growth necessary to accomplish the healing.

In the months following Peter's death, events conspired to bring me to just that point of assent. Many of them were entirely ordinary and practical. I was not going to be allowed to take off on any flights of unreality which I might mistakenly have called "spiritual." The business matters confronting me were calculated to bring me back to earth with a thud.

Peter—to the surprise of all who had known him well—had left no will. Apparently he had thought that since he possessed little other than insurance, making me the sole beneficiary of that took care of the situation. If only he had known how much it left to be taken care of! Yet in thinking a will unimportant for those with a small or moderate estate, my husband was not unusual. I learned later that an estimated 70 per cent of American property owners die intestate.

The first business complication developed when Peter's checking account (we did not have a joint one) was frozen. Consequently, no money could be drawn out even for funeral expenses or immediate needs. All of the insurance policies were in a strong box at the bank. That box was immediately sealed by the bank under the Internal Revenue Department's regulations. It took three weeks of cutting red tape before even the insurance agent could get into the strong box "to initiate the collection of death proceeds," as the insurance term has it.

Then I learned that, under District of Columbia law, when a man dies without a will, after all the debts are paid, his widow receives one-third of his estate, his child or children, two-thirds. It was necessary for me to appear in probate court to post an expensive bond and to be made administratrix of Peter's affairs. Everything thereafter came under the jurisdiction of this court. Not even funeral expenses, doctor or hospital bills, nor ordinary household expenses could be paid until the court passed on them.

Following this, some of my husband's possessions had to be appraised —his car, his stamp collection, a few power tools. The appraisal of something like a stamp collection is a highly technical matter. It has to be handled by men who know the value of stamps. But all appraisers had either to be appointed by the probate court or specifically approved by them. Such appraisal can be time consuming, a great deal of trouble, and costly.

I found it hard to keep my mind on these business affairs, because my heart kept intruding. The businessmen who were trying to help me would have found many of my thoughts highly irrelevant. . . . How much are a few British colonial stamps worth? So many dollars and cents? A hundred hours of pure pleasure?

I could see Peter bending over the stamp books spread out on a card table in our living room. To him the stamps were not just stamps. They were cargo ships on their way to romantic, far-flung places—Antigua . . . Barbados . . . the Cayman Islands . . . Grenada . . . Montserrat . . . Trinidad. The very names were music . . . ! The commemorative issues were some of history's most dramatic moments. . . . The stamps were beautiful. . . . "Catherine, take a look at this new St. Kitts's ultramarine on blue violet—and this magenta, this carmine rose. . . ."

And sermons? How could sermons be appraised? So much lift and lilt to the human spirit? So much bowing down of the heart in adoration to its Maker? Yet the sermon manuscripts were an integral part of the estate and the next thing that had to be appraised. Obviously how much they were worth commercially was anyone's guess. But even after some arbitrary value had been placed on them, then what disposition was to be made of them? It took several lawyers a little over four months to figure out that one.

It seemed that almost daily, everywhere I turned, legal proof of my husband's death was required. Finally I had a whole sheaf of photostats of his death certificate made. To the uninitiated in grief, this may seem like a small matter. Still it scarcely has a soothing effect on the bereaved.

Then came the day when I had to reappear in probate court to be made Peter John's guardian. Since then, I have been required to give a detailed financial accounting of my guardianship to the court each year. This will go on until my son becomes of age. Each year the account figures must be sworn to before a notary public. Each year a fee must be paid to the office of register of wills for the accounting.

The amount of cash in Peter's checking account at the time of his death was not large. Most of this had been given to us as a gift on the occasion of our tenth anniversary at the New York Avenue Presbyterian Church, and had been meant to pay part of our expenses for a trip abroad. Yet by the time the final accounting is made to the probate court, almost every cent of that original sum will have been drained away in legal and court costs.

When I discovered the amazing amount of red tape involved even with such a small estate, I almost ran to a lawyer to get help in making a will of my own. Not only that, but I began urging my parents and close friends to consider the same move. Though in my case there was little to leave anyone, I reasoned that the tiny sum involved in making a will might some day save many times that amount in fees for dealing with quite unnecessary legal technicalities.

Of course, Peter had no idea of all of this. Yet some of his close friends were lawyers. And often he himself had been called on to help the recently bereaved in practical matters as well as spiritual ones. I marveled that he had never even once encountered some other widow entangled in the same difficulties with which I was wrestling.

Another question of a different kind still waited to be decided. It was the decision as to where Peter would be buried. He and I had owned no cemetery plot. Thus when the suggestion had been made that I make temporary use of a receiving vault, I had gratefully agreed.

Part of the relief I felt about postponing this decision was based on emotion so faulty that even at the time I would have been ashamed to discuss it with anyone. Yet I know now that many sorrowing individuals experience the same set of feelings.

Peter had died in January. Climatically that month is usually the worst time of year in the District of Columbia. In the first shock of my grief every shred of emotion in me protested the thought of placing that beloved body—no matter how tenderly—in the wet, icy ground. I would stand at my bedroom windows watching the cold slanting rain falling on the bare bony branches of the trees, and feel relieved that Peter's body was in a dry receiving vault.

Then at the next moment shame at such a thought would pour through me. I understood quite well that reason did not prompt it. I also knew that it dishonored the faith I held. Had I not known for a certainty, standing in the hospital room that morning of January 25, that the man I loved was no longer in the shell of a body? Of course I had. It was an obvious fact—indisputable. Yet during the weeks that followed, very wisely I refrained from lashing myself too severely about feelings I could not help. Intuitively I sensed that to castigate myself would merely have been to make matters worse. My ragged emotions needed gentleness, time to catch up.

Part of the shame I felt about these emotions came from the realization that I was but reflecting clearly the trend of my time in its pagan attitude toward death. We give lip service in this regard to what we like to believe is a compassionate Christian approach. We think that if some Scripture is read and some prayers said at a funeral or interment service, this proves that we are Christian. Actually, if we Americans really believed that the spirit of the person is not extinguished by death, we could not then view death as unmitigated tragedy.

We reveal our hand in many small ways. One of them is in our accepted social and medical mores concerning last illnesses. The patient must not be told the true seriousness of his case. Undoubtedly there are instances where this withholding of information is justified and desirable. On the whole, physicians in our day are compassionate, dedicated men who make such decisions thoughtfully.

But have we become so soft and cowardly in the twentieth century that we will go to any extreme to avoid facing up to the transition called "death"? Are we not really handing the grossest insult imaginable to the dying when we assume that they have not the spiritual or character resources to handle this test courageously and victoriously?

Every modern person would shrink from the idea of maudlin, falsely sentimental, overdramatic death-bed scenes of the type described in many a nineteenth-century novel. But then some of life's experiences, among them birth and death, *are* dramatic. And isn't it possible that, by going to the opposite extreme and forcing most humans to spend their last moments on this lovely earth in ignorance of what is happening or in a drugged coma, we are denying them and ourselves one of life's most precious experiences?

At the very least, we are withholding from them the privilege of making their last plans in their own way, of saying the things most deeply in their hearts and minds to those whom they are leaving behind. On occasion, it has seemed to me at once ludicrous and tragic to watch a husband and wife—each of whom knew that the parting called "death" was imminent—keeping up a pretense, each trying to deceive the other, letting only falsely cheery superficialities pass the lips when the heart was about to burst with things waiting to be shared.

I have even heard one physician say after it was all over, "I wish now that my wife and I had talked things out. Looking back, our pretense seems stupid, childish. We fooled no one—not even each other."

The same acting out of our feeling that death is the end of everything—the final disaster—is shown in our morbid concern with the cast-off body left behind.

> We are assured in the words of the New Testament that
> ... it is the spirit that quickeneth; the flesh profiteth nothing.
> (JOHN 6:63)

If we believed that, then we would know that consciousness *is* life; that when the living spirit that looked out through the windows of the eyes has gone, what is left behind is like the chrysalis which the winged moth has abandoned. Therefore, we would find it foolish to make a fetish of the deserted chrysalis—to try to preserve it indefinitely, to spend huge sums of money on it.

Yet out of the science of the preservation of that nonprofitable flesh, of which the Apostle John wrote, has been built the huge business of the modern mortician, who deals in profits of a very different kind from any the first-century writer had in mind.

The idea of burying the human body at all originated with primitive pagan man. He believed in some sort of life after death, but subscribed to the superstition that it would be the same sort of material life that he had known on this earth. Hence food, weapons, tools, and money were carefully buried with his dead.

The emphasis on glorifying and trying to immortalize the body reached its height under the ancient Egyptians. Their greatest monuments, the pyramids, were houses for the dead, and embalming was regarded as a fine art during the time of the Pharaohs. For long centuries after that, it was scarcely practiced at all. In the Western Hemisphere it was revived by a certain Dr. Thomas Holmes, a Brooklyn druggist, during Civil War days. Since that time the preparation of the dead for burial has been made increasingly elaborate and expensive. Now it is carried to such an extreme that the services of beauticians and hairdressers are often required in addition to the work of the mortician.

Peter, who, like all clergymen, had seen a lot of funerals, felt strongly that we moderns are on the wrong track in our death customs. He had incisive words to say about it:

> Why, in our day, do we shun the fact of death?
> We try so hard to disguise it.
> We are so stupid about it.
>
> We rouge the cheeks of the corpse and dress
> it up in its best suit.
> And then we say with ridiculous gravity,
> "How natural he looks . . ." as if there
> could be anything natural about a corpse!
>
> We, who call ourselves Christians, act in
> a very pagan way.
> We gaze upon the lifeless, human clay. . . .
> We touch the cold cheek. . . .
> We line up to pass by the casket and "view
>   the remains" as the stupid phrase has it,
> as if we had never heard of the soul and never
> understood what personality is.
> If this thing called death were some
> leprous calamity that befell only a
> few of us. . . .
> If it were something that could be avoided,
> then our conspiracy of silence concerning
> it might make some sense.
>
> But it is life's great and perhaps its only
>   certainty. . . .

This conspiracy to disguise death goes on in a score of ways. There are, for instance, the expressions we use . . . the dead are just "asleep"; they have only "gone away."

Then custom dictates that the body must be preserved as long as possible. To this end, there must be a costly moisture-proof casket or metal vault. Even the grave must be camouflaged. A canopy of artificial grass is laid over it during the graveside rites.

Much of this is done in an honest attempt to smooth the way of the bereaved. There is, however, danger in these deceptive techniques. The danger is that facts not faced, but pushed down below the level of conscious dealing with them, tend toward creating real emotional difficulties.

This pagan concern with the body is reflected in the fact that steadily, year by year, the cost of dying is rising as funeral customs become more and more elaborate.

Many times undue and unfair pressure is even brought to bear on the sorrowing, emotionally vulnerable members of the family to force them to purchase an expensive casket, cemetery plot, niche in a mausoleum, or a tombstone which they can ill afford.

We in the United States are now spending more on burials than on seeing that our babies are brought into the world safely, more on funerals than we do on hospitals. The figure has now risen to more than 500 million dollars a year. On top of that, we spend another 60 million dollars on funeral flowers.

One modern nation finally became sufficiently alarmed about the gigantic waste implicit in funeral flowers to do something about it. Since 1921, Sweden has had a national organization called the "Flower Fund." Money that would be spent for flowers is sent instead as a memorial to the Flower Fund. This money is then used for modern housing developments for needy old people. The fund has long been a gigantic success, shedding light and joy into the lives of the still living.

Our own nation has no such plan. Still there is an increasing trend toward making a contribution to a favorite charity in memory of the one who has died instead of sending expensive flowers that will wilt in twenty-four hours. This trend has grown to such proportions that the organized florists are feeling threatened. Hence, during the last year and a half, at least two such organizations have been spending big sums on national advertising, trying to repersuade the American people that nothing can possibly take the place of flowers for comforting the bereaved.

Many times I had seen funeral flowers banked twenty to thirty sprays and wreaths deep all the way to the ceiling of church vestibules or chancels. I felt that it would be wrong to let this happen at the time of Peter's death. Therefore, I asked that, instead of flowers, gifts should be made toward an endowment fund for students for the gospel ministry at Columbia Theological Seminary, the school from which Peter had graduated. Of course, some flowers were sent anyway—some very lovely ones, and they were deeply appreciated. But there was not the wasteful display that might well have been. The Memorial Fund initiated at that time has been steadily growing ever since and is a living memorial to Peter Marshall.

Spring came to Washington early that year. The forsythia seemed a more brilliant yellow than usual; the azaleas were punctuation marks of flaming coral and cerise. The Tidal Basin was adrift in pale pink blossoms. Out in the residential section of Kenwood, one drove through fairy-feathered avenues of pink-and-white dogwood and cherry trees.

The weeks that had passed since January had wrought changes in me. For a time grief had made me tone deaf to the harmonies of earth. Now I could hear music again. Hence, Easter had fresh meaning that year. In my heart was a new peace. It was the kind of peace that comes, not from the absence of any pain or difficulty, but rather from knowing that I had gone through flames and had survived the ordeal.

From that travail I had been left with a crucible of conviction that, since Christ is beside us, the worst that can happen to any one of us in this life need not overwhelm us. I realized that out in my future somewhere there might be other sorrows, other crises. But there was also the sure knowledge that I need never meet any future difficulty alone, that help from a loving God would ever be available for the asking, that resources beyond imagining are always at our disposal—provided only that we are willing to put ourselves in the stream of God's purposes. Thus, that Eastertime, I knew that we human beings who are still grappling with life on the planet earth, need have no fear of any unknown tomorrows. In my heart I could kneel before the Risen Lord and promise Him to try to live in the present—joyfully.

And so I knew that the time had come to make my decision about where Peter would be buried. I was ready for that step in a way that I had not been in January.

Several trips were made to a cemetery on the edge of the District of Columbia—an uncrowded one set in a lovely rolling countryside. A new and costly mausoleum had been erected on the highest point of ground in the cemetery. The owners were anxious to sell me a crypt there.

I was shown through the mausoleum and told in some detail why the crypt type of burial was recommended. There was a certain atmosphere of luxury in the place—subdued indirect lighting, deep-piled rugs on the stone floor, long rich draperies, soft "canned" music coming over hidden loud-speakers. There were very beautiful stained-glass memorial windows, much marble, and somewhere in the distance the singing of imprisoned canaries.

The crypts were in the walls. It was explained to me that both the humidity and temperature were sharply controlled to ensure the best possible preservation of the human body. There would be, of course, both in the mausoleum and outside, what is called in cemeteries of this type "perpetual care."

In all fairness, I should say that the men dealing with me were courteous and gentle. In my case there was no high-pressure salesmanship. I sensed, however, that particularly because the mausoleum was new, the men were eager to persuade me to bury Peter there. They had no intention of using my husband's name in any overt way in advertising. Still I knew that they would like to be able to say privately, quietly, to future visitors to the place, "Now you probably know that Dr. Peter Marshall is buried here—right over there off the chapel floor gallery."

As I stood there in the dim light, with the stained-glass windows making little colored patterns on the stone floor, I could see Peter's face— laughing at me. I thought of how he had hated dim light anywhere—the subdued, supposedly glamorous lighting of cocktail lounges and some restaurants, even certain churches and cathedrals. "Who wants to grope his way through life?" he would ask. "God made brilliant sunlight—not this duck-soup atmosphere." I could see him making an elaborate pantomime of striking matches to read a restaurant menu—to the openmouthed consternation of many a waitress.

Now he seemed to be saying to me, slangily, with merriment in his eyes, "Catherine, leave us not be silly. You're taking this much too seriously. Don't let's make a production out of it. *I'm* not in that box. I dare you to think that I am."

So I knew that the atmosphere of the mausoleum was not for him. It would have mocked him, betrayed him. The fetid, closed-in feeling of the place, its artificiality—no—definitely not. In comparison there was something clean and releasing and right about being buried in God's out-of-doors—January weather or not.

That's how it came about that I chose a spot on a hill in the gently rolling countryside just across the Maryland border. Over the site were the spreading arms of a stately elm tree. From the hillside one could see for miles in all directions—a panorama of a good land.

On a mild afternoon in the late spring, a group of us gathered under the elm for a graveside service. We heard those imperishable words:

> Because I live, ye shall live also. . . .
> Let not your heart be troubled; ye believe in
> God, believe also in me. In my Father's house
> are many mansions; if it were not so, I would
> have told you.

As the words rang out—vibrant with the promise of life—it was a voice with a Scottish burr that I was really hearing. For how often those same words had been on Peter's lips for other people! And always he had spoken them with an inflection of his own that had given depth to their meaning. . . . "If it were *not* so, I would have *told* you."

As we turned to leave the cemetery, the plaintive notes of an ancient Scottish bagpipe lament sounded across the hills. Among many other kindnesses, some of Peter's fellow Scots in the St. Andrews Society had wanted to pay that last tribute. The pipers were playing that *most* soulful of all the laments, the one with a sob at its heart, "The Flowers o' the Forest. . . ."

> The prime of our land lie cauld in the clay. . . .
> Women and bairns are heartless and wee. . . .
> The Flow'rs of the Forest are a' wede away.
> The Flow'rs of the Forest are a' wede away.

Yet the rugged face that I kept seeing, the voice that I kept hearing, was impatient with, indeed simply would not tolerate, any sadness in us who were left behind. Somehow in the weeks since January, Peter had succeeded in getting at least one basic lesson through to me. . . . "*I'm* not in that casket, Catherine. I dare you to think that I am." It was because I knew that—finally—deeply—that what we were doing that spring afternoon was bearable for me.

The next time that I visited the cemetery, there was an old man standing by Peter's grave. Tears were raining down the deep furrows of his cheeks and falling on the newly gashed earth. I had never seen the old man before. Whatever had prompted his visit and had released his tears was obviously too intimate for intrusion. So I went on without making myself known to him.

As I drove away, I was thinking about the difference in the way grave sites affect individuals. I doubted that any tears of mine would ever fall on Peter's grave because I had no sense of reality about his being in that particular spot. Therefore, there was no special solace for me there. Nor did I find it a particularly good place for thoughtful appraisal or meditation—as some people do for the last resting places of their beloved dead.

Even as I headed the car out of the cemetery gates, I was once again hearing that resonant, confident voice:

> We do not well, for this is a day of good
> tiding and we hold our peace. . . .

> It is only when we know Christ that we are not
> afraid, for there is then nothing to fear.
> Only when one is no longer afraid to die, is one
> no longer afraid at all. . . .

> To be free—free as a bird—simply means
> to be unafraid, in the fullest awareness. . . .
> which awareness includes the recognition of death.
> And when we are no longer afraid, do we begin to
> live . . . in every experience, painful, or joyous
> in gratitude for every moment, to live
> abundantly. . . .

"To live abundantly. . . ." I remembered the promise I had made on Easter Sunday morning to try "to live in the present—joyfully." I thought of the editing work on the manuscript of the book of sermons waiting for me back at home, of the immense satisfaction that work was bringing to me, of the friends who had come as if from nowhere to help me. And I had strong suspicions that Peter himself had had more to do with bringing me to that point of grateful acceptance than I had any way of knowing.

Six

The Woman
and the Book

I DON'T KNOW how the woman sitting behind the green baize-covered table appeared to other people. I do know that on the inside she was at once both exhilarated and bewildered. For I was that woman.

The occasion was the publication-day autograph tea for the book of my husband's sermons that I had edited—*Mr. Jones, Meet the Master.* The day was November 28, 1949. The scene was being enacted on the second floor of the Federation of Churches building in Washington.

Two rooms had been thrown together for the tea. The line of waiting people stretched all the way across both rooms and down the stairs. Almost every person in the queue was a resident of Washington who had sat under Peter Marshall's preaching. There had been much anticipation of the day when his book of sermons would be released.

Nobody, however, had expected such a crowd. The line moved slowly because almost everyone had something special to say to me. Out of great gratitude they spoke of my husband. The eyes of some were moist with emotion. Yet many spoke with humor, clearly reflecting Peter's light touch. Often they asked for some special inscription on the flyleaf of the book.

On the table beside me was a vase of flowers, a bottle of ink, the ever-present water pitcher and glass, and a tall stack of copies of *Mr. Jones.* Behind me hovered three beaming representatives of the publishing house. At one point in the afternoon a lady spotted Peter John standing near me and asked him to sign his name underneath mine. That started it! Soon Peter John was sitting beside me, busily signing his name in book after book in a large, round, childish scrawl.

After a while, someone brought me a cup of tea and some cookies, but there was never time to sip the tea. I was much too conscious of the patient guests who had been waiting so long, and whose feet, I thought, must have begun to ache intolerably. For four hours the line passed in front of me.

Between saying a few words to each person and autographing the books, there was scarcely any time for thinking. Still, I couldn't help reflecting, somewhat wryly, that the situation was ironic. After all, Peter Marshall was the author of *Mr. Jones, Meet the Master*—not I. They were his sermons. What business had I autographing his book? Yet that was what the guests wanted and were waiting for—that personal contact.

It began to dawn on me that I was there merely as a channel—a go-between. Since Peter had begun his new life, I was as close as his friends felt that they could get to him. In a way that I had not sought nor bargained for, I was being thrust into the peculiar position of representing Peter to other people.

In several ways, that publication day was a preview of the years immediately ahead. Certainly there was to be success as the book world measures success. Three thousand copies of *Mr. Jones* were sold in Washington on that one day. Before publication day was over across the nation, the entire first printing of 10,000 books was gone. The day after that the publishing house in New York received by telephone, wire, and mail, orders for another 4,000 copies. Paper had already been ordered for the second printing (another 10,000 that sold out immediately), but even with all the rushing possible, it took 13 days to get that printing to the bookstores.

Before those books could be printed and bound, there were advance orders for every one of them. From then on for over a year, it was a mad scramble to get *Mr. Jones* off the presses fast enough. The third printing, ready 6 days after the second, was stepped up to 15,000 copies; the fourth, to 25,000; and so on.

In one of his broadcasts, Walter Winchell called *Mr. Jones* "the book surprise click." Booksellers began tagging it a "runaway best seller." So new was I to all the commercial aspects of the book world that I scarcely knew what that meant.

Therefore, when just after the turn of the year I received a letter from the Revell Company informing me that on January 8 the book would make both *The New York Times* and the *New York Herald Tribune* nonfiction best-seller lists, I was not as impressed as I should have been. I had never paid any particular attention to the best-seller lists; I knew only that books of sermons rarely do that well. But I soon began to realize that the reception that this particular book of sermons was receiving was any author's or editor's dream.

Yet for me, the real success of the book was measured in an altogether different way—by what the message of the sermons meant to individual men and women. This was dramatized through the mail that began pouring in. On any given day there would be letters from many who apologized for writing and confided that this was their first fan letter. Their letters were direct and simple expressions of deeply felt gratitude. For example, one from Villa Ridge, Illinois, began:

My dear Mrs. Marshall:

On my eighty-second birthday I was given a copy of Mr. Jones, Meet the Master. *For almost seventy years I have been a church member. Yet Christianity as Dr. Marshall preached and lived it was unknown to me.*

By the time I had finished the book my soul was flooded by a downpour of revelation. . . . I thank God that I have lived to come face to face with the Master through Dr. Marshall's living words. . . .

Or from a housewife in Conrad, Montana:

Out of a grateful heart I would thank you deeply and sincerely for making it possible for us "little people" to share the love and wealth of expression of Peter Marshall. . . . Just think! How poor the rest of us would have been if Mr. Jones, Meet the Master *had not been published, if Dr. Marshall's own congregations had been the only ones ever to receive these sermons and prayers. . . . And please, would it be possible to publish more sermons . . . ?*

The title for the book, *Mr. Jones, Meet the Master,* had originally been a sermon title of Peter's. It seemed that the publisher and I had made the right choice of title, because running like a refrain through all the letters was the thought that out of the pages had stepped a living Lord. . . .

From Schenectady, New York:

I have just finished reading Mr. Jones, Meet the Master. *This comes to you to thank you from the depths of my heart for publishing this book. . . . From the opening word the book has been hard to put down. . . . For sheer beauty of language . . . the book is unsurpassed. . . . But far beyond that, its real value lies in its amazing ability to bring my Lord into my own living room. . . .*

And on heavy vellum paper from Park Avenue in New York came a memorable letter:

This book was like a shaft of brilliant sunlight on the dark path I was treading. Thank you. Thank you. . . .

Very soon, mail began coming from abroad too—from the British Isles, from Ceylon, from a woman missionary—a "hen medic" as she described herself—in Potifunk, West Africa, even a letter written by a young American student in Germany. . . .

Heidelberg, Germany

. . . Peter Marshall really had the stuff on the ball. . . . I haven't read a book in a long time that's put me to thinking like this one. Now don't laugh, but I've decided to take the Man up on a few of His promises. . . .

I could scarcely have read letters like these day after day without their having a profound effect on me. Daily I was receiving proof that *Mr. Jones* really had been God's idea and His project. The substantiation lay in many little human-interest vignettes, as varied as the facets of Peter's personality, that kept coming back to me. . . .

In Cranford, New Jersey, an elderly woman was found dead in bed with one hand stretched out resting on a much-thumbed page of *Mr. Jones*. The book had been read and reread to the woman and had been of particular comfort to her during her last days. The relaxed fingers of one outstretched hand were lying like a benediction on the words:

Let us therefore act like believers,
live like Christians so that we can die
like Christians
with songs and rejoicing. . . .

For those we love are with the Lord,
we believe, and the Lord has promised
to be with us,
   never to leave us nor forsake us:
      "Behold I am with you always."

Well, if they are with Him,
   and He is with us. . . .
      they cannot be far away. . . .

About that time an American correspondent in the European theater had to submit to an inspection of his baggage at the Czechoslovakian border. The Communist guards confiscated two articles as being "inflammable material"—a small file of letters to American clergymen and a copy of *Mr. Jones, Meet the Master.* In telling me about the incident later, the newspaperman commented: "I can't be too sorry about the loss of the book, because I'm glad the Commies had enough sense to think of *Mr. Jones* as inflammatory material. It certainly is! I hope that it wasn't destroyed. Somehow I'd be pleased to think of that particular book being behind the Iron Curtain."

But almost the best story of all came from Asheville, North Carolina. A pleasant-faced, gray-haired woman sitting behind a desk in one of the branch libraries was busy sorting cards one morning. That was why it took a small boy on the other side of the counter quite a long time to get her attention. The child was freckle-faced and pug-nosed, with a shock of blond hair that kept falling in his eyes.

The bobbing up and down at the counter finally caught the librarian's eye. It was the little boy jumping on tiptoe, trying to see behind the counter. The woman looked up and smiled at what she saw.

"What can I do for you, sonny?"

"I'm Dick Beamer. My mother said—would you please send her a copy of *Joe's Mixmaster* home by me? She said I was not to come home without it." The eyes under the tousled blond hair were very serious.

The attendant was genuinely puzzled. *"Joe's Mixmaster,"* she murmured half to herself. Some kind of a book on small appliances? A cookbook? But she couldn't remember any title like that. She decided to telephone the child's mother.

A minute later, laughing, she hung up the phone, and reached for a book.

"Here you are, Dick. The customer is always right. Just what you ordered."

The book she handed over the counter was, of course, *Mr. Jones, Meet the Master.*

Trips for autographing followed—to Atlanta, Birmingham, New Orleans, Cleveland, Columbus, Boston, Detroit, and Richmond, Virginia. I soon found that the autograph party as such is as American as the hot dog stand or the New York Giants. It is a child of American business promotion.

I soon discovered that all such parties have certain common denominators. The bookstore people are always nervous lest the author's or editor's hand not write fast enough or give out on them. Therefore, they want a pile of books signed ahead of the scheduled hours for autographing. This is also designed to take care of those astute customers who have ordered their autographed copies of the book the easy way—by telephone.

The publisher and the author must lean over backwards to give all the major retail booksellers in any given city equal treatment. If books are signed for one, usually they must be autographed for all. That often means tramping from bookstore to bookstore, meeting the personnel, and signing a pile of books in each store.

At each party, there are always a few individuals who do not really understand what an autograph is. I remember one sweet-faced elderly lady who thrust a book at me, saying, "This one is for a birthday present. I wonder if you would be so kind as to write something special in it for me?"

"Of course, I'll be happy to. What would you like?"

"Well—suppose I just sort of dictate it to you. . . . 'To Aunt Emma Cartwright, who means more to me than—' "

My pen hovered over the fresh page. I asked gently, feeling for words, "Are you sure that you want me to put it just that way? You see, Miss Cartwright is not *my* aunt. Won't that inscription seem a little odd over my signature?"

But the face before me merely smiled more sweetly still and went blithely on, "Oh, my dear, I've known Emma for *such* a long time. She *really* is a dear. You would *love* her. It just doesn't matter a bit that it's over your signature. You go right ahead and put your name *right* there. Emma will treasure it *so.*"

After a few such feeble protests and attempts to explain—which I found equally futile in Richmond or in Atlanta, in New Orleans or in Cleveland—I just gave up and dutifully wrote anything that people requested—short of blasphemy or libel. The result is that I have inscribed astonishingly tender and intimate messages for scores of people on whom I've never laid eyes.

It is a rare party, I found, which the average bookseller can handle in orderly fashion. Americans do not like lines; I can't say that I blame them. They would rather crowd around, poking books in all directions, first come, first served. The autographed—sunk down in the middle of the melee, feeling like a target for bow and arrow practice, gasping for a breath of fresh air, her right arm aching, the flowers on her left shoulder tickling her nose, the corsage pin scratching her shoulder—sits there, writing furiously, her signature getting more and more illegible, wondering if the smile on her face looks as mechanical as it began to feel a full hour ago. She meanwhile has one eye on the bookstore clock and the other on the still-unsigned piles of books which must be autographed before an escape can be made back to the hotel room.

It should not have surprised me that I was finding details of my new life—such as sleepless nights on jerking trains or bumpy plane rides—a hurdle and a challenge. The truth was I couldn't even read a plane or train schedule. During twelve years of marriage, all training and motivation had been in quite the opposite direction. During these years I had stayed in the background—a behind-the-scenes wife. So definitely was this true that there were those in my husband's congregation who did not know whether or not the minister was married, or at best, had never seen me.

This was quite in keeping with Peter's ideas and ideals on the subject of marriage. He took a dim view of feminism. But he was able to articulate this in a way that had attracted rather than repelled most of the feminine sex who heard him. His credo of marriage was spelled out—indeed, spread all over the landscape—in his sermon "Keepers of the Springs." Yet during all his years in the ministry, this had been by far the most popular sermon he had ever preached.

The emancipation of womanhood began with Christianity
and it ends with Christianity. . . .*

When women in this country achieved equality with men,
it was accomplished only by stepping down from the pedestal
on which Christianity, chivalry, and idealism
had placed her. . . .

So she copied the vices of men—in the name of progress!
But it is not progress to go in a downward direction.
It is not progress to lower moral standards and to
lose ideals!
No woman ever became lovelier by losing her essential
femininity.

There is no substitute for goodness . . .
    nothing can take the place of purity.
To be sweet is far better than to be sophisticated.
America needs young women who will build true homes,
    whether they live in two rooms—or ten . . .
    whether starched white organdy curtains
        hang at the windows—or silk damask.

We need homes where harassed husbands may find peace
                                        understanding
                    refreshment of body and soul . . .
where children may find the warmth of love . . .
where friends may find hospitality
                    graciousness
                    and joy.
Only out of such homes will go men with strength and
courage to help the United States build a new and a
better world.
To make such homes is therefore, any woman's supreme
contribution to her country and to her generation. . . .

There might well have been some conflict between Peter and me
over his strong views on the role of women in marriage had I not discovered early in our life together that putting these ideas into practice

---

*Marshall, Peter, *Mr. Jones, Meet the Master*, p. 150, Fleming H. Revell Company, New
York, 1949. Following lines are from unpublished manuscript. Used by permission.

brought me joy and satisfaction at a deep level. Such nonfeminist ideas meant that I was single-eyed in the marriage relationship. I was not a divided personality. All the talents I possessed, all energy, all creativeness, were poured into the marriage partnership, and no effort was made to channel any part of it in other directions.

For any minister—who must preach twice or three times every Sunday and often prepare several weekday talks—a steady stream of new ideas is the breath of life. Therefore, I handed over to Peter any ideas that came to me or that I stumbled across in reading that might be sermon material, as well as any thoughts I might have on the ever-present church organizational or personnel problems.

Nor was any of this a hardship or a sacrifice. I felt in need of neither credit nor approbation for it. For I was discovering for myself during those years the profound truth of that ancient and inexorable law that "he that loseth his life . . . shall find it."

Would the law have been stated more accurately had its pronouns been cast in the feminine gender? I don't know; I am no expert in feminine psychology. I only know that in giving all of myself to our marriage, with no reservations—in losing my life in that sense, I found it again in a fulfillment of every shred of femininity in me.

Furthermore, almost three years of ill health had given me a special kind of training in the quiet life. Anyone who has had to go to bed full time finds it an irksome adjustment. I was no exception. The first three months were the worst. Every muscle in my body ached in protest against too much bed rest. The minutes held their breath; the hours dragged their feet. Every inner resource available had to be mustered to fill those halting days. Then, too, all of life looks different, takes on quite another color, when viewed from a horizontal position.

I finally succeeded in making the adjustment. Some natural bent toward the secluded life rose to meet the need. Rush, flurry, and tension fell away from me. Great chunks of time for reading, undisturbed thought, and making notes filled up pits of emptiness in me so that they became reservoirs of mental and spiritual resources. That was all to the good. The filling meant that, henceforward, all of life could be built on a more solid basis.

How completely the adjustment had been made became apparent when the time finally came for me to get out of bed and pick up active life again. At first, the presence of more than two or three persons in a room tired me rapidly and left me confused, like one who watches a rapidly moving object—galloping horses or a roller coaster—on a movie screen. With relief, I would go back to my quiet room to clear my head, to get perspective again. It took many months to retrain nerves, reflexes, and emotions back to the accelerated pace that most of us think of as normal living.

Then only a little over a year after I had recovered and picked up the threads of normal life again, Peter's death and the publication of his sermons thrust me into the public eye.

It was no wonder that I found the reversal of my position with my husband somewhat difficult. Peter had gone on to greater things. Yet for him, as for all in that other life, death now hid his new mission with a cloak of anonymity.

It is as if at the moment of death the sword of self must be laid down along with the flesh and left outside the gates of timelessness. In that sense, therefore, Peter was now the one in the background; I, the one forced to the forefront.

My reaction to this was that, more often than not, I felt like fleeing. Psychologically, I was still reacting as I had as a child. In the house where we had lived for most of the growing-up years, there had been narrow, curving back stairs off the kitchen leading to the second floor. These proved to be a most convenient means of ready escape. When grownups whom I did not relish seeing or for whom I did not consider myself presentable came to the front door, I would bolt up the back stairs two at a time. Thus, so far as my emotional reactions were concerned, during the first few months of the publicity that followed the success of *Mr. Jones*, I found myself fleeing up the back stairs again and again.

The secret desire to flee was no passing emotional phase. Nor was it just the kind of fear of public appearances that comes from ineptitude or inexperience. I had been making impromptu talks in my father's church since childhood. During high school days I had won local and then statewide speaking contests. In college, it had been an exciting experience to be on the debating team and to match wits with representatives from other women's colleges, even with teams from British universities—Cambridge and the University of London.

No—this was not simple shyness; the difficulty went deeper. Its symptoms appeared before I was even aware that there was any problem.

A few days before an autograph party in a department store in Richmond, Virginia, I acquired a bad cold which developed into laryngitis. By the day of the party I was unable to speak above a whisper. Since the occasion had been widely publicized and many hundreds of books had been ordered, there was nothing to do but to appear as scheduled—voice or no voice.

Appear I did; it was certainly an incongruous situation. Silent and apologetic, I could only sit there at a little table in the middle of the book department of the store, trying to make my eyes and a smile say what my lips could not. The book-department personnel took turns standing solicitously beside me, explaining my voiceless plight to the people in the line before me.

The autographing had been scheduled from two to four in the afternoon and from seven-thirty until eight-thirty that evening. In between times, I had dinner at a nearby hotel with a salesman from the publishing house who had come down from New York especially for the party.

After we had decided on our orders—I, by pointing and gesturing at the menu—he asked, "Did you notice that I skipped out on the party for a while this afternoon? Or were you too tied up to notice?"

I tried to whisper, "I'm afraid there were too many milling—" Suddenly, even the whisper died on my lips.

"Better write your words of wisdom—," and he shoved a pencil toward me and groped in his pocket for a scrap of paper. "I can see that for once in my life when I'm with a woman, I'm going to get a chance to talk as much as I want to—well—anyway . . . whether you noticed or not. . . ." Here his voice sank to a whisper, too. "I skipped out, found the nearest Catholic church, and said a little prayer for you. I even burned a candle. I was worried about whether you could hold out for tonight."

I wrote on the paper, "I'm touched and grateful. . . . But why are *you* whispering?"

"Hey! Why *am* I whispering . . . ?"

The voiceless autographing party in Richmond would scarcely be worth mentioning were it an isolated incident. The trouble was that, as invitations—not only for autographing, but for book reviews and other types of talks kept coming in—the frequent colds became even more frequent. All too often I would become ill shortly before a scheduled trip for some kind of public appearance.

There was no pretense in this; the viruses that felled me were real enough. Sometimes I would keep the engagement anyway, as I had in Richmond. But usually my doctor would step in and positively forbid the trip. This was embarrassing, because always there had been local advertising of the event, and the cancellation inconvenienced other people. It wasn't any fun several days later to receive clippings from a local newspaper in which a notice had been prominently displayed in a box on the front page:

NOTICE

CATHERINE MARSHALL

is ill and will be unable to keep her

speaking engagement at

SMITHFIELD ST. METHODIST CHURCH

tonight

The meeting is therefore canceled

Finally it began to dawn on me that the colds and the laryngitis, the viruses and the flu, were much too conveniently timed; the correlation between the illnesses and the public appearances was too high. I knew that this was no conscious ducking of obligations on my part. But pondering it, I had strong suspicions that the colds were the result of some kind of inner rebellion and conflict.

Recognizing the psychosomatic character of the small illnesses was half the battle in eliminating them. The rest was done through prayer, applying a little humor to the predicament, and resolving firmly that when I had made a date, it had to be kept—period! Under this treatment, colds and viruses practically disappeared from my life.

Yet the basic conflict—of which the colds had been but a minor sign—did not disappear so easily. It took a long time for me even to realize what the emotional upheaval was all about. I only knew that it was there and that it was making me unhappy.

Was there in me, I wondered, a deficiency of love for other people that was making me yearn after the back-stairs escape routine? Could the trouble be traced to a despicable lack of gratitude to God for the part I had been enabled to play in the publication of *Mr. Jones, Meet the Master* and its subsequent success?

The fact that I could represent my husband to the public had been at first not only acceptable to me but very satisfying. I was glad that I could be used in any way to carry a bit further the work that Peter had begun.

About that time, I read a statement that seemed to underwrite what I was doing. It was a paragraph or two in a book that had been published three years before and was still popular—Rabbi Liebman's *Peace of Mind:*

> When death destroys an important relationship . . . equilibrium will be restored when the bereaved person discovers some situation demanding the same or similar patterns of conduct. . . . We must act as the ambassadors of our departed, their messengers and their spokesmen, carrying out the mission for which they lived and strove and which they bequeathed to us. . . ."*

I had no idea whether or not Rabbi Liebman, in this point of view, was really presenting a sound principle. Certainly I had not undertaken the project of compiling and editing the book of sermons with the conscious motive of finding a pattern of conduct that would aid my own recovery from grief. Still it was good to have this assurance that I had been on the right track.

But the probing went on. . . . Was the difficulty that I felt at this time a rebellion against any intrusion of the innermost citadel of my private life by the public? A covert guarding of the heart's door? An instinctive feeling of—"you may come this close, but no closer." Could it be that all of this together was a lingering emotional mutiny over widowhood—a sign that there was still some grief-repair work to be done? Or was the trouble all this and more?

In time the outlines of the "and more" began to emerge. My ideal inner image of woman's role in the world—formed partly by the femininity with which I was born, partly by a Southern heritage, and partly by the years of my marriage—was definitely not that of the career woman. I had spent my childhood in a Deep South Mississippi town. In me still was the child who had reveled in the *Little Colonel* series, replete with the beautiful woman reigning supreme over the domestic

---

*Liebman, Joshua Loth, *Peace of Mind*, pp. 115–117, Simon and Schuster, Inc., New York, 1946.

concerns of her own domain—in that case, a Southern mansion. Still not far under the surface was the little girl who had never had enough perfume, bracelets, and undergarments lavish with lace to satisfy her; who had disdained playing cowboys and Indians but had adored her dolls.

The aggressiveness and independent attitude necessary to make a sally out into the world of successful careers seemed to me a contradiction of everything feminine I had ever known; therefore, it was emotional anathema to me. Yet now circumstances which I had not sought were thrusting this genuinely distasteful role upon me.

While in the midst of strong resistance at the emotional level, I was too much involved to analyze my feelings objectively. Looking back now, I know that this was only the beginning of a conflict that was to go on for a long time and become even more poignant before it could be resolved. There was no clash between my ideal of a woman's role in the world and the writing itself. Always the pencil in my hand meant joy. My difficulty was that of reconciling myself to the commercial aspects of the book world, to my writing being in any way connected with earning a living. The conflict in me was therefore basically a clash between femininity and the career that pressed in upon me. The woman and the book were in headlong collision.

Seven
They Walk
in Wistfulness

EVERY SORROWING PERSON has difficulty in returning to places uniquely connected with the one who has died. So I had found it in going back to the church on the Sunday following Peter's death. So I found it the following summer in returning to Waverley, our Cape Cod cottage.

Since Peter and I had always lived in manses belonging to the churches we had served, Waverley was the only home we had ever owned. The sea almost at the front door; the fogs that rolled in off the Atlantic; the cool nights when the rest of the country was sweltering in a heat wave; the little arm of land that is Cape Cod all but smothered in rambler roses—Peter had loved it all, perhaps because it spoke to him of home and Scotland. The cottage was *his*. He proved it by planning and planting a garden of hybrid tea roses, by building fences, and painting the shutters his favorite Chatham blue.

Our son had spent every summer of his life there. As spring had melted into early summer that year of Peter's death, our nine-year-old was all eagerness to return to the cottage and the seashore. He wanted to leave the day after school closed. I, in turn, could offer no excuse for not going that Peter John would have understood.

Friends offered to help me drive up. As we left the parkways of New York and Connecticut behind and crossed the Bourne Bridge from the mainland to Cape Cod, suddenly I remembered what had been in my mind

at the same spot the year before. Peter had been driving. He had been gay
and eager to begin his vacation, and had let out an exuberant shout as soon
as we had crossed the bridge and were on Cape Cod's sandy soil.

Sitting beside him, watching his face, all at once I had had a stabbing premonition. I had not even allowed it to jell into thought, but had
thrust it from me with the opposite idea, "One more year—and we've
made it—together." Now, a year later, I remembered.

Our friends stayed with us in the cottage for a few days and then
had to return to Washington. With Peter John and me alone, there came
a procession of agonizing days. At Waverley I could not dodge the reality of my husband's death. Everywhere I turned there were reminders.

Under the bed were the old white shoes Peter had used for garden
work, with his socks still stuffed in them. The shoes would never again
walk under the rose arbor and into the garden. On the closet shelf in the
front hall was a summer hat with its blue band fading to lavender; the
hat was enjoying no trips to auctions or to summer theater matinees
that year. In the wastebaskets were scraps of letters Peter had answered
the previous September. They were eloquent with the message, "No one
will ever again receive a letter from Peter Marshall." On the table was a
game score with neat figures, and beside it, a list of perennials Peter had
planned to plant. Now he would do no planting that summer or any
summer. In the garage was a pair of canvas gloves, thrown carelessly on
the workbench, still almost in the shape of their owner's hands—but
now the gloves were empty.

One evening after young Peter—tired from a whole day of swimming and crabbing—was asleep, I headed toward the beach. A brisk
breeze, acrid with the smell of seaweed, was blowing in from the sea.
Off in the distance was the blinking lighthouse of Chatham Point. The
moon shining on the water and the white sand made it almost like day.
Always I had found soothing the rhythmical swish of waves beating on
the shore.

"On this particular night of all nights," I thought, "I need something soothing." By that afternoon the cumulative effect of our days on
the Cape had reached a climax. The result was a tempest of emotion.

Standing there on the wide beach, a solitary figure in the night, there
was wrung from me an unspoken prayer. . . . "Oh God, I want to believe
that Peter is alive somewhere. But all I can feel is a great aching void, a
gigantic emptiness."

There was no answer at the time—only the cool air on my cheeks, the still moon shining down, and the rhythmical march of the waves to my feet.

But back at the cottage sometime during the night, after several hours of sleep, I awakened. The confusion in my mind was gone. Clear, rounded thoughts were waiting there, as if they had been dropped into my consciousness during sleep. . . .

Once again you have been trying to put feeling before faith. Because you haven't been able to feel Peter's presence, you have assumed that he is lost to you forever.

Simply have faith that he is with you whenever you need him. Assume it—and the feeling and the proof will come later. Accept this on faith. Accept it though you have no idea how it can come about.

That was all.

The need was to love and to be loved—that ultimate of life. Could I, and all those like me who walk the earth in wistfulness, find the way to trust God even for that?

Yes, I would try.

I thereupon made a quiet little act of receiving the message at face value. Why should I doubt it? I have nothing to lose, I thought. Otherwise there is only emptiness.

I lay there with one arm under my head, staring into the darkness, thinking of how Christ had told His closest friends that "it was expedient" that He go away. Probably, I thought, they had stifled the retort that had sprung to their lips: "Expedient? How could it be? We like being with You. What could possibly be better than the peace, the joy, and the satisfaction of Your physical Presence?"

And then I thought of an incident that had taken place seven days prior to Peter's death. He and I had been visiting friends in a nearby city. Their guest room had twin beds. Sometime after the lights had been turned out and we had gone to bed, long after the house was quiet, suddenly I had put out one hand toward the other bed, and had found Peter's hand stretched out in the darkness waiting for mine.

He had whispered, "How did you know that my hand was there?"

And I had answered, "I don't know. *I just knew.*"

So now the space between us was wider, much wider—greater than the distance between any twin beds. It stretched all the way across the eternities that divide the world of the seen from the world of the unseen. Somewhere out in that emptiness, an outstretched hand was waiting for me. The promise of it was implicit in the message I had just received. But so far, I could feel only the darkness and the emptiness. And I missed the reassurance of those strong fingers.

Having resolved to accept the message on faith, I felt that I had done my part. The next move was up to God. In that I was mistaken. Not a single one of us can fly across the Valley of the Shadow; we must walk its rocky paths step by step. Being creatures of free will, we must assent to each step in recovery and live it out.

Day after day that first summer I found that my journey through the Valley was a running battle with self-pity. Several of the couples on our street would often take a stroll toward the beach on an early evening. Sometimes seeing them, I would think, "Here Peter and I were, the youngest couple on the street, and our marriage is over." Or at a summer-stock performance at the theater in Dennis, I would see a gray-haired man reach for his wife's hand, and I would wince with a passing pang of self-pity.

Or at a dinner party I would find myself the only single person there. Always I knew that my hostess had not meant to be thoughtless. It is hard for anyone who has known only an unbroken family to imagine how this particular situation makes the single person feel. Try as I might to overcome it, I would find that being in the presence of couples threw my aloneness into sharpest perspective.

In spite of such experiences, the lonely person often makes the mistake of thinking that physical nearness to other people is the answer. Yet some of the most solitary people in the world live in great cities— London, Paris, New York, Los Angeles. One can feel utterly alone, have no sense of belonging, even in the midst of a jostling crowd.

I remember once when the loneliness of a mutual acquaintance, a widow, was mentioned in a group of her friends. One of those present was a married man. An odd look came into his eyes. "Don't make the mistake," he said, "of thinking that the only lonely people are single people. Loneliness doesn't fly out the window in the wake of the marriage ceremony. A man and a woman can live in the same house, in fact lie side by side in the same bed, and still be worlds apart." Of course, he was right. Our divorce courts testify that in many marriages no water of life has been found for the thirst of the solitary spirit.

What then is the solution? It must lie somewhere in the realm of relationship. As solitaries we wither and die. We long to be needed; we yearn to be included; we thirst to know that we belong to someone. The question is . . . how can we achieve that sense of belonging?

There is a price to be paid. The first tribute exacted is a modicum of honesty with ourselves. Do we so want to be rid of self-pity that we will allow ourselves no more wallowing in loneliness? How badly do we want to make connection with other people? Do we really want to find happiness again?

In the light of honest answers to questions like these, suddenly we find that we do not ever need to be lonely, unless we choose to be. For there are always others eager to receive our friendship if only we will take the first steps out of our solitary shell.

For several months my family and friends had seen me happily engrossed in the editing, prepublication work, and launching of *Mr. Jones, Meet the Master.* What they had not seen was my continuing inner struggle to fill up that great void now at the center of my life.

The church's Order for the Solemnization of Marriage recognizes the problem by including in the marriage service the poignant words "till death do us part." And Christ once commented in speaking of marriage, ". . . and they twain shall be one flesh." Did He mean that only in the spiritual sense or just mystically? Not at all. Perhaps only those who have lost a mate know the stern reality that those simple words represent.

One takes an arm or a leg or an eye for granted until it is gone. When in good health, one has no reason to be preoccupied with different parts of the body. It's only in pain or disease that awareness comes. Even so, those who have lived through the disseverment of a marriage through death become acutely aware of how real the "one flesh" was. With the death of a marriage partner, there is an awareness of dismemberment. Moreover, this tearing asunder has taken place at such a deep level that its healing will yield to no superficial therapy.

I was still groping to find what that answer might be when one afternoon I went to my doctor's office for a routine cold shot. Most of his appointments were over for the day, and the doctor was in a leisurely talkative mood. He was a tall, fine looking man close to retirement age whom I had known for years. Having helped me through many a difficulty, he was more inclined to treat me like a friend or a daughter than a patient.

Suddenly in the midst of our conversation he fell silent, leaned forward in his swivel chair, and looked at me closely. His eyes were searching my face as if trying to see what lay underneath.

"Catherine, enough chitchat. Suppose you just relax and drop that gay mask you've been wearing since you came in here. Now—look at me. How are you? Really?"

I half turned to gaze out of the window at trees tossing in a sudden thunderstorm. The room was quiet now except for the pelting rain against the windowpanes, the ticking of a clock on the mantle, and the nurse's muffled telephone conversation beyond the outer office door.

Finally I turned back to look at my physician friend. What I was feeling poured out in a rush of words. . . . "Do you really want to know what it feels like to be a widow? God made men and women for each other. Any other way of life is wrong, because it's abnormal. The last few months it's been like having a gnawing hunger, a haunting wistfulness at the center of life. I can forget about it for short periods—ignore it sometimes. But it's always there—always—and I'm afraid not even you can prescribe any pills that can cure it." Suddenly I became a little defensive, "There now, that's how I really am. Does that answer your question?"

"Partly—I could see all that clearly in your eyes. You didn't need to spell it out. It helps you though to be able to talk it out. Now—there's more. What else?"

"Do widows and widowers simply have to learn to live with this aching emptiness at the core of their beings? Some days it's worse than others. But it's always there. Do we just have to come to terms with it? It seems to me that the immense satisfactions of daily living are gone forever."

Gently the doctor answered, "No, not forever. It only seems that way." He paused and his voice became a little stern. "Look, Catherine, you aren't the first person in the world to lose someone you love by death. This too will pass. The world won't always seem formless and gray to you. You'll just have to take my word for it. I've watched many friends, many patients, go through this stage, and I've helped a little—I hope. And it is a stage. You still have a lot of living to do—happy living. Just believe that, even though right now you don't see how."

For days after that my thoughts kept returning to what the doctor had said. I fervently hoped that he was right, that the gnawing hunger of the inner person was just a stage out of grief. But if so, I kept wishing that this particular mood—or stage—would pass.

It was true that the bittersweet wistfulness ebbed and flowed. I quickly discovered that certain things brought it to full tide—a convincing love scene in a movie, a sensuous passage in a book, certain songs, even certain fragrances. For me it was English lavender, the sweetness of Nicotiana—heavy on the night air of a garden—and, oddly, the smell of fresh tar on a street.

Funerals I could now take with surprising equanimity; weddings I found emotionally devastating. Something about the wedding ceremony touched a deep chord at a level where I had no control over the emotions connected with it. Since it was embarrassing and unfair to other people to weep my way through what was a joyous occasion, usually I made excuses and stayed away. Often I would just drop in to greet my newly married friends at the reception after the ceremony.

Sometimes the situation that precipitated these floods of emotion caught me unawares. There was the night of a mother-daughter banquet for which I had agreed to make an informal after-dinner talk. Before my part in the program, a young baritone rose to sing a group of semiclassical songs. The last in the group was "Drink to Me Only with Thine Eyes."

I had heard Ben Jonson's words sung and read many times. It held no special memories for me, and I had never felt in the least sentimental about it. As the words of the lyric rose and fell . . .

> Drink to me only with thine eyes,
>   And I will pledge with mine;
> Or leave a kiss within the cup,
>   And I'll not ask for wine.
> The thirst that from the soul doth rise
>   Doth ask a drink divine—

suddenly I felt myself tighten. My hands, hidden under the edge of the table, began alternately twisting the edge of the tablecloth and clutching the evening bag in my lap until my fingers ached.

This won't do, I thought. I'll just have to stop listening. My eyes roamed over the scene before me—the mothers in all their finery sitting with their daughters beside them at the round tables, all listening intently to the tall young singer. I was searching desperately for something not at all sentimental on which to concentrate. Suddenly I spotted a redheaded teenager's hair-do. Deliberately, I studied it, trying to decide how some beautician had created the sleek turned-under effect.

By the time the last notes of the song had died away, the tension in my hands had relaxed, the fullness in my throat had disappeared. I was able to get to my feet calmly and even put a little humor into my talk.

In this sort of reaction, I was experiencing what almost every person goes through who has known bereavement or deep disappointment. My doctor had been justified and wise in reminding me—a little sternly—that my situation was not unique. Acknowledging that fact helped, not because "misery loves company," but because there is solace in understanding that there is such a thing as a fellowship of suffering.

After all, millions of other human beings down the centuries have known the snuffing out of their dreams and the medley that is grief—the tears, the feeling of being forsaken and bereft, the loneliness, the self-centeredness, the self-pity, the self-accusation, the physical frustration, the wistfulness, the loss of zest for life. Somehow other people have survived it; the rest of us can too.

My doctor made it clear to me that the physical adjustment required in the change from married life to a single life accounts for much of the emotional upheaval, even aspects of grief that may seem to have no connection at all with the physical. He urged that I be clear-eyed about it and not try to explain it away on other terms.

"Honesty, even with yourself, helps." I remember his saying with a twinkle in his eyes, "Those who go through life pretending that sex doesn't exist or that it doesn't matter are either deceiving themselves or they're abnormal. Often these same people think that they are being lofty and spiritual in that attitude. Whereas if I read my Bible correctly, it has a surprising amount to say about the flesh. Above all, Catherine, don't be ashamed of your feelings. You are flesh and blood. Just thank God for that!"

In the years since then, an occasional widow, often shyly feeling her way, has talked to me about this delicate point. Always I knew that human beings and their emotional reactions could not be pigeonholed. Any generalization in this area would be dangerous. Still I find that the feelings of those to whom physical loneliness is a problem follow a certain pattern, though the timing may vary.

At three months after the death of her husband, the average woman thinks, concerning the physical adjustment, "This is easy. What's all the hullabaloo about? Why all the insinuations and snide remarks, the lifted eyebrows about widows and their needs? If there's anything to it at all, I must be some sort of an exception."

At about five months the same widow begins to feel differently. She too may have begun to find it difficult. At six months the battle toward some sort of physical adjustment is on in earnest. The happier the particular woman had been in marriage, the more thoroughly she had adapted herself to married life, the greater her physical loneliness and her need will be.

One self-help book written for widows insists that sexual adjustment difficulties have been grossly exaggerated, often whipped up to an unnecessary froth, as if the widow concerned enjoyed making a problem where one did not exist. The writer's main contention is that the female of the species is made to respond to specific sensual and sexual stimuli. Withdraw the stimuli and the woman is supposedly then in a state of blessed quiescent peace.

It's a neat theory. But just where within the confines of our modern society can the widow shelve herself these days in order to avoid sensual or sexual stimuli? I do not know the spot. Our society, influenced by Hollywood and the entertainment world generally and further egged on by modern advertising, does quite the opposite. It goes in for all the stimuli it can manage. Exit the state of blessed quiescent peace!

I have known several widows who have sought and found some release through music. One of these used to sit at her baby grand piano and play and sing her heart out. Through the open windows of a summer afternoon her neighbors would see her, hear her filling the empty house with music. After a while, she would rise, go out into her yard, and search for weeds in the lawn with intensity, pull them out with determination. Then she would go back into the house for more music. It was a good combination—the singing and the weeding—but as later events revealed, it did not solve her problem.

Other widows or widowers have told me that, from the first, they recognized the physical vacuum in their lives for what it was. Then as time passed, they sensed that the frustration was sinking deeper, through level after level of the personality. The hunger to share life intimately with another human being, the deep need for love then began to emerge in all sorts of ways, sometimes in such devious disguises that the individual did not always recognize the masks it wore.

With a woman, the family cat or parakeet, pet poodle or cocker, the mastiff, or German shepherd that had belonged to her husband may become the object of her lavish affection. Those of us who love pets find this quite understandable. Fortunately, however, most women do not carry it as far as the one I heard bemoaning in a horrified tone the fact that her miniature schnauzer "had gone without a bath for three whole days." Or the French poodle I saw in a Washington department store whose owner had lacquered the dog's toenails red, put a rhinestone choker around its neck, and sprayed it with Chanel No. 5.

Most pets will lap up the affection and come back for more, none the worse for it. But when one's children suddenly find themselves all but drowned in a superfluity of love, then the situation is more serious. I have watched children come to feel restricted, even threatened by this smothering kind of love. They may start resisting it—either violently, according to the particular child's temperament, or by fleeing it.

One day, a few months after my husband's death, I wrote a reminder to myself on this point in my Journal. . . .

> I am now inclined to want to pour out too much love on my child. . . .
> Any tendency toward smother-love must be resisted at all costs. I must
> not penalize my child's development because of my own need, and ratio-
> nalize it as mother love.

A kindred reaction of the bereaved is the loss of all zest for life. The sense of futility about everything is like a thick gray blanket smothering all initiative, stifling laughter, snuffing out hope, drugging energy. The smallest task becomes a gigantic effort. Why cook a meal when there is no one to share it? Entertaining looms as an impossible effort. Why dust or polish the furniture when there is no one to see or care? Anyway more dust will have settled by tomorrow. Why bother about clothes or grooming when there is no man around to notice a new dress or to comment on a becoming hair-do? Why bother? Why go through the motions?

The male is equally vulnerable to this kind of lethargy. As one businessman whose wife had died commented to me, "I have a thriving business and a fine income. But now that Fran is gone, it's all sawdust in my mouth. What's the point of success if you have no one to share it with? Why knock yourself out to make money when there's no one to spend it on?"

Such a sense of futility is often accompanied by desultory daydreaming. It may be a reliving over and over of certain scenes out of the past, or it may be conjuring up fantasies for the future. In either case, it saps energy that should be given to daily tasks, to the rebuilding of life, to the working out of new patterns of action.

Another symptom of physical loneliness for a woman is a new and surprising set of reactions to the opposite sex. One woman commented, "When I was with a man, I found myself suddenly and acutely aware that he *was* a man in a way I had seldom experienced before Jim's death. I found that I had to keep a sharp check on my reactions to men friends, leash my emotions in, lest I give undue response to the most routine and insignificant attentions."

The same woman may find that after this "leashing in," tears are too often just under the surface. This discovery frightens her; probably she has always prided herself on not being the crying type. She wonders if she is actually becoming emotionally unbalanced.

Or she may be horrified one day to realize that she is thinking about sex quite a lot. Suddenly it looms too large. Her own reactions in this regard seem alien to her; she cannot remember having been that way before her husband's death. Secretly, she wonders if she has more than her share of sexual energy or is abnormal in some way.

What has happened is understandable. When one is happily married, the physical aspect of marriage falls into place as but a part of one's total life. That is as it should be. But the soldier lost in the desert can think only of water. The explorer, caught miles from his base in Antarctica, is preoccupied with a mental picture of lolling luxuriously before a cozy fire.

I remember one man who had taught for many years in a men's college saying to me, "After years of observation, I'm not sure but what I think coed institutions are to be preferred to all-male schools. When the boys are isolated from girls, they finally get to the point where they can't think about much *except* girls."

What then? It is not enough to acknowledge that this is a common, perhaps unavoidable dilemma for the single person. What is one to do with the superfluity of creative energy pulsing through his veins? There must be some healthy right answer to it. But what?

The first answer that may occur to the widow or widower is remarriage. The single person suspects—probably rightly—that there is no final perfect solution to the physical problem for the unmarried person.

"It is not good that man should be alone," is the wisdom given us from God Himself in the second chapter of Genesis. We would be foolish indeed to pretend that it is good. When we live alone for any length of time, an inevitable warping takes place. It is only in living closely with another person that we find our own identity and that the rough edges of selfishness are smoothed away. Every widow or widower who thinks about marrying again thinks about it in the abstract long before the thoughts are linked to any particular person. He wonders if it would be possible to fall in love again. And if immortality is at all real, he wonders how the one in the next life would feel about his remarrying?

Other widows and widowers immediately shut the door even on the possibility of second marriage, like a slim attractive woman who came to call on me one afternoon. Somewhere in her forties, she had been utterly desolated by the recent death of her husband.

I sensed that her need at that time was to talk out her grief. So she did talk—for two hours. Then just as she was leaving, she said, "Of course, I know that I'll never marry again. I could never replace Jim."

For days afterwards her words echoed in my mind—"Replace Jim. . . ." Of course not! Not Jim nor anyone else. The mold was broken when each of us was born.

Yet this casual remark revealed something fundamentally wrong with that particular widow's concept of remarriage. The idea that Jim could not be replaced seemed close to the idea that remarriage would somehow be a repudiation of Jim, would betray his love.

Another woman who wrote to me seemed about to reach the same conclusion by a different line of reasoning:

> *After all, real marriage is a spiritual union as well as a physical one. And two people in a true marriage do indeed become one. My love for my husband has long since been written into my being. Therefore death had no power to disturb that. . . .*

But Ted has now been gone three years. A fine man wants me to marry him. I can't seem to get my thinking straight on it.

My sticking point on second marriages is this: Since marriage is a spiritual union, too, doesn't the idea of second marriage put an undue emphasis on the physical side of marriage? If one's husband were physically incapacitated, would a woman worth her salt divorce him because the physical was denied? Is death very different from that . . . ?

These thoughts are not unusual. No doubt a person like Queen Victoria, who for forty years never gave up mourning her Albert, had many of the same thoughts. The interesting thing is that my correspondent and others like her are being more "spiritual" on this point than the Scriptures. For one of the foundation stones of the Bible is the assurance of life after death. Yet in its clear approval of second marriage, it understands our human need of companionship and recognizes that there is a difference between the physical and the spiritual.

There is another, quite opposite danger—that of thinking that remarriage will automatically mend the hurt and solve all problems. Perhaps this danger is partly the result of what I believe to be a mistaken concept of marriage. It is a concept well dramatized in a Greek legend. One Androgynous—a four-legged, four-armed creature—is said to have tried to scale heaven to challenge the gods themselves. Zeus thwarted the threat by splitting this strange creature in two, thus creating man and woman as they are today.

Plato, in his *Symposium*, describes the results:

After the division the two parts of man, each desiring his other half, came together . . . longing to grow into one. . . . Each of us when separated, having one side only, like a flat fish, is but the indenture of a man, and he is always looking for his other half. . . . And when one of them meets the actual half of himself . . . the pair are lost in an amazement of love and friendship and intimacy, and one will not be out of the other's sight. . . .

It is true that when death removes the one from the other's sight, the one left does indeed feel like half a person. Yet death also dramatizes the deeper truth—that marriage as it is meant to be is not the coming together of two halves, but of two whole mature people, each a separate though interdependent entity.

We who have been bereaved are in a peculiar position to understand this, and with that understanding to take a new step toward maturity.

The widow sees as never before that only when she is a whole person does she have enough to contribute to any marriage relationship. She sees that in marriage or out of marriage, she will be lonely unless she is taking definite steps toward finding herself, toward becoming the whole person she is meant to be.

In my case, I was early pushed into asking many of these questions by the vivid dream I had had soon after my husband's death. At that time, my deepest questions had been . . . Where was Peter now? And what was my relationship to him now?

My answer was that as love is progressively purified, possessiveness is dropped out. The deeper and truer the love, the more completely it releases the beloved. The bereaved usually think of this from the earthly side, from a selfish point of view. Not often enough do they consider the fact that the possessiveness inherent in their continuing sorrow fails to release the ones who have gone on into the new life, in a sense holds them bound to the wheel of sorrow.

As my child was growing up, I saw an analogy in my love for him. The highest function of my mother love would be fulfilled when my love was strong enough to cut the apron strings and let my adult child move off into his own life. I would succeed as a mother only when I had so reared my child that he would no longer have need of me. Yet this is not tragedy; it is growth. This is no betrayal of love. This is love.

But what if the events of life so arrange themselves that the bereaved person does not remarry? The first question that every widow or widower must then face is . . . do I really want an immediate solution to my sexual frustration or my loneliness? Or am I clinging to it? To what extent do I actually enjoy wallowing in self-pity? Am I too fear-ridden to venture into new situations that might offer some creative solutions?

Clear-eyed answers to these questions are essential because help is available when and if we really want it. Moreover, God knows the minute we stop playing around the edges of the problem and really begin wanting His help.

What we must *not* do is to assume that the only right way to handle the problem of physical longing is to be rid of it entirely, in order to be at peace. Such repression can be a carryover from an abnormal Puritanism.

Is it possible that we in our day are too enamored of peace of mind? We can be so peaceful that the edge is gone off living; that we hear no birdsong, see no lavender-tinted sunsets, shed no tears, forget the rough edge of pain, no longer know how to laugh. In fact, when we feel nothing at all, then we are dead.

My experience has been that it is only out of a state of tension that growth can come. It is a strange paradox that we have to be willing to suffer the tension for a time, knowing that it is the bridge to the next step in our lives. Even sexual frustration puts the sparkle in the eyes, the warmth in the voice, the lilt in the step. If we can manage to thank God for it, thank Him that there is still enough life in us to burst the old bonds, however painfully, in order to create something new—then we shall find even the tension a blessing.

The solution, at least for a given period of an individual's life, may be in the rechanneling of the creativity that is sexual energy. This energy in us is always seeking a way to express the spirit that is the real person. Such expression *is* creativity. Sex is only one of life's expressions for it. There are many others—singing, dancing, writing, painting, speaking, cooking, gardening, flower arranging, woodworking, dressmaking, giving a child joy or planting a dream in his eyes.

Yet this rechanneling of emotional energy is tricky. Peace of mind, happiness, contentment, and all their first and second cousins come to us only as by-products. The paradox is that he who tries basket weaving, not because he is fascinated by weaving, but in order to avoid his emotional problem, will end up a still-frustrated person, loathing his baskets.

Thus creativity will satisfy the inner hunger only if the individual finds the natural channel of expression for him. No artificially made work, just to fill up time, will suffice. For the task will satisfy the inner need only if the total person—will, body and soul, mind and emotions— can be given to it.

But the person tethered to loneliness and frustration is likely to be impatient with an answer like this. "This 'live creatively' theory of yours is a stopgap measure," he replies. "Not a final solution."

His impatience may be justified. It is true that this is only a wayside stop on the road to a more complete answer.

The problems of loneliness and sexual frustration are inextricably intertwined. They who walk in wistfulness have need of belonging, of being loved for themselves. How then, is that quality of love found?

Most of us make self the center of reference. . . . What do I want . . . ? What's in it for me . . . ? What will make me happy . . . ?

When we live this way, we treat other people not as persons, but as things. We use everyone else, as we would a commodity, for our own purposes. In doing so, we renounce life's precious law of relationship.

Even though such a person finds romance, the result will not be love, but lust. And lust titillates, but does not satisfy. Moreover, the law of diminishing returns always sets in. It takes more and more romantic adventures to satisfy less and less. Thus the belongings that we think we have set up, often fail us in the end. We are left lonelier and more frustrated than before.

Many another belonging must fail us too. Death can snatch parents and relatives from our sides. Even the groups of friends in clubs and organizations to which we have given our loyalty, change through the years.

In the period immediately following my husband's death, I felt that much of the structure of my life was gone. I tried going down many roads in an effort to find a solution. I found every road a dead end but one. My conclusion is that there is only one belonging in the universe on which we can finally depend—our belonging to Jesus Christ.

The reason that many a hungry-hearted person does not know this is simply because he has never entered into the relationship. He is still on the sidelines reading about it, thinking about it, appraising it.

Long ago one Paul, from the Cilician city of Tarsus, after searching down many a road himself, tried to put into words for the rest of us the indestructibility of this final belonging. After cataloging some of the troubles that can plague us in this life, Paul gave his conclusion:

> I have become absolutely convinced that neither Death nor Life
> neither messenger of heaven nor monarch of earth,
> neither what happens today nor what may happen tomorrow,
> neither a power from on high nor a power from below,
> nor anything else in God's whole world
> has any power to separate us from the love of God
> in Jesus Christ our Lord! (ROMANS 8:38, 39)*

---

*Phillips, J. B., *Letters to Young Churches*, The Macmillan Company, New York, 1951.

So what must we do to enter into this highest relationship?

Entering into a marriage relationship is an almost perfect analogy. We want to enter into it. We make a decision. We take a definite step at the moment of the marriage ceremony.

We take that step, even though we know that a risk is involved. We cannot know what the future may hold; we cannot guess all that may be required of us. But we guess that the joys of the comradeship will outweigh the risk.

Instinctively, we feel that there is risk involved in entering into a relationship with our God. How can we know what He may require of us?

But when we guess that the joy of the relationship and having His love in our empty hearts may outweigh the risk and we take the step anyway—that is taking a step in faith.

Then, wonder of wonders, our feeling of the futility that has enshrouded life as in a fog begins to evaporate. Life has structure again. A sense of mission returns. Once again we know that we belong. We have come home to our world.

What does all this have to do with physical longing, sex? Quite a lot. Because sex is not unspiritual; it is part of life. It is only our earthly expression of the spirit that is us, reaching out to love and to be loved, to belong in an intimate way.

And loving is giving ourselves—not just our bodies—but the real us, the essence of us. Not until we have entered into that highest Relationship, do we find a self to give. Only then do we become a warm-hearted person capable of giving love; only then can we receive it.

And after we have entered into this highest Relationship, we discover the best thing of all—that our God is indeed a personal God. His directions could not get through to us before. We could not understand His plan; now we can. We find that His solution for us is designed to fit our special needs and that it is consistent with our earthly happiness.

The answer to all my questioning that summer on Cape Cod seemed to be that a new pattern of action, one tailor-made for me, was just around the corner. It would—at least for the next period of my life—answer the deep needs with which I wrestled.

Eight

"Go Ahead and Write It,
Kate. . . ."

FROM WHERE I stood in the doorway, Peter John's room was quite a
sight. Three ancient, dearly loved stuffed animals were lying sprawled
at his feet, with Jeff, our cocker spaniel, beside them. Some books had
been piled up carefully. I could see *The Wind in the Willows* and *Misty
of Chincoteague* on top. There was another stack of comic books. A cardboard carton filled with train track blocked the door. Peter was standing in the midst of the disorder, holding a plane model in each hand, his
blond hair tousled, a bewildered look on his face.

"What's got you stopped?" I asked.

"Mom, do I *have* to give some stuff away?"

"Yes, you do. The apartment only has four rooms. Your room is
small. There just won't be space for all this."

"But gosh! I've gotta keep the books, the trains, and the airplane
models."

"The books can be thinned out. Children's Hospital will be delighted
to have some. Better get on with the sorting."

"Holy cow! I'm not sure we'll like the apartment."

I was not sure myself. I was finding moving out of the Manse even
harder than Peter John. It was no wonder. . . . This was the first move of
my new life, that life I had not wanted. The Cathedral Avenue house
had been our home ever since we had been in Washington, through
twelve happy significant years.

110

Still, in three days the moving men would be on our doorstep. This was early March, 1950. We were leaving the ten-room Manse for a second floor, walk-up apartment in one of Washington's immense developments. We would still be in the northwest section of the city, not far from the Cathedral Avenue house.

There was the problem of what we would have room for in the apartment, what should be given away or sold, what should be stored. Each decision took its own emotional toll.

But before I had taken down the seascapes, packed the books and linen, the china, the glass, I had asked a friend to take some interior flashbulb snapshots of our home. . . . The breakfast nook with its yellow organdy curtains and the miniature potted plants on the window sills; the sunroom with its shelves of colored glass; Peter's big chintz-covered chair by the radio; a corner of the front bedroom. . . . I wanted to be sure that each detail would be captured. Yet—how could I ever forget? These rooms had been the setting for a lot of happy living.

The apartment development had been built on hilly terrain. On moving day four men staggered up the hill and down, then up the two flights of stairs with our spinet piano and numberless cartons of books. They grunted and complained about the books. . . . "Why—so many? Books are—heavy."

I carried the boxes of carefully packed antique glass myself. Peter was just as solicitous about his plane models, all three cartons of them.

The moving men finally dragged themselves up the stairs with the last load and drove away. They had left us with boxes piled halfway to the ceiling of our tiny living room.

Eventually, some order was brought out of the chaos. We finally got to the place where we could walk unimpeded across the living room. But we were still crowded. With every day that passed we were becoming more space conscious, learning what every apartment dweller knows—that space is one of the most beautiful things God ever made.

This was dramatized by the way one of our apartment neighbors stored her extra blankets in the trunk of the family car. The only trouble was that the blankets were not exactly accessible at times when they were ten blocks away in the parked car. Our own space problem resulted in my using the kitchen food chopper in the bathroom linen closet. A thorough search had uncovered the odd fact that a linen-closet shelf was the only place to which the food chopper could be attached.

I also found that the manless household has its unique difficulties. I had no knowledge of how to keep the car in good repair, how to fix a leaking faucet or repair a burned-out electric cord, or even how to set a mousetrap. As for emptying a mousetrap—no, a thousand times no! One morning, when Peter John was not there to dispose of the unfortunate mouse for me, I pressed the milkman into service.

Soon Peter and I got to know our neighbors very well. If a baby had gas pains and kept his parents awake, all of the neighbors stayed awake too. If the occupants of apartment C-3 were having a party, the rest of us shared the hilarity. If some of the neighbors went through a period of battling damp bugs or roaches in the kitchen, all of us battled bugs. Unitedly we bore with the man who liked to listen to prize fights and wrestling matches far into the night, and the Britisher who religiously tuned in the 12:00 A.M. short-wave newscast from London.

With a front as solid as any Macedonian phalanx, we bore up under the strong smell of disinfectant used in the halls, the wide cracks in the floor, and the vociferous cuckoo clock in B-5.

Peter John appeared to take the change from house to apartment living in his stride. He took his turn at walking Jeff often enough to make up for the fact that even the cocker's quarters were cramped. He thought it very funny that to the other children who lived in our court, I was known simply as "Jeffrey's mother." By careful planning, Peter had found a place in his bedroom for all twenty-eight plane models, though that meant he had to duck, dodge, and sidestep on the treacherous path from door to bed.

I noticed, however, that Peter rarely invited any of his friends to our apartment. Often after school, he would disappear for a while. Investigation revealed that on these afternoons he was going back to our old home on Cathedral Avenue. The new minister, Dr. George Docherty, Dr. Marshall's successor at the church, had by then moved into the Manse with his family. His two boys were considerably younger than Peter, therefore not the playmates he would ordinarily have chosen. But apparently the Manse was still home to Peter. Like a homing pigeon, he kept returning to familiar haunts.

Peter was missing more than the house. I knew that he was homesick for the family fun—the special nonsense game he had played with his father at mealtimes, their work together on the electric-train layout, their discussion of sports that "you, Mom, just don't understand." He was missing, as I was, all the guests, the teas, and church meetings, the constant procession of friends in and out of our old home.

He and I were having trouble persuading ourselves that one woman and one child could still make a family.

That month I received a letter from someone unknown to me. It was from an Edward C. Aswell, editor-in-chief of the trade department of the McGraw-Hill Book Company in New York City. He was writing, he explained, at the instigation of one of the book world's most respected and widely known buyers, Peggy O'Neill of Miller and Rhoads in Richmond, Virginia.

Later, I was to find out more details about what had happened. During a visit to her book department from one of the McGraw-Hill salesmen, she had told him, "I have a message I want you to deliver to Ed Aswell. We've had two very successful autograph parties here for Peter Marshall's *Mr. Jones, Meet the Master."* *Mr. Jones,* it developed, was one of her favorite books.

The salesman seemed surprised, "But you're not a Presbyterian."

"No, I'm not . . . but *Mr. Jones* appeals to all faiths. Well, anyway . . . Mrs. Marshall mentioned that she has a lot more sermon manuscripts. . . ."

The message was faithfully delivered. Mr. Aswell suggested in his letter to me that his publishing house would like to know more about those other sermons.

That spring we exchanged letters. I suggested a theme for the next book, a compilation of Dr. Marshall's sermons on immortality. But by early June another idea—exciting, frighteningly ambitious—was taking shape in my mind. Slowly, I had come to the conviction that the next book should not be a book of sermons, but Peter Marshall's own story. The sermons had grown out of the life; the story of the life held a message that I felt should not be lost to our time.

Mr. Aswell seemed interested in the new proposal. He wrote:

Why don't you write a chapter of the book you have in mind, and send it to me, together with a fairly detailed outline of the entire book . . . ? I shall await the sample material with eagerness.

There was no time even to think about the sample chapter until after Peter John's school was out and he and I were back at the Cape Cod cottage. In the early summer of 1950, as in the previous year, the return to Waverley reopened emotional wounds. At the cottage everywhere I turned, I was reminded of Peter. I tried to handle the situation by keeping busy.

During the New England winter, the paint on our garage doors had weathered. One day I undertook to repaint them. By evening, Chatham blue paint was under my fingernails, even in my hair.

But during all the hours of physical work, I had not been able to turn off my mind and my emotions. Finally by evening, exhausted, I went to bed earlier than usual. But I could not sleep. Suddenly I sat bolt upright in bed, startled by an altogether new idea.

What were the last words that I had ever said to Peter? Yes, I remembered. He had been lying on the stretcher in the first-floor hall where the two orderlies had put him down for a moment. And as he had looked up at me through his pain, I had said—of course! "See you, darling, see you in the morning. . . ." Why had I never thought of it before? Words began stringing themselves together in my mind, spinning themselves into clauses and sentences.

Suddenly the tears spilled over, as if they had been lying in pools behind my eyes for many months and were now glad of release. I switched on the night light and grabbed a piece of paper and pencil. Words poured onto the paper. I wrote steadily with never a pause, though at times tears blurred my eyes and dampened the penciled lines. Ten minutes later I fell back against the pillows—emotionally drained.

I could not have known it then, but the ending—the last page and a half of a book later to be known as *A Man Called Peter*—had just been written. Hardly two words of what had flowed out that night were ever changed.

Later that week, while I was planting window boxes, sunning and brushing blankets, and getting lawn furniture washed, I was pondering the question of what the sample chapter should be. The page and a half was not enough manuscript to send to Mr. Aswell. Finally one day I sat down and began writing. . . .

> I was twenty and allergic to figures. Unfortunately the required college algebra had figures, lots of them. . . .

My pencil sped along the page. What was being set down were certain lighthearted, gay incidents of courtship days. Immediately, I found myself reveling in the humor of the experiences as I relived them in the writing. So long as I worked on the chapter, a weight was lifted from me; it was almost as if Peter were alive again.

Then I put my portable typewriter on the old drop-leaf mahogany table that Peter and I had refinished together and laboriously typed out the pages—hunt and peck. The brief ending, written in tears; the single chapter, written in happy memories; and a loosely woven, crude outline of the book were then mailed to Mr. Aswell.

I had not the slightest idea what his reaction would be. After a few days I began nervously haunting the little white-frame post office in West Harwich for the editor's reply.

Within the week I found the letter lying in my mailbox. Standing in the middle of the post-office floor, I ripped open the envelope. What I read astonished me:

July 21, 1950

Dear Mrs. Marshall:

Your outline of the book on Dr. Marshall, together with your draft of Chapter 6 and the end of Chapter 16 arrived safely a few days ago. I read over the material promptly and was delighted with it. I then had several of my colleagues read it and they shared my enthusiasm for it.

There is not the slightest doubt in our minds, that this will be a good book and a very deeply moving one. It is one we should be most proud to publish. . . .

As for the writing, I compliment you on its sincerity and its deep emotional integrity.

We are now prepared to offer you a contract. . . .

I was exhilarated by such encouragement. Still I marveled that Mr. Aswell had so much faith in my ability that he was willing to offer me a contract before seeing the completed manuscript. How did he know that I could write a book? I didn't know myself. But there it was in black and white. . . . "We are now prepared to offer you a contract. . . ."

So far my only contact with the editor had been through correspondence. Though I knew little about the usual relationship between author and editor, I sensed that there would have to be close teamwork. Thus, before considering a contract, I decided that my next move should be to meet Mr. Aswell.

Peter John stayed with one of our neighbors on Pleasant Road while I made the trip to New York. Going down on the train, I reviewed what I had learned about Edward Aswell. He had been Thomas Wolfe's editor during the last part of the novelist's life. After Wolfe's early death in 1938, Mr. Aswell had been responsible for editing and publishing *The Web and the Rock*, *You Can't Go Home Again*, and *The Hills Beyond*. He had also worked with Richard Wright, Betty Smith, and many others. He had moved to McGraw-Hill only a few years before, and was one of those responsible for building the company's reputation in the field of trade books. And now he wanted to see me. I could only marvel.

The New York, New Haven & Hartford train slowed down at the outer rim of the gigantic, sprawling metropolis that is New York. Now we were going through the slum districts with their forests of television aerials, their pocket handkerchiefs of back yards cluttered with debris, the lines of wash swung out from second- and third-story windows, the children playing stick ball in the streets. As the tram got closer to Grand Central station, something inside me began to tighten. Just making a sally by myself into New York was still a new and terrifying experience. And this was one of the nation's largest publishing houses which I was invading. . . .

The McGraw-Hill building on West 42d Street was an impressive, modern, green-and-chrome structure thirty-four stories high. The executive offices of the trade book department were on the twentieth floor, and my feeling of tension increased as an express elevator whizzed me upward.

I did not have to wait long in the reception room. A secretary took me past a battery of clicking typewriters to a quiet corner office. There I met the editor—a graying, balding man with alert and kindly eyes. He was friendly, easy to talk to. He soon put me at ease. We talked for over an hour. I shared with him some of my ideas on the proposed biography of Dr. Marshall. Mr. Aswell, on his side, told me about his philosophy of books in general. From time to time he would go to the bookshelves that covered one wall and pull out some recently published book to make a point more vividly.

On another wall was a large original cartoon by Thurber, a memento of one of his earlier publishing experiences. As the editor and I talked, we could look over the whole lower part of New York. The two walls of windows were wide vistas, like live murals of the city. Looking west, there were the ramps connecting the Port Authority Bus Terminal with the Lincoln Tunnel, the ocean-going liners at their berths, and across the river, the mist-blurred New Jersey hills. Looking south, there was the Battery, the Statue of Liberty, and the Bay beyond.

During the conversation with Mr. Aswell, I had an intuitive feeling that in him I had found the right editor. Even so, I did not sign the contract that afternoon, but took it back to the Cape to study it at my leisure and to check it with other people. After the contract was changed in a few details and signed, it pledged me to deliver the finished manuscript of a biography of Peter Marshall to the publisher by May 1, 1951—ten months hence.

That fall, the day after Peter John's school started, I got out the outline of the proposed biography that I had sent Mr. Aswell during the summer. I cringed (as I thought Mr. Aswell must have) at the romantic title—*Heather in My Heart.* Terrible! Couldn't be worse! The outline itself was a rough one . .

CHAPTER 1—"Under Sealed Orders"
Peter Marshall leaves Scotland as a quota immigrant. . . .

CHAPTER 2—"The King Is in the Audience"
This shows P. M.'s unique and dramatic approach to Christianity. . . .

CHAPTER 3—"Sagging Balconies"
A personality sketch of P. M. as man and preacher. . . .

Something more basic than sketchiness was wrong with this "P. M. leaves Scotland," "P. M.'s unique and dramatic approach," "A personality sketch of P. M." . . .

Suddenly I felt the necessity of asking myself some pointed questions. . . . Why am I writing this book? What am I trying to accomplish?

I saw immediately what was wrong with the outline. The hero of the biography had to be God—not Peter Marshall. What I was to write was no ordinary Horatio Alger story of the successful immigrant. What Peter Marshall alone had done was not important; what God had done through him—a man with faults like the rest of us—was important. Jesus Christ would have to tower as the central figure of the book if the biography was to be anything more than a wife's fond recollections. I saw that the life of no human being has lasting significance apart from his relationship to God.

The need of all of us—whether we realize it or not—is to know whether there really is a God, and if so, to know Him in a direct and personal way through Christ. When we know Him and understand something of His love for us as a person, then we can trust and follow Him. Only then shall we lose the pang of our loneliness and our heart hunger.

The life of this one man then, this fallible man, Peter Marshall, could be used to answer the average person's questions about God and how He deals with each of us.

I discarded the old outline and started over, asking myself two questions about each chapter . . . what is the theme, the cohesive idea? And what will this chapter tell about God that people really want to know?

CHAPTER 1—"Under Sealed Orders"
Does God still guide people today as the Bible says He did in other ages?

CHAPTER 2—"Singing in the Rain"
Can God still provide material help in our day . . . ?

Such an approach to the writing of a biography was unusual. I knew that. But then the nonprofessional writer either has to be himself completely or else a slavish imitator of somebody else's techniques. I didn't even know enough to be an imitator, so I was nothing if not individualistic.

That fall, if a space man had paused in an interplanetary flight to peer in through a window of our second-floor apartment, he would have stared at a curious sight. . . . A woman propped up in bed writing, with scrapbooks and papers cluttering the bed and the floor; pencil smudges on her face and hands; on the floor beside her a cocker keeping sleepy sentinel. On one side of the bed was an olive-green filing cabinet; in a corner, a dictating machine. Sometimes the woman would jump out of bed to get a cookie or an apple; at other times, to search the file for a missing paper.

During my long illness several years before, I had learned to write in bed. I had discovered then that my thoughts flowed more easily when my body was relaxed. The bedroom, however, was scarcely the ideal place to work. Papers were everywhere, even among my lingerie in the dresser drawers. Most mornings there were from four to twenty-three preschool children playing lustily under my windows. Then there were the ever-ringing telephones. And, of course, the cuckoo clock in B-5.

Each forenoon, Monday through Thursday, I began work at nine. By twelve-thirty or one I would be limp, written out for the day. The afternoons I saved for revision, interviews with people close to Peter, and reading the longhand manuscript into the dictating machine. A part-time secretary would then do a typewritten copy. This, in turn, would undergo several revisions.

Experience soon taught me not to work on an evening if I wanted to sleep. The mind can act like a high-powered machine. Start it going, and it's hard to turn off. Moreover, I found that I needed to see my friends in the evenings. With the continuous work that a book entails, a change of pace is necessary to keep one from going stale. Fridays were reserved for my housework and weekly grocery shopping. Saturdays I devoted to my son.

Two factors enabled me to take my writing schedule so seriously. The first was the signed contract resting in my files. At moments when I wondered whether I was merely indulging myself with delusions of grandeur about being a writer, I would remember that I was legally pledged to deliver a finished manuscript by May 1.

The second was my continuing sense of destiny. There is no bulwark like the conviction of being under orders. Without that, I would have fallen by the wayside a thousand times.

A series of events vindicated my faith that Someone Else's hand was on the project, and that His help was always available. At one point I needed some detailed information about Peter's stepfather. He had died in Scotland one week after Peter. Mother Janet, my husband's mother, was still living, but her memory often failed her on early details. There was not time to take a trip to Scotland to gather information. It seemed as if all possible sources had been exhausted.

Then one night an English couple whom I had met casually invited me to dinner. In the course of an enjoyable evening with them I felt an urge to tell my host about the facts I needed. Suddenly he interrupted me excitedly.

"Surely, you couldn't be speaking of Peter Findlay?"

"Yes, certainly. Why?" The atmosphere in the room became electric.

"I worked beside him in the same office at Stewarts and Lloyds in Glasgow for years. I knew him well. What do you want to know?"

That night I went back to our apartment as excited as a child on Christmas Eve. There are over 800,000 residents of the District of Columbia proper. It's a safe guess that the man to whom I had been led was the only one of the 800,000 who had ever worked in the same office with Peter Findlay. It was as if God were saying, "I'm in this with you. Let this little incident give you courage when the task seems too big for you."

I needed that courage, because sometimes I grew very much afraid. For example, the chapter about Peter Marshall's early life was still unwritten. I was uneasy about it. A straight narration of facts, dates, places would make dry reading. For this chapter I had to describe events that had happened long before I had known Peter. But how could I write vividly, except out of experience—mine or someone else's? I had no background to help me understand a Scottish boy growing up in an industrial suburb of Glasgow, and later, working as a machinist in a tube works.

Once again, in a childlike way, I asked God for help. My answer came in a long-distance call from one Jim Broadbent. He was coming through Washington soon, he said. Could he see me? Jim Broadbent was a cousin of Peter's who had known him always. He was a world traveler and adventurer, long associated in business with the Anglo-Iranian Oil Company. It was he who had first turned Peter's thoughts toward the United States.

There was no doubt that Mr. Broadbent had the information I needed. Among the writer's treasured raw materials is the anecdote lifted right out of life. Firsthand stories provide those graphic details which allow the reader to see, feel, hear, even smell a scene. Many interviews had already taught me that some people have the feel for the good story and the vivid detail, while no amount of prying can get it out of others. I held my breath, hoping that Jim Broadbent would, miraculously, turn out to be one of those tale spinners.

On the afternoon he arrived, I saw at once that he was the rugged, unself-conscious type. Of above average height, sturdily built, he gave an impression of repressed vitality. His Scottish accent filled the room like a buzz saw.

The Scot is by nature clannish; he will do anything for "his ain folk." Jim's warmth toward me suggested that he had already taken me into the clan. He would probably have given me anything, even half of his oil shares. When he found out I wanted reminiscences, he settled himself, put his feet up, lighted his pipe, and prepared to spend the afternoon. All he asked, he said, was a spot of tea later on.

"Tell me what Peter was like as a young boy," I began. "What did he look like?"

"Tall . . . shot up too quickly . . . shock of curly blond hair, inclined to be unr-r-ruly, never slicked down . . . stubbor-rn as a MacDonald or a MacTavish . . . idealistic . . . impetuous."

Only a few questions were needed to keep him going. Jim Broadbent had a photographic memory. More than that, detailed descriptions began pouring out—how a Mr. Ash, Peter's foreman at Stewarts and Lloyds, had looked; the picture of Peter's tidy boardinghouse room; the look of an iron bedstead; the iron, cold to the fingertips in the Scottish winter, the quiet ticking of an old-fashioned clock on a wall, with Peter's kilts hanging on a peg under it. . . .

Bit by bit, the missing pieces of my "Under Sealed Orders" chapter were falling into place. Excitedly I took notes, at the same time soaking up the atmosphere of the scenes Jim described. I could not have imagined a more adequate answer to my plea to God for help than was Jim Broadbent. Once again I had been put in contact with just the right person.

But God's help is not limited to such dramatic episodes. Some of it has to be of the everyday, run-of-the-mill variety. As a housewife trying to write a book, I needed some help in craftsmanship and professional writing techniques.

One day in the course of an informal talk in a Washington church, I mentioned my book. Afterward a slightly built woman of middle years came up to introduce herself. "I am Ruth Welty," she said, extending her hand. "I wonder if you would give me your address? I'd like to write you."

In a few days the note came. . . .

Dear Mrs. Marshall:
Last Wednesday afternoon I asked for your address in order that I might send you several thoughts. . . .

Your book, I feel, will be an interpretation of the great soul, Peter Marshall. You will relive your association with him, in order that he may live for thousands now and in the future.

For the next few months you will not be living in 1950 at all. You will be tempted many times to flee Washington and the many demands made upon you by people who do not understand what it means to write a book. But your source materials, your familiar tools are here, and so you will try to be both the writer and the sweet, accessible adviser. May you have the strength of twins . . . !

You probably have many literary friends. But I'm moved, nevertheless, to suggest that if you should desire impartial comment on your manuscript, or want to discuss it in process, I should be happy to cooperate with you—gratis. It's all part of the Father's work.

Most sincerely,
(Miss) Ruth Welty

The offer in the last paragraph of the letter was an unusual one. But who was Ruth Welty? She had apparently never known Peter or me and had never been connected with our church. I put out feelers among my friends; no one had heard of her.

Finally I telephoned Miss Welty. She explained that in the past she had done editorial work in one of the government agencies and had herself once written a play that had been produced on Broadway. Recently she had retired from government work.

"I wrote you," she said, "under a sort of inner prompting. If I can help with criticism, I'd like to. Naturally, you'd be free to take or leave my suggestions. And I couldn't accept anything for the work."

I protested . . . "But that wouldn't be fair."

"That's the only way I'd agree to do it."

"But why?"

"Well, you see, I believe that there's a sort of reservoir of good will in the world. I call it a spiritual blood bank. Those in need can draw help from it. But the reservoir can be added to only through good deeds done without personal gain. I may not have too many more years. I'd like to feel that I've added my bit. That's all."

The spiritual blood bank idea was new to me and sounded a bit odd. I thanked Miss Welty but hung up without committing myself.

I was still so unsure of myself as a writer that the wrong kind of criticism might bog me down completely. Mr. Aswell had warned me about that. "Get a first draft down on paper," he had said. "I don't even want to see it until it's finished. Critical work will come later."

How could I know what Miss Welty's criticism would be like? I wanted help, but the right kind. In my dilemma, I again tried prayer, asking God—quite simply—to tell me what to do. After several days, there came the quiet assurance that my unknown friend's "compulsion" about contacting me had been authentic, that I should accept her offer. I waited a few more days. Still it seemed clear and right. Finally I dared to accept her offer.

I need not have doubted that God could give me specific guidance on even such a technical matter as this. Miss Welty took the manuscript several chapters at a time. She sent them back with pages of typewritten suggestions . . . page ———, line ———, my suggestion is . . . She caught poor sentence structure, fuzzy writing, dangling modifiers, misspelling, bad transitions, places where I had taken too much reader knowledge for granted. Never did she tear the manuscript apart in a destructive way. She gave encouragement when it was needed. Always she made it clear that it was my book; the final decisions were mine. In short, I had been sent the perfect adviser—expert, prompt, businesslike, kindly.

By then, some four months' work had taught me a little about the process of creating. A person writing a book cannot wait for times of inspiration. Usually the spurts of inspired writing come as dividends from hours upon hours of grinding labor every day.

Another encouraging result of the daily writing schedule is that the work gains momentum with time. Any interruption in the schedule decreases this momentum. Thus I always found it harder to get started on a Monday morning. After a vacation longer than Friday to Monday, it would sometimes take me days to get under way again. I discovered what many writers know, that it was well to end a day's work in the middle of a paragraph, even in the middle of a sentence. Then one's mind is forced to carry the unfinished work until the next work period, and the picking up is easier.

The other side of the writer's schedule is that it can imprison one. For me, much of writing involves catching on paper those will-o'-the-wisp ideas and impressions that come up suddenly out of the subconscious mind. They can rise up at odd times, ruthlessly interrupt sleep, work, even periods of relaxation. Often I would get an idea while walking Jeff along the woodland trail behind our apartment. Then I would rush home to get it down on paper. Or I might wake up in the night with a full-blown sentence in my mind. I soon learned to keep a pad and pencil on my nightstand.

I found that listening to music—different moods of music—affected the feel of what I wrote. In the same way, I had to screen what I read because different authors affected my own style. Did I want to sound faintly tinged with Shakespeare or Edna St. Vincent Millay? *Time* magazine or the King James version of the Bible? A gushing society column or a terse Hemingwayesque novel? It was tricky.

Sometimes it was annoying to have authorship become so tyrannical. I did not always like having to follow docilely where it led. For example, by December I had written the ending of the book, five chapters out of the middle, and some scattered passages. I had no idea what the opening chapter should be. The book still had no title. All this irregularity frightened me. Surely most books, I thought, must be written in orderly and chronological fashion, from the first chapter to the last.

Finally, in despair, I went out and bought a book on how to write nonfiction. The author was a professor in a western university. Eagerly I began to read. The author said that a real writer would discipline himself to outline his book completely before starting, that this was the only way he could know where he was going. I had tried. But my outline was still sketchy. So I gave myself E for effort on that.

The author then recommended doing an abbreviated version of a biography at top speed—say in three days. This version, which would merely hit the high spots, could then be used as another type of outline. I found the idea unappealing. Besides I didn't have the three days to spare. So I decided to pass that one up.

Sooner or later the reader is going to tire of your style, the writer contended. I had strong suspicions that he had something there. For one thing, I had already tired of *his* style, and there were mornings when I all but gagged over my own. I read on eagerly to find out what to do. One might give the reader a change of pace by quoting from some other author—but make it a good author, the book warned. I could just see lengthy quotations from Shakespeare or Dickens interspersed with excerpts from Peter Marshall's sermons.

At that point I tossed the book on how to write a book across the room and told Jeff that he could chew on it. It was not for me. I'd have to do the biography in my own way.

Even so, I became increasingly unsure of my own way. I was getting material down on paper. But what if it wasn't good enough or written well enough?

At first, I shared my fears with no one. I was ashamed to confess them to Mr. Aswell or Miss Welty. Finally I mustered up the courage to take what I had written to a friend whose judgment I trusted. "Will you read it," I asked, "and give me your candid opinion? No flattery, no soft-pedaling. I want it straight."

He gave it to me straight. "You're writing too objectively, too factually. Your stuff lacks warmth. You still haven't gotten inside the man Peter Marshall. He—he just isn't here." And for emphasis he thumped the manuscript.

This was devastating. Yet I knew it was true. The difference between a book that would be as dry as dust and one that really lived would be the presence or absence of a strong glow of emotion. Not trumped-up emotionalism but honest emotion.

I asked myself . . . how does one write without emotionalism but still reach the reader's heart as well as his head? I hadn't the remotest idea. I was at a dead end.

This was a major crisis. My discouragement was so complete that my daily output slowed to a trickle of words on a page. What if I just didn't have what it took to write a book? Indeed, it now seemed rank presumption that I had ever thought I could write.

One morning I awakened shortly before six. Everything was quiet. Miraculously, even the baby overhead was sleeping later than usual. This would be a good time, I thought, to try to get some answers. And I had to have answers—or throw in the sponge.

Because I meant business, my praying that morning was at least honest, if not exactly phrased in theological language. . . . "Dear God, I believed that You told me to write this book. In that belief, I undertook it. But what I've done so far is no good. I'm whipped, helpless. What can I do now?"

Helpless? Your problem is helplessness? The words seemed to echo. I remembered a verse in the New Testament about that. I turned to it and found that I'd already underscored it. . . . Jesus was speaking:

Without me, ye can do nothing. (JOHN 15:5)

Was helplessness, then, not such an unusual state? Could it be that we human beings actually are helpless, but most of the time don't know it? Could the realization of it be the first step out? Could our inadequacy become our greatest asset when it becomes the open door to God's adequacy?

I remembered that the clearest response I'd ever gotten from God had come out of the most abject helplessness of my life. It had been the turning point of my long bout with tuberculosis. One by one every resource had failed—the healing powers of nature, the prescriptions of medical science, even my belief that God could heal me. When my dejection had gotten down to the emotional level—which had meant bitter tears—and when I had presented it to God as all I had left to give Him, then I had received my answer—His presence—and health.

Could it be that it was only out of an emotional as well as an intellectual realization of my inadequacy that I could get outside of myself enough for God to help me? Though I did not get all my answers that morning between six and seven, I had glimmerings.

A few days later a friend came to Washington. She was the wife of an Episcopal rector whom I had met three years before. I knew her as a courageous experimenter with prayer, a tiny woman with a wonderful sense of humor. I spent part of an afternoon with her. We had talked about some of her latest discoveries about prayer, and I had told her about my book. As I was rising to leave, she asked, "How would you feel about our having prayer together about your writing?"

"I'd be so grateful." I sat down again.

My friend's prayer was short and informal, though its content was startling. Her request was specific. "Oh, God," she prayed, "write this book through Catherine. She and I join now in asking You so to write it, that the words will reach out from the printed page to touch the emotions of all who read. Then use these emotions as a springboard to divinely directed action. Amen. So be it."

I was astonished. I had shared none of my thoughts about getting emotion into the writing with my friend. How had she put her finger so surely on the heart of this particular petition? Coincidence? I didn't think so. I felt that the Spirit of God had directed her prayer.

Then in another early morning hour I received a more complete answer about the way in which my friend's prayer was to be fulfilled.

The summer before at Waverley I had asked God to tell me what a widow is to do with her surplus emotional energy, with the great vitality which she used to spend in love for her husband. Now, though I saw no writing in the sky, through an inflow of vivid thoughts I came to know what His answer was for me. "There is a definite connection between strong emotional writing that will touch the reader and your own need of an outlet. Find the connection and use it. The book is My project. I did tell you to write it. For this particular period of your life, use the creative energy that I've given you for My purposes for the book. Allow me to channel it in a steady stream into your writing."

This made sense. The pieces fitted together. I gave the request back to God. When God has dictated the prayer, it is easy to have faith that the prayer will be answered. That January marked the turning point for the book. After that, the writing was lifted to another level. God took over; more than ever I felt myself only an instrument.

Emotion did rise in me—rich and deep and flowed into the words that sped across the pages. There was much pure joy. Peter Marshall had been an exuberant man, and one with many lovable foibles. It was fun to get the foibles down on paper, to relive many a funny scene. Sometimes I enjoyed the work so much I felt self-indulgent. I had all but forgotten the frustrations of the previous summer.

There were other times when feeling what I wrote was costly. That was true during the week I worked on the chapter about my husband's death. Not only did I have to reexperience every vivid detail, but there was the necessity of restraining the emotions. Complete communication in writing depends, at least in part, on discipline. Trying to avoid both sentimentality and diffuseness was as exhausting as reining in a pair of runaway horses. By the time the week was over, I felt as if my spirit had been plowed and harrowed.

My part-time secretary was a fine and eager sounding board for each chapter as it was finished. Several afternoons a week she typed on a card table in our living room. From the next room, I would sometimes hear her chuckling as she worked. Or on the day that she was typing "See You in the Morning," I went to the doorway to ask her a question and was astonished to find her crying unabashedly, tears rolling down her cheeks and dropping on the typewriter keys.

As the spring progressed my project became more and more absorbing. Miss Welty had been right. I wasn't living in 1950 at all. For the first time in my life I became so absent-minded that my friends grew alarmed. "There are times," one of them said, "when you just don't hear what I'm saying to you."

The absent-mindedness reached a climax the day I drove through two red lights—one on Connecticut Avenue and one on Wisconsin. I discovered that it isn't wise to say to a District of Columbia policeman, "I'm awfully sorry, officer. It was my fault. But you see, I'm writing a book."

The officer in question pushed his cap back and scratched his head. There was a quizzical look in his eyes. Then he let loose a blast of sarcasm that all but blistered the paint on my car. "Yeah, lady? I've heard all kinds of excuses in my time. Sure—oh—*sure*. Writing a book, huh? Well, I'm standing here conducting the National Symphony—. Tsh! Tsh! Us artistic people have so-o much trouble!"

Then there was the evening I made biscuits without either baking powder or salt. At dinner I noticed that Peter John seemed puzzled as he bit into one of them.

"What are these?" he asked.

I thought he was trying to be funny. "What d'you think? Biscuits, of course."

I had not yet tried one. After the first mouthful I decided it might be wise to hire a cook until the book was finished.

My eleven-year-old turned out to be one of my best critics. He couldn't be bothered reading the manuscript, but he listened to it on the dictating machine. He would make serious comments, as if he were a senior editor.

"Mom, come here. Listen to this." I came, forced to listen to my own recorded voice:

Finally, I would come out, with a toidy seat in a laundry bag flung over one shoulder, a Sterno stove with cans of baby food—assorted spinach, peas, and prunes—in one hand, juggling with the other Peter John Marshall himself. Then wedged in between boxes, bundles, and suitcases, Peter would drive off, muttering that he really did not think a few days away from the office was worth all this, and that this car might not be a truck, but it surely drove like one today. The car was so loaded, the rear end was hardly off the ground—

My son snapped off the machine. "It's that last sentence, Mom. Since when does a car ever ride with its rear wheels up in the air?"

I was duly abject. "You're absolutely right. I can't imagine how I missed that. Thanks for the correction."

The completed biography was due in New York on May 1. All through March and April I watched the neatly typed pages piling up in an old typewriter paper box.

On the 29th of April I wrote the short preface:

"It's all right, Kate. Go ahead and write it. Tell it all, if it will prove that a man can love the Lord and not be a sissy. . . ."

Then on the last day of April, I walked to the post office to mail my manuscript. It seemed to me that the man on the other side of the window was handling my precious bundle much too casually—as if the box contained a few yards of calico and not my life's blood.

"It will have to go first class," I told him. "It's manuscript—not merchandise—" That should teach him!

It didn't teach him a thing! Carelessly he slapped on some stamps and then tossed the package over his right shoulder into the nearest mail hamper.

I walked out with a letdown feeling. Then I discovered how tense I had been and how tired I still was; how drained and yet how glad. For good or bad—I had done it. I had written a book. . . .

Suddenly that particular set of feelings seemed like familiar ground. Then I remembered. It's the way I had felt just after Peter John was born. That's it! Writing a book is so much like having a baby. No wonder I had wanted the man at the post office to handle my precious bundle with gentleness!

Nine
Like a Thank You
to a Friend

IN THE SPRING of 1951, I had written to my editor:

> . . . I am planning on going to Scotland the middle of July, coming back in
> mid-August, provided this will not interfere with anything important
> about the book, such as seeing proofs.
>   Let me explain that Dr. Marshall had a family jaunt to his home in Scot-
> land all set up for the Summer of 1949. Because he had so looked forward
> to giving this trip to my mother and father, it seems like unfinished busi-
> ness. Therefore, if at all possible—I would like to carry out the plan for
> him. . . .

It pleased me to know that the trip would still be Peter's gift. For
without the royalties from his book of sermons, *Mr. Jones, Meet the
Master*, our going abroad would not have been possible.

There were other reasons, however, for the return to Scotland. All
his life Peter John had heard about his father's native land. It would be
great fun to show it to him, to have him meet his cousin Jennifer, who
was just his age, and his Aunt Christina. Peter's mother, Mother Janet,
seemed delighted that I planned to bring him. She could never see enough
of "her laddie"; Peter John was the living perpetuation of her Peter.

Then, too, in my book I had written of many incidents that
had occurred before my husband had come to the United States. I had

written about still-living people, some of whom I had never met. I had written of his family. After having been married to a Scotsman, I well knew that Americans and Britishers could have quite different points of view.

I felt strongly that, while the book was in the proof stage, when changes were still possible, the early chapters in question should be discussed and checked with Peter's family. A wife, though she sometimes may think so, is not the sole owner of her husband or her husband's memory. Others had loved Peter, had shared him with me.

Our sailing date was set for July 14. My publisher had managed to get *A Man Called Peter* processed as far as the galley proofs. Page proofs would have to follow by air mail. Thirty-six hours before we were to sail, I was still going over the proofs and had done no packing. In the end, a miscellaneous assortment of clothes was thrown into a bag.

Our party of four never knew how we managed to board the *Queen Mary* in time. As the giant ship slipped from her pier 90 berth, I stood on the afterdeck, still breathless, almost too limp to feel anything. "Never again," I vowed, "will I let myself work under pressure like this for the homestretch of a book."

During the quiet days at sea, I lived in the immediate past. I had my first chance to evaluate the weeks just gone by. Once the manuscript had been mailed to the publisher on April 30, events had moved swiftly.

During the first week of May, Mr. Aswell had telephoned me. . . . "I took your manuscript home with me. I've read it twice. As much as I believed in it, it far surpasses my expectations. Could you come to New York soon? Say, sometime in the next few days?"

"For a conference about revision?"

"No, not that. No real revision is necessary. Just minor corrections. If you and I could sit down together, we could do the job in short order. Then we'll go to press."

I had been almost too surprised to speak. "But—but—you can't do that. I mean—it isn't polished. It needs lots of work. This is only the first draft. I mean—I thought you'd ask me to rewrite whole chunks of it."

Mr. Aswell had laughed at my bewilderment. "No—no. Beyond a point a book can suffer from too much revision."

I had a mental picture of my editor grabbing the pages of manuscript from me and rushing for the printing presses. "But—but—I've written it so hurriedly. Eight chapters since February."

"Let me explain. You know, I'm married to an Englishwoman. There's an old British Army term she uses a lot. Not too elegant—but graphic. 'Spit and polish.' Well, you want to 'spit and polish' your book. A natural enough feeling. . . . But just take my word that it needs precious little. Now—when can you come to New York?"

The necessary changes had then been made in one afternoon. In between handling things like . . . page 167, will Americans know what a *glaikit lump* is . . . ? page 173, who is Miss Mary . . . ? page 175, spelling . . . page 239, wolf has a bad connotation . . . my editor had made some interesting comments.

He had admitted that it was unusual for him to ask for so few changes. "But then my experience with this book has been different from the beginning."

"How do you mean?"

"Hard to explain. It's had a different feel about it. As I told you over the phone several of our editors have already read the manuscript. Maybe I shouldn't tell you this . . . but frankly, we've all been amazed. We didn't quite expect what we got."

My heart sank. "You mean it's worse in some spots than you expected?"

"Quite the opposite. You haven't had any training in writing. How did you know certain techniques? Instinct? That doesn't answer it. There's an unknown quantity here." And Mr. Aswell had looked at me with frank curiosity in his eyes.

The "unknown quantity" had, of course, been God. But I had been shy about parading my own deep convictions. Besides I had a horror of sounding stuffy, pious. What had happened had been quite simple, though wonderful. Out of my helplessness, a book had been written through me. I knew my limitations. The period of black discouragement in the middle of writing *A Man Called Peter* had brought home to me my lack of ability. Had I not almost rung down the curtain on the book because of it?

Yet the last eight months had taught me that God, always the Creator, helps us with our creative tasks when we ask Him to. Should it have surprised me to find that this could be very practical aid—in

my case, help with sentence structure, transitions, and craftsmanship generally? It shouldn't have appeared surprising. All too many
people still think of God as interested only in their morals and church
attendance.

The next step had been that the people at McGraw-Hill had asked
if I would put in an appearance at the June sales conference to talk about
A Man Called Peter.

At eleven o'clock on the morning of June 4, all of the company's
sales, promotion, and advertising personnel, together with the officials
and editors of the trade-book division, had been gathered in a conference room on the top floor of the McGraw-Hill building. I had slipped
inside, curious and a little nervous, and had taken a seat near the door.
The men were grouped around an immense mahogany table, discussing
sales techniques.

The talk had whirled and eddied around me. I had tried to listen but
couldn't follow the thread of the commercial book world jargon—"quantity order discounts . . . back list titles . . . prepub offers . . . suffering."
So I had used the time to try to size up the people at the table. It wasn't
easy. The salesmen, each of whom was responsible for a specific section of the country as his book-selling beat, were obviously of all ages,
of every imaginable background. I guessed that almost every religious
faith and denomination—as well as men with no religious affiliations
at all—were represented there.

I had expected book salesmen to be a hard-boiled lot, interested not
at all in the product but only in making the sale. How wrong I was! When
I was introduced and rose to speak, I found them easy to talk to, responsive, obviously enthused. In chatty fashion, I told them some of the
behind-the-scenes details of the writing of *A Man Called Peter*—of the
last pages being written first; of my favorite writing position propped
up in bed; of my son's stern editorial criticisms—and then something
about my purpose in writing the book.

Later on that day I learned that copies had been made of my manuscript and that all of the salesmen were being given a chance to read it.
This was a revelation. I had not dreamed that even a book which they
thought had a chance of success would be given such serious, individualized treatment.

After getting back to Washington, I received a letter from Mr. Aswell
that left me glowing:

You will be pleased to know that by now all of the salesmen have read
A Man Called Peter. Their enthusiasm for your book is without parallel
in my experience. They are realists, these men. Their experience has taught
them what is likely to sell and what is not. With complete unanimity they
confirm the hunch I have had from the beginning that this book is going
to be bought, and read, and cherished by thousands upon thousands of
people in all walks of life.

Prediction, I know, is always hazardous. . . . Yet already this book has
the unmistakable feel of success about it. . . .

Thus, I sailed for my husband's native land with a feeling that something momentous was in the wind. Perhaps *A Man Called Peter* would
indeed be read by the wide audience I had pictured. At least this was my
publisher's guess—and he backed that guess with a first printing of 75,000
books.

By July 21, we were on our way from London to Glasgow by train.
As the *Royal Scot* left the grimy industrial city of Carlisle and sped
toward Gretna Green and the Border hills, I saw the heather bending
before the wind, the black-faced sheep, smoke curling from the chimney of a stone cottage nestled in the shoulder of a hill. It began to look
like the Scotland I remembered, the Scotland that Peter Marshall had
so proudly shown his bride back in 1937. . . .

Then the Border country became mountainous, craggy, desolate. The
Royal Scot crawled upward between jutting rocks and tumbling streams.
Once Peter John excitedly called me to a window to see a sandy-haired
shepherd with his dog. He stood by a mountain path staring at the chrome
and blue monster that shattered his solitude.

In half an hour we would be pulling into the Glasgow station. I
imagined that Peter's eighty-one-year-old mother and his sister Chris
were probably already there waiting for us.

All at once, with no warning, as if a spring had released it, a freshet
of tears overflowed. I put my head down on the table before me and sobbed,
crying as I hadn't since that first Sunday in church after Peter's death, when
the Chinese woman had opened her heart in silent sympathy. I was as
surprised as the rest of the family, because I had had no feeling of holding
emotion in check. The intensity of it shocked me.

Then it was over. This trip to Scotland was the last and biggest hurdle of going back to places fraught with special memories. But my tears were healing tears, and the experience was actually another big stride forward.

When Mother Janet saw us on the station platform, she tried to enfold both Peter John and me in her warm arms all at once. As she looked into my face for the first time since her son's death, I was the one who comforted her. And because of what had happened on the train, I was emotionally prepared for the rest of our visit.

Peter John, who was sometimes not too talkative around grownups, found his tongue within minutes after he had met Jennifer. On the way out to Airdrie, where Mother Janet lived with Chris and her family, he shot a running barrage of questions at his blond cousin. Some of them provoked lively discussion; some made wonderfully little sense.... Why is a pence so much bigger than a shilling...? Why is all your ice cream vanilla...? Do you play Monopoly? You have a set? Good! I suppose yours has British money.... When I was a little boy, one of my favorite stuffed animals was a wire-haired terrier named Airdrie. Isn't that funny...? Could you help me find a store that sells British soldiers? I'm looking for a set of the Black Watch...."

At Airdrie and elsewhere in Scotland and England where we wandered, the page proofs of *A Man Called Peter* followed me with dogged determination in four separate chunks. They had to be returned promptly, sightseeing and shopping notwithstanding. It appealed to my sense of drama to deal with them as I sat on a rock by a trout stream in the Trossachs, in a hotel room in London, in an inn on the Isle of Wight. I thought doing the proofreading in such romantic spots ought to give my book a special flavor, like garlic rubbed on the salad bowl or a hint of rosemary in the soup.

One July morning I sat on a wall above the ramparts of Edinburgh Castle looking over the latest spate of page proofs, while my parents took Peter John on the 10 A.M. tour of the storybook fortress. The view was so good that it was diverting. When I turned sideways, there were the Princes' Street gardens with their manicured flower beds, the flower clock, and the Sir Walter Scott memorial.

Before me in the cobblestoned courtyard, a pantomime was taking place. A lady tourist, dressed in flashy tweeds, was about to take movies of the guard on duty. Dressed in his Argyll and Sutherland kilt, with his chest thrown out, the guard was colorful camera material. At first he didn't see the photographer. Then when her camera started whirring, he threw his chest out still further, tilted his cap at a more rakish angle, and tried to look stern. At that point, I dropped the proofs, and took a picture of both the tweedy lady and the Scots guard.

On August 14, we sailed for home. I had had satisfying talks with Peter's family about the book. I had had the fun of playing guide to my mother and father and Peter John, showing them many of the places Peter had shown me thirteen years before—Robert Burns's village of Ayr, Sir Walter Scott's home at Abbotsford, historic Stirling Castle, John Knox's house in Edinburgh, the Trossachs at the edge of the Highlands . . . and the page proofs for *A Man Called Peter* had long since been sent back to New York, for better or for worse.

Peter John was triumphantly bringing home his own strange booty— a hard roll off the *Queen Mary* (to see how long it would last); a bottle of different colored sands from the Isle of Wight; a wall plaque of Tam O'Shanter and Sauter Johnny ("Tam lo'ed him like a vera brither"); a toy reproduction of a London double-decker bus; a set of the Black Watch soldiers and also the Queen's Bays—the Second Dragoon Guards.

It took us four hours to get through customs, but they didn't find that hard roll.

My first conscious thought on the morning of October 5, 1951, was— Publication day! This is publication day. . . . I had looked forward to it for so long!

Yet, in retrospect, I can't imagine what I expected. Church bells to toll? Headlines in the Washington *Post?* Booksellers to put placards in their windows? People trampling one another in their eagerness to read *A Man Called Peter?*

Actually, as the day progressed, not a thing happened. October 5 seemed no different from any other day, except that I did receive a routine telegram of congratulations from the publishing house. Having dealt with green authors before, my friends at McGraw-Hill undoubtedly knew what a letdown feeling publication day can bring.

Every author, green or not, is anxious to see the first reviews of his book. I was no exception, though I was equally curious about reader reaction. The reviewers who mentioned the book at all were kind enough. My chief impression, however, was that the publication of *A Man Called Peter* had caused very small ripples indeed in the world of book reviewers.

It was kindly reviewed by Clarence Seidenspinner in the *Chicago Tribune:*

> The best stories are those that really happen. None of the novels concerning the ministry, written during the last few years, touches the heart and appeals to the mind in the way that Catherine Marshall does in telling the story of her husband's life. . . .

The *Boston Herald* called the book "luminous and moving . . . a dimensional portrait. . . ." A reviewer in the *Houston Chronicle* wrote that "no matter what your religion . . . you cannot help but thrill to this story." *Newsweek* said nothing about style or craftsmanship, spoke only of the biography's content.

A. Powell Davies in *The New York Times* wrote:

> It can scarcely be claimed that any man's wife is well equipped to be his most objective biographer. . . . Nevertheless, Catherine Marshall writes extremely well. Those who do not accept her religious viewpoint will nevertheless admit that she presents it with grace and charm. . . .

And Alvin Morris in the *Des Moines Register* said:

> There is more than either Peter Marshall or Catherine Marshall in this book. There is God—God not in abstract idea, but in life. This is the story of a man who served God with all his heart because he knew Him, and yet sought Him with all his heart because he felt that he did not sufficiently know Him. It is this paradox within the man that accounts for the true greatness of Peter Marshall. . . .
>
> You will be sorry when the story is over; only you have a feeling that it isn't over. You know that the last chapter of A *Man Called Peter* cannot yet be written.

A reviewer in the *Saturday Review of Literature* commented about what he called my "Palmer method of English." (I hope it has become a little less Palmer as time has passed. . . .) The only thorough panning I

got was to come a little later from a British newspaper under the headline, "Unfair to Peter":

> It is sometimes necessary to be harsh if only to persuade some women
> not to repeat the mistakes other women have made. Mrs. Catherine
> Marshall, for instance wrote Peter Marshall's biography. It is selling well
> in the U.S. Why it was published here I do not know. . . .
>
> Mrs. Marshall has written an embarrassing book about a good man who
> deserved better. The sermon extracts are very ordinary. Peter Marshall
> could do much better. We even have the last words Mrs. Marshall ever
> spoke to her husband. We have them in italics *"See you, Darling, see you
> in the Morning. . . ."* I'm sorry Mrs. Marshall wrote this book and I'm sorry
> this note is cruel.
>
> But Peter Marshall was a good minister of the Gospel and a man who
> would have been acutely embarrassed by this kind of emotional nudism.
> She would have been wiser and kinder to allow some good friend of Peter's
> to write a small book on a good man. But she was not. The good and wise
> Peter Marshall is a shadow seen through the substantial presence of his
> biographer, who never stands aside. The book might be called "A Woman
> Called Catherine"; but we have A MAN CALLED PETER, by Catherine
> Marshall.*
>
>   J. G.

I soon learned that there are two barometers of reader reaction. One
is the actual sale of the book as gauged by the bookstore reorders to the
publishers and the best-seller lists. The other is the author's fan mail or
lack of it.

On October 28, within three weeks of publication, I opened my
Sunday *New York Times* to find that *A Man Called Peter* had a toe hold
on the nonfiction best-seller list. By the end of the next month, it had
climbed to fourth place. Through subsequent months it vied with Rachel
Carson's *The Sea Around Us*, Millis and Duffield's *The Forrestal Dia-
ries*, Tallulah Bankhead's *Tallulah*, Norman Vincent Peale's *The Power
of Positive Thinking*, the new Fannie Farmer *Boston Cooking-School
Cook Book*, and the new Revised Standard Version of the Bible.

The climb up the lists was exciting to watch, heady wine for a new
author. Every Sunday morning I would rise early, slip on robe and slip-

British Weekly, Aug. 21, 1952.

pers, and grab the papers, wondering who my nearest competitor would be that week—Tallulah or Dr. Peale. Then, juggling a cup of coffee in one hand, I would curl up in an easy chair to study the lists more carefully. Was Tallulah creeping up on me? Was Fannie Farmer faltering? Peter and Dr. Peale were neck and neck. . . . It was a lot of fun.

On April 23, 1952, seven months after release, I received a wire from my publisher:

YOUR BOOK GOES TO NUMBER ONE ON HERALD TRIBUNE BESTSELLER LIST OF MAY FOURTH. CONGRATULATIONS.

The *Reader's Digest* published a condensation of the book. Then the U.S. Information Agency asked to do its own condensation for publication abroad. I was particularly pleased, because the books the Agency chooses for possible foreign publication are supposed to portray the best in American life.

The book sold and sold. The sales passed the 180,000 mark by the end of the first seven months. Meanwhile, *Mr. Jones, Meet the Master,* out more than two years, had sold some 230,000 copies.

At the end of 1952, *A Man Called Peter* was still going strong. *Time* magazine's round-up, "The Year in Books," for its December 15, 1952, issue said:

The year's true bestseller was the Bible . . . the new Revised Standard Version. . . . Next to the Bible on the bestseller list stood Catherine Marshall's warm, clear-eyed biography of her husband, the late Chaplain of the Senate, *A Man Called Peter.*

This was just another indication that something had happened with the sale of books in the United States. Fiction was not doing well; religious titles were selling in phenomenal fashion. Columnists wondered whether this was a sign of some sort of a religious revival. Or was it due to the uncertainties of the international situation? To the continuing cold war? Or to fear of the atom bomb?

I had to believe that there was more to it than fear. Could it not be that the public's taste for religious books indicated that a thirst for answers to the riddle of life was at an all-time high?

The sale of religious titles was three and a half times as great in 1947 as it had been in 1937. In February, 1953, as an example, the four top titles on the *New York Herald Tribune's* nonfiction list were all religious: *A Man Called Peter*, Murrow's *This I Believe*, Peale's *Power of Positive Thinking*, and the new Revised Standard Version of the Bible. A quarter century earlier this would have been unthinkable.

Eugene Exman, religious editor of Harper & Brothers, analyzed this phenomenon of religious-book buying in an article "Reading, Writing and Religion" in *Harper's Magazine** about that time. He suggested four reasons ... an element of fear, the fact that science has failed us as the god we once thought it was, a renewed interest in psychology, and the one-world consciousness that has been forced on us.

Whatever was behind the interest in religious books, it was obvious that one of the reasons for the success of *A Man Called Peter* was that it had hit the country at the right time. I took this to be one more sign that God's hand was on the book.

All of this was heartening. But figures make arid reading. Much more heartwarming was reader reaction as it came to me through the mail. Every day my mailbox was stuffed with letters. Though fan mail had poured in after *Mr. Jones* was published, this seemed different, more personal. Something had been added.

Whenever I think of the letters, I see a procession of pictures.... A blind woman in Atlanta, laboriously typing a letter, with many mistakes. Often she had not known when she had reached the edge of the paper. ... A sixteen-year-old girl writing on pink paper at four in the morning. ... A Senator dictating his letter in his office where scores of autographed photos looked down from the walls. ... An interne in his Baltimore rooming house. "I'm in the eye section of Johns Hopkins Hospital...." A Boston shoe manufacturer, en route to Washington by train, reading in his roomette until almost dawn. ... A soldier near the front lines in Korea, sitting on an upturned keg, laboriously printing his letter. "I'm not sure you will ever receive this...." An Iowa housewife writing in her farm kitchen.... A Japanese girl in her college dormitory room. "I am a foreign student from Tokyo. In the bitter experience of World War II, we lost our house and all our possessions...." An Illinois business-

*May, 1953.

man. "I handle auto parts. For the past several years I have been groping for God. Don't misunderstand me. I'm not particularly emotional. . . ." A prisoner in the Insular Penitentiary of the Philippines. "I am a terrible sinner, but I am trying to seek and know God like your Peter did. Humans like you can help me. . . ."

What did these correspondents, of all colors, races, and backgrounds, have in common? Nothing. Everything. They had each read a book. But it had been more than reading a book. Often it had been an experience in worship. Something had stirred in their hearts. Haltingly they expressed it. From border to border of the United States and from all around the world they shared their hopes and fears with me. Their common humanity blended into a common longing. And as I read their letters, I felt wrapped around with that common humanity—warm, precious, pulsating.

As 1951 passed into 1952, an increasing amount of my mail bore foreign postmarks. There were as yet no foreign editions of *A Man Called Peter*. The book was being mailed from this country to far corners of the earth, from friend to friend, passed from hand to hand. And so I heard from

> A man from Hrisey, Iceland;
> A family in Johannesburg, South Africa;
> A man writing from a hotel room in Brussels, Belgium;
> A woman in Taechung, Formosa;
> A couple in Haifa, Israel;
> A woman with almost undecipherable handwriting
>   in Lausanne, Switzerland;
> A missionary in Ceylon;
> A girl in Nagercoil, India . . . "I am an Indian.
>   An American friend loaned me the volume . . ."
> A boy in Paget West, Bermuda;
> A man from Lisbon;
> A woman in Dublin;

and on and on.

I noticed that our postman often had a quizzical look on his face as he delivered our mail. One morning I happened to meet him at the door. He pushed his cap back on his head, shifted his pack to a more comfortable position, and started shuffling through the pile of letters in his hand. As he gave me one stack, I thanked him and started to shut the door.

"Wait a minute—there's a lot more." He sighed and continued to shuffle. "I don't mean to be nosy, but what goes on here? Are you starting a Lonely Hearts Club or something? The men at the Friendship branch of the post office say—well—they're puzzled too." He handed over another fistful.

"It is quite a pile! Well, it's like this . . . I wrote a book. Some people have read it and—well—they write to tell me so."

The postman stared at me, his mouth hung at half-mast. "Some people—*some.* . . . Umph! Well, lady, I dunno—. See ya when I stagger back tomorrow—"

During the writing of *A Man Called Peter*, I had hoped that it would help ordinary men and women with their everyday problems. The prayer for the book that my friend, the wife of the Episcopal rector, had prayed that afternoon had been a request for specific results. She had asked that the printed word reach through to the emotions of all who read, that the emotion would become a touchstone for action.

As the letters continued to come, I saw that those twin dreams for the book—mine and my friend's—were being fulfilled to an extent that I had not dreamed possible. Someone with a knotty problem in his life had read the book. He had laughed and wept. He had come to know one Peter Marshall. But far more important, out of the pages had stepped a living Lord. Somehow the Spirit of God had spoken directly to his particular needs.

Was his problem alcoholism, a mental breakdown, bereavement, the adjustment of a man to the armed services, a shaky marriage? I had not written of those problems specifically. Yet the reader seemed to get insight into himself and his needs. Often he was able to solve his problem.

Delightedly, he wrote to tell me about it, sometimes in crude longhand on ruled paper, sometimes in neat script on engraved stationery. Often the writer was self-conscious, not sure how to begin, fearful lest his sharing be an intrusion. Yet each had something he so wanted to say that, without being aware of it, he wrote with the freshness of newly turned earth on a spring morning.

In letter after letter, the heart showed. And I, reading these letters, often with a lump in my throat, knew full well that I, the author, could take no credit for such results. It was God's doing. I could but thank Him and marvel at the stories that came back to me. . . .

A dark-haired boy on duty in sick bay was reading a book. Most of the patients were asleep, and the big carrier off Eniwetok was quiet. Only the groan of the ship's plates as she rolled slightly and the scratch of the doc's pen broke the silence of the night.

The doc was writing his wife back in Akron, Ohio. "Not really much to tell Mildred.—What's the book, Don?"

"*A Man Called Peter.* Got it this afternoon in the ship's library."

"How'd you like it?"

"Okay, so far."

When Don had finished the book, he wrote to me:

Dear Catherine. . . . Hello there!

Please forgive me for being so bold to call you Catherine, but I feel as if I have known you for a long time. This is a sort of fan letter I guess, but it's really more than a thank you to a friend. . . .

Your book was read in still of night in sick bay. Two of our boys were injured seriously in swimming when an LST accidentally ran over them. It was then we turned to God. Strangely enough I had started your book the night before.

Your Peter came alive and very real to me, and with Peter you brought God along . . . or Peter and God came hand in hand. All this sounds trite and artificial I know, but this is what I've been thinking.

Several of the boys here are reading your Peter and now stop and think. This helps when our thoughts get all jumbled up, and there are no emotional outlets. . . .

And from a college dean in the Deep South:

Last week a tragedy struck our campus. A student died suddenly during class. This had a subduing effect on the innate gaiety of our young people.

The day after the funeral, I read to my English class Peter Marshall's sermon "Go Down Death." The students sat quiet and attentive. The message got through.

Thank you for sharing A Man Called Peter *with the rest of the world. . . .*

There was a letter I shall always treasure from Babs, who was a minister's wife in a small Iowa town. She wrote me one January 3. Her miracle of a changed heart had happened, she said, on New Year's Eve. "As I closed the book," she wrote, "I knew I could never be the same person again."

The story started back in college days. During that period, the young girl was a romantic and an idealist. She had a long list of qualifications laid out for her dream man. Every night she knelt by her bed and prayed, "Oh God, if You will just send me this man to love, I'll do anything You ask me to."

It happened; the man appeared on her horizon. He had all of Bab's requirements, plus a few she hadn't thought of. Dennis was an industrial engineer with Eastman Kodak Company. He had a fabulous salary and what seemed like an unlimited future.

They had a deliriously happy first year of marriage. Babs was looking forward to the building and decorating of their first home. After that, she planned to have a baby.

Then Dennis began to talk about going into the ministry. At first Babs couldn't believe that he was serious. She hoped this was a passing fancy and that the idea would die a natural death. She thought, "When I promised God back during college days that I would do anything He wanted if He would send me the right husband, I surely didn't mean this." How could Dennis even think about giving up his wonderful position with its great future?

Yet after a nine-month struggle the young husband quietly but firmly informed his wife that there was no other way for him—he felt compelled to answer the call.

The couple went to the McCormick Theological Seminary in Chicago. Babs postponed having the baby and took on a secretarial job. Financially things were not so good, but otherwise they came through with flying colors. "Surprisingly the three years of preparation for the ministry were the happiest of our lives," Babs confided to me. "We were sharing everything and made lifelong friends."

Finally Dennis was ordained. He was offered a call to the Iowa church. They went there with high hopes, one card table, and a $1,000 debt. The church had paid the last minister $1,800 a year; they stretched a point and offered Dennis $2,400.

Babs had the baby—a daughter, and then two years later, a son. The church work flourished, and Dennis became more and more absorbed in it. Too often Babs had to stay at home with the children alone. Dennis seemed no longer to have time to talk everything over with his wife as once he had. The month the young minister was out on church business every night and was home only one afternoon, Bab's resentment boiled over. She raged, "This isn't any marriage. Am I married to a church or a man?"

On both sides barriers went up; lines of communication went down. Whenever Dennis suggested that he and his wife pray together as they used to, Babs would stiffen and change the subject. Dennis felt pulled in two directions. Where did his duty lie? The quality of his preaching and his contacts with people suffered as the conflict grew.

On New Year's Eve there was to be a party and watch-night service. Babs wanted very much to go, but at the last minute her baby-sitting arrangements failed. Her husband was sympathetic but could offer no other solution and went off without her. Babs's mind was full of rebellion and self-pity. "Thirty and too young to be put on the shelf. . . . Once again the church comes before me . . . it always does. . . . It just doesn't matter to Dennis how lonely I am. . . ."

After the children were in bed, Babs settled down to her solitary vigil. She sat before the fire in the living room—bored, restless. And then her eyes fell on a book on the table. Its title was *A Man Called Peter.* It had been a Christmas present. Unable to think of anything better to fill the long hours till midnight, she opened it and began to read.

Her letter told the rest of the story:

> *Somehow reading your book, something in me melted. I felt so ashamed when I thought what I could be and haven't been. All at once I saw myself clearly. The demand in me, the pettiness, the self-centeredness. In those hours, I grew up. That night Dennis and I knelt down together and with unashamed tears turned it all over to God and started a fresh chapter in our marriage. I have never known such serenity or felt the Presence of God so continually.*
>
> *May I thank you for being willing to write this book—for sharing all the beautiful memories you and Peter had with people like me. . . .*

There were other true incidents. One concerned a college boy who suffered a nervous and mental breakdown. He turned ruthlessly against those who loved him best, particularly his parents.

His parents could afford fine doctors and psychiatrists. But the experts were unable to help because the boy had withdrawn completely into himself. He would not even talk to the psychiatrist.

Institutional care was recommended, but his mother still insisted upon keeping him at home. The withdrawal grew worse. After two years, the young man would scarcely leave his bedroom. He even insisted that his meals be served there.

A family friend thought that reading *A Man Called Peter* might be of some comfort to the heartbroken mother. On one of the rare occasions when the son ventured from his room, his mother noticed that he kept eying the book in her lap.

Something about it intrigues him, she thought.

But she knew that if she suggested that he read it, that would be the last thing he would do. Then her love gave her a rare insight into his twisted temperament. She hid *A Man Called Peter* underneath the cushions on the davenport. The next morning the book was gone. Apparently her son had found it and was reading it.

He stayed in his room for the next twenty-four hours. Then, the following morning when the father and the mother were eating breakfast, their son appeared in the doorway. He had shaved and was immaculately dressed. There was a smile on his face and a new look in his eyes.

"Good morning, Mother," he said. "Hello, Father. May I have some breakfast?" He chatted happily over his bacon and eggs as if the three of them had dreamed the last two years. Later, the mother, using the excuse of a checkup but really overwhelmingly curious about the sudden change, took her son back to the psychiatrist. The doctor was frankly astonished.

"What's happened?" he asked the mother.

"You'll never believe this. A book did it."

"For God's sake—what book?"

"A biography—*A Man Called Peter*."

It was the mother who divulged the story.

The minister who lived near Wapwallopen, Pennsylvania, knew that the General Store nearby stayed open each night until 9:30. Just before closing time one evening, he walked up the creaky wooden steps of the store, nodded pleasantly to the two farmers still lounging on the porch.

The interior smelled agreeably of crackers and soda pop, but no one seemed to be around. Finally the minister called, "Anybody here?"

After a minute the proprietor came out from the back room. "About seventy," the clergyman guessed. The old man had been crying and was obviously embarrassed to have anyone see him with bloodshot eyes.

"Been readin' a book," he explained. "Maybe you've heard of it—*A Man Called Peter*. It's a good'un—sort of got me. You know about my wife adyin'—"

"Yes I do. That's really why I'm here. Your daughter asked me to drop by."

"Mighty nice of you, Reverend, to come and see me—"

I heard about the minister's visit and a whole lot more in a letter the old storekeeper wrote me—one of the nicest letters I've ever received. . . .

> *Your book came at a time when I needed it most. It just about saved my life. My wife died Dec. 26, '52. I just felt I couldn't go on living without her. . . .*
>
> *I started to read it Thursday afternoon. I cried so much while I was reading it, I was ashamed to go in the store when a customer came. . . .*
>
> *One of those who saw me was our minister. He's a Lutheran. I told him what I was reading. . . . But I also noticed a tiny bit of moisture in his eyes, so I didn't feel so ashamed any more.*
>
> *Sometimes I had to laugh through the tears, like where you spoke of the turkey hash. That's one thing I don't like either—stuff all chopped up— like that. . . .*
>
> *I hope you'll excuse my mistakes and a stranger writing to you like this. But you don't seem like a stranger any more. . . .*
>
> *Respy yours,*
>
> *P.S. Someone said that man is like a tack—useful if he has a good head on him and is pointed in the right direction. . . .*

One morning the first letter on the pile was from a teenage girl in Atlanta, Georgia:

> *. . . I feel, and I know many teenagers who feel that Dr. Marshall's ministry was not cut off with his death, but rather extended and augmented.*

You see, Mrs. Marshall, through this book, the lives of many young people have been changed. Many of our problems, trifles as they may seem, have been solved within the pages of this book. Yet we are too young to have seen or heard Dr. Marshall. . . .

On down the pile was a letter from a minister in Ohio:

Then with the sudden passing of Dr. Marshall, I felt that God must care very little for His work to take away one so effective. But now I think I know "Why." His ministry is now far wider than ever it could have been. . . .

In those first weeks after Peter's death, I too had asked why. I had asked it desperately, confusedly, almost every hour of every day. Why did this have to happen to me? Why did the one I love have to die so soon? How can you reconcile a God of love with all the tragedy in the world?

I had received no answers then. That had left me with the alternative either of trusting God blindly on the assumption that He would give me some answers in His own good time, or of letting go all faith in the love of God. I knew that the latter would have netted only total darkness, abysmal grief.

Therefore, out of no answer I had reached for the only answer. I claimed that extraordinary promise that God has made to His children in the midst of tragedy,

All things work together for good to them that love God.
(ROMANS 8:28)

I asked Him to work His miracle of bringing "good" out of Peter's death.

Almost two years had gone by. Now, in the wake of *A Man Called Peter,* part of God's answer came into sight. Over and over my correspondents expressed it for me:

God moves in mysterious ways. Had Peter lived, you would never have written this book. Then I—and thousands like me—would never have known of his life. . . .

Did this mean then, that it had been God's will that my husband die at forty-six of a heart attack? I did not think so. With all my heart I believe that a loving Father wills health, happiness, love, and joy for His children. But on this imperfect earth, we rarely achieve these goals. In fact we stumble into hole after hole. Given our stubborn wills, our limited spirits, our refusal to listen to God or even the message of our consciences, we often make a mess of our lives. Our fondest dreams come crashing down in wild desolation.

Then what? It is as if God says, "Never mind. I understand. Even as you sit in the midst of your wrecked playhouse, don't despair. The mess can be cleaned up. Hand the grief, the failure, the disappointment, over to Me. I'm the only One who can take the broken things from life's rubbish heap, and by a divine alchemy make them better than they were before. Try Me and see."

Isn't this the meaning of the Cross? An old hymn expresses it:

> In the cross of Christ I glory
> Towering o'er the wrecks of time. . . .

Yes, that's it! Wrecks . . . the wrecks of our lives, the wreck we make of our world—that's what the Cross towers over, as a symbol that something can be done about the rubble of frustration, poverty, war, disease, heartache.

I could not believe that Peter's early death had been in God's ideal plan. There is a difference between God's ideal will and His permissive will. But given a set of circumstances which ended in death, then God was able to step in and turn those circumstances upward to an alternate plan—toward breathtaking good.

Ten
The Reservoir of Love

EVERY HUMAN BEING needs love. Most of our troubles spring from the lack of it. Like thirsty men in a desert, we perish without it.

In one way, love had been withdrawn from my life at the time of my husband's death. By the beginning of the year 1952, as one result of the publication of A *Man Called Peter*, love in another form was being returned to me a thousandfold. I first became aware of it through the avalanche of fan mail.

Typical was a letter from a seventy-year-old woman from Boulder, Colorado:

> *Dear Catherine,*
> *I know you won't mind me calling you Catherine, for since reading your book I feel you are a very dear friend. . . .*

Or the same thought expressed by a high school girl in Aurora, Illinois:

> *. . . I had never heard of Peter Marshall until I read your book, but now I feel as if I have known him all of my life. And I have the same feeling about you. . . .*

150

Friendship and love can follow only in the wake of the heart's articulation. Mind must speak to mind; spirit to spirit. Somehow, this had happened in *A Man Called Peter*.

Out of a sense of compulsion, I had written a book, written it almost solely on the instinctual level, from the heart. At the time, I could not imagine how the public would receive it; for all I knew, few people would ever read it. The immense popularity of *A Man Called Peter* was as much of a surprise to me as to anyone else. I could only marvel—and marvel some more.

Letters from readers made it abundantly clear that one of the secrets behind that popularity was that heart had spoken to heart.

A Marine in Korea wrote:

Reading about Peter's life has definitely changed mine. I want you to know that . . . Mrs. Marshall, your spirit has touched mine all the way over here in Korea. I love Peter and you and Wee Peter with a love that only Christians can know. . . .

Those who read *A Man Called Peter* took it personally. There was a surprising identification with the Marshall family. This transcended all barriers of creed, dogma, or nationality. A Japanese man wrote me from Nagasaki:

I've just finished your book A Man Called Peter. *First I started to read it with a dictionary in hand around Christmas. Then I forgot I was reading in a foreign language and stopped looking up words. There existed no longer the barrier of language. I was happy with you, I was desperate with you. I have sobbed and cried with you, and now I am filled with the same bliss and gratefulness and happy memory that you are. . . .*

What a dearest friend of us, Peter Marshall! The impact of him will not let me go again to despair or hatred of other men and myself. I found in him a fellow-Christian who really understands the daily presence of God in our common life, a G.G.P. who encourages and understands my enthusiasm to Volley Ball, table tennis, Japanese chess, and photography. . . .

The identification was so complete that our family jokes became the readers' jokes. For example, a girl in India picked up the two sentences from *A Man Called Peter*—"Peter John requests that he not be called Wee Peter any more, since he is growing so big. So he suggests that he be called Big Peter and that I be called Enormous Peter. . . ." and closed her letter with "I do hope you and 'Big Peter' are doing well."

In the same way, readers from across the world often remembered the birthdays, anniversaries, and special occasions of our family. A native of Taipei, Formosa, wrote:

> As the third anniversary of your dear husband's Heavenly Birthday draws near, I wish to send you this little note to remind you that friends over here remember. . . .

Reader friends even hugged "Enormous Peter's" foibles to themselves:

> St. Paul, Minn.
>
> Dear Catherine Marshall:
>
> You have shared the personal life of a great man with the public who loves him in a tender and beautiful way. I have just finished reading and re-reading A Man Called Peter.
>
> I have wept over many of its pages, chuckled over others—especially that part about the boiling of his egg. Would you please let me know— did you ever get that egg boiled just right?

So complete was the identification that many a reader all but took Peter John and me in as members of his family. One man wrote from Buenos Aires:

> I sail ships under the Swiss flag. My home is in Lausanne, Switzerland. . . . By the way, tell Peter John that we have five children, the third one just his age, another boy called Peter. We would love to have you and your Peter visit us sometime. . . .

A letter from a teen-age girl contained an invitation:

> Dear Mrs. Marshall:
>
> . . . I know you are a very busy woman, but would it be possible for you to attend my graduation in June? I am asking you early. You could stay at my home. I'm sure my Mother wouldn't mine. Graduation is June 26th. . . .

Sometimes the family feeling got surprisingly cozy, as from an eleven-year-old boy:

Dear Mrs. Marshall,
. . . I pray each night to God that you would sent me a letter, and you did. . . .
. . . I thank you again for writing to me and I am sending you one of my school pictures. Now I have to go for I have an in-grow toe nail in my toe, and I have to soke it.

Then came a continuous stream of letters, telling me of newborn babies named for Peter Marshall. . . .

Spring Valley, N.Y.
Dear Mrs. Marshall,
I think you would be interested and maybe pleased that I named my new son after Dr. Peter Marshall, whom I met and fell in love with when I was fifteen. I shall always remember the two weeks he visited in my hometown, and will always remember Dr. Marshall as a wonderful man with beautiful curly sandy hair and a Scottish burr. . . .
I would be delighted if you have a picture of Dr. Marshall you could send me to put in Baby Marshall's baby book. . . .

At first I tried to keep track of Peter's namesakes—one in Spring Valley, New York; Warner, New Hampshire; Tarrytown, New York; Marion, Mississippi; Oak Park, Illinois. After a while the bookkeeping overwhelmed me. Only God and Peter finally know the latest count on how many little Peter Marshalls there are.

As these letters poured in, the world began to seem like one big family. Then came the realization that my growing family of correspondents was making demands. And one has to give time to one's family. This came home to me very soon, because so personal were all the letters, so warm, so human, often containing such remarkable stories of lives lightened and lifted, that I wanted to answer every one. That alone meant changes in my life. The first was that it was no longer possible to get along with a part-time secretary and a bedroom office.

Therefore, in March, 1952, Peter John and I moved from the apartment into a house. The most pleasant bedroom, one with a bay window, was turned into an office. Open bookshelves with cupboards below were built, floor to ceiling, on three sides. At last I had a place for the books which had always overflowed the apartment. The cupboards were big enough to house the boxes of Dr. Marshall's sermon manuscripts and the voluminous scrapbooks that had been such a help to me in writing *A Man Called Peter.* Now I even had a place for the olive-green filing cabinet; no longer did it have to stand beside my bed.

There was also a place of special retreat for Peter John. He appropriated part of the third floor. There he unpacked the toy soldiers he had brought back from the British Isles and lined them up in brigades and regiments. He papered the walls with baseball pictures and favorite pennants. From the ceiling he hung his fifty-odd plane models. Now that he had space . . . space . . . space . . . he set about constructing more models—adding dozens of ships to the planes.

But often during those days, our new home seemed like a glass house. The telephone rang constantly. Out-of-town visitors appeared at the front door without warning. There were requests for autograph parties, speaking engagements, magazine articles, pictures, interviews, radio and television appearances; for awards, even honorary degrees. The demands from my reader family piled up and up. My private life was in danger of being squeezed to extinction.

My publishers tried to help in various ways. To meet the requests for autographing, they suggested that I sign the end sheets before they were bound into the books. This meant that, instead of my making dozens of personal appearances, preautographed books could be mailed to the bookstores. The end sheets would arrive at the house in bundles of several thousand to sit in the front hall, mute testimony to the work ahead.

Only those who have tried to sign their way through a pack of paper several feet high can know what an uninviting, even terrifying task this is. After the six hundred and fifty-seventh signature, I always began to wonder if my mind might not start playing tricks on me. At any moment I might misspell my name or sign someone else's. Instead, the signature would only get larger and larger, more and more scrawly. Of one thing I'm sure. No autograph of mine could possibly be worth anything to posterity. There are too many of them!

The typewriter in the new office was in use eight hours a day by my new secretary, Peg Bradley. Many of the requests were more amusing than earth-shaking. But since they were important to those who made them, they could not be ignored. . . . Would I please autograph the enclosed scrap of material. It was to be embroidered for one square of a "famous names quilt" and would then be auctioned off. An organization wanted some personal possession to auction off—costume jewelry, a scarf, a pair of gloves, even an old hat—always for a worthy cause.

Women's groups were always wanting my favorite recipe for a cookbook they were printing. Usually I would send them Mother Janet's recipe for steak and kidney pie, the one that began . . . "First you inquire at the Fleshers for two puir wee sheep's kidneys and a half pound o' steak, cut 'em up, brown the pieces in a wee saucepan with a wee pat o' butter. . . ." I thought that this would lift any cookbook out of the doldrums.

That book I had mentioned in the closing pages of *A Man Called Peter—The Case of the Perfumed Mouse*. . . . Did I know the author and where could it be obtained? The bench Peter John and I were sitting on in the picture on the back of the book jacket—could I send a detailed drawing or pattern for it? My fan-mail friend wanted to copy it for his back yard. Would I select the beauties for a high school annual?

How was our dog Jeff? An unknown fan-mail friend, a dog lover, had fallen in love with our cocker. If I would send a picture of him, she would like to do a pastel of Jeff. The artist was as good as her word. After a few weeks, the picture came. It was beautifully done, artistically framed. Jeff's doggy personality had been faithfully captured. To this day, he is the only member of our family whose portrait hangs in our home.

Of course many requests were more serious. It was surprising to me how many teen-agers had read *A Man Called Peter*. Some of their letters were difficult to answer. I soon discovered that teen-agers have a positive genius for pouring earth-shaking questions into one sentence with the calm expectation that all of life's problems can be solved pronto in an answering sentence. Letters like this one from Greer, South Carolina, could throw me into a tizzy. . . .

Dear Mrs. Marshall:

In our English class we are studying individuals who have attained success. I'm writing to ask you, if you would please tell me, "What makes an individual great?"

Or one like this would have me walking the floor:

Dear Mrs. Marshall,

I am a senior in high school and have decided to write my theme on Peter Marshall. Would you please answer these questions for me:
1. *Where did Dr. Marshall get his ideas for his sermons?*
2. *What did he think of the crime wave going on in the teen-age world?*
3. *Did he have any important likes and dislikes?*

I found it difficult to restrain myself from putting tongue in cheek and answering to (1) from life; and (2) he was against it; and to (3) yes, several.

Still the teen-agers came on. . . .

Phoenix, Arizona

Dear Mrs. Marshall:

I am a 17-year-old Junior in high school. . . . This is a personal question. But did you ever wonder why God called Dr. Marshall home at such an early age? Will you please write and tell me why or why not?

Often friends asked me, "Do you get many problem letters?" My answer was—not as many as Mary Hayworth or Norman Vincent Peale, but always more than I could adequately handle.

Every type of difficulty was represented in these letters—financial problems; marital and divorce questions; parents with the heartbreak of a mentally deficient child; childlessness; questions on courtship; the problems of people who wanted to immigrate to the United States; illness and how to pray about it; and always and always, bereavement.

The last-named was a reflection of the fact that there are over 100,000 new widows added to the population in the United States each year. The total has now reached almost 8 million. Add to this the war casualties, the toll of about 40,000 killed on our highways each year, the deaths caused through cancer and other diseases. The net result is that the agonizing problem of bereavement is all around us, threatening us at every turn.

Isn't it odd that, in a century where medical advances have prolonged longevity, we are more conscious than ever of our mortality? Life seems like a golden gossamer thread, precious, beautiful, but snapped, so easily snapped—finally, irrevocably.

Many who had seen that thread snapped wrote letters in which they stripped all bandages from sorrow's wounds. As I had shared intimate experiences with them, so they wanted to share with me. They paid me the priceless compliment of believing that I would understand. . . .

Hibbing, Minn.

Dear Mrs. Marshall:

I, too, lost my husband and know all the anguish, heartache, and lone-liness that only such a bereavement can bring. I want to tell you how it happened. . . .

There must be many others who feel maybe this waiting and longing wouldn't be so terrible if our faith were so deep that we would never doubt that we'd be reunited in the hereafter. Won't you please write us about your husband's teachings on the life to come?

Yes, I, too, feel Lou's nearness. I feel it when I sit alone, out at our cabin at the lake—a beautiful place he built and loved. But I want to see him, touch him, talk to him. Will I ever?

I would read a letter like that and see the world's anxious, sorrow-ing heart bared before me. For we never see the bared heart in generali-ties, only in particular. The letters always gave the specific—the three-year-old crushed beneath the wheels of a truck; the tiny boy who had died of sleeping sickness; the couple who had wanted a baby for so long, only to have the young husband die two months before the child was born; the widow who had lost her only daughter.

What can one say? How does comfort come? I found it hard to min-ister to the troubled individual whom I had met only in the sentences of a letter. For all those sorrowing people who wrote me, I felt some-thing so unbearably tender that even now I grope for the words to de-scribe it. And I knew that what I felt was but a spark blown off the altar of the love of God.

God loves these people. God cares about the three-year-old dying under the wheels of a truck. He yearns over each of us. He stoops to help. That was why a Man who was yet God died on a cross. These things I know. It is of the love of God for each of us that the grieving most need reassurance.

And yet, and yet—over and over the letters posed questions hard to answer, containing in a few sentences all the tangled skeins of the prob-lem of evil in our world. . . .

Dear Mrs. Marshall:

Last September 27th, we attended our church picnic at a local park. My young sons, David, 13½, and John, 9 years, were playing baseball. I went over and leaned against a eucalyptus tree to watch them play. David saw me and left the game to run over and tell me something. On his way, he passed a microphone that had been set up on the damp ground to announce some games. As he passed, he reached out and touched it. He was instantly electrocuted. There before my eyes, my handsome, tall, blue-eyed son, with his gleaming potential for greatness, was turned to clay. Nothing could be done for him; my David was gone. . . .

I have found no benediction to my grief. My child has been deprived of his life on earth, of his chance at fulfillment. God has placed desolation on me, and I can only respond with desolation. . . .

There is no pat answer to such a letter. Nor to this one. . . .

Buffalo, N.Y.

Dear Mrs. Marshall,

. . . My wife passed away suddenly and wholly unexpectedly last April 25. She loved life and the living of it with the same fierce intensity that she detested dirt, evil, ugliness. . . . She was a brave and gallant soul if there ever was one. . . .

And now for my question . . . I cannot believe in personal immortality much as I yearn to. . . . My faith is too weak to accept it, just as my reason is so strong to rebuff the belief. Do you believe in it?

If I have presumed too much in writing, just ignore this letter. . . .

How could I ignore such a letter? But my problem was how to compress into a few sentences my personal reasons for a belief in immortality. And still the letters came, like this one from Highland, Ill.

Dear Mrs. Marshall,

You and I have a great many things in common. May I write you about it . . . ? Our little girl, Nancy Lee, only four and a half, left us so suddenly, so unexpectedly. . . . We did not know that a slight fever would, in a few hours, develop into the dreaded bulbar polio, so swiftly to silence the gay laughter.

The great pain of this loss quickly bound its heavy chains about my chest, scarcely allowing me to breathe. This lasted months, each morn-

ing awaking to an awful emptiness. . . . Oh, Catherine, she was beautiful
with big brown eyes so full of love and laughter.

If it were not for my deep faith that my little one is waiting for me to
come, I couldn't stand this thing called life. . . . I know you must feel the
same deep hurt with me this Yuletide season. The songs, the snow, the
very air are poignant with memories that keep a deep hurt throbbing. Do
you have any suggestions at all as to how I can stand this day after day . . . ?

As I would read letters like this, often I would have the sinking feeling that some who wrote to me nursed the secret hope that I could send
them by return mail some magic prescription that would solve their
problem. I sympathized. How many times I have wished for that kind
of an answer to my own problems!

Yet in all truth, life is not that simple. Christianity is a day-by-day
walk, not a shot in the arm.

There are solutions—plenty of them. But in my experience, they
have come only when I have been willing to open my total life to receive them.

Always, whether the problem was bereavement or something else,
I felt that my answers were inadequate. I am neither a minister nor a
trained counselor. There were times when I, forgetting that Christ alone
can be the Burden-bearer, tried to shoulder other people's problems and
all but went down under them.

Apparently to some readers the closing pages of *A Man Called Peter*
had given the impression that I was scarcely human, that my brush with
death had been all victory. A Britisher expressed this by saying, "Your
references to God seem a little too glib, if I may express it so, for those
who, like myself, have experienced a great loss. . . ." And an American
woman wrote, "After finishing your book, it somewhat surprised me
and others to whom I have talked about it, that you could so readily find
resignation. I haven't found it that easy. . . ."

It wasn't easy. It never is. I had traveled the same road that everyone travels. The searching, sometimes bitter, always poignant questions
that others ask, I also had asked. Then out of the universality of my
experience, I reasoned, might it not be of some help to other people if I
were some day to retrace my slow steps along the way out of grief—
perhaps in a book?

One summer morning at Waverley, a happy bobwhite had awakened me early, his loud clear notes ringing out over the garden, hanging almost visibly in the still air. Lazily I opened my eyes to see a pink hollyhock nestling against the windowpane. Outside it was a typical foggy Cape Cod morning, but the sun was trying to break through.

A good day to start on the window boxes, I lay there thinking. Peter John and I had arrived at Waverley the afternoon before. Planting the boxes had always been one of my first tasks for the summer.

I put on shorts and a blue denim shirt and went to get the pots of coral geraniums and vines. The planting was messy work because last year's dirt and dried roots had to be dug out and new top soil put in. To reach two of the boxes, I had to use a step-stool. Since the ground was uneven, my balance was precarious. Soon there were dirt smudges on my face, and a brisk sea breeze that had sprung up had my hair blowing in all directions.

About an hour later, I heard a car stop in front of the house. Surely they can't be coming here, I thought. Too early in the season to have visitors.

I was wrong. Out of the corner of my eye, I saw a young man looking at the cottage, opening the blue gate, starting up the curving flagstone walk. Then he was beside me, looking at me curiously.

"Are you—is this 'Waverley'—the Peter Marshall cottage—are you—" He looked at the shorts. "You couldn't be. . . ."

Carefully I climbed down from the step-stool and pushed a wisp of flying hair out of my eyes. "Yes, I'm Catherine Marshall." I held up grubby hands. "Sorry I can't shake hands with you."

"We asked at the flower shop in the village—They told us where to find you—I hate to disturb you like this—during your vacation and all— I'm Stanley Benton; this is my wife Flora—we're from Logan, Ohio— first time we've ever seen New England."

I invited the young couple into the cottage. Mrs. Benton paused in the doorway of the living room. Her eyes were taking in the white organdy curtains, the old-fashioned Christmas lights with ivy in them in the windows, the procession of Scottish Highlanders marching across one wall. "This is the house you wrote about! I remember your writing about the Highland Regiment with their kilts swinging. Look—Jim, there they are! You can't possibly know what it means to us to see this—"

My guests were delightful people. Mostly it was Stan who talked. I wouldn't have missed hearing his story. . . .

"I worked my way through Emory University in Atlanta—with Flora helping me, of course. You may remember that Dr. Marshall was down there in 1944 for a week's preaching mission. Flora and I went to hear him on the last night. We were thrilled!

"Then I went into the ministry—ended up in Ohio. Well, when I heard about Dr. Marshall's death, I couldn't understand why God would take away someone who was doing such wonderful work.

"So when your book came out, I only read half of it. It hurt too much. It went back on the shelf unfinished.

"Later I had a tough problem to solve. One evening, on impulse, I grabbed the book off the shelf and took a beach chair to the back yard. Flora was busy with something else and, as it turned out, I was glad to be alone. I needed to be by myself to let the tears flow unheeded.

"That night I found the answer to 'why. . . .' Why had God let Peter Marshall die? Immediately I knew that it was because Peter's ministry was far wider now than it could ever have been before.

"I knew a lot more too—that the One who wrote the book and guided it into the hands of so many readers was greater than the man who preached the Word.

"I've had a lot of discouraging moments in my ministry. A minister's dreams are often crushed, his church programs stalemated. You know, it's positively uncanny, though, how through the years, every time I've just about thrown in the sponge, this man Marshall has crossed my path again.

"I guess the biggest thing I want to say to you is—well—thank you for reminding me Who still runs the universe."

That summer a constant procession of people came by to see Waverley. Not all of them rang the ship's bell on the front door; some merely stood in the road, whispering and taking pictures.

I kept thinking that all this must be temporary. Surely life would soon return to normal, the mail would slough off, and I could go back to occasional secretarial help. But when nothing of the sort happened during the following fall and winter, I began to see that the situation would not adjust to me. I was going to have to adjust to the situation.

Sometimes one instinctively flees a superfluity of love. There is always the fear of being stifled by it. So the question was . . . could I open my heart wide enough to accept all the overflow of affectionate good will? Could I let it warm rather than constrict me?

I was able to make only a partially satisfactory adjustment. For one thing, I began to resist lectures and personal appearances. At the time the resistance seemed justified. I was a housewife who had written a book. My life had always been a quiet one. During the months of writing *A Man Called Peter*, it had been a secluded life. It was little wonder that I was again finding painful the transition to the public eye.

There was much inner conflict over the requests for speaking engagements. I knew full well that as a Christian I did not belong to myself, but to God, for any way He wanted to use me. Usually that involves people. And in my case, it could mean speaking.

Yet my son was my sole responsibility. He needed me, and I could not, did not, want to leave him to take to the road. Besides, it was the writing I enjoyed most, and that I could do in the mornings while Peter John was at school.

Then, too, there were far more requests than one human being could fill. I never understood why there are so many such groups except that the United States is organization-happy. And each organization has a monthly meeting. And apparently the American eagle would scream, and never stop screaming, if each meeting did not have a speaker. It was difficult for me to fit into this pattern. I was simply not an organization person and had a poorly concealed horror of becoming tagged as a lady lecturer.

Other tags were already securely tied to me. I was a clergyman's widow and had written a book in which God was central. Therefore, quite rightly, the public cast me in a religious mold. There was only one trouble. I soon found that the public's concept of religion is not mine. I see life as all of one piece. To some people, religion is an isolated compartment, so narrow as to be stifling. Perhaps that is why so many flee it.

For example, if I were invited to a motion-picture party, inevitably it would be for such a picture as "The Robe." When friends who were traveling in Europe would send me postcards, they would carefully pick pictures of churches or cathedrals. Often publishers would send me books in proof, asking for a comment. Never once would it be a novel or even a so-called "secular" book; always, the latest religious tome. Television and radio people were always contacting me around Christmas and Easter when they were eager for programs with religious themes.

One incident was typical of many. I had accepted an invitation for an after-dinner talk at a men's banquet in a Southern city. "Make it light and gay," the banquet chairman said. "Not too serious."

That was fine with me. I was looking forward to it, relishing the idea of letting myself go for once.

Three days before the engagement, the chairman telephoned. "Our wives want to hear you too," he explained. "So we've decided to adjourn after dinner to the church auditorium. Your talk will be there."

"I can't win," I complained to my secretary as I hung up. "I accepted an invitation for an airy, informal talk. Now it has to be part of a church service, and they will expect it to be deadly serious."

A letter from an unknown friend about that time said:

Dear Catherine Marshall:
You and I have so much in common. I don't smoke either. I don't drink. I don't swear, nor play cards, nor dance the rumba. I feel so close to you. . . .

Reading this, I couldn't help thinking of Peter Marshall's reaction to such a negative approach to Christianity. To this type of person, he was inclined to reply, "Well, now that's fine. But there's a difference between being good and being goody-goody. You have to be good for something. You don't do this, and you don't do that. What do you do?"

For me, the mold began to confine. Life when Peter was alive had never been so narrow. Why should it be now? During this period, I thought I understood how adolescents feel. Often their rebellion is caused by too much pressure to do this or not to do that.

Of course, this invasion of privacy is experienced by every person who catches the public's eye. It takes several forms, one of which is the feeling on the public's part that the well-known person—whoever he may be—belongs to the public. Thus the President of the United States becomes "Ike," and his wife, "Mamie." Their souls are scarcely their own. Americans feel free to criticize them and openly to discuss every known detail of their private lives—Mamie's bangs, Ike's golf game, even the way he may be spoiling his grandson.

How Princess Grace of Monaco spends her days, the colors in which Princess Caroline's nursery is decorated, the latest news about Queen

Elizabeth and her dashing Philip—all this becomes bridge-table conversation in a thousand homes.

In a small measure, I too experienced this. Though in my case, the public was lavish with its good will, I nevertheless received quantities of well-meaning free advice. . . .

> *Dear Catherine Marshall,*
> *I saw you on* I've Got a Secret. *It was a surprise to me that you are so young. Were you a lot younger than Dr. Marshall? Wasn't it fortunate that the Panel did not guess your secret . . . ?*
> *I must say, though, I was shocked that you would appear on a program advertising cigarettes. I thought better of you than that. . . .*

Sometimes the advice took a practical turn. . . .

> *Dear Mrs. Marshall:*
> *I want to tell you how thrilled we all were out here in the Midwest to see you on* Person to Person. . . .
> *When you showed Dr. Marshall's 500 sermon manuscripts, it looked like they were in a wooden cabinet. If they are, don't you think for protection they would be safer in a fireproof cabinet? I do think you should tend to this right away. . . .*

No detail was too small for the American public to notice. . . .

> *Dear Mrs. Marshall,*
> *I must confess to my disappointment in your interview on television with Ed Murrow, the little mention you made of your late husband, Dr. Peter Marshall. . . . Maybe I was expecting too much, but I did not even see a picture of him in your lovely home. . . .*

Living in a glass house opens one to inevitable criticism. As always I found that a sense of humor helps. It wasn't too difficult to apply the humor to some of the free advice. One day, after a small informal talk in Washington, I received an anonymous letter. It must have been from a man, because it read . . .

> *Dear Mrs. Marshall:*
> *I heard you speak yesterday for the first time. . . . If I may be excused for my bluntness, I think you should put more Sex into your presentations.*

There is a quality about you that I feel you are "putting the wraps on" so to speak.

I believe maybe you are too self-effacing. You are a good-looking young widow, and I think you should act the part.

Sincerely,
An Admirer

Or on another day . . .

Dear Catherine Marshall,

On October 24 this year, I shall be 74 years young. I am still quite vigorous. I feel sure that I have many years ahead of me still. Perhaps some of this is due to the fact that every day I have a workout in a gym down the street from my home.

Day before yesterday, I chinned myself 14 times, yesterday 16. When I have worked up 20 times, may I come up to Washington and see you . . . ?

Along with humor comes a sense of proportion. Many of my correspondents, I realized, did not think of me as an individual but as a symbol. By remembering that, I could keep some sort of equilibrium. And the warm and affirmative responses so outweighed everything else. People in many countries had read *A Man Called Peter*, and through some divine chemistry they had glimpsed the love of God. Inevitably, that great warm love had drawn them—American or Japanese, British or Indian, Swiss or Australian.

Dear Catherine Marshall:

Since you and Dr. Marshall entered our home through your book, I have thought of you often. I can't help wondering how you are getting along! Is it sometimes lonely for you . . . ?

Mr. Jones, Meet the Master and A Man Called Peter have something that reaches way into one's heart. They're unforgettable, so they're always traveling, never resting on my bookshelves.

You made me want more than anything else in the world to know Jesus and to have faith in Him. Your writing has made it the most desirable quality one might ever have. . . .

And I, reading letters like that, could but conclude that if any words of mine had increased by even a little the reservoir of love in the world or pointed others to the Source of that love, then who could mind—even a glass house?

Eleven
Is There Life after Death?

ONE EMPHASIS KEEPS recurring in many of the letters that come to me. A typical expression of it was in a letter from a young widow:

> On June 28, my husband died. I couldn't see why he couldn't have been spared at least long enough to see our baby.... For I am writing this from the hospital. Last Friday morning a little girl was born to us....
>
> Your book gives a person the thought that you think that Peter is still alive. Do you think my Erwin is alive too? He was just a farmer, but he loved God, and he loved the land.... I could be comforted and contented if I could be sure that Erwin still lived....

This groping to believe in life after death is the need of every bereaved person. Some can accept immortality on faith without questioning. Others would like to believe; they hope it is true, but can get no further than hope.

I, too, have had the same need of reaching beyond hope to proof. My search was made in several directions.

The philosophical approach did not greatly interest me. For instance, some contend that immortality is an instinct buried deep in the race; therefore, immortality must be a fact. Others use the argument of analogy pointing to seasonal death and rebirth in nature. Or the juridical

166

argument . . . sometimes good people suffer and the evil prosper; therefore, there must be another life to equalize these wrongs. Then there is the moral and ethical argument . . . the higher and more worthy a man, the more incomplete his life seems. Since he cannot achieve his ideals this side of the grave, he has a right to expect to achieve them on the other side of death.

None of this is proof, at least to me.

I have found more conclusive the evidential testimony piled up through the ages. I do not mean spiritualism, but these experiences that have come—unsought—to thousands of people.

Sometimes a person crossing the threshold between life and death gives those watching a glimpse of what lies beyond. The universal testimony in these instances is that death is nothing to be feared; that there is beauty—often rapturous music, reunion with those who have gone before, recognition, warmth, and love—on the other side.

A man recently widowed wrote me of just such an experience. . . .

In June, 1952, my wife of 19 years was taken by coronary thrombosis. . . . I left the house at 1 P.M. . . . When I returned at 5:30, she was lying on the bathroom floor. There were no good-byes. She was gone.

It was probably between 1 and 2 A.M. before I got to bed and to sleep that night. However, at very early dawn I began to be conscious again of the world around me and of another world. Our bedroom is an enclosed sleeping porch at the rear of the house with windows on three sides.

Margaret had loved the out of doors along with music and birds.

How can I try to describe to you my experience of that dawn? All I can say is that Margaret was there and I was there at a little distance observing it all. As a Navy officer during the war, I found myself thinking of the ceremony when an admiral is piped aboard. It was as if the boundaries between earth and heaven were obliterated and Margaret was being piped aboard. She was entering her heavenly home in a blaze of glory with the birds singing that morning as I have never heard them sing before or since. It was as if ten thousand angels were crying "Joy! Joy! Here comes Margaret! Everybody out! Everybody out! Here comes Margaret!"

Strangely, my dominant emotion was not grief, but a thankfulness that I had had her for 19 years and a fierce and uncontrollable pride in having been her husband. Only one word can describe my mood at that time— exaltation. . . .

Another letter I received records a similar testimony, only in this case, the dying man was pulled back from crossing the threshold:

> *In 1944, came my first heart attack ... in 1949, a second. This time I almost slipped through the velvet curtain that shuts out our sight of the world to come. Now I know that death is not to be feared; the pain ceases, you know what is happening, but it does not matter; you sink into a soft velvet restful blackness and consciousness is gone.*
>
> *I want you to know that your husband did not suffer. One just slips through the curtain, leaving the tired, worn body behind.*
>
> *Since my experience, I am convinced that consciousness is the only reality. By this I mean self-awareness, the persistence of the I-ness of the individual, the mind, the soul, the spirit, the character, the nonmaterial elements that distinguish one person from another. ...*

As a little girl in Canton, Mississippi, I had a brief glimpse of the continuation of this I-ness into the next life. It came through the eyes of a dear elderly friend whom I called "Auntie Chamberlain." She was a wealthy New York aristocrat who had come South to be near a married daughter. She was often lonely, and my parents befriended her. Soon she was spending every Wednesday and every Sunday in our home.

Auntie Chamberlain was tall, and as a girl in finishing school had been taught to walk erect by practicing balancing a book on her head. The head held so proudly wore two braids of hair encircling it, and always around her neck there was a narrow velvet band, sometimes clasped with a diamond brooch, sometimes an amethyst one.

She gave me fluffy dresses, hand-embroidered by nuns in a convent. At other times, her gifts would be beautiful editions of carefully selected books, and she taught me to love and care for them. ... "A book is a friend and has its own personality. Treat it with consideration. Always wash your hands before handling it." She taught me precision in the use of words. ... "Never say 'lost' when you really mean 'misplaced.' Any article that is recovered was only 'misplaced.'"

But Auntie Chamberlain's greatest impact on me came at the end of her life. She had suffered a stroke and was bedridden in her apartment up Peace Street. Often my mother would ask me to take her some soup or custard or delicacy. Holding the offering carefully, I would walk along the uneven brick sidewalks, under the arching trees, to Auntie Chamberlain's.

On one of these occasions, a few days before her death, I saw her suddenly sit up in bed, speak the name of her long-dead husband, and throw out her arms in glad reunion. Caught up in the drama taking place before me, I knew I was witnessing something that was no hallucination. I've never been able to forget the reality of that scene.

There is another type of experience, equally unsought, that has come to people in every century. This constitutes a body of evidence that we cannot laugh off or disregard. . . .

In a hospital in Atlanta, Georgia, a young wife, the mother of two small children, lay desperately ill. Her doctors, feeling that the end was near, had summoned her relatives. Hers was a loving and closely knit family. Her father had died several years before. But all the rest of the family had come—her husband, her mother and her husband's parents, brothers and sisters, and several aunts.

Suddenly the young woman, only thirty-five, in great pain, became hysterical. "I don't want to die," she screamed. "I don't want to leave my children. Why can't somebody help me? I don't want to die."

Her screams tore the emotions of those who loved her. They tried to comfort her, but nothing they could say helped. The hysterical sobbing only grew worse. Nurses on the floor heard and summoned the resident physician. He rushed to help in the only way he could—he gave her a hypo to plunge her into unconsciousness.

She was out for seven hours. When the drug wore off, her devoted family was still huddled near, loving her, praying, hoping they could find some way to help.

But the sick woman woke with a smile on her face. "I'm sorry I acted so badly," she said. "Everything's all right now. I've seen Dad. He came and told me that there's nothing to be afraid of. He promised that he'd stay with me every minute and hold my hand. Don't worry about me. I'm all right now."

There were no more hysterics. That night the girl slipped over into the next life. There was a smile on her face and one hand was outstretched.

If such experiences are valid, why do only a few people have them? No one knows. Sometimes they must be granted—as in the case of the young mother—because help is desperately needed. In other cases, it may be that some have the gift of a type of spiritual sight, even as others have an ear for music or a talent for mathematics. I have known several people with this gift. One of their characteristics is that they are not necessarily spiritual people as church people usually mean that term. That is, they are anything but otherworldly. The ones I know have in common a robust sense of humor, a twinkle in their eyes, and give the impression that their feet are planted firmly on earth.

One such friend, Olga Worrall, must have been born with the ability to see into the world of the spirit because she first noticed it at the age of three. As a young girl she decided to give the gift to God for His use. She has never taken a cent of money from anyone for it. She uses it only to give other people the confidence that at death there is no interruption to life. At times she has been able to help even clergymen to anchor their hope of immortality in the utter confidence of sure belief.

One of these is a minister whom I know and who told me of this incident himself. . . .

Several years ago in Baltimore, Lynn Youngman, a student at Goucher College, became ill with lobar polio. The minister some years before had regained his own health through prayer. Lynn was a member of his church and her case lay heavily on his heart. He believed that she could be cured, and night and day stormed heaven in her behalf. He also asked Olga and her husband Ambrose to pray. They did, though they had neither seen nor met the girl. But one morning while in prayer, they came to know that Lynn would not recover.

The next day the girl died. The minister felt that he had failed her and sank into a state of black spiritual discouragement. His depression lasted for days.

Sometime after that he brought another person in need to see Ambrose. While the two of them were in an upstairs room, the minister, very tired, stretched out on the davenport in the living room. Olga was sitting quietly in a chair across the room. For a moment there was silence. Then Olga said, "There is a tall girl, blue-eyed, blond, smiling, standing beside you. She says to tell you that she is Lynn, and that you must stop grieving. You did not fail her. You were unable to heal her body, but you healed her spirit. Strange"—here Olga paused—"now she is bending over, kissing you on the forehead. She says, 'Tell him I'm returning his kiss.'"

My friend, the minister, jumped to his feet. "How could you have known that? No living person could know it. A few days before Lynn died, she had a sinking spell. Just the two of us were in the hospital room. As she lay there with only her head sticking out of the iron lung, I bent over and kissed her forehead." For the first time in days, there was joy on the minister's face.

Still another Washington friend of mine, Jane, also possesses this gift and has frequently had similar experiences when she was least expecting them. Jane was named for an aunt who was a beautiful blonde. When the aunt was in her thirties, she developed diabetes.

In that late summer long ago, Aunt Jane came to visit in the family home. It soon became apparent that she was a very sick woman. This seemed the more tragic because Aunt Jane was to have been married in the fall.

For convenience, the sick woman's bed was moved to a first-floor parlor. This was the era of heavy damask portieres and draperies, of dresses with taffeta petticoats.

One day the family physician decided to give an injection of glucose because the invalid was rapidly sinking into a coma. As he worked over the patient in the parlor-bedroom, he asked young Jane to hold a light for him. An ether anesthetic was being used, and its odor permeated the room's hangings. It was weeks before the smell of ether disappeared.

Later the aunt died. Two weeks after her funeral, the family wanted to take some flowers to her grave. But the teen-age Jane and Stella, a friend, decided to stay at home. The two girls were left alone, sitting in rocking chairs on the front porch.

Suddenly both girls heard the rustle of taffeta petticoats in the front hall. Jane, nearest the door, ran to the screen door. There she saw her Aunt Jane starting up the stairs, wearing a black dress, looking chipper, very flesh and blood, not at all ghostlike.

Involuntarily the girl called out, "Aunt Jane! It's you! What do you want?"

There was no answer. The woman continued on up the stairs, her petticoats rustling with every step. Then as she got within three steps of the landing, she turned her head slightly, so that Jane saw her face clearly. Then she disappeared.

In telling me of this incident, my friend commented, "At the time, I couldn't see any reason for the experience. Then I remembered that my aunt had willed me a lovely garnet ring, and the ring was missing. At first, I thought perhaps she had come back to show us the ring's hiding place. But we never recovered it.

"Then for ten years after that, at intervals, a strong odor of ether would reappear in the parlor—but only for me—not for other members of the family.

"What has bothered me most about this and a whole procession of like experiences is that I can't see any reason for them in the Christian scheme of things. I don't seek them. In fact, I'm impatient with them. Yet they keep coming to me. What good purpose do they serve?"

Yet it would not occur to us to ask, "What good purpose does physical sight serve?" We see the faces, the smiles, the gestures of our friends; the wagging tail of a dog; the tapestry of leaves against a darkening sky. We see—and it is enough.

Just so, there are those who seem to be able to see just as naturally into the world of the spirit that lies all about us. The early church may well have had members with this gift. Is it possible that the Apostle Paul was speaking of it when he referred to the gift of "discerning of spirits" (1 Corinthians 12:10)?

In spite of that, the church has frowned on any probing of life after death. Her traditional position has been that Christ told us what He wanted us to know about the life to come and that, because that world of spirit is real, excursions into it can be dangerous if they are not centered in Christ.

A friend of mine who is a physician with a large practice in Richmond, Virginia, had an experience that was exactly that—Christ-centered. It is one of the most astonishing stories I have ever heard. Had I gotten the story secondhand, I might have doubted its validity. But knowing my physician-friend as well as I do, I cannot.

"As a doctor," he said, in telling me the story, "I have learned that there is more to human beings than their bodies. But I'd know it anyway because of an extraordinary experience I had when I was nineteen."

This experience revolutionized the basis of the young man's life. Moreover, there are parts of the incident that he feels he cannot yet reveal to anyone.

Even as a little boy, George had wanted to be a doctor. By nineteen he had completed his pre-med work.

Then came World War II. November, 1943, found him a private in the Army, stationed at Camp Barkeley near Abilene, Texas.

But the Army needed doctors. So George, still a private, was given the glad news that he was being transferred to the Army's Specialized Training Program to complete his medical training. What was even better fortune, on December 20, he was to be sent back to his home town—Richmond—to the Medical College of Virginia.

Nine days before he was due to leave Camp Barkeley, the boy became ill with pneumonia. After a week in the Army Hospital, he was much better. In fact on the night of December 19, he and a friend left the recuperation ward to go to a picture show. They got back to the ward about nine o'clock.

Five hours later, at 2 A.M., George had a relapse. When the ward boy took his temperature, it was 106.5. Hastily the boy summoned a nurse and the O. D.

They saw that the patient was too ill to walk, but insisted that they should try to X-ray his chest. "Do you think you could stand just long enough for us to get one film?"

His face flushed with fever, his eyes a little glazed, George nodded that he thought he could. The last thing he remembered was the humming of the X-ray machine. Then he crumpled into an unconscious heap on the floor.

Later he was told what happened from the viewpoint of the hospital staff. . . . He was carried to a bed in a new ward section—not back to the recuperation ward.

He remained desperately ill and unconscious for two days. The hospital routine specified that the ward boys were to make four rounds each night for checks. At three o'clock on the morning of December 22, when the ward boy got to George's bed, he was shocked at his appearance. He looked—dead. A closer scrutiny revealed that there seemed to be no pulse, no respiration.

The boy ran for the captain, the O. D. in charge. After the captain had examined the patient, he straightened up—sighed—"Blood pressure at zero, no pulse, no respiration, body temperature falling rapidly. I'm sorry—"

The ward boy standing on the other side of the bed was shocked. "But it can't have happened that suddenly. He was so young—"

The doctor left. A few minutes later, the ward boy sought him out again. "I'm sorry to bother you, sir, but that private—I can't get him off my mind— Shouldn't we make one try to do something, sir? Maybe adrenalin—or something?"

The O. D. looked at the youngster with compassion in his eyes. He saw that the ward boy was shaken. "All right, I'll go and examine him once more. Prepare a large hypo with adrenalin and bring it along in case I decide to use it."

Once again George was examined. Once again the O. D. sighed. "It's no use. He's gone."

"Please, sir. Let's use the hypo anyway."

Without saying a word, the O. D. plunged the needle directly into the heart muscle. . . .

While all this was going on, George was having quite a different set of experiences. As the X ray was being taken, he had been preoccupied with just one thing . . . the next day he was to leave for Richmond and medical school. That would be the fulfillment of a lifetime dream. What if he couldn't go? What if—because of the delay—someone else would get his place in the Specialized Training Program?

He remembers sitting on the edge of his hospital bed thinking, "I've got to get out of here—but fast."

As he got to his feet, he glanced back at the bed. What he saw was shocking. Someone who looked like himself was still lying there. He had seen a few dead people in his life, and this one looked—dead. It was himself all right. He recognized his familiar class ring on the left hand of the one on the bed.

He started toward the door. A ward boy was coming in. George thought that they were going to collide. He tried to step aside, only to find that the ward boy did not see him. He walked right through him.

George didn't understand it. He went out into the corridor and wandered around, trying to figure things out.

Nobody who passed him seemed to see him. He felt totally unable to communicate with anyone alive. This separation from his fellow human beings caused him an acute anguish of loneliness.

Then he looked down at his hands. If he was to be a doctor, he would need his hands. But he couldn't touch things. Material objects—substance—did not seem solid any more. He tested this out by leaning against the guy wire of a telephone pole. His hand went right through the wire.

That decided it. No man in this fix could become a doctor. He decided to go back, find his body, and somehow make connection with it again.

He retraced his steps along the hospital corridor. But his body had been moved. The soldier went in and out of one hospital corridor after another. Finally he found it in an isolation ward. His class ring was still on the left hand. But what a ridiculous situation! How did one get back in one's own body?

"Then," George said in relating the incident to me, "suddenly I was no longer alone. Someone stood there. I knew that it was Christ, though my chief impression was of light—dazzling, blinding light.

"He asked, 'What have you done with your life?'

"'Well—I—got to be an Eagle Scout.'

"'This glorified you.' There was a long pause.

"'I tried to help some boys and girls in high school.'

"He said, 'What have you done to tell them about me?'

"I changed the subject. 'I'm too young to die.'

"Very kindly the One immersed in light said, 'Nobody is too young to die.'

"A lot more passed between us," George says. "I've never felt free to tell anyone the rest of it. I saw how selfish my life had been, and that Christ held me personally responsible for how I had wasted my time on earth. I made up my mind right then that, if by some miracle, He would let me live on earth awhile longer, I would do better in the future.

"The miracle happened. Suddenly I found myself back in the familiar housing of flesh. With my right hand I touched the class ring and turned it round and round—and marveled. A little later I discovered that four days had passed. It was the morning of the twenty-fourth of December."

George was in the hospital until the third of January. His weight had gone down from 178 to 135 pounds. During his last week there, the head nurse, knowing how curious he was about what had happened to him, let him see his chart. Everything was recorded—the 106.5 temperature, the collapse, the two examinations, the injection of adrenalin into the heart muscle.

"It's true," the nurse said, "all true. There was no sign of life at all. I saw you examined."

"I don't know what others will think of all this," the prominent physician says today. "Let them explain it as they please, put their own connotation on it. I only know that it remains the most vivid experience of my life. From that day on, I have not been the same person."

Peter Marshall's father had died when his son was four, and ever afterward Peter eagerly sought information about him. In addition, anything about that other life "behind the curtain," as he called it, fascinated him.

When Peter was eighteen, before he emigrated to America, he and two friends went one night to visit a man who had what the Scots call "second sight." That evening the man claimed that he could receive messages through table-rapping. There were various messages, including one said to be from a man who had lived in France 200 years before. He told his name (Peter always remembered it; I do not), some facts about his life, where he was buried.

Then the table rapped out the name "Peter Marshall." Some facts followed which jibed with what Peter knew of his father's early life . . . the date of his marriage to Peter's mother in Switzerland; the full names and certain facts about long-dead relatives. Then came this message for Peter: "You must never again toy with spiritualism. For you, it is very dangerous." That was all.

Peter took that as authoritative and obeyed it to the letter—not because he was certain that the message really had come from his father, but because an instinct told him that the warning was authentic. Though to the end of his life he found the subject compelling, thereafter he never went outside the framework of the Christian church to investigate it.

Within that framework, Peter arrived at an absolute assurance of immortality. Where others might hope it was true, he knew it was true. Often, by the simple, matter-of-fact way in which he spoke of the next life, he was able to transmit his assurance to other people.

One day at the Willard Hotel in Washington, during a luncheon talk to a national convention of music teachers, Dr. Marshall tossed this in. . . . "I love music and have always wanted to study it. But I've never had the opportunity, the money, nor the time. In my next existence, I look forward to the study of music as one of the satisfactions I'm going to have."

One woman present that day later wrote to tell me what Peter's comment had meant to her:

There was such confidence in his assurance, that for me it bridged the gap between this life and the next. Never before had I felt that reality....

On the tape that recorded Dr. Marshall's last pastoral prayer and last Sunday morning sermon two days before his death, were these words:

Father, we join our prayers in asking Thy help for those, who bereaved, still feel lonely. They have not even yet found the joy of Thy Resurrection and the sense of the presence of those they love who are with Thee.

Grant that those who have loved and lost may feel their loved ones near; may somehow be persuaded that they still live, that they are happy, that they still love us as we love them.

May such assurances come to all the hearts that need them today....

Then, after Peter's death, I found among his papers a copy of a letter he had written to the young widow of a physician in Atlanta. It contained these paragraphs:

Doubtless many times before the doctor had left you and the children to answer a call, and he may have been detained longer than you expected. You, as a doctor's wife, had known what it was to be left alone at all hours of the day and night.

This time the doctor went in answer to a call—the last call which we must all obey, but this time he is not coming back—at least not in the way he used to do. That he will come back is a deep conviction of my own faith.

I believe that those who have died are with us still in different form and communicate with us in different ways. It takes time and also the grace of God and a simple Christian faith to feel the presence of our beloved departed, but that in itself is a comfort and consolation that will fill up the vacuum left in your life....

It was one sentence in this letter plus one clause in the Apostles' Creed that sent me on the second part of my search. The sentence was

... "I believe that those who have died are with us still in a different form and communicate with us in different ways. ..." I wondered ... what ways? How? And the clause in the Apostles' Creed was ... "I believe in ... the communion of saints. ..."

The minister of a church where I sometimes worshiped always ended his pastoral prayer by thanking God for the communion of saints. One Sunday I lingered after the benediction to ask him just what he meant by the communion of saints.

Immediately he lapsed into traditional theological jargon. ... "We are told that we are surrounded by a great cloud of witnesses. Of course, you know that in New Testament parlance, any member of Christ's Body, the church, is called a 'saint,'—not just 'good' people in an earthly sense. Therefore, the communion of the saints refers to the interaction, the fellowship, between the Church Militant—the saints here on earth—and the Church Triumphant—the saints already in the next life."

That did not satisfy me. ... "Yes, but what kind of interaction? What kind of fellowship? And how can someone like me have fellowship like that?"

At that point, the minister's answers became shadowy, vague. At last he confessed that I was asking questions beyond him. "Perhaps," he admitted, "because death has not brushed me personally." I admired him for his honesty.

Then I started searching on my own. I knew that the Apostles' Creed in its present form dates back to the fourth century. What experiences of the early church had crystallized into that clause about the communion of saints? Did Christians then know something about personal contact across the dividing line of death that we do not know today?

The first fact I uncovered was that, from the establishment of the church after Pentecost to the Protestant Reformation in the sixteenth century, prayer for and with the dead had been universally practiced by Christendom. This followed naturally from two bedrock beliefs of the Apostolic Church: (1) that of immortality, that Christ—through His resurrection, to which the earliest Christians claimed to be eye witnesses—had forever conquered death; and (2) that the unity of the church—the Body of Christ—was such that death could not dismember it.

The prayers of the first Christians for the dead were not mere petitions that the departed be delivered from some state of eternal punishment. To them, prayer was as natural as breathing. It was the life of the spirit; it was their life line with the Risen Lord. He had taught them that they were "members one of another" of an organic fellowship; that His riches in glory were their individual and corporate heritage; that they should confidently and joyously present their needs to Him.

Therefore, they prayed for all sorts of things: for the forgiveness of sins and the breaking of sinful habit patterns; for strength in temptation; for the healing of sickness and disease; for specific directions from God; for their enemies; for those still outside the Christian fellowship, that they might find the joy of the faith.

They lived in days of upheaval with death all around them. Often members of their families or friends, who had been an integral part of their prayer fellowship, would be there one day, and the next day would be thrown to lions in the arena or bound to stakes on one of the roads outside Rome to become blazing human torches. In the midst of such terror, they were able to keep their sanity only because they were so sure that the pain of dying was brief, that death was only an incident in continuing life. To them it was unthinkable that the incident of death should sever their communion with each other and with the living Christ.

The epitaphs of the martyrs under the Emperors Nero, Domitian, Trajan, Hadrian, Antoninus Pius, and Marcus Aurelius in the catacombs of Rome dramatize the hazardous life of the first-century Christians....

IN CHRIST, IN THE TIME OF THE EMPEROR ADRIAN MARIUS, A YOUNG MILITARY OFFICER, WHO LIVED LONG ENOUGH AS HE SHED HIS BLOOD FOR CHRIST, AND DIED IN PEACE. HIS FRIENDS SET THIS UP. . . .

Another reads . . .

IN CHRIST ALEXANDER IS NOT DEAD, BUT LIVES ABOVE THE STARS, AND HIS BODY RESTS IN THIS TOMB. HE ENDED HIS LIFE UNDER THE EMPEROR ANTONINE. . . . FOR WHILE ON HIS KNEES, AND ABOUT TO SACRIFICE UNTO THE TRUE GOD, HE WAS LED AWAY TO HIS EXECUTION.

Some like Alexander may have been snatched into martyrdom so suddenly that there was not time to finish the "sacrifice unto the true God," no time for any last confession or any tender words of parting to family and friends. What then?

Did someone else, perhaps the one who cared enough to make the inscription, then undertake a last confession for Alexander? Though it seems reasonable to suppose so because of the closeness of the fellowship, still the New Testament is sketchy on this practice. We have only one clue, given us by Paul. He was writing about immortality. . . .

> If Christ did not rise, your faith is futile, you are still in your sins. More than that: those who have slept the sleep of death in Christ have perished after all. . . . But it is not so! Christ did rise from the dead . . . Otherwise, if there is no such thing as a resurrection, what is the meaning of people getting baptized on behalf of their dead? If dead men do not rise at all, why do people get baptized on their behalf?
>
> (MOFFATT; 1 CORINTHIANS 15)

Here, in a chapter whose whole thesis is immortality, Paul mentions a common practice of the Apostolic Church—that of being baptized on behalf of the dead.

Apparently events were moving so swiftly that sometimes one like Marius, the young military officer, may have taken all but the last step into the faith—that of baptism—only to be cruelly wrested from his Christian friends. In such a case, a friend would be baptized on behalf of the martyred person. Paul does not argue about this; he takes it for granted.

Other evidence of a strong belief in the fellowship of prayer is given us in the earliest liturgies surviving, those from the first part of the third century. From the Liturgy of St. James comes . . .

> We implore of Thee, O Almighty Lord, to unite us without delay to the company of the first-born, who are written in heaven.
>
> We remember them so that they also may remember us before Thee, and may communicate with us in this spiritual sacrifice for the preservation of those who live, for the consolation of all who are in trouble, and for the repose of the faithful departed, our fathers, brethren, and rulers, by the grace and through the mercies of Thy only Son. . . .

And from the Liturgy of St. Ignatius . . .

> Because of Thy great goodness, O Lord, receive peacefully and calmly the spirits and souls of Thy servants and worshippers who out of this present life have departed to Thee. . . .

Because of Thy great love to mankind, grant them that life that knows not old age; give them the good things that pass not away, and the joys which are endless. May they obtain mercy through Thy clemency, and rest through Thy mercy. Hide them under the shadow of Thy wings. . . .

The writings of the earliest church fathers who came after the apostles—such as Tertullian and Cyprian—also bear unanimous testimony that the fellowship of prayer with those in the next life was taken for granted. Then in Augustine's *Confessions* we have his prayer for his mother Monica, written after her death.

In the Anglo-Saxon church the communion of the saints seems to have taken three forms—prayer; a special, tenderly beautiful Eucharist for the dead; and the giving of alms on behalf of the dead, much as we today give a memorial gift to a favorite charity.

According to descriptions that have come down to us of social gatherings, when the loving cup—originally a symbol of good will and Christian charity—went round, a prayer for the dead was always included in the ceremony. Some of these prayers are engraved around the rims of the loving cups and can be seen today in museums in the British Isles. The thought was that the living should remember the dead in the midst of happy times and on special anniversaries.

Then through the Middle Ages came the corruption of what had been pure and loving practices, a corruption that finally brought about the Protestant Reformation. Were the abuses widespread? Or did a flagrant spark here and there kindle a great fire? The distance of the years makes it difficult to tell.

One Dominican monk who helped to kindle the flame of righteous indignation in Martin Luther's heart was John Tetzel, the son of a goldsmith in Leipzig. He had been put in charge of indulgences by Albert, Archbishop of Metz. For a fee, Tetzel claimed to be able to forgive any sin—for the living or the dead.

In England the reign of Henry VIII was a hideous procession of corrupt practices. The Reformation was almost inevitable.

At first, there were those within the church who tried to sift out the bad, keep the good. For example, in 1536, the Ten Articles appeared. The last of the Ten dealt with the abuses that had crept into the Apostolic doctrine of the communion of the saints . . .

... for as much as due order of charity requireth ... and all these ancient documents clearly show that it is a very good and charitable deed to pray for the souls departed, for as much also as such usage as has continued in the church ... even from the beginning, we will ... that no man ought to be grieved with the continuance of the same. ...

Wherefore it is much necessary that such abuses be clearly put away, which under the name of purgatory has been advanced, as to make men believe that through the bishop of Rome's pardon, souls might be clearly delivered out of purgatory and all the pains of death ... and other like abuses.

Conciliatory men tried to retain the practice of praying "for the souls departed," but their voices were drowned in the rising emotional tide of the Reformation. At the crest of the tide, frenzied mobs wrecked cathedrals and abbeys, destroying priceless, medieval stained-glass windows and irreplaceable art treasures. In Scotland, I have stood in the shells of some of those wrecked abbeys, the empty bones of the windows, like patterns of fragile old lace, so exquisite that only patient, dedicated hands could have chiseled their cobweblike traceries.

It is not too surprising that the wrecking mood resulted in some strange decisions. From the Protestant point of view the reformers were justified in their zeal for purifying the church. But they were emotion-blinded, and much good was thrown out with the bad. Men had begun to worship art treasures instead of the living Christ, so many churches were stripped bare. Some of the ceremonies, including the masses and music, had become an end in themselves. So in many Reformed churches, no musical instruments were permitted, only tuning forks; nothing but psalms could be sung.

And what of the communion of the saints? It had been corrupted by indulgences. So the Reformed church taught that there was no need for any fellowship of prayer with and for the dead. The inference was that to pray for the dead was a sin.

Yet at least two vestiges of the communion of the saints escaped the wrecking. In the *Book of Common Prayer* are still remnants of this universal practice of the early church. In the service of holy communion are these words:

And we also bless thy Holy Name for all thy servants departed this life in thy faith and fear; beseeching thee to grant them continual growth in thy love and service, and to give us grace so to follow their good examples, that with them we may be partakers of thy heavenly kingdom. . . .

And in the service for the burial of the dead are a number of such prayers, among them:

O God, whose mercies cannot be numbered; accept our prayer on behalf of the soul of thy servant departed, and grant him an entrance into the land of light and joy in the fellowship of thy saints, through Jesus Christ our Lord. AMEN.

Then there is that one clause in the Creed—"I believe in . . . the communion of saints"—that somehow survived the Reformation. It comes down to us like a few bars of a half-remembered melody.

When I first became aware of it, I could not escape the feeling that it should mean something special. In my own need for comfort and assurance, I kept groping for something that seemed to be missing in the church's teaching in our day.

We stand at an open grave. It seems that our memories, hopes, and dreams—a part of us—are being buried there. In our anguish, the church says to us, "There is no death. Christ has forever conquered it. Believe that your husband (or wife or brother or child) is not in that grave. You will get all the comfort you need from accepting that."

Then the sorrowing leave the cemetery and go back to an empty house. Desperately the mind tries to fathom those soaring words, "There is no death." Then where is the one whose body was left in the grave? And how—in the daily round of life—do the rest of us live out our belief in immortality?

Even children wonder about it. A certain little boy always named each member of his family in his bedtime prayers and asked God to bless and to take care of each one.

The child's father had long been ill. On the night he died, an aunt was hearing the boy's prayers. The child started to include his father as usual. But the aunt interrupted, "You mustn't pray for your father any more. He is with God now and doesn't need our prayers."

She meant well. But many years later, the man, recalling the incident, said, "The effect of her words was like a curtain coming down, or a heavy door being shut between me and my father. He was behind that door, forever lost to me. Yet the minister who had called at our home had taken me on his knee and told me that my father was still alive and that he still loved me. And my childish mind reasoned that I certainly loved him as I always had. So why couldn't I ask God to bless him?"

Why indeed? Is that heresy? I don't think so.

For a time after death invaded my life, this feeling of something missing in the church's credo about immortality went no further than an intellectual conviction. Then came a personal crisis, a big one, one I was not equipped to handle. It was a problem involving my husband and his work, too complex and painful to write about even now.

One day in a prayer tinged with desperation, my petition took a strange turn, surprising even to me. . . . "O God, You've asked me to accept by faith the fact that Peter is still alive. I've tried, but it isn't real to me. But if he is, then he will be as concerned as I about this problem.

"I don't know how this works—but if it's possible, then I ask that Peter join me in this prayer asking for Your specific help. And I ask that he and I together claim that wonderful promise (ROMANS 8: 28) that You will take this messy situation and bring real good out of it—not just for us, but for Your Kingdom."

From one point of view, such an untraditional prayer made me feel like a fool. Yet if ever there was a desperate effort to act out a belief in immortality, that was it.

Within two months the crisis passed. One door closed; another opened. The good appeared. It was significant beyond imagining. The crisis led directly to the writing of *A Man Called Peter.*

Had this fellowship of the spirit across the barrier between life and death been real? I was not sure. I only knew that never before had I experienced such a far-reaching answer to prayer.

It made me wonder even more about that clause of the Creed whose meaning had been all but lost. On earth, human fellowship always involves the inner person, the spirit. Then what about after death? Either there is simply oblivion, or else the spirit that is the real person lives on in conscious awareness. If the latter, then the only possible communion across the barrier is through spirit. And for the Christian, the most potent vehicle of spirit—as well as the safest—is prayer.

About that time, an old friend told me of two of his experiences. This man had been a teacher of English in a small college. "In observing my students through the years," he told me, "I always saw some with more sensitivity, more creativity, than others. One might expect that. But when I probed into the lives of the most creative ones to find out what made them tick, I discovered that almost always someone near to them had died.

"I can't prove this. But it's as if death had opened doors to life. As if those who had gone on into the next life were able to bestow added capacities, added awareness, added creativity."

"That's too big a thought for me," I told him frankly. "I'm skeptical. But what was the second experience?"

"That came after the death of my mother. Always I had wanted to write. Up to that time, I had tried to be content with teaching my students to write. Then after mother's death, suddenly things began happening in my life. The prayers that were my deepest desires were answered, as if my mother was somehow able to open the way for me."

"And the result?"

He paused and smiled. "In thirty years I've had fifteen books published."

Since then I have learned of several others who have done some experimenting of their own with the communion of the saints. Most of them do not talk about it readily; if they did, they wouldn't dream of calling it by any such high-flown theological term.

One of these—a well-known minister—lost his father not long ago. The father also had been a minister, the founder of twelve churches, a man with a vital mind and an agile sense of humor. Always father and son had relished pitting mind against mind, batting ideas back and forth.

"Since my father's death," the minister told me, "there have been times when I've been aware of this same process. That is, I toss an idea out. Presently a counter idea is tossed back with the stamp of my father's personality on it, with his characteristic twist of humor. This isn't anything I've consciously sought. Yet it's happened a good many times."

Another person, Helen Chappell White, the wife of a retired university president, began searching out of her deep need when her elder son, a bomber navigator, was shot down over the Baltic Sea in 1944. It was a young chaplain who supplied the first clue. The sorrowing mother had admitted to him that neither God nor prayer was real to her any more.

"Then talk to your boy," the chaplain advised her. "Ask him to help you find and know God. He's closer to God now than you and I are—he'll lead you to Him."*

The mother felt that nothing could be lost by trying. She began by setting aside a few minutes in her bedroom each morning, relaxing her body, quieting her mind, silently affirming her faith on the promise that her son was alive.

She has had no startling experiences. "I don't think that it is for 'signs and wonders' that this companionship across the line is permitted or should be cultivated," she wrote to me. But she has found more precious things—healing for her grief; a feeling of daily companionship with her boy; and like the minister, at times a tossing of ideas back and forth amounting almost to conversation. "There's a solid, steadily growing core of utter reality in this spiritual companionship," she says. "Often just a kind of happy sharing. . . . I should not care to live at all without it any more; the past would hurt, and the future terrify me."

One of my correspondents, a widower from Kansas City, the one who had insisted upon being so honest, had asked:

I cannot believe in personal immortality. . . . You seem to believe it. . . . Can you offer the rest of us any proof?

And my answer had been . . . no, not final proof as the scientist means proof, not yet in our day. When I sought that proof, I found that the best reasoning of the finest minds, plus all the piling up of evidential testimony, can take us only part of the way.

The work of Dr. J. B. Rhine of Duke University has taken at least the first tentative steps toward proving extrasensory perception, telepathy, and clairvoyance, and thus that there is something more to life than the material.

But until science can finally prove life after death beyond evidential experiences, we are backed up against faith. For anything relating to the spirit, the irreversible order is faith first, then knowledge. That is because faith has a way of slicing through prejudicial and intellectual barriers and opening the eyes of the spirit.

*White, Helen Chappell, *With Wings As Eagles*, p. 198, Rinehart & Company, Inc., New York, 1953.

I am a child of the scientific age and do not find this order easy to accept. Yet the order is a fact.

Christ has told us . . .

> Whosoever liveth and believeth in me, shall never die.
> Believest thou this? (JOHN 11:26)

Not only did He tell us, but to prove immortality He rose from the dead, and over a period of forty days appeared and reappeared to more than five hundred witnesses.

All that is without the bounds of my experience. Yet if I disbelieve what Christ said about immortality, then I have no right to credit anything else He said or did. And I have experienced too much to believe that He was a fraud.

Moreover, though I do not understand the resurrection *with my mind,* the proof to me lies in what believing it did for those first Christians. Men do not have their characters reversed, bisect history, make an impact on generations to come, because of something they have imagined.

So there came the moment in my search when I had to get down on my knees to get through the low door of faith; I had to accept immortality on faith because Christ has assured us that it is true. I knew that if any proof were to come to me, it would have to follow, not precede, that acceptance.

I am not a mystic nor do I have any psychic gifts. I have no experiences to report that could not have happened to anyone. That night on Cape Cod, during the first summer after Peter's death, I had been told that if I would believe in Peter's presence when I needed him, the feeling and the proof would come later. Exactly that has happened. A strengthened faith has replaced the feeling of irremediable loss through death. My crisis prayers have been answered in an extraordinary way. There has been a steady stream of help, directions from without.

There has come the restoration of perspective on life; the knowledge that our world is connected with joy and hope to another; that we who refuse to explore its spiritual and physical boundaries with zest and a sense of adventure, who will not lift our eyes to its far horizons, cheat only ourselves.

Twelve
Adventure in Hollywood

It WAS AUGUST in California—one of those days when low clouds were playing hide and seek with the sun. Three people in the Buick on highway 101 were traveling from Oceanside to Los Angeles—two teen-age boys and a Negro woman, the family cook.

Lamar, the older boy, was at the wheel. His fourteen-year-old brother, John, was in the front seat beside him, and Hattie, the cook, was in the back.

Suddenly, in the midst of lively conversation, a fruit-truck trailer was hurtling toward them. There was the screaming, grinding crash of metal on metal. Then men shouting and running, the sound of sirens. . . .

The *Los Angeles Evening Herald and Express* reported the next day:

FILM PRODUCER'S SON FIGHTS FOR LIFE AS CRASH
KILLS BROTHER

One son of film producer Lamar Trotti fought for his life today while his brother and the family maid were dead of injuries received in a head-on auto-truck collision yesterday at San Clemente. Lamar Trotti, Jr., 18, and the Negro maid Hattie Johnson, 50, were killed instantly. John Trotti, 14, suffering a spine fracture and other injuries was taken to St. Joseph's Hospital in Santa Ana.

The younger boy was operated on and he was given transfusions early today. . . .

The boys' parents took it hard. Lamar Trotti's friends at Twentieth Century-Fox studios, who knew that he had suffered a heart attack two years before, watched him battle his grief, struggle to piece his life together.

A clergyman friend, Dr. Albert Harris, from Macon, Georgia, sent him a book that he thought might help.

Mr. Trotti wrote his friend to thank him:

Dear Dr. Harris:

I am . . . taking a six months' leave of absence in the hope that in that time I will be able to adjust myself to all the things that happened to me when Lamar died.

This is a prelude to saying that as soon as I get to the beach, where we are spending the summer, I will very carefully read A Man Called Peter. . . . *Frankly, that may be just what I need to do. . . .*

Lamar Trotti evaluated any book in terms of potential movie material. He began to make notes on *A Man Called Peter.* Though this man had come into the motion-picture industry by an unusual route, he was where he belonged. He saw all life in terms of drama.

He was a native of Atlanta, Georgia, a former newspaperman. Then he had had a stint of writing and directing publicity for the Motion Pictures Producers and Distributors Association in New York. Intrigued by the problems peculiar to the writing of screen plays, he had himself written fifteen.

In 1942 he had turned producer. Such successful movies as "Wilson," "The Ox-Bow Incident," "Cheaper by the Dozen," "Razor's Edge," "Captain from Castile," "My Blue Heaven," "Alexander's Ragtime Band," and "Guadalcanal Diary," had brought him to the top of his profession.

Several things about the Peter Marshall story intrigued Mr. Trotti. Much of it had an Atlanta setting. That struck a responsive chord. Then there was the story's strong emphasis on immortality. For example, the Sunday of Pearl Harbor Day Dr. Marshall had preached at the Naval Academy in Annapolis, and had talked about death—and life. What a stirring scene that would make! Since his son's death, Lamar Trotti had come to know how deep and widespread the need was for reassurance, for strengthening on this point.

But Mr. Trotti was not to be the one to use these notes. Suddenly on August 28, 1952, two years after his son's death, a second heart attack struck. That one carried him away.

Lamar Trotti's notes passed into the hands of one of his fellow producers at Fox—Samuel G. Engel. They were to play their own part in the movie "A Man Called Peter."

The wire delivered to me aboard the westbound "Chief" read:

WOULD YOU PLEASE ARRANGE TO GET OFF TRAIN AT PASADENA STATION AT 7:55 A.M. STUDIO CAR WILL MEET YOU THERE. THIS IS A SMALL STATION AND IT WILL BE EASIER TO RECOGNIZE YOU AND TO HANDLE YOUR LUGGAGE THAN AT THE LOS ANGELES STATION. REGARDS.

> JOHN ADAMS
> TRANSPORTATION DIVISION
> TWENTIETH CENTURY FOX STUDIOS

The hand holding the telegram trembled a little. There had been some surprising adventures since Peter's death; surely this was the strangest.

The procession of palm trees flying past the train windows told me that I was not only in California but was nearing my destination. Thoughts chased themselves through my mind: Here I am—all alone . . . I don't know anyone at the Fox studios . . . I've never set foot on a movie lot. . . . Who do I think I am, making this sally into Hollywood? And along with these realizations came an upsurge of emotion quite like stage fright. Suddenly the palms of my hands were moist; my stomach was doing a series of flipflops.

For a moment just before the "Chief" came to a gentle stop in the Pasadena station, I felt like someone standing in the wing of a theater, waiting for her cue to go onstage. What does an actress experience during those moments of waiting? I thought I knew . . . mounting tension, a wary uneasiness interlaced with fear, a strange lifting of the senses in an effort to catch the mood and measure, the receptivity of the people out beyond the footlights.

My stage fright lasted only until the action began. Mr. Adams, the studio representative who had come to meet me, was young and easy-going. Meeting and squiring assorted actors and actresses, authors and publicity people, was obviously just part of the day's work—nothing to get excited about.

"The studio car is right over there, Mrs. Marshall. We've made reservations for you at the Beverly Hills Hotel. I'll take you there first. Then we'll go on to the studio later this morning to meet your producer, Sam Engel."

We were scarcely settled in the studio limousine before I made my first *faux pas.* "My former college roommate lives in California now," I said. "She's anxious for me to visit her—lives in Menlo Park. Mr. Adams, maybe you could tell me—how long would it take to run over there?"

The man looked at me in tolerant amusement. "Well—you see, actually—Menlo Park is some five hundred miles away. It's a suburb of San Francisco, not Los Angeles. You could make it to San Francisco overnight on the train. About two hours by air." And his eyes seemed to be trying to take the measure of the woman who had written *A Man Called Peter,* but who didn't know the difference between Los Angeles and San Francisco.

The room to which I was shown in the luxurious Beverly Hills Hotel was an immense one with wide windows and a balcony overlooking a swimming pool—quite in keeping with my preconceived ideas of Hollywood glamour. The bedroom was decorated in shades of pinky taupes—subtle understatements of femininity. It had thick carpeting; French Provincial furniture in light fruitwood; heavy hammered-satin bedspreads and draperies; many mirrors; and an oversized vanity table in the bath–dressing room, its mirror surrounded by fluorescent lights—obviously for women who took their make-up seriously.

And when I opened the top bureau drawer, an exquisite fragrance floated out. Immediately it set my imagination working. Had the last occupant of this room been a famous actress? I thought not. Just a beautiful woman whose costly, personally blended perfume had lingered behind her.

But I had to pull my thoughts back to the business at hand. Soon I would be walking into the inner sanctum of the Fox studios. I recalled the events that had brought me to this moment. . . .

It was in the late fall of 1952 that I had first heard from a certain producer at Twentieth Century-Fox who was interested in *A Man Called Peter*. Hollywood's attention had been directed to the book because it had then been on the best-seller list for more than fifty consecutive weeks, and that fall had reached the top.

Even so, I had been told by my publisher's agent on the West Coast that the professional movie makers were skeptical that this particular book could be made into a successful movie. After all, the element of conflict—the catalyst for drama—was mostly missing from the Peter Marshall story. True, there was sweeping across the nation such a revival of interest in religion that some analysts were unabashedly calling it "a spiritual awakening." But Hollywood remained skeptical. The truth was that previous motion pictures about the lives of ministers, even the most popular like "One Foot in Heaven" and "Stars in My Crown," were not the most successful financial ventures.

Moreover, in the fall of 1952 the studios were cautious about buying book rights. The nation's mounting interest in television had Hollywood's collective teeth chattering. Obviously this was not gambling weather—especially for a religious book. No other studio was bidding against Fox for *A Man Called Peter*.

All of this added up to the fact that the overtures made to me for an option on the book were not financially alluring. Still the men at Fox seemed reasonably eager to have the option and kept pressing me by wire and phone for a decision.

During those days I wrote my thoughts down to try to clarify them:

> I am not interested in the money that has been offered me if the option is eventually picked up. . . .
>
> Nor am I interested in more publicity. I have more than I can handle now, or have any taste for.
>
> The one thing I *am* interested in is what the movie could mean in constructive help to thousands of Americans, perhaps to the nation as a whole. This is the possibility I want to explore. . . .

On the other hand, I knew that turning a book over to the movie men is always a calculated risk. If they Hollywoodized the Peter Marshall story and ruined it, I could forget about its being a constructive help to anyone.

While I pondered all this, Louella Parsons in her column for November 25 let out the news that Fox was negotiating for the book—only she made it appear that it was all settled:

> *A Man Called Peter*, the life of the late Peter Marshall, chaplain of the U.S. Senate has been bought by 20th Century Fox. . . . Sam Engel who will produce the story, has chosen Richard Burton, the British actor, to play Peter, while Jean Peters will be seen as Catherine (Mrs. Marshall). . . .

Immediately I began to receive a flood of mail. . . .

> *Can any good come out of Hollywood? I've got my fingers crossed. . . . Please don't allow it to become too Hollywoodish. . . . Who in the world could ever play Peter Marshall . . . ? My family and I have enjoyed this story so much that we feel that it is too sacred to be imitated or substituted. . . .*
>
> *I don't want you to be disappointed in your project. . . . Mrs. Marshall, let me give you some good advice. You speak right up "in meetin'" out there in Hollywood. . . .*

I could understand why my friends were so uneasy. They seemed to feel that Hollywood's forte was the physical and the material. Would the movie industry have the sensitivity to handle material dealing with the human spirit?

Such was my questioning also. I knew that in this as in all situations, there were imponderables. Obviously something more than my best judgment was needed. So—very simply—I asked God to tell me what my decision should be.

There came the day when I knew the answer; it came as a strong and unmistakable feeling. I was to keep the door open to the possibility of a movie. Therefore, I gave Fox the option in the faith that if God did not want this movie made, the option would never be picked up or the legal negotiations would bog down; if He did want it, then it would be His project just as the book had been. He would then see to the final result.

I had agreed to this first trip to Hollywood as a private scouting expedition. I was not there to be dined, feted, and soft-soaped, but to examine the situation for myself, to observe and to be observed. The big question was . . . could Mr. Engel and I work together to translate A *Man*

Called Peter into a fine screenplay? If so, I felt that something would have to be added to what I had always been told was Hollywood's usual attitude toward authors: "We'll treat you like a queen for a few days and then get you out of our hair as quickly as possible." If this was really true, then I felt that a special effort would have to be made to achieve rapport between the producer, the script writer, and me.

By eleven that morning I had been whisked down Beverly Drive to the Santa Monica Boulevard entrance to the studio. The watchman at the double gate recognized the driver of the studio car and signaled us through. We drove down a narrow road lined with warehouses filled with props—all manner of doors, thousands of window frames, columns, mantles, and architectural gewgaws—past well-kept flower beds to the Administration building.

Mr. Engel was a middle-aged man with dark hair and black horn-rimmed spectacles. His setting was a suite of offices in early American style, decorated in greens and tawny beiges. Behind a large desk was a bookcase filled with leather-bound copies of the screenplays of movies Mr. Engel had produced—"Come to the Stable," "Follow the Sun," "Sitting Pretty," "Frogmen," and many others. That first day's meeting held surprises on both sides. There was curiosity in the producer's eyes. Was it that I didn't quite fit his preconceived mold of the minister's widow?

And marvelously, within hours after I had first set foot on the Fox lot, my question about Hollywood's handling of spiritual material was answered in an unusual way. I had brought with me some of the tape recordings of Peter's sermons made the last year of his life. Mr. Engel was eager to hear Peter Marshall's voice. Immediately he ordered a tape recorder brought to his office. He shut the door, selected "The Rock That Moved," and settled himself in his swivel chair.

Soon the musical voice with the familiar Scottish burr filled the office. Mr. Engel seemed absorbed and chuckled frequently during the colorful description of the St. Andrews Society dinner with which the sermon opened. . . .

My, what memories came back, as the drumsticks twirled above the drum, and the kettledrums rolled . . . and our feet tapped out the time to *Cock o' the North*,

The Forty-Second
and *Hieland Laddie.*

In memory I saw a battalion of the Gordon Highlanders,
swinging down from Edinburgh Castle to Princes' Street
when I was last in Scotland—the pipes skirling
    and the kilts swinging,
with the pride that only Scotsmen fully know.

I thought of home . . . and long ago. . . .
We sang the old songs . . . and many an eye was misty. . . .

But then, after this light beginning, Peter plunged directly into the heart
of his message . . .

Memories . . . they come surging back into the heart to
make it clean again . . . or to accuse it.

Yes . . . to some it is music . . . or a song.
    To others it is a picture or the face of a friend,
but to Simon Peter it was the crowing of a cock.

He had seen the last flickering torch disappear round the
turn of the path that wound down hill.
Only once in a while could the lights of the procession
be seen through the trees like giant fireflies. . . .

There swept over Peter the realization that his Master
had at least been captured and was marching away to die.
The icy fear that gripped—*

Suddenly Mr. Engel flicked off the machine. "My wife Ruth is coming
to join us for lunch. I'd like her to hear this. Suppose we wait. We can
hear the rest later."

I was surprised, uneasy. He had seemed so impressed by the sermon.
But the three of us had a pleasant lunch in the studio commissary, and
I forgot my disappointment.

On the way back I got glimpses of the sets from movies I had seen—
the bridge for "My Cousin Rachel" was pointed out to me; a cobblestoned
French village that looked familiar; the gigantic tank used for "The
Titanic"; some sets from "Daddy Long Legs." But all of the sets were
deserted; nothing was shooting. The lot was like a ghost town. As we

*Marshall, Peter, *Mr. Jones, Meet the Master*, pp. 79–80, Fleming H. Revell Company, New
York, 1949. Used by permission.

walked down the long corridors of the Administration building, I noticed that many of the executive offices were empty. I asked why.

"I've been here a long time," Mr. Engel said. "I've never seen production at such a low ebb."

"Why? How do you account for that?"

"TV," he said simply. "Something's got to break soon or this industry's a goner. The wide screen could be one answer. By the way, your picture may be the first one made in CinemaScope."

Back in the producer's office, once more the recorder was turned on. Clearly Mr. Engel was engrossed all over again. Yet as the voice with the burr began building the drama of Simon Peter's denial to its climax, once more Mr. Engel jumped up and flicked off the recorder.

"I've a friend here in the studio, David Brown, who really ought to hear this. If you two don't mind . . . I think I'll wait. He may be able to join us later this afternoon."

But the same procedure was followed with the friend. He too heard only a portion of the sermon. By then I knew something strange was going on. Peter Marshall's voice and message held a fascination for Sam Engel. Like a moth to a flame, he came back to it again and again. But there was something else—some agony in it. I thought I knew. The bedrock reality, the incisiveness of the message underneath the music of the words was creating fear, spiritual tension, pain.

Later I learned that after dinner, when the lot was deserted except for the night watchman, Mr. Engel had closeted himself in his locked office and had listened to the end of "The Rock That Moved."

> The same Jesus, who called Simon, is calling you.
> The same Jesus, who saved Simon, can save you.
> The same mighty hand will hold you up.
> The denials that you have made were made by Simon.
> Yet he was restored; so may you be restored.
> Christ changed Simon into Peter,
>   The sinner into the saint.
>
> He can change your life, if you are willing.*

---

*Marshall, Peter, *Mr. Jones, Meet the Master*, p. 88. Fleming H. Revell Company, New York, 1949. Used by permission.

After that, the producer was all enthusiasm for the tapes. He had copies made for himself—one set for his home, one for his office. For weeks to come, he would insist on playing them for anyone who would listen.

This episode was a key to the character and personality of the movie producer. Sam Engel had been born into the stream of a rich and authentic religious heritage. His grandfather had been an orthodox Jewish rabbi. One of the childhood memories that had impressed him deeply was that of his grandfather dropping a warm Lincoln penny into his hand on the days when he had successfully completed his Hebrew lesson. "An angel from heaven sent this," the venerable old man would say. "If you'll believe in God and learn His holy Torah, you'll be blessed a millionfold."

There was in Sam Engel a sensitivity to spiritual matters that could only have been the fruit of such a heritage. He longed to leave the world a better place than he had found it. Religion drew him. Yet in this materialistic world, particularly in Hollywood, his religious heritage sometimes ran head-on into other values. Giving the spiritual real priority might jeopardize those other values. That he knew.

The next morning Mr. Engel showed me his personal copy of *A Man Called Peter*. It was dog-eared, copiously marked with red pencil.

"I want you to see something else. Did you ever hear of Lamar Trotti?"

"Yes—yes, I have."

"Well, these are his notes on your book in his own handwriting. Mrs. Trotti sent them to me after his death."

"What made him that interested in the book—enough to make notes, I mean?"

"He needed a lift himself." Then I learned from Mr. Engel the story of Lamar Trotti's last days—the death of his son in the automobile accident, his terrible grief, and finally his own death from a heart attack.

Mr. Engel leaned back in his swivel chair, his eyes on the ceiling. "Funny thing . . . far too many men around here dying of heart attacks . . . frightening. . . . When death comes to my friends, I try so hard to think of something—uh—really helpful—comforting—to say to those left."

"It *is* hard."

"Sure—sure is. That's one thing about your book. Peter had a real message about death. Everybody needs it. If we didn't do anything else in this movie but give help like that, it would be worth everything."

That afternoon I met the girl who had been assigned to work on the screenplay. She brought along a step sheet for "A Man Called Peter" bound between blue covers.

Mr. Engel knew that I'd never before seen a step sheet. "This is the first go-round in writing a screenplay," he explained. "To take a book and make it into a motion picture, we have to see the story as a sequence of scenes. A step sheet is just what it says—the scenes step by step, in progression, numbered. Now let's go over it."

1. Establish Agnes Scott College for women, Decatur, Georgia—southern atmosphere of the campus, etc.
2. Tennis courts at college. Catherine and another girl playing doubles with two young men. . . .
3. Dissolve to exterior of Westminster Church as Catherine and friend approach bulletin board. It announces Dr. Marshall's sermon "Praying Is Dangerous Business."
4. As Catherine and her friend enter the church. . . .

That was fine, except that in step 10 we suddenly took off into pure fiction. A colored boy named Phillip Humes was introduced. He was supposed to be the son of the church janitor in Atlanta. His story was to run all through the movie, ending with his death in the Pacific in World War II.

I objected. The subsequent discussion between Sam, the writer, and me revealed a sharp difference of opinion. To the producer and the script writer, fiction was as good as truth, provided it was plausible.

My viewpoint was that truth was often more exciting than fiction, sometimes had more dramatic possibilities. Moreover, I felt that the film would wield its greatest impact only if the movie audiences knew that they were seeing what had really happened. The dilemma was not resolved that day. It was to haunt us.

Before I left for Washington, Mr. Engel offered, if Fox picked up the option, to give me the position of technical adviser to the script. That meant that he trusted me enough to let me be a party to all decisions about the screenplay. I would be included in further conferences. But it did not mean that he would be obligated to accept my suggestions.

He and I parted good friends. He was so hopeful that the option would be picked up that he instructed the script writer to proceed with a first-draft continuity taken from an expanded step sheet. In time I would hear from Fox's lawyers about the option.

Back in the East, I made some inquiries to find a lawyer who had had some experience with motion-picture contracts. Knowing my lack of business know-how and how difficult it was for me to make sense of the legal terminology in any contract, this seemed only common sense.

It was not until August 12 that I learned that Twentieth Century-Fox had decided to exercise their option. A contract followed by mail. I knew nothing about contracts, but that one seemed hardly fair. My impression was that it was a trial balloon sent up to see just how gullible I was. For instance, they asked for all drama rights to *A Man Called Peter*, including television rights stretching ten years into the future. Later I found that these were standard clauses in most movie contracts.

My lawyer took nine months to negotiate the changes that we considered important. He tried hard to get final veto rights in case anything turned up in the movie script to which I objected. We did not win that. But I did get veto power over anything libelous or detrimental to the character of Peter Marshall. In the end, the contract was at least reasonable, though the buying price was what it had been from the beginning.

In the meantime, the script writer's first-draft continuity had been sent me. It was conscientious work but had more fiction in it than truth. For example, I was supposed to be shocked out of tuberculosis back into health by seeing an automobile accident from my bedroom window. This was not only fiction but scarcely plausible fiction!

Increasingly, though I liked the girl personally, I began to feel that she did not understand the basis of the Peter Marshall story and therefore was on the wrong assignment. "Should I," I wondered, "share that conviction with Mr. Engel?"

I decided against it; that would be overstepping my bounds. The producer knew his scenario writers under contract—their interests and capabilities. Frequently during those weeks he telephoned me. Since he seemed quite happy with the writer chosen, I kept quiet about how I felt.

I did however pray about it. The essence of my prayer was, "Oh, God, if this is the writer for this job, then fine. If not, then will You please get that point across to Sam Engel? I leave the matter in Your hands."

About ten days later an airmail special delivery came:

Dear Catherine:
  After much deliberation I have come to the conclusion that the script writer on the job for "A Man Called Peter" is not the one for the project. . . .
  I have for the past two weeks discussed "Peter" with another woman writer whose work I am familiar with and respect. She is an extremely capable craftsman and is highly enthusiastic about undertaking the job.
  Already I have had several conferences with her and we have made excellent progress. It is my hope to have a stepsheet of the new lineup ready by the time of your next visit here.
  I hope that this change I am making won't cause you any anxiety, and that you will be pleased with the new writer when you meet her.
    With every good wish,

                                                          Sam

P.S. Incidentally, the new writer feels very strongly the need to stick pretty close to the biographical facts contained in your book. I know this will please you.

Far from causing me any anxiety, I was so elated I almost took off in all directions. Rarely had I received such a prompt, incisive, and specific answer to prayer. This was the reassurance I needed that the movie really was God's project, and that He was quite capable of handling all complications.

My next Hollywood trip was set for November 10. I had been asked to stay for at least a month of daily script conferences. These would be crucial, policy making. My growing feeling for the movie and my emotional investment in the final result can be judged by a letter I wrote Sam Engel about that time:

  To be sure, moving, inspirational entertainment is not discounted. But, Sam, I long for this particular movie to be far more than that. And I think you do too. I long for this picture to show movie audiences all over America what God can do for modern men and women, and so to change lives and set feet on the right track.
  Now I know that what I'm asking for is virtually a documentary film— one that's true to the facts, not of a book but of life—only handled with

all the artistry of fiction. That would not be an easy scenario to write. I
know that. I think I understand some of the difficulties. But I'm convinced
that it could be done, and that it would make movie history. . . .

What I did not share with Mr. Engel was any mention of a spiritual
problem involved. It might have seemed irrelevant to him; to me, it was
basic. . . . Peter and I had had evidence in our lives that God can guide
modern men and women. But God has also given us freedom of choice.
He won't violate that. He can certainly direct those who want Him to
direct. But can He guide those who aren't aware of any need for His help
and don't seek it?

I was trying to be realistic. It seemed probable that some of those in
the movie industry who would be making "A Man Called Peter" would
fall into the category of those who sought no help from God. What then?
Is prayer for other people effective only if those for whom we pray are
dedicated men of God?

About that time I was reading parts of the Old Testament. Certain
things impressed me as never before—the God-centered view of history—
God standing in the shadows keeping vigil through the long centuries
of civilization's slow upward progress; the Bible's unwhitewashed heroes,
presented as sinners like all men; the lusty sex, unabashedly set forth,
taken for granted as a part of life; the continual rap-rap of the ancient
writers' insistence on the Almightiness of God.

This last gave me pause. Those early writers really believed that
there were no limits to God's power. No problem about man's freedom
of will bothered them. For example, out of jealousy and anger, Joseph's
brothers sold him into slavery in Egypt. Yet God's hand was above all,
overruling, so that later, as the "ruler over all the land of Egypt," Joseph
could say . . .

> . . . be not grieved, nor angry with yourselves that ye sold me
> hither. . . . It was not you that sent me hither, but God. . . .
> (GENESIS 45:5, 8)

In the same way, God overruled the Pharaoh of the bondage.

> He removeth kings and setteth up kings. . . . (DANIEL 2:21)

Like a gold thread this reiteration of the Omnipotence of God runs through all Scripture. . . . A man's heart

> is in the hand of the Lord, as the rivers of water,
> he turneth it whithersoever he will. (PROVERBS 21:1)

Either God lives—or He doesn't. Either He has real power—or it is all delusion. If God could overrule Joseph's brothers and assorted Pharaohs and kings, then He could manage modern rulers—and Hollywood. At least, I thought, now I have a good chance to find out.

But the Bible also insists that we have to ask for God's help in order to get it. That is the point of petitionary prayer. And the asking seems to have more power when many join their petitions in agreement on "what they shall ask."

It was out of that background that I decided to write to each of those who had sent me letters after reading *A Man Called Peter* to ask for their specific prayer about the movie project. I told neither my publisher nor Mr. Engel that I was doing this. . . .

November 1, 1953

Dear Friend:

I remember with gratitude the most thoughtful letter which you wrote me sometime ago, in which you shared with me how God spoke to your own life through Peter Marshall's story and sermons.

Now I want to ask a personal favor of you. Twentieth Century-Fox plans to make a movie of A Man Called Peter. *This movie could speak to the heart of America. It could mean a great deal to our time and generation—using this modern movie medium.*

I can visualize movie audiences—made up of whole families—alternately laughing and shedding a few tears as they relive certain episodes of A Man Called Peter *on the screen, as they see God Himself shining through one man's life. I can see vast audiences streaming out of the theatres onto the sidewalks of a hundred thousand Main Streets, entertained, uplifted, inspired, with the thought singing through many a mind . . . "If God could solve Peter Marshall's problems, maybe He can solve mine—and my nation's. I'm going to give Him a chance. . . ."*

I can see the scenario writer, the producer—Mr. Samuel G. Engel, the director, the entire cast given by God inspiration and ability quite beyond all natural talent.

But all this can happen only if this whole project is literally floated on a gigantic wave of prayer. It is precisely because I well know what a difference prayer can make, that I am writing this letter to you and 1800 other choice friends, requesting your specific prayer about the movie "A Man Called Peter."

The next two months will see many crucial decisions made. The scenario is not yet completed. The movie has not been cast. The director has not been chosen. I leave for Hollywood on November 10 to make what suggestions I can. . . .

Usually most people pay little attention to a form letter. Yet this one drew an amazing response. I heard from almost everyone who received it. Most of the replies were written in longhand. It was evident that my request for prayer was being taken as seriously as I had hoped. . . .

From Toronto, Ohio:

Your fine circular letter has just come. I am so grateful to be one of the many hundreds who will be praying with you about the filming of A Man Called Peter.

Both you and he already belong to America. I think of you as "Catherine." . . .

From Cincinnati:

Your letter came just an hour ago. I found it on returning home from my day's work in a steel shop. . . . I am nobody special. Lady, I'm just an uneducated steel worker, 38 years at this trade. . . .

I was never one who could express myself in prayer. But I've searched my mind. . . . With God's help, Lady, nothing can fail. . . .

From Winona Lake, Indiana:

I prize highly your request for my prayers that "A Man Called Peter" may be directed by our wonderful Lord Himself . . . I hope I'll be able to get out and see the picture when it's ready. At seventy-one I was stricken with my second coronary. . . .

From Tyler, Texas:

Your letter was very welcome. I'll not only pray, I'll ask my prayer group to. . . . My husband and I have talked it over and we think Clark Gable would be perfect for the part of Peter. . . .

From Springfield, Pennsylvania:

Our first reaction to your letter was one of immediate opposition, fearing that Hollywood would insist upon injecting its polish into the biography of a man who was far more concerned with inner composure than with exterior appearances. Unless we do Hollywood and the movie industry a grave injustice, Mrs. Marshall, their motive for making a movie of Peter's life would be almost purely monetary; your motive, on the other hand, was spiritual. The fact that your biography has been a financial success was incidental. . . .

At the same time our hearts and our common sense suggested that you yourself would not accept any situation that would compromise the sanctity of Peter's life. . . . Thus our prayers have not been for the production of the movie, but for your guidance. . . .

From a businessman in Dayton, Ohio:

How can my prayers for your movie project be of any help when God does not seem to listen to my prayers for myself? But at least I can try. . . .

While I was away, Peter John stayed in Washington with friends who had two children themselves. This kind couple moved their whole family into our home and kept house for Peter.

This time Twentieth Century-Fox provided me with a three-room apartment on Wilshire Boulevard, close to Westwood Village, within six minutes' driving time of the studio. The living room, with its two walls of windows, opened on a swimming pool. Flowers had been placed in the apartment as a greeting from Sam Engel and his wife.

As I unpacked that evening, my thoughts were on the first script conference set for the next morning. An idea kept plucking at my mind . . . "That conference should open with a prayer asking God's blessing on the work. You're the one to suggest it. You've asked other people to pray. Now it's your turn."

I tried to brush the thought aside. The last thing I wanted was to seem like a religious eccentric to Mr. Engel. Nor did I want him to think I was suggesting such a thing for effect.

I went on hanging up dresses and putting lingerie in the drawers. The thought returned.

It was easy to think up excuses. . . . What if I did suggest that we start the conference with prayer, and word got out? People in Hollywood are publicity conscious. They might think the whole thing a publicity stunt.

I dismissed the matter and deposited my toothbrush and some toiletries in the bathroom. The idea came back. It stuck like flypaper. I had a sinking feeling that the minute before that conference began in the morning, I would have an opportunity I'd never have again. And if I passed it up, I might be failing not just myself, but Christ. I had trouble going to sleep that night.

At ten the next morning three of us joined Mr. Engel in his office— Eleanore Griffin, the script writer, a Catholic; a secretary who was a Mormon, and I, a Presbyterian. Mr. Engel was, of course, of the Jewish faith. Apparently the Lord had something cosmic in mind.

I was seated in a wing chair before Mr. Engel's desk. Miss Griffin was sitting on the davenport, scanning the material abandoned by the other writer. The secretary was poised to take notes. The moment I had anticipated had arrived. My mouth was as dry as cotton. The words would surely stick in my throat.

"Sam, I've something to ask you."

"Sure, Catherine, shoot."

"Well, you know how I told you that every morning while I was writing *A Man Called Peter*, before I began, I said a quick little prayer and asked God to write that book through me. Seems maybe He did, judging by the results. . . . We've got a big job ahead of us. We'll never do it right on our own hook. Would you think me goofy if I suggested that we pause for just a minute and ask for God's help?"

For half a minute no one said anything. Time hung in space. The brown eyes batted once behind the spectacles and then looked straight at me. There was no embarrassment in them. A sober look flicked across the mobile features. Then . . . "I'd love that, Catherine! Will you do it?"

The prayer was short, informal, and to the point. When I had finished, I found Eleanore Griffin's eyes glued to my face. For a minute there was a hush in the room. Then the shop talk began.

The goal of the ten-to-five conferences every day was to hammer out the story line. Our biggest problem was that of selectivity. Most motion pictures run only an hour and a half to an hour and forty-five minutes. How could we effectively portray a man's life in so short a time? What should we put in, what leave out?

I soon saw that there was a difference between fictionalizing for its own sake and the legitimate modification of facts necessary to translate a book into a screenplay. There would have to be some time compression, some shifting of the sequence of events, some changing of details. For example, in real life Peter and I had spent our honeymoon in New York, not on Cape Cod; in the script there was the necessity of introducing Cape Cod early in the story. In real life Peter John was born on January 25, 1940, not in December of 1941. Yet this time shift simplified the Annapolis sequence in the movie, and so on and on. Changes of this sort did not bother me, because they did no violence to the spirit of the truth.

We talked the story out—scene by scene. Some sessions were exciting. Mind sparked mind. Inspiration flowed. Ideas piled up. At such times, Sam would pace the room, gesturing, spitting words like bullets. Whenever he was forced to pause for breath, Eleanore and I would leap into the breach. Sometimes Sam would throw off his coat and walk up and down, plucking at his suspenders as if they were fiddle strings. Often he would get carried away, try to dramatize a scene, taking all the parts himself. He might drop to one knee, change his voice to falsetto . . . "This is Catherine speaking—" swing his arms, sit on the desk, take his glasses on and off, drink glass after glass of water, shoot questions at me.

Often these questions would go beyond what I had written in *A Man Called Peter.* Sam was using the book as a jumping-off place. Sometimes they would be as penetrating as psychoanalysis. He probed motive and thought, seeking to get beneath the surface. He wanted to know my emotions under given circumstances . . . "Think back, Catherine. How did you feel at the moment the doctor called? See this scene. What should the actress feel?"

For me the probing days were wearying days. I was talking about myself; yet I wasn't. Soon it seemed natural to say "Catherine" rather than "I." . . . "Well, if Peter leaves without proposing, and Catherine goes to her dorm room, weeping—don't you think—?"

Over and over, Sam appeared to be amazed at this objectivity. "I don't know how you do it. You've made an amazing recovery from Peter's death—or you couldn't. Besides, most authors battle for their stuff like tigers, consider every word straight from Sinai."

Eleanore and Sam turned to me for all theology, for anything pertaining to hymnology, for information about the Protestant church and a minister's life. At various times they asked me to explain deacons, elders, the Presbytery, the General Assembly, preludes and postludes, a minister's call, what a manse is, an every-member canvass, the whys and why-nots of the ministerial collar, the Geneva gown, etc.

One morning Sam leaned back in his chair and said, "Catherine, there's something I've just got to ask you—"

"Of course—"

"You know that formal dinner the church gave you and Peter right after you went to Washington?"

"Yes, in a private room of the Mayflower Hotel."

"Well, tell me . . . didn't they serve any liquor at all? None at all?"

"No, Sam, they didn't."

"Well, I'll be—! Sorry!" And he said nothing more, just clucked his tongue.

At another time, Eleanore asked, "Catherine, I'm curious about something. How much salary did Peter make?"

"A very good one, as ministers' salaries go. At the time of his death, $11,500. That would be plus some fees and honoraria."

"But that's not possible—"

Sam interrupted, "A man like Peter—$11,500! Why, in any other job under the sun he could have pulled down—"

"But Sam, the average minister gets something like $3,000 a year. And don't forget that he has the expense of three years of postgraduate work on top of college."

That news about Peter's salary proved to be quite a bomb-shell. Obviously, Sam and Eleanore were oriented to the salary scales of the entertainment world. Nothing else I might have said could have so convinced them of the authenticity of Peter's call to the ministry and of his sincerity.

I soon learned the jargon of script writing and enjoyed flinging it around—montage . . . establishing shot . . . narration . . . fade in . . . fade out . . . dissolve to . . . echo chamber . . . reverse shot . . . cut to . . . a tag. Always there was a secretary to take notes, but I took some for myself— in between doodling. I became a master doodler. One day it would be geometric designs; another day elaborate flowers. One morning I designed five new flags.

But sometimes it was as if we were walking barefoot on hot cinders when the story line seemed to be veering in a wrong direction. There was the time when Sam toyed with the idea of injecting an incident about a frustrated woman taking sleeping pills. We had been talking about the dilemmas and temptations suffered by most professional men through designing women. Mr. Engel wanted to crystallize this problem in Peter's life through a fictional vignette. . . . Several scenes would reveal a woman's scheming to get close to her minister. Her plans would fail. Then she would take an overdose of sleeping pills and be rescued just in time.

"Sam, we'd be on dangerous ground," Eleanore objected. "People won't bother to separate truth from fiction. They'd always think 'where there's smoke, there's fire.'"

I agreed with Eleanore. But Sam had dreamed up so many nice details for the vignette that he was loath to drop it. "Let's think about it," he suggested.

The second day he was still in favor of using it. Nothing Eleanore or I could say moved him. It looked as if the poor woman and her sleeping pills might be in the screenplay for keeps.

Yet on the third day Sam announced, "About that sleeping pill incident—something tells me 'no' on that. It won't really add anything. We can do better. Let's just forget it."

This process was repeated at several crucial points. Soon I learned to rely on it. Sam made his own decisions from the inside—sometimes wavered—but in the end, made them right.

Increasingly, Eleanore became aware of the process too, believed in it, leaned on it. "This is the greatest experience of my life," she would say to me privately. "We're sure getting help from some place. Golly, you'll never know how glad I am I didn't miss this assignment!"

On several mornings she would ask that we begin with prayer. "Other people don't need to know about it. Anyhow, who gives a hang what they think? The prayer does make a difference."

As the conferences went on, Sam became eager to include actual sermon material in the script. "You wouldn't make the Jolson story without songs," he would say. "And Peter Marshall was first, last, and always a preacher. Preaching was the music of his life. All right then, can you tell his story without letting him preach?"

"Right." Eleanore and I nodded.

"But, of course, you realize," he paused, frowning, "—this is daring. It's never been done. It will be a trail blazer. And another thing—I want one of those sermons to deal with immortality. Maybe some of 'Go Down Death.' That's terribly important. I couldn't let Lamar Trotti down on that."

My visit to Hollywood wasn't all work. The studio loaned me a car— a big unwieldy Lincoln. On holidays or days when we couldn't work, weekends, and after hours, I played. There was a weekend at Laguna Beach, a drive to the Old Mission at San Juan Capistrano, a meal at Knott's Berry Farm, a visit to friends in the San Fernando Valley, a morning spent wandering through the Farmer's Market. I soaked up sunshine, drank gallons of fresh orange juice, ate fruits flown in from Hawaii, and bought an evening dress at Bullock's, Westwood, that was so right for me that it quickly became my favorite.

I spent a delightful evening with Margaret Lee Runbeck, the author, and drove out to Monrovia to see Starr and Marie Daily. At Ciro's one evening George Burns and Gracie Allen were at an adjoining table (I concluded that Gracie's pictures don't do her justice), and Cary Grant was just across the room. There was a dinner party in the home of Dennis Morgan, the actor, and an evening with the Hollywood Christian Group, where I met Dale and Roy Rogers and Jane Russell.

Hollywood is a place of strange contrasts. One day Queen Frederica and King Paul of Greece came to see the Twentieth Century–Fox studios. That morning I watched Marilyn Monroe and Debra Paget jockey—

female fashion—for top position in the receiving line, and that same evening attended a formal dinner given for me by Dr. Edgar J. Goodspeed, the Bible scholar and translator. Such is the fascinating variety of personalities in the Los Angeles area!

At a Literary Celebrities Luncheon in Pasadena, I sat next to James Hilton, the author of *Lost Horizon* and *Good-bye, Mr. Chips*, and had a memorable conversation with him.

"I saw the movie 'Lost Horizon' in London in 1937," I told him. "I'll never forget certain scenes—particularly that one in the pass where the beautiful girl turns into a hideous old woman. Mr. Hilton, where or how did the idea for Shangri-La come to you?"

In his eyes was reverie. "Funny thing that you should ask that. The idea came to me as a little boy. Ever since, it's been a part of my life. You know, I think the idea matured in me as I grew up."

There were certain fleeting impressions . . . that Hollywood's glitter is that of tinsel—not diamonds; that in this area must surely be the world's greatest concentration of roses, Cadillacs, sports cars, and mink stoles. Where materialism is rampant, people judge and catalog one another according to life's trappings. Thus a rush business is done renting mink stoles, capes, and coats for important dates or interviews.

In the midst of this materialism is great loneliness. Popularity as the stars know it doesn't preclude desperate aloneness. To most of the motion-picture executives, the stars are not people, but commodities, worth such and such on the box-office market. To the fans, the stars are idols. Even idols can have wistful eyes.

Yet loneliness as a Hollywood disease is not limited to the stars. Its all-pervading presence was dramatized for me by an organization called "Listeners, Inc." For a fee, one could purchase an hour's time in which to pour one's self out. The conferee was there only to listen. He was obligated to offer neither advice nor comment. Such a business could prosper only in a city where friendship does not.

There in the movie capital is the greatest spiritual hunger and thirst I've ever felt anywhere. People hunt greedily, hunt everywhere, for some meaning to life, some answer, some structure. Alcoholics Anonymous, and more recently, Divorcees Anonymous, thrive. In addition, the religious fringe groups and pseudo-religions draw crowds in Los Angeles— along with the established churches—as nowhere else in the nation. A

Science of Mind Church fills the Fox Wilshire Theatre each Sunday morning. Yet God's name is scarcely mentioned at all there, or if so, half apologetically, it seemed to me. A Church of All Religions tries to live up to its name by encompassing every faith and creed.

Yet Christianity flourishes, too. A church like the First Presbyterian Church of Hollywood pulsates with vitality. Dr. Raymond Lindquist's preaching and Dr. Charles Hirt's music draw overflow crowds for three services each Sunday—alert, expectant, open-hearted congregations. Genuine conversions, changed lives, cures from alcoholism, crowds of enthusiastic teen-agers and young married couples are not at all unusual.

The script conferences were finally over. We had not covered all the story, but Christmas was approaching. Wilshire Boulevard had blossomed into an avenue of pink boudoir-looking Christmas trees! Besides we were being pushed for an early deadline. Since Eleanore Griffin would be starting over with the screenplay, it was necessary to drop the conferences and let her start on the first-draft continuity. She would send me pages for criticism as she went.

I left Hollywood grateful for one of the most stimulating experiences of my life, with many wonderful new friends, and armed with lists of material to send Eleanore:

Excerpts from my college journals;
A copy of the Senate prayers;
A copy of the sermon that Peter had been preaching
    when he had his first heart attack;
A list of favorite Scottish songs;
Copies of Peter's sermons printed in the *Congressional Record*;
Several sermons on young people and marriage; etc.

I got back to Washington in time to celebrate Christmas with my son.

Thirteen
"The Lord God Omnipotent Reigneth"

MANY PEOPLE THINK of the camera work as the hard work of movie making. Actually with most pictures the shooting takes from one to three months; the preparation of the screenplay many times as long. With "A Man Called Peter," the shooting took two months, the screenplay, one year and nine months.

One of the reasons for such a long-drawn-out process is that the script writer has so many people to please. Other forms of the arts can be solitary work—poetry, the short story, the novel, painting, sculpture, certain kinds of music. But making a movie requires teamwork to end all teamwork.

When I left Hollywood, Eleanore Griffin had nothing but several hundred pages of typed notes from our three-way conferences. Her first step was to turn out a rough writer's working script from those notes. After that, the screenplay went through four drafts, covering ten months of continuous work on Eleanore's part, and hundreds of suggestions from Mr. Engel and me.

The first draft was some fifty pages too long. Thereafter each revision was directed toward cutting and tightening. I kept protesting the cutting in my letters to Mr. Engel:

Dear Sam:

It is good news indeed that Mr. Zanuck likes the First Draft Continuity. However, I cringe, hold my breath, and keep my shoelaces crossed at his saying that "drastic cuts must be made." In my wildest dreams I can't imagine where.

Let us hope—and hope—and hope some more that he will not want us to drop out most of the sermon material. I predict that's what the movie audiences are going to eat up. . . .

Having just seen "Gone with the Wind" again—three hours and forty minutes of it—I am impressed all over by the scope a longer screenplay allows for character development, and how it gets over the hurdle of the choppiness of many movies.

How can real artistry be poured into the mold of a set number of pages? Should all other values be sacrificed to length? Is no compromise possible? . . .

And Mr. Engel answered:

Good news! I have gotten Mr. Zanuck's comments. Like you, I had kept my fingers crossed, fearing that he might suggest deleting, or at least drastically cutting the sermons; the Youth Rally; and some of the religious content. Happily that is not the case. . . .

Over and over again, I have had to debate with myself as to what values are to be retained, and where to take a legitimate, dramatic license by omitting some of the facts. Mind you, I said "omitting"—not distorting. And more and more I have become convinced that Peter's continuing ministry must not be sacrificed to so-called documentary facts or chronological developments. . . .

Length was not the only problem. As the months went on, my suggestions crystallized in several specific directions. I battled (1) putting too much emphasis on the love story; (2) presenting a distorted picture of the Protestant ministry by, for example, giving it too much glamor; (3) putting Peter up on a pedestal where he merely snapped his fingers and God's directions came clear and all his prayers were immediately answered. This last would have been discouraging to the movie audiences, and above all, unrealistic. Prayer had never been that easy for Peter. He had often felt inadequate, had had seasons of agonizing over his inability to get through to God.

Mr. Engel was always patient in considering my point of view. In the beginning of our work together, he had said, "Catherine, this project has to be founded on mutual trust. I know you've had some warnings from people who have had dismal experiences in Hollywood. That doesn't lay much of a foundation for trust. But you've got to believe in my good will, because it's a fact."

It was a fact. Whenever Sam Engel and I failed to understand each other, it wasn't for lack of trying.

In the spring of 1954 the producer decided that he and Miss Griffin should come East. We needed more of the three-way conferences; he wanted to scout out shooting sites in Washington and Atlanta, and he felt that it would help Eleanore to see the places she was writing about and to talk with people who had known Peter.

It was up to me to bring together Eleanore and the people who could help her. Accordingly, the first event was a small dinner party at my home. That evening Eleanore and Sam had two reactions which they made no effort to conceal. . . . They were amazed at how modestly I lived in Washington; once again they appeared surprised with the discovery that people could be so gay and have so much fun without the lift of liquor.

On subsequent days a group of men—including some of the officers of our church—gathered for a luncheon with them in a private dining room in a Washington hotel. Then some thirty young people spent an evening with Miss Griffin. She asked penetrating questions. They answered them all and reminisced about Peter with humor and gusto.

The mornings we devoted to script conferences, the afternoons to seeing the sites connected with the story. Then suddenly Sam announced one morning that he was giving up the Atlanta trip and would be starting back to California the next day.

"It isn't really necessary," he said, "to see the Georgia sites. We can do just as well making our own sets for the Agnes Scott campus and Peter's two Georgia churches."

This, I felt, was bad news. "A Man Called Peter" was recent history. Why build sets when the real spots were available? Far too many people would know the difference. Eleanore and I were convinced, even without discussing it, that the picture would suffer without those authentic scenes. I also knew that seeing Peter's first little church in Covington, meeting some of the folks who had known him there, and feeling for themselves the flavor of a Southern woman's college, would bring Eleanore and Sam—and therefore the movie—that much closer to the realities of Peter's life.

We pleaded, but Sam was adamant. Finally we could say nothing more. The atmosphere was a little grim as we parted for the day.

Eleanore's months of reading Peter Marshall's sermons and working on the screenplay had given her a growing conviction that prayer does change things, that it is the appointed way of cooperation between man and God. That afternoon she leaped into the breach in a way that shamed me. Secretly she wired a mutual friend of ours, Haywood P. Sconce, a minister in Oregon. "Just pray," she asked, "that Mr. Engel will do— even without knowing it—what God wants him to do about the Atlanta trip." A reassuring wire came back.

That evening Sam telephoned me . . . "I've been thinking. Maybe I was wrong. There isn't any real pressure about my getting back to the studio this week. Eleanore says she could be ready to leave for Atlanta tomorrow. Can you?"

Could I . . . ! The visits to Atlanta and Covington turned out to be as crucial as we had thought. To this day I can't quite imagine what the movie would have been without them.

Miss Griffin and Mr. Engel saw the Westminster Presbyterian Church and Stone Mountain in Atlanta, the Agnes Scott campus and Columbia Seminary in Decatur, and the church in Covington. The result was that, when the cameras started grinding in late September, the scenes in these places were shot on location.

But what charmed Eleanore and Sam most were the people they met. This was the first taste either of them had ever had of the warmhearted hospitality of Christian folk in the Deep South. In Covington, they met the men who had known Peter Marshall fresh out of seminary when his Scottish burr was still thick, his hair always tousled, and his knowledge of life in the United States meager. The doors of the Stephenson home where he had roomed, and the Gardner home where he had boarded, were opened wide to the visitors. At Agnes Scott they were included in a faculty dinner, and Sam, basking in the atmosphere, rose and delighted the group with a spirited analysis of what really goes on behind the scenes in movie making and of what he planned for the fall when the cast and camera crews moved onto the campus.

The three of us also had several days of script conferences, trying to hammer out more story line. A secretarial agency recorded the talks and later delivered a copy of the notes to each of us, 318 pages of them. It looked like a court transcript.

I had often toyed with the idea that this same procedure might be one way for a writer to learn how to handle dialogue—that is, secretly record actual conversation, transcribe it to paper, and study the result. But after seeing the scrambled gobbledygook of our conversations, I was far from sure that the would-be writer would learn much. A look at almost any page was a humbling experience, enough to make a person decide never to open his mouth again . . . !

MR. ENGEL: That's right, when he speaks there—but, you know, that's all very good, but I'm just thinking now, also, -how-how-how this gal can work for us, whatever we'll call her, Miss Pemberton, or—

MISS GRIFFIN: Miss Pemberton will be her name. I'll make a note. . . .

MR. ENGEL: But, but. . . .

MRS. MARSHALL: Did you ever study tombstones for names?

MR. ENGEL: (Apparently ignoring me) But supposing—supposing that—you see—here's how—here's how Peter became beholden to her. Just supposing he needs very badly certain things, song books, or hymn books, or things that—that the board hasn't appropriated money for, and. . . .

MISS GRIFFIN: Or she pays for the choir director.

MR. ENGEL: Ummmm, Ummmm—Well, I think—You see, anything that he wants to institute, and. . . .

MRS. MARSHALL: Yeah, I understand that. I also have a question though. And I'm just trying to save y'all trouble you understand. Now—

MISS GRIFFIN: Fine, yeah.

MRS. MARSHALL: And he could get that cocker spaniel look on his face like he used to, you know—

MR. ENGEL: Now Peter can feel—that she's a good soul, after all—

MISS GRIFFIN: Silly, but a good egg. That kind of thing.

MR. ENGEL: That kind of thing. Well, on the other hand, Catherine, doggone, well, that's fine, if she wants to buy little books or Bibles or whatever.

MISS GRIFFIN: Catherine just has to be eliminated.

MRS. MARSHALL: Uh huh. Why honeychile! I don't object to being eliminated. . . .

Already my days were punctuated with communications by wire and phone from production people at the studio. The director of research wanted to know:

1. What kind of a car Peter Marshall drove in Washington.
2. What type of suits he wore for everyday.
3. Did he wear a business suit in the Senate or a Geneva gown?
4. Did he have a clan tartan?

The studio was unable to get clearance on *The Case of the Perfumed Mouse* mentioned in my book. Did I have any suggestion? They could not find the music of "Oh, You Beautiful Doll." Could I help? The wardrobe department wanted to know what kind of a wrist watch I would have worn during college days. The thoroughness with which the movie people went after these details was amazing.

It never occurred to me that after the picture went into production, this interchange would not continue. There had been so much of it! So far, I had surely been needed; I thought I would be needed to the end. I was to find out differently.

My first intimation of this was in relation to casting. I was not consulted. That was easy to accept, because I had had no experience with it and was not sufficiently well acquainted with available talent anyway. Events were to prove that no help from me was necessary; a better Hand than mine was directing casting as well as a lot of other things.

One of the modern translations of the New Testament speaks of everything fitting "into a pattern for good"* for those who love and acknowledge God. The New Testament writer was not just stringing words together. This is the "how" of God's omnipotence—an awe-inspiring fact.

Sometimes it works like a play set on a cosmic stage. People of whom we've never heard are added to the cast. They may be summoned from across the world. Sometimes there are time lags between the scenes, but always the characters are at the bidding of the Master Director. The right props appear at the right time. The hand fits the glove. The chessmen are moved with precision. Every piece of the jigsaw puzzle finds its place. . . .

*Phillips, J. B., *Letters to Young Churches*, p. 19, The Macmillan Company, Inc., New York, 1951, Romans 8:28.

A case in point was the casting of the male lead in the movie "A Man Called Peter" and the part that one of the props—some tape recordings—played in that casting. The first scene was set in the winter of 1948. . . .

It was twenty minutes to eleven on a Sunday morning. The two men in the dimly lit kitchen at the New York Avenue Presbyterian Church in Washington were working swiftly, saying little. Finally one of them, Jack Ingram, spoke. . . . "That just about does it. The wiring's been tricky. Of course the podium would be over the kitchen!"

The other, Charles Chapman, shrugged. "And what a spot! It doesn't take much imagination to see Abraham Lincoln right over there—by that antiquated stove maybe—delivering a postscript to the Gettysburg address."

Mr. Ingram smiled. . . . "Well, anyway, I'm glad we got the trustees' okay on setting up the equipment. Did I tell you I won this the hard way?"

"How d'you mean?"

"I had lunch with Peter on Thursday. When I asked about tape-recording his sermons, he laughed in my face. Pooh-poohed me."

"How did you persuade him?"

"Out of nowhere I had an idea. . . . The shut-ins and old people. Record the sermons, then take the tapes to them. Peter finally agreed on that basis. What a guy!"

S. Jack Ingram was and is in the aviation engine business in Dallas, Texas. He had come to Washington in 1942. Until a few months before, he had not been inside a church for years. Then his wife, Pat, had persuaded him to go and hear Dr. Peter Marshall. That did it! From then on, he tried never to miss a Sunday morning service.

That winter he had sought out Dr. Marshall, and the two men had become friends. "I never knew," Jack had told Peter, "that Christianity could be such fun. I'm happier than I've been in years. It's like getting a good meal every Sunday. But I don't want to keep such exciting preaching to myself. Would you be willing—if I bought some tape-recording equipment myself—?"

What Jack Ingram could not have guessed was the precision of his timing. The sermons that he had methodically recorded Sunday after

Sunday turned out to be those of the last year of Peter Marshall's life. On January 23, he sat in the kitchen over his controls and captured "The Sin of Silence" on tape. On Tuesday morning he got the news that the voice from the pulpit was still.

The next scene took place four years later in Hollywood. A movie producer was being interviewed by Celestine Sibley of the *Atlanta Constitution*. She had come to talk about the proposed film on the life of Peter Marshall.

"Mr. Engel, you probably know that Atlanta has always claimed Peter Marshall. Atlantans are all agog over the movie. What everybody wants to know is—who's going to play Peter?"

"I wish I knew. One thing sure. It's going to have to be a Britisher. I've said that from the beginning. Nobody else can handle the King's English as Marshall did.—But before we talk about casting, there's something I want you to hear—"

Miss Sibley later reported in her column:

Mr. Engel had a tape recorder by his desk and as I settled down he turned it on, and the rich, deep voice with its pleasant Scots' burr poured into the room. . . .

"You see," said Mr. Engel, turning off the machine, "the voice is magnificent—and it's going to take an English actor to play the role. I'd like Richard Burton, but nobody knows how long he'll be tied up on "The Robe." And then he has an engagement with the Abbey Theatre in Ireland. And of course, there's Lawrence Olivier. . . ."

Whether or not Olivier who has been playing Shakespeare with his wife, Vivian Leigh, would be interested, is something Fox is now trying to find out. . . .

"We'd thought of Richard Todd (of the 'Hasty Heart' and 'Robin Hood')," Mr. Engel added—

The girl standing in the doorway of the house in Pinkneys Green was small, blond. "Anything interesting in the mail?"

Her husband, Richard Todd, waved a letter at her. "Oh—so, so. A letter from America—Beverly Hills."

"One of the studios?"

"Fox. It's a formal query as to my being available—"

"For what?"

"Something I never heard of. 'A Man Called Peter.'"

"Well—are you—available?"

"Don't think so. I've more interesting things to do right here."

Five days later a copy of *A Man Called Peter* arrived by air parcel post. The actor read the book, but felt that he was not physically suited to the role. Peter Marshall had been of above-average height, broad-shouldered, originally a blond whose hair had darkened. Todd was inches shorter, a brunet.

Mr. Todd was also secretly afraid of what approach Hollywood might make to the story. He talked it over with his wife. "If they were to pull out the integrity and put all the emphasis on the love story—as they're likely to do, the picture would be a dud." Therefore he insisted that he would not even consider the role without seeing the finished script.

The script was at that time far from finished, but Mr. Engel sent the latest draft. Richard Todd was not impressed. The treatment seemed too long, unwieldy. He wrote Sam Engel, turning the part down and suggesting two other British actors who he felt could do it better than he. That, he thought, ended that.

But the studio persisted. Two weeks went by. One day a flat package arrived from Beverly Hills. It was a copy of one of Jack Ingram's tapes—"Were You There?"—a sermon on the crucifixion.

Later by transatlantic telephone Dick Todd told Mr. Engel, "I've played it over and over. Each time I'm more stirred. What an inspired word painter that man was. And what a sense of timing! The material is any actor's dream."

"You'll do it then?"

There was a pause. Then the voice with the clipped British accent said hesitantly, "I still can't commit myself. There's one more test I'd like to make. I wonder—may I have your permission to deliver part of one of the sermons over here and have the scene put on film?"

"Certainly. By all means. And we can use it as we would a screen test."

One evening at six, after a hard day's work in the studio, Mr. Todd rounded up some forty people. Deliberately, he picked an odd assortment. There were technicians, wardrobe and makeup people, some of the camera crew, several old-time character actors. In the front row was a hard-bitten blonde off the street, with her boy friend on her arm. None of the group knew why they were there or what was coming.

Dick Todd mounted a makeshift pulpit and looked out over his hastily gathered congregation. What he wanted was not only a screen test but a reaction from human beings. If Peter Marshall's sermon material could move this group, it would move anybody!

The words poured out over the Elstree sound stage. For eight minutes Todd spoke. When he had finished, the blonde in the front row was in tears. So were several others. An electrician came down off his perch and gripped the actor's hand, "You must do that picture. I never heard of it. But you must do it."

Dick Todd cabled the Fox studios that he would take the role.

It was from Mr. Engel that I got the news:

Dear Catherine:

By the time you receive this, Richard Todd will have been signed. He made a great, very great test for us! Everyone who has seen it was thrilled! Mr. Zanuck sent me a note saying, "I was simply mesmerized. I couldn't believe this was something on film." Todd's diction, accent, and delivery strikingly resemble Peter's. . . .

It would be very nice indeed if you would drop Mr. Todd a note. I enclose his address. . . .

Everything is going forward splendidly.

> *All the best,*
> *Sam*

I did write Mr. Todd. In his reply he mentioned the now famous tapes:

> *Pinkneys Green*
> *Maidenhead*
> *Berks.*

My dear Mrs. Marshall:

I was very pleased and very touched by your letter, and indeed by your kind thought in writing to me at all. . . .

I feel great humility and diffidence about my choice for this role. I am still very conscious of the fact that in appearance I cannot be as close as I would wish to the ideal person to personify Peter Marshall. . . .

I look forward very much indeed to meeting you while I am in America.
. . . In the meantime, I would appreciate very much indeed any pointers
which you could give me to help me with my characterisation. If you have
any other recordings, might I borrow them from you for a time during the
initial part of the progress on the film . . . ?

In the meantime, again very many thanks for your kindness, and my
sincere hope that our film will match up to the excellence of your book
and to your memories.

Yours sincerely,
Richard Todd

What Mr. Todd had in mind in asking to hear the other recordings
was not a forced imitation of Dr. Marshall's accent and delivery. Todd's
ideal characterization went much deeper.

"Each man is unique," he was later to say to me. "I'm not Peter
Marshall. But I can saturate myself with the timber of the man's voice,
with the sparkle of his personality, with the inner essence, until something of the man's spirit shines through. It's the difference between a
photograph and a painting. If I try to imitate rather than create an impression, my characterization will fail."

I was impressed by his sound and intelligent approach. In order to
achieve it, the British actor made several uses of the tapes. "I'm trying
an experiment," he explained to me. "I listen to Peter Marshall's voice
for a while just before falling asleep. That way, perhaps an impression
will be made on my subconscious mind that will come out later in depth-
dimension portrayal."

And when the time came for shooting, Todd was to order a tape
recorder brought to his dressing room. Often he would listen to a portion of a sermon between takes.

Mr. Engel was relieved to have the male lead settled. The matter of
the director had also been decided. Henry Koster, who had directed many
successful movies, including "Désirée" and "The Robe," had been chosen. As for Catherine, Mr. Engel had never been too concerned about
who was to play the part. He felt that a number of the younger actresses
could do it adequately. Shooting was scheduled to start in September.
July was drawing to a close—and still no Catherine.

Finally in late August, Eleanore wrote me that Eva Marie Saint and
Elizabeth Taylor were being considered for the role of Catherine. ". . .
Wouldn't you like to be played by the most beautiful girl in the world . . . ?"

I replied that I found it hard to understand the ways of the movie studios. I was appalled by the fact that the feminine lead had still not been chosen. Surely the September 20 starting date had been postponed. As for Elizabeth Taylor, she was, I feared, too beautiful—so beautiful that it might obscure the role itself.

After that, other actresses were considered—Jean Simmons, Dorothy McGuire, Donna Reed, and Jean Peters, who had recently starred in "Three Coins in the Fountain."

From the beginning, it had been Miss Peters whom the gossip columnists and movie magazines had reported as having captured the part. Many of these rumors were reported as fact months before the studio had even begun casting. This time, however, the rumors, no matter how premature, proved prophetic. Miss Peters was offered the role. Six days before shooting started, she accepted it.

Covington and Atlanta enjoyed their contact with the movie personnel. The day that the stars arrived, the *Atlanta Journal* ran headlines:

MOVIE CAMERAS WHIRRING AT NORRIS

Filming of Catherine Marshall's book *A Man Called Peter* began Friday morning on the shores of Norris Lake in DeKalb County following the arrival of Jean Peters and Richard Todd Thursday night. . . .

In Covington, hundreds of citizens dressed in the fashions of the 1930s acted as extras for the crowd scenes in the church, while most of the rest of the town watched. The *Journal* reported:

FILM FOLK CREATE UPROAR AT SCOTT

The usually quiet and serene campus of Agnes Scott College Saturday was in an uproar.

Stars Richard Todd and Jean Peters arrived early with the supervisor of the second unit, James D. Clark, and a small army of technicians and paraphernalia to begin filming campus sequences.

Following in their wake were some seventy-five extras (most of them Agnes Scott students) and dozens of fans wanting autographs. . . .

For three days all academic work was practically at a standstill. The professors were very patient. How else could they deal with 500 starry-eyed, movie-struck girls?

Then, by September 28, the campus shots were completed. The old cars had been driven off. The last camera had been loaded into the last truck. In the middle of the quadrangle stood one of the freshmen who had been used as an extra, gazing mournfully after the camera truck as it disappeared round the bend of the road. At that moment, the dean of women walked by. She saw the wistfulness written on the girl's face, the slim shoulders sagging. She heard the girl sigh, "And *now* what is there to live for?"

As soon as I had heard that Jean Peters was to play Catherine, I had written her, welcoming her to the cast. Probably the note went astray. At any rate there was no reply. I sent another note to her Atlanta hotel, saying that I hoped to meet her when the cast moved on to Washington.

The cast arrived in town, but Miss Peters was not with them. Mr. Eckhardt, the unit manager, explained that the star had for urgent personal reasons gone back to Hollywood. A stand-in was to be used for the Washington scenes.

Dick Todd telephoned me, came to dinner, and spent the evening talking out his role. Though I had been told about his height, I was not prepared to find him as short a man as he is. Already I knew how the studio planned to handle this—lifts in his shoes and carefully angled camera shots.

His personality and attitude delighted me. He was refreshingly candid and clear-eyed about himself. . . . "We cinema people aren't always realistic about ourselves. I try hard to be. I'm not brilliant, far from it. Therefore, in handling my roles, I have to do some plodding—just plain hard work."

It was also obvious that Mr. Todd was taking his Peter Marshall role seriously. There was no false sentimentality. He had a deep respect for the person he was portraying—for Peter's virility as a man, as well as for his gentleness and spiritual sensitivity.

He was also concerned about fine points. For example, he had begged from his London studio a skimpy, poorly cut suit which he felt would be just right for the immigrant Peter to wear for the shipboard scenes.

The British actor studied all the photographs of my husband in my possession; he questioned me carefully about Peter's pulpit gestures and mannerisms. By the time the evening was over, I had a secure feeling that Peter's part was in the right hands.

During the company's stay in Washington, I was impressed with how hard the crew had to work to make relatively small scenes.

Sometimes for a scene that had to be shot in semidarkness, like the one in which Peter, newly arrived in Washington, takes Catherine to see his church at midnight—shooting had to start as early as five-thirty in the morning. Since make-up took an hour and a half, this meant that Dick Todd and Marion McDonough—Miss Peters's stand-in—had to roll out of bed at 3:30 A.M.

Another Washington scene was a sidewalk shot of a line of people waiting on a rainy day to get into a church service. A local modeling agency was tapped for extras. The girls, feeling that this was their big chance, knocked themselves out with fresh hair-dos, make-up, and their prettiest clothes. But they were photographed with umbrellas hiding their faces, their backs to the cameras!

Actually, the historic old building in which Peter Marshall had preached had been torn down soon after his death and another church built on the site. The new building was enough like the old so that the exterior could be used for the movie. For the interior, a studio set had to be built in Hollywood, carefully copied from photographs taken on the last day of the old church's life.

Nor could the actual manse be used. It had by then been sold, and the new owner had made extensive changes. Therefore, a house of about the same architecture near Capitol Hill was chosen. There, with the Capitol dome in the background, more of the flavor of Washington could be packed into less film footage.

One morning I visited the Capitol Hill set. Huge trucks and vans were parked across the street from the "Manse." The car that Dick Todd was to drive stood in front of the house. Clouds obscured the sun. Mr. Todd, Miss McDonough, and the camera crew were standing by, waiting for the sun to break through. It never did, so work was postponed until the next day. It turned out that the clouds that day cheated me of the one chance I might have had to see a bit of my movie being shot.

During the waiting that day, Mr. Eckhardt had asked me to pose for some pictures with Mr. Todd. Naively I had agreed. Naively, because I should have asked how the pictures were to be used.

The Fox publicity people sent that particular picture to newspapers all over the nation. Usually the caption read:

On Hollywood set—Mrs. Marshall, technical director, with Richard
Todd, who portrays her husband in the picture "A Man Called Peter."

This was misleading. It was true that I was technical advisor to the
script, but not to the movie. There is a vast difference. As events turned
out, I never saw a single scene shot, and I was not in Hollywood while
any of the filming was going on.

I knew that if the men at Fox wanted me on the sets, they would
not hesitate to say so. But I did not want to force the issue. I also knew
that they would be receptive to suggestions from me only if they really
wanted those suggestions.

No such invitation ever came, so I stayed in Washington. For me it
was a difficult time. I was too intimately bound up with the movie project
to tell myself that it didn't matter how it turned out. Already I had given
it two years of my time and thought. My heart was with the work going
on in Hollywood. Try as I might, I couldn't extricate myself from it.

Only one recourse was left—prayer. Faith was needed. That's what
God was asking of me.

I had thought that I had to keep my fingers on the progress of the
movie venture. Sheer presumption probably! At any rate, denied that, I
must somehow muster enough faith to believe that God could take over
on the sets of "A Man Called Peter." I concentrated on that, remembering those hundreds of memorable letters promising prayer from my
friends.

Though my faith may have been small, it was deposited in the right
Source. It was rewarded. But there was a price to be paid. The price was
a lien on my pride. Later, much later, I learned some of the things that
happened on the sets.

One evening at the close of a day's work in one of the churches, Dick
Todd surprised everyone by making a special request. . . . "Would it be
possible for me to be left alone for a while here tomorrow before we start
shooting? I'd like to practice my sermon, really get into the spirit of it."

The director, Henry Koster, had had much experience with the tem-
peramental quirks of movie stars. He wondered if Todd's request was
temperament. If so, at least it was a new kind.

Aloud he said, "Okay. It will hold things up a bit. But I'm game.
How long do you want by yourself?"

"At least an hour and a half."

"All right. Then the rest of you won't report back here until ten tomorrow morning."

The next day a policeman on duty at one of the gates asked for time off to hear Todd preach. Wardrobe people, electricians, and mechanics quietly made their way to the church set. Afterwards, one of the mechanics described what happened. . . . "You should've seen the crowd listenin'. Practically everybody on the lot was there—from the lowliest mechanic like me to the directors and producers—everybody. You could've heard a pin drop. There was a kind of hush in the air. Then when Mr. Todd finished, and the director yelled 'Cut,' all of us started applaudin'. . . . I'll tell you somethin' else too. This is downright peculiar . . . I haven't heard a single cuss word on that set. Man, that's somethin'!"

Mr. Koster, the director, said it in another way during an interview, "There was a happy cooperative feeling on the set of 'A Man Called Peter'—something so rare that—well—Anyway, it's the happiest picture I've ever been connected with."

He went on to supply details. "It was like an aura around the picture. Everything good happened. We would go out on location. The rain would come down. Time was important. We would decide to get ready to shoot, anyway. When we were ready, the rain would stop, the sun would come out. . . . We hired two special people for the cast. They turned out to be all wrong. Sam Engel and I talked it over, trying to decide the best way to get rid of them. First, one resigned voluntarily. Then the other.

"I'm not superstitious, nor would I dare call these incidents divine intervention for our benefit. But things like that happened over and over. It gave me an odd feeling about the picture. Take that break we got at Annapolis, for instance."

Mr. Koster was referring to a scene in which Richard Todd, after preaching at the Naval Academy, had to leave the chapel and stride across the grounds toward his car. Just as the actor got halfway to the car, the doors of the building behind him burst open and all the midshipmen came pouring out. The movie crew had not dared to inconvenience the Academy by requesting anything like that. As it was, the uniformed cadets in the background added the perfect touch.

That same day another incident occurred, this time inside the chapel where Dr. Marshall's Pearl Harbor Day sermon was to be filmed. Twelve hundred midshipmen were in the pews. In the finished film, this scene turned out to be the longest single take in the history of the Fox studios. Mr. Todd was before the camera without a break for eight and a half minutes.

Everyone thought it unwise to put the cadets through that much. Therefore, Dick Todd was to start the sermon, let the cameras pick up shots of the chapel with close-ups of the men's faces as they listened.

James—fourth chapter—fourteenth verse: "For what is your life? It is even a vapor that appeareth for a little while and then vanisheth away." What a queer thing for James to say. . . .

Then the actor would do only the concluding sentences the rest would be shot in Hollywood. . . .

That life that shall never end . . . shall be the journey's end for the heart and all its hopes. It shall be the end of the rainbow for the child-explorers of God. We have His promise for that. . . .

But that was underestimating both the sermon and the cadets. The midshipmen became so interested in the content of the sermon that they started clamoring for more. Mr. Todd gave them the eight and a half minutes' worth. Then they called for the rest. In the end, Dick Todd had to preach the whole sermon before they would let him go.

These were small incidents. A more important one was something that happened to Marjorie Rambeau. "A small miracle," she called it. Miss Rambeau is a veteran actress with fifty-seven years of stage and screen experience. Still a beautiful woman, in "A Man Called Peter" she took the part of the fictitious character, Miss Fowler.

At twilight on a winter's afternoon in February, 1945, the actress and her sister Thelma were in an automobile accident. The sister was killed. Nine days later Miss Rambeau regained consciousness. She had been cruelly hurt—her right shoulder broken, fifty-six stitches in her head, her right leg opened to the bone, thigh to knee, the left hip socket crushed.

Three months later she left the hospital a cripple, confined to a wheel chair. After five years of constant pain, a corrective operation was performed, then a second. Her left leg was still three inches shorter than her right. The pain in the hip socket was gone, but there was muscular pain. Any undue strain or tiredness produced muscular spasms that could only be relieved by intermuscular injections. The doctors gave Miss Rambeau no hope of ever walking without her crutches.

Then Mr. Engel summoned her to the Fox studios. "You'd be perfect for the part of Miss Fowler. Can you walk without crutches?"

"I'm sorry to say—no. But do you remember 'Torch Song' with Joan Crawford?"

"Yes, of course."

"Well, you may remember that I did my entire part seated on a sofa. The best I can manage is a step or two with a cane for an entrance or an exit. But I'd like to have this part. I must have been one of the first to read the book. It came at a time when it meant so much to me. . . ."

Miss Rambeau left that afternoon with the script under her arm.

Production had been in progress for two weeks when the actress was called for her scenes. Special arrangements had been made, so that no walking would be required. She was to be photographed sitting in a church pew, then standing at the front of the church, leaning on her gold-headed cane.

The director asked for silence. Richard Todd started preaching. . . .

> Surely, He had power to lift from the dust
> of disease the flowers whose stems had been crushed
> or withered in the mildews of human misery!
>
> As this thought burned itself into her mind her faith
> was curiously stirred as it wrestled in the birth-throes
> of a great resolve.
>
> It was daring—fantastic, perhaps.
> Her heart thumped
> but it was worth trying.
> It could only fail
> and she was no stranger to failure. . . .
>
> *She touched Him in faith—in desperate believing*
> *faith and He stopped!*
> The touch of one anonymous woman in a crowd halted
> the Lord of glory. That is the glorious truth of this
> incident. She touched Him so can we. . . .*

*Marshall, Peter, *Mr. Jones, Meet the Master*, pp. 181,184, Fleming H. Revell Company, New York, 1949. Used by permission.

Suddenly, sitting there listening to Peter Marshall's words, the actress said to herself, "Marjorie, you do believe. Put yourself in God's hands. You *can* walk down that aisle."

The extras—acting the part of the congregation—stood up and started toward the front of the church. Marjorie got to her feet. No one paid any attention at first. But when she started walking down the aisle without her crutches, there was a concerted gasp.

Miss Rambeau motioned for silence; the rehearsal could not be interrupted. She walked the entire length of the aisle, 100 feet of it. As she reached the chancel, a stagehand, unable to believe his eyes, came running forward with a stool. He was so agitated that he almost knocked her over with it.

Marjorie's husband, Francis A. Grudger, a retired vice president of the E. I. du Pont de Nemours Company, was on the set and saw the incident. Practically holding his breath during her long trek, he had expected his wife to fall at any moment. By the time she reached the end of the aisle he was at her side, begging her to get off her feet immediately.

She refused. She had done it once. She would do it again—and again—for as many rehearsals as were necessary.

Her husband watched in agony. In vain, he pleaded with her to stop. He was sure that she would pay for her foolhardiness with hours of agonizing pain that night. Finally, unable to bear the sight any longer, he turned on his heel and left the set.

That night Miss Rambeau was tired, but there was no pain. Her maid prepared a hypodermic and put it on her night stand.

"Mr. Grudger said to have it ready just in case, madame."

"In case of what?" the actress asked. "There isn't any pain. I feel nothing but good healthy tiredness."

After the movie was released, the actress wrote to tell me about it. . . .

A miracle did happen to me while making the picture. A blessing from you and yours and our Saviour. I discarded my crutches one day after listening with my heart—not my ears—to one of Peter's sermons. To the utter amazement of everyone in the cast, I walked. God took over. I have never gone back to my crutches. There is no need.

Forgive this long letter. But I did so want you to know about it.

Gratefully,
Marjorie Rambeau

Of course, at the time I knew nothing at all of this. Back in Washington, I could only wait and wonder and hope. My first intimation of how the picture had turned out came in a note from Eleanore Griffin. It was a copy of a memo sent to everyone on the lot—a memo originally to Mr. Darryl Zanuck by Harry Brand, the head of publicity and exploitation:

> I just looked at a rough cut of "A Man Called Peter" and was held spellbound, and came out exalted. . . .
>
> This picture can't help but be a memorable achievement, and, because it is so unusual, you should be highly lauded for your courage in having it produced.
>
> I will write to New York to convey this information. . . .

Eleanore's accompanying note said, "This is just an echo of the feeling on the lot. There was never so much surprise and enthusiasm over a picture. . . ."

This was wonderful news but I still had mental reservations. After all, Mr. Brandt's memo had been for his boss's consumption.

Then on January 24, eighty clergymen, Catholic, Jewish, and Protestant, saw the same rough-cut version in a special showing on the Twentieth Century-Fox lot. No musical score had yet been dubbed in.

Later that day I had a telegram from Dr. Louis Evans, the former pastor of the Hollywood Presbyterian Church:

> WE SAW THE PREVIEW AND FELT WE HAD BEEN LIFTED BY THE ARMS OF A GREAT SWELLING SEA OF COURAGE AND FAITH. HAVE NO FEARS, AND IT WILL BLESS MILLIONS. GOD BLESS THE TEAM THAT MADE IT POSSIBLE.

I had enthusiastic comments from others who were present that day. While I was relieved at the good news, still I wanted to see for myself. But I had to wait another five weeks. By then, the picture was set in concrete; no more changes could be made. Already fifteen minutes' worth of the rough-cut version had hit the cutting-room floor.

Finally I was invited to a special meeting in the New York offices of Twentieth Century–Fox. I asked my long-time friend, A. D. Fuller, to go with me. On March 7, as we flew to New York, I kept wondering what I would say to Sam Engel, if the picture was not what I hoped. I was not willing to be a hypocrite. In any case, he knew me too well for me to deceive him.

The private theater on the fifth floor of the old Fox office building turned out to be an ornate baroque setting. There was only a handful of us in a room meant to seat several hundred. Several representatives from my publishing house were among those invited. On one side of me sat A. D.; on the other, my editor, Ed Aswell. In the row in front and across the aisle were a dozen or so Fox executives who had not yet seen the movie.

Only a few days before, Hedda Hopper had reported to the nation that "A Man Called Peter" was emotion-packed, a "six handkerchief picture." This had alarmed me. What if it were maudlin emotion, overdone, in poor taste?

On the other hand, if it was well done, I might break down completely. For that reason, I had been hoping that my first viewing might be private, with only my family and a few friends present.

The situation on March 7 was scarcely that. The publicity men there seemed as much interested in my reactions as in the picture. Knowing that, I was tense. I did not realize how tense until later that day. Every nerve was stretched taut; every emotion dammed up behind a wall of resolution; every hope steeled against disappointment.

The lights went off; the musical score came on. The name of the book that had become a part of my life flashed before me, set on a deep blue background. It was a peculiar feeling seeing my own name there in gold letters on the wide screen. The moment toward which I had worked and prayed was upon me.

The deep slashes of the cutting-room shears were immediately apparent—at least to me. Some memorable scenes had been sacrificed to length. We were catapulted all the way from Peter digging ditches in New Jersey to his graduation from Seminary.

Then came Dick Todd's first sermon material. . . .

There are men and women in the world today who say that God orders their lives—guides them in making decisions, answers their prayers, provides for their needs—in ways that are often strange and unexpected. That is the testimony of my own experience. And there are many here who can make the same statement. But if you, yourself, have not had that experience in your life, do not be too quick to jump to the conclusion that we who say these things are daft—mad. . . .

I couldn't believe what I was hearing! The voice was authentic. The message rang true. The words were vibrant with power. The spirit of the man I knew so well was there, coming through, spilling over, glowingly alive again. From that moment, I knew that whatever small faults the picture had, it was all right. The miracle I and hundreds of others had prayed for had happened.

When the lights came on, most of the rough-hewn Fox executives had their handkerchiefs out wiping their eyes. I had not wept; I was still much too tense. It was not until I saw the picture for the second time under quite different circumstances that my tears flowed too. Later I found out that the men that day were dismayed that I had not cried. They feared that my lack of obvious emotion meant that the picture was not a success.

In Hollywood Sam Engel was awaiting my reaction. On the way back to Washington, I carefully composed a wire to him:

THIS MORNING AT FOX'S NEW YORK OFFICE I SAW A MAN CALLED PETER. . . . PETER'S SPIRIT AND PERSONALITY COME THROUGH WITH COMPLETE INTEGRITY. EVEN THE MOST EMOTIONAL SCENES HAVE THE RESTRAINT OF REAL ARTISTRY. MAY THE PICTURE BECOME A MILESTONE BOTH IN MOTION PICTURE HISTORY AND IN THE SPIRITUAL LIFE OF THE NATION.

I could not forget my fan-mail friends. Surely they deserved the next word. . . .

In November, 1953, I sent a letter to many of my friends asking for specific prayer in connection with the making of A Man Called Peter into a motion picture.

Sixteen months have passed since then. The movie is finished and in most cities will be released shortly before Easter. I wanted to wait until I had seen the finished product to report back to you. . . .

Out of this experience, I have learned one of the greatest lessons of my life. The lesson is that our God is still an Omnipotent God.

In the two years "A Man Called Peter" was in process, I went through some very bad moments. At times, those concerned were on the verge of very wrong decisions. My faith often wavered and faltered. . . . I was Technical Advisor for the screenplay. But from the moment that shoot-

ing started, I was not Technical Advisor for the movie itself. I saw none
of it shot.

Yet God's Hand was on the project, so He did not need mine. He still
reigns in His World! In response to prayer, He can still rule and overrule;
can still have His way with His creatures—even in Hollywood. It has been
an awe-inspiring and humbling experience to have seen this worked out
step by step. The Lord God Omnipotent still reigns . . . !

Fourteen
"All That Glitters. . . ."

AT THE BYRD Theater in Richmond, Virginia, the special preview showing of "A Man Called Peter" was just over. I had not been able to attend because of radio and press interviews in New York, but Peter John was there with my mother.

In the theater lobby, a newspaper woman elbowed her way through the crowd toward a tall blond boy. "I understand that you are Peter Marshall's son. How did you like the picture?"

"Okay—very good."

"How true to the facts is it? Do you have any criticisms?"

"Well—maybe—our Cape Cod cottage is bigger and nicer than the one in the movie—"

When the article came out the next day, March 25, in the *Richmond Times-Dispatch*, it reported . . .

They gave their unqualified approval to the picture, although Peter John stated that the Cape Cod cottage in the film is larger and more elaborate than the one he and his parents occupied during summer vacations. . . .

Peter was furious. This was his first brush with publicity, and he felt that he had been grievously misquoted on an important point. The cottage had always been his favorite place. "The one in the movie was

235

just a box," he railed. "If ours were smaller than that, it would be a *dog* house."

"You'll have to get used to being misquoted," I laughed at him out of a little recent experience. "It happens all the time."

My trip to New York included six press interviews, three radio broadcasts, newsreel pictures in Mr. Spyros Skouras's office, the recording of a speech greeting for the Glasgow opening and one for Japan.

The newspaper people were consistently gracious with me. I found them easy to talk to, perhaps because I have never been on the defensive with the press. Always my viewpoint has been that reporters have a job to do, and that I want to give them the best possible interview.

However, my baptism of fire was still to come. On my last day in New York, reporters from a national weekly news magazine contacted me. My time was filled, but they were insistent. Finally it was arranged that they would interview me on the way to La Guardia Airport. Two brisk and businesslike women reporters were sent for the job.

After some preliminary questions, one of the women said, "We'd better be frank with you, Mrs. Marshall. We're here for one purpose above all others. We have emphatic instructions from the top brass to uncover the facts about your finances. There are some people who think that you've made a good thing out of the book—and now the movie—who question your motives—"

The other woman added, "Of course, it's entirely up to you how you'll answer. You can give us the usual blunt 'no comment' and tell us it's none of our business. But in that case, we'll dig up the facts anywhere we can get them, and you'll have to take the consequences. Or you can square with us."

I could feel the blood rushing to my face. It sounded like an inquisition. This type of approach made the rest of my interviews seem like milk toast. Despite my annoyance, I tried to think fast.

Suddenly I knew that frankness and putting myself, along with the facts, at the mercy of the reporters was the only intelligent course. Some of the things they would want to know undoubtedly were none of their business, but I knew that the minute I clammed up, I risked their hostility.

"Look," I said. "I have nothing to hide. Suppose I state the facts, and then leave to your discretion what you'll print. I ask only that you stay within the bounds of good taste. But first, as to the sale of the movie rights, I don't even know whether or not I have the right—so far as Fox is concerned—to reveal the figure."

Both reporters laughed. "Don't worry about that. We've already dug that up. Not exactly whopping—$30,000. But do you get any percentage of box-office receipts in addition?"

"No—none—$30,000—period. And I'm sure you know that my publisher, lawyer, agent, and Uncle Sam got hunks of that. I tried to take an even smaller amount plus the percentage plan, because I believed in the movie. But my lawyer couldn't swing it."

An exceedingly frank talk followed. My openness seemed to win the women. Still I scanned the next issue of the magazine with some misgivings.

Their report used most of a page. It was restrained and sympathetic. . . .

From her Washington, D.C., home this week a . . . woman headed for New York to see a movie. Seven years ago, Catherine Marshall was the mistress of the manse and the happy wife of Dr. Peter Marshall, pastor of the New York Avenue Presbyterian Church in Washington and Chaplain of the U.S. Senate. This week she was to attend the premiere—simultaneously presented in Glasgow—of "A Man Called Peter," the film version of her best-selling biography of her late husband. . . .

For one thing, she receives between 150 and 200 letters a month and has had to hire a full-time secretary. She has made no great fortune from her writings (the movie rights, for example, sold for only $30,000) and while she is comfortably situated, she cooks all the meals and employs only a part-time maid. . . .

The simultaneous premieres to which the magazine referred were to be on the night of March 31, 1955, at Roxy's in New York and at La Scalla in Glasgow, Scotland. The Roxy opening was to be for the joint benefit of the Highland Fund (for the economic and social development of the Scottish Highlands, of which Lord Malcolm Douglas-Hamilton was chairman) and for the Caledonian Hospital in Brooklyn.

Jean Peters had sent word that she could not attend either premiere; therefore I had agreed to appear with Richard Todd at Roxy's. I had no idea what this "appearance" was to entail.

On the day before the premiere I flew to New York for an appearance on Garry Moore's *I've Got a Secret*. The rest of the family was to follow later. The trip up was rough. In the midst of what the airlines call "turbulence," a voice came over the intercom . . . "Message for Mrs. Morell, on landing at La Guardia, will she please remain on the plane until all other passengers are off, and deplane last?"

Since the name "Mrs. Morell" meant nothing to me, I paid no attention. The sign "Fasten Seat Belts" was on all the way, so there was no chance to freshen up. Before we landed, I didn't even bother to powder my nose. Feeling very casual about the whole thing, I started to get off with the rest of the passengers.

It was raining, and there was a cold whipping wind. Suddenly through the sound of the wind and the rain, I heard the unmistakable wail of a bagpipe. Then I saw a group of people coming toward the plane, several of them dressed in kilts, with the bagpiper in their midst. As soon as they spied me coming down the plane steps with the rest of the passengers, the group began frantically waving me back.

An airlines official standing at the bottom of the steps asked, "Are you Catherine Marshall?"

"Yes, I am."

"Would you please go back into the plane and wait until everyone else is off? We tried to send a message to that effect but apparently it got garbled."

So that was it! Docilely, I retreated and sat down, wondering what was coming. Finally even the pilot and the navigator left the plane. Then I timidly started down the steps for the second time.

The lone piper took a deep breath, started up again. He was succeeding in making an incredible amount of noise for one man. Two photographers yelled above the noise of the wind and the rain, "Hold it." So with the pipes screaming in my left ear and the blowing rain pelting down, I waited while two girls dressed in kilts rushed forward to thrust a huge wet bouquet of roses into my arms. On the other side of me stood a man whom I did not know. He turned out to be Lord Malcolm Douglas-Hamilton, straight from Scotland to represent his Highland Fund.

Meanwhile, any feminine pride in appearance left to me was being borne away on the screeching wind. Wisps of my hair were blowing across my eyes. The ribbon ties at the neck of my blouse were standing straight out. On my nose were glistening raindrops. Looking more like a drowned rat by the minute, I managed a sickly smile.

The publicity stunt over, I was taken to the Warwick Hotel, where Fox had reserved a suite of rooms. Several messages were waiting, including one informing me casually that Roxy's was sold out for the next night—6,000 people; that I was to appear on the stage with Richard Todd and would be asked to say a "few words"; that Fox had a standing arrangement with a certain furrier; and that I was to be given the loan of any fur wished to wear to the premiere.

The next morning, half wondering if someone was having a little joke at my expense, I took a cab around to the fur salon—one of New York's oldest and most famous houses. Since I had a full schedule, including an appointment at the hairdressers, I planned to take only thirty minutes to select the wrap.

A frock-coated gentleman met me at the elevator and led the way through a deeply carpeted foyer to a room with gilt French furniture and many mirrors. There he introduced me to two salesladies.

They looked me over carefully, while pretending not to look at all. "Tell us—your gown for tonight—describe it," one of them said.

"It's white lace, simple lines, a molded, off-the-shoulder bodice, floor length, very full skirt."

"White—mm—hmm—Well, dear, first of all, do you have any particular type of wrap in mind?"

"I don't think I'd like one of the fluffy furs—like white fox. I thought it might be fun to try white ermine first."

"All right then, ermine—perhaps also white mink. We'll have some modeled for you—"

Two models appeared wearing the most gorgeous furs I had ever seen. Quickly I decided that the white mink left ermine far behind. My exclamations of delight drew other members of the establishment into the room.

Soon one of the men standing watching said, "You say that you have to appear on the stage at the Roxy tonight? Then this has to be right. And we really can't do it correctly without seeing your gown. Why not let us send a messenger around to your hotel for the dress?"

I couldn't imagine their wanting to go to that much trouble, but I agreed, and gave them the information about my room number and where the dress was hanging. Then we sat down in the gilt chairs to wait. Eagerly they asked me about the book—how long had I taken to write it?—and the movie—what was it like to see yourself portrayed on the screen? When finally the messenger arrived with my white lace over his arm, we were good friends. Now they insisted that I model the dress and furs.

We started all over. There seemed to be no other customers that morning, so the entire staff stood around making comments. After much discussion, the consensus of opinion was that none of the white furs would do. They were too creamy against the chalk white of the dress. Then too, pictures—newsreel and stills—were to be taken. Contrast was needed.

Wrap followed wrap . . . ranch mink and Emba blue mutation mink. "Not the right shades for the dress. Try something darker." A hooded stole of autumn-haze mutation mink . . . "Style not right for her, not young enough—"

Then one of the men interrupted, "We haven't yet tried sable. Try a tiny wrap in Russian sable."

So the sables were brought in, deep-skinned, glossy, precious. I slipped into a waist-length jacket with a stand-away collar. It felt just right. But then, curiously, I looked at the price tag—and gasped.

One of the men clapped his hands. "That's *it*! Beautiful! Perfect!"

"It really is," a woman said more cautiously. "Very youthful. And just right with the dress."

So it was decided. Someone took away the little fur and my dress to box them. Four people escorted me to the elevator! "It was such a delight to meet you. Have a wonderful night—real Cinderella night. We'll send a messenger for the jacket in the morning."

Haltingly, I tried to thank them, still scarcely believing what I had just experienced. . . . All that enthusiasm, warmth, interest, and outgoingness in the City of New York . . . three hours of it . . . when the furriers knew that nothing more than the loan of a wrap was involved. . . . Who could have believed it?

Peter John had asked for time off from school for the premiere. Mother and Father had also been easy to persuade, but I had some trouble with the rest of my family. From both my sister Em and my sister-in-law Mary, I received almost identical replies, "We'd love to go, but since the last several years have been given over to babies instead of social life, we haven't anything to wear."

Then some of their neighbors and friends began insisting, "You just have to go. It would be a shame to miss it. Don't let clothes stop you. We'll lend you anything we have."

Their offerings poured in—evening dresses, fur wraps, evening purses, gloves, and costume jewelry. The two girls relaxed and took it in stride.

After days of trying on and swapping, Mary ended up with a dress of my secretary's, a neighbor's fur coat, and some of her sister's jewelry.

Em finally decided on a dress and wrap of mine, a neighbor's jewelry, and a pair of Mother's gloves.

Compared to this, the men had no problem. They simply rented tuxedos, though we had some trouble in finding one for Peter John with long enough sleeves. And Father, being rather stout in the middle, had to have careful tucks taken in his cummerbund so that it didn't stand up straight just above his stomach like a kangaroo's pouch.

With this odd assortment of possessions, my family arrived at the Warwick Hotel about noon on the day of the premiere. Then there was enacted a little drama for which the Warwick personnel were ill prepared.

Before the rest of the party was out of the two cabs, Father had charged into the hotel lobby and up to the desk. His deep-throated ministerial voice rang loud and clear, "I'm John A. Wood. Mrs. Marshall is my daughter, and we want to check in."

"Yes, sir. Do you have reservations, Mr. Wood?"

"Yes, we do. Someone from Twentieth Century-Fox made them. I don't know whose name they're under."

The clerk looked puzzled. Then as if resigned to the hazards of his occupation, he said patiently, "Wood? Let me check, sir— We have nothing under the name of Wood. What did you say the other name was?"

Dad boomed, "Mrs. Marshall, Mrs. Peter Marshall."

By that time everyone in the Warwick knew that someone by the name of Marshall had arrived. After several more exchanges, four keys were finally produced. Father appropriated them and, with the air of a conquering hero, led his little army to the wrong rooms on the wrong floors.

After another half hour of stewing, Mother and Father were installed in 1407; Em and Harlow in 1203; Mary and Bob in 1411. But the luggage was still mixed up. The total effect of the hour's maneuver had the hotel management so confused that they were leaving Father and his luggage strictly alone.

Still Father was not satisfied. He felt that the hotel would want to know which couple now had which room. Once again he galloped up to the harried desk clerk.

"Young man, I want to report a change in the Marshall party's rooms."

"Yes, sir, if you don't like your rooms, perhaps we can arrange—"

"They're fine. It's just that we moved my daughter and her husband into room 1203, when you had reserved 1407 for them. Mrs. Wood and I are now in—"

"Now I don't quite get all that. Aren't your daughter and her son in a suite on the seventh floor?"

"Yes—no—you misunderstand me. I have another daughter, Mrs. Hoskins. She and her husband are now in 1203, and—"

"Mr. Wood, let's start all over. There's something I don't quite—"

That session didn't end the matter. Each time during the next twenty-four hours that Father walked through the lobby, he and the desk clerk had a workout at getting the record straight.

The havoc Father wrought with the Warwick's bookkeeping system was clearly reflected in the final bill. It read simply: "Marshall party. Rooms for two nights—$96.42."

That evening we had ringside seats from which to observe the showmanship that goes into a movie premiere. Three limousines were to be sent around to the hotel at seven-thirty. Every detail had been planned—which member of the family was to sit in which car, the route, the moment at which we would arrive at Roxy's.

The three long, black limousines proceeded slowly. As soon as we turned into Seventh Avenue, we could see the searchlights and hear a bagpipe band. For the last three blocks, the cars had to inch their way because of the crowds. At ten minutes to eight we double-parked around the corner from Roxy's to wait until the exact moment we were due to arrive. At three minutes to eight we drew up before the theater. Cordons of police were holding the people back in order to keep a cleared space on the sidewalk. Both the outer and inner lobbies were decorated with tartan and heather, and there were scores of photographers and radio interviewers with portable microphones.

A Fox man took me by the elbow and tugged me from place to place through the closely packed crowd—to be introduced to this person—"to say a few words, please" into that microphone.

I was as interested in watching the celebrities arrive as everyone else. I couldn't help wondering how much pressure had been put on some of them to be present in order to have "names" there—Jayne Meadows and her sister Audrey, Gloria Swanson, Monica Lewis, Rudy Vallee, William Reid—the royal chief of the Scottish clans in the United States and Canada—Lord and Lady Douglas-Hamilton, Mr. Skouras, the president of Twentieth Century–Fox, and his wife, Mr. and Mrs. Richard Todd.

Once I almost lost my tall son when he lingered behind to stare at Terry Moore.

By eight-thirty the hullabaloo was over, and we were shown to our seats. The theater lights went out; the stage lights went on. Richard Todd, now wearing a pointed goatee for the filming of "Sir Walter Raleigh," came to escort me to the stage. Others joined us there—William Maclair, the executive director of Roxy's; Lord Douglas-Hamilton; and some representatives from the Caledonian Hospital.

Standing there on the stage, I had an impression only of light—light—light—from the blinding footlights. When my time came to step up to the microphone, my heart was beating wildly. There was the feeling of being stranded, engulfed in white incandescent heat. I was groping through a blazing sea of light to make contact with an audience whose faces were out there somewhere, but were lost to me.

I spoke of the fact that almost three years of dreaming and hoping, of resolution and hard work, of teamwork unparalleled in my experience, had gone into the picture; of the debt that I owed to Mr. Engel, Mr. Koster, Jean Peters, Richard Todd, and many more. . . .

Then it was time for the movie. Throughout that particular showing I had every antenna out, alert to audience reaction. Very soon I became aware of the sophistication of the New Yorkers. They laughed at some of the wrong places and did not laugh when they were supposed to. The thought crossed my mind that perhaps this wasn't a "big city" movie. Later this impression was verified by the fact that the picture was not the success in New York that it was in smaller cities and towns.

I had seen the movie but once before. For this second viewing, I relaxed enough to let myself be swept into it. I wept at times; yet had little sense of reality that I had lived out the role I was now seeing on the screen. I had trouble identifying myself with Jean Peters, even though this was a girl with my hair-do and a gesture or two typical of me. Todd's role was a little more real to me. In one scene—the first one in which he did some preaching—I could hear Peter. Then in a scene lasting a few seconds—portraying Peter in an oxygen tent after his heart attack—I could see my husband. For me these were two completely authentic moments.

Still, when the light came on, I must have been in quite a fog because I struggled for several minutes to get my arms into the sleeves of the borrowed sable jacket. Finally I discovered that I had been trying to put it on upside down.

The rest of my family came down to earth more quickly. Back at the hotel, Peter said that premieres always made him hungry, and couldn't we please get something to eat?

So at almost midnight, the eight of us trouped into the nearest drugstore—tuxedos, trailing dresses and all. We perched on stools at the counter while Peter John nibbled on a three-decker club sandwich and gulped down a double vanilla malted. I had considerable trouble hanging on to a soda with one hand and the sable jacket with the other, while trying to keep the voluminous skirts of my white lace dress off the floor.

Meanwhile the talk flew back and forth as we shared our varied impressions of the evening. . . . "Who was that distinguished-looking couple sitting behind you, Catherine? They seemed to know you." . . . "I like Dick Todd with a goatee." . . . "Jean Peters was at her best in the Youth Rally scene. She's just as cute as a bug's ear. . . ."

Finally curiosity got the better of one of the soda-fountain boys. "Look, this is none of my business," he blurted out, "but are you people refugees from a night club? Or where in t'thunder have you been?"

The trip back to Washington the day after the premiere was in sharp contrast to the trumped-up fanfare of my arrival at La Guardia. The rest of my family was returning by train, so I joined them. By nine the next morning, Cinderella had shed the sables and had sent them back by bonded messenger. Ten o'clock found her in her own clothes, sitting on her suitcase in Pennsylvania station, waiting patiently for the ten-thirty train to be called—not a photographer nor a Fox man in sight.

I sat there reading William K. Zinsser's account of the premiere and his critique of the movie in the *New York Herald Tribune* . . .

. . . there is no reason why it shouldn't please all the people who like the book and several million more . . . told simply . . . acted well . . . refreshingly free of the sticky piety that mars so many Hollywood ventures into the spiritual life. . . .

So far so good. One reviewer on our side. But already I was wondering how the nation as a whole would receive this movie.

The first reports were disheartening, and as it turned out, misleading. In Los Angeles the picture opened at Grauman's Chinese Theatre. A week after the New York premiere, I received a note from Eleanore Griffin:

Dearest Catherine:
Just a stricken note. For all the wonderful reviews, "Peter" is flopping at the box office. This just can't happen. You prayed for it to be a wonderful picture—so pray that people will go to see it. Love,

Eleanore

No, it just couldn't happen. Though it would mean nothing to me financially, I naturally had hoped that the picture would be a real success at the box office. This alone would prove something about American tastes to the Hollywood movie makers that I longed to see proved: that spiritual help related directly to people's real problems would draw movie audiences as strongly as Hollywood's two favorite magnets—escapist entertainment and unabashed sex.

A few days later came another note from the script writer:

Dear Catherine:
Sam just called to tell me that AMCP is turning into a smash. Simply fabulous—and from word-of-mouth advertising. I am so happy. I hope you heard Bing Crosby interrupt his radio program to rave about "A Man," probably the nicest thing that has happened. Love,

Eleanore

The reviews of which Eleanore spoke were consistently good—with a single exception. I read scores of them, and so far as I know, only *Time* magazine's was adverse:

. . . And yet, for all its big talk about God, Peter Marshall's story as it emerges on the screen has depressingly little to say about religion. On the evidence given in the film, the man was more to be praised for his social than for his spiritual qualities. The film, much more strongly than the book, gives the impression that Peter Marshall was a great salesman, who sold Christianity the way another man might sell frontage in an exclusive suburb. And his death at 46, which is apparently intended to move one like the death of a martyr, has instead a kind of sorry unimportance on the screen, as if Connecticut, and not Heaven, had been his destination.

This acid account brought me some curious little experiences. Several people (who apparently still believed everything they read in print) wrote me, saying that they had read *Time*'s comments and were bitterly disappointed that I had thus betrayed Peter Marshall. They had no intention of going near this picture.

In my reply, I pointed out that there was at least food for thought in the fact that *Time*'s reaction seemed to be a minority report—in fact a minority of one. I was surprised that they were willing to judge and condemn something on secondhand evidence. I suggested merely that they see the movie and let it stand or fall on its own merits.

To a person, each correspondent went to see the picture, loved it, wrote to tell me so, and to apologize for the tone of the letter he had written earlier.

A letter from Mr. Engel summarized for me how the picture was doing . . .

Dear Catherine:

In this country and Canada it is a solid hit everywhere. . . . Word-of-mouth is so good that invariably the returns are greater the second week than the first. Typical of this capability to build on itself is this cable which Mr. Skouras received the other day from Ernest Turnbull, our Fox representative in Australia . . .

"'Man Called Peter' has established remarkable performance by breaking all time nonholiday first week record. Stop. Second week exceeded first week. Stop. Third week exceeded second, and fourth week exceeded all previous three weeks. Stop. . . ."

Unfortunately and inexplicably, the picture is turning out to be financially disappointing in Scotland and England. In the latter case, it got a bad break. It was released during the London newspaper strike. Consequently movie-goers never saw the reviews, which were excellent. In the British Isles, movie goers pay much more attention to critics than they do in the United States. . . . However, the picture's ability to generate good-

word-of-mouth opinion may indicate that there was a more serious rea-
son why it hasn't done as well there. . . .

Whatever the reason for the growing interest in the picture, I felt sure it was not due to the ads run by Twentieth Century–Fox. About this time I was contacted frequently by Fox's advertising department, who were eager for me to make public appearances. During one of our telephone conversations, I requested that they let me see some of their advertising copy. They sent me a package of sample blurbs, but not until after they had been released to national periodicals and newspapers. To say that I was shocked at some of them and felt that they were mislead-ing is to put it mildly. . . . "Their love surges with exaltation from the first second to the last sigh. . . ." "It could only have been written by the woman who loved him. . . ." "Let yourself glow with 'A Man Called Peter.'" They might have been blurbs for any torrid love story.

Life magazine, in its issue of April 4, gave a five-page spread to the picture but was caustic in its comments on Fox's advertising:

Now "A Man Called Peter" is to be released in a sentimental though credibly artistic form, as a movie which will certainly be even more suc-cessful. It will owe no thanks, however, to some ads by 20th Century–Fox ("He was a lovin' kind of guy. . . ." "He was God's kind of guy") that set something of a record for plain bad taste and skirted close to blasphemy.

Soon it became apparent what was happening. The picture, like the book, was not reaching its greatest success in the large cities. But when it hit grass-roots America, and when the word-of-mouth reaction began spreading, then everywhere theater managers had to hold it over. To the surprise of most of the movie industry in that year of 1955, "A Man Called Peter" was to chalk up Fox's largest box-office take.

The movie won a new group of friends that my book had not seri-ously touched—the teen-agers. Across the nation, they flocked to see "A Man Called Peter." They went and went again—three times, four times, seven times. The record—so far as I know—is twelve times.

The picture seemed to call forth all their latent idealism, their long-ing for someone to put on a pedestal. It launched their own private dream-ing, and sometimes swung the dreaming into surprising action.

Their letters piled into the Fox studios asking for copies of Jean Peters's Youth Rally speech. . . .

I've seen the movie four times. But I want to know and keep every word of Jean Peters's speech—especially that part about learning from a man what it means to be a woman. Will you please send me a copy of that talk. . . ?

They wrote to me exuberant, bubbling over, telling me about themselves, asking me for this and that, especially for a picture of Peter Marshall, expecting an answer in the next mail. Always Peter had won the teen-agers in life; now he had his favorite audience back. . . .

Pottstown, Penn.

Dear Mrs. Marshall:

I will be 15 on November 3. I have just come back from seeing "A Man Called Peter" for the seventh time. . . . I think that sermon Peter gave at Annapolis was the best he ever gave. Could you send me a copy of it so that I could memorize it?

Also, would you please send me a picture of Dr. Marshall—wallet size will be fine—for my very own.

Yours truly,
(with a cramped finger)

South Wales, N.Y.

Dear Mrs. Marshall:

I am 14 and away at boarding school. Recently I have seen the movie "A Man Called Peter" and after that I read the book. I have greatly admired Peter and the way he was close to God. . . .

On Monday night, December 2, I received a call from home saying that my father had had a heart attack. I immediately became panicky. Then I remembered what you did when Peter had a heart attack. So I prayed the way you did. Then my being scared left, and I felt a peace of mind that was so welcome. . . .

I am writting you this letter, because you are the one who taught me this through your sturring book A Man Called Peter.

Thank you for everything.

Love, your friend and admirer,

Des Plaines, Ill.

Dear Mrs. Marshall:

I'm 14 years old, and last summer I saw the movie "A Man Called Peter." Since then, I have read the book four times, and the story seems more wonderful to me each time. . . .

It would be impossible to tell anyone how Peter has changed my life, but God knows. . . .

Now my one ambition is to enjoy life as Peter did, to have his faith, to know God as he did, and to serve God as he did. Then I know I'll be happy. . . .

Very sincerely yours,

And from a somewhat older boy . . .

Anderson, S.C.

My dear Mrs. Marshall:

I realize the contents of this letter will be startling. . . . I work for a newspaper. I'm the assistant sports editor. . . . I had planned some day to be a teacher-coach, that is, until last April. . . .

Then one night in April, I was alone. It was 8:45. Something within seemed to say "Go and see 'A Man Called Peter'." I did.

Then came the scene where young P. M. was walking across the moors in a fog. Suddenly I felt as if there was nothing in the theatre but a Voice and me. "So, it's You, God. So it's You." The words pounded in my heart. It frightened me.

Afterwards I drove out to the lakeside, seeking some sort of answer. It's a long story, but I want to tell it step by step. . . .

Well, the net result is that I've found my real vocation. I'm going to be a minister. I'm to enter Columbia Seminary in the fall. It's strange and wonderful and all because I went to see a movie. . . .

May I ask you this one favor? Will you pray for me as you did for Peter Marshall?

Sincerely,

The ultimate touchstone of the movie's success for me did not lie in the realm of money, but in human values.

When I had written that prayer letter to my correspondents even as the movie was being conceived, I had dreamed of "vast audiences streaming onto the sidewalks of a hundred thousand Main Streets, entertained, uplifted, inspired, with the thought singing through many a mind . . . 'If God could solve Peter Marshall's problems, maybe He can solve mine—and my nation's. I'm going to give Him a chance. . . .'"

And Mr. Engel, the movie producer, had dreamed of "A Man Called Peter" helping especially with those universal problems that prod all men into uneasiness—death—grief—immortality.

He and I had dreamed more accurately than we knew. Ultimately our dreams had been clothed in reality, had lived and breathed. The true stories that came to me spoke for themselves. Those dreams had walked straight into human hearts. . . .

At the Miracle Theater in Miami, the special preview showing of the picture was just over. A dozen men, most of them strangers to one another, were in the men's room.

"I'd heard only vaguely of this guy Marshall," one man said to another. "How old was he when he died?"

His companion seemed to be thinking about something else . . . "I don't know—pretty young."

A tall man in the corner said, "He was forty-six."

Someone else commented, "Those Senate prayers were sure pungent—most unusual. But that one scene, where Peter was shown praying in the Senate, was curiously chopped up—"

Several agreed. The tall man said, "I have it straight from the horse's mouth— One of the chief problems of making this movie was with length. That chopped-up feeling was the fault of the cutting room."

Another man said, "You know, I'm a naturalized American. That scene towards the end—when the Marshall family was walking the little cocker—what was his name—with the Capitol dome in the background—that was beautiful. Something about that scene got me. I felt a great surge of gratitude for being an American—"

No one spoke for a minute. Then the tall man in the corner said laconically, "The cocker's name is Jeff."

As one man, the group turned to the tall one. "Hey, how do you know so much about it?"

"I'm Bob Ingraham. I gave Jeff to the Marshalls. I'm their neighbor on Cape Cod."

A tight little knot of interested men gathered round. The questions flew. Time passed; Mr. Ingraham was an interesting talker.

Outside in the theater lobby score of impatient wives stood cooling their heels, wondering what on earth was going on behind the sacrosanct door marked "Men." . . .

The letter was postmarked "Lynchburg, Virginia." "This is a true story," the young woman named Violet wrote. "You should know about it. . . ."

"A Man Called Peter," which had been held over for some time, was in its last few days in Lynchburg. All week I had tried to get my mother and father to go. But each time they had said that it just didn't suit that day.

Then early Saturday morning I was tidying up, vacuuming. Something seemed to insist "Try again today."

Mama said, "I'll ask Father. But I know he won't go on a Saturday."

"But tell him that it's the last day."

When Mama returned to the telephone, she seemed surprised, "Father said he'd try to go. He'll deliver his eggs before noon."

So the three of us went to the 2:30 show. Afterwards as Papa let me out at my front door, he said, "I like that movie more than any I've ever seen— especially the way Peter Marshall spoke of dying."

Well, Catherine Marshall, at eight o'clock that night, Papa was watching the Jackie Gleason Show. He had his shoes kicked off, his feet up on the big ottoman, his bride of fifty years by his side. And suddenly, he just closed his eyes and joined Peter Marshall. As simple as that.

I wouldn't trade that Saturday afternoon for all the money in the world. I just thought you'd be grateful to know the contribution you and Peter Marshall made to the last day of my father's life. . . .

In late October and early November, 1955, seven Russian journalists visited the United States. A public relations man whom I know was asked by the State Department to be one of those to squire the visitors around the nation.

On Saturday afternoon, November 12, he telephoned me. "We're just back from our tour," he explained. "It's been quite an experience! I've a favor to ask of you. It will take a little explaining though—"

"I can't imagine—Go ahead—"

"Well when we were in Hollywood, the seven editors were shown three movies. Each of the three major studios was asked to choose one as being representative of the industry. They were "Harvey," "An American in Paris," and "A Man Called Peter." Did you know that?"

"No—I certainly didn't."

"Your movie was translated for them as they saw it—even the sermon material. When the translator finished, he was in tears, and so were several of the Russians."

"But aren't they usually pretty emotional?"

"On the contrary, that was the first time all the way across the country that I'd seen them really touched. Well, after that, they couldn't seem to get that picture off their minds. They kept bringing it up, kept asking me questions. When we got to Phoenix on our way back, one day out of a clear sky, one of the men said almost defiantly, 'I don't think that Catherine Marshall exists.' I said, 'Sure, she exists. I know her. Would you like to meet her?'"

After a little pause he went on, "You see, they were intrigued—very curious as to whether the story you wrote could really be true. Well, then I had a brainstorm—'I go to a certain church in Washington,' I told him. 'If I could clear it with the State Department and arrange it with Mrs. Marshall, would you like to meet her there and attend a typical American church service?'"

"I think I know what's coming—" I said.

"Probably you do—the State Department has given its blessing, though they seemed a trifle astonished. Would you be willing to meet us at my church tomorrow?"

The next day I was at the church at a quarter to eleven. Five of the seven Russians were there, together with my friend and one interpreter. The Russians were big, energetic-looking men who seemed a little uncomfortable in city clothes.

The introductions were garnished with much bowing and scraping. One of the Russians, Boris Izakov of *International Life*, spoke English.

Mr. Izakov asked, "Was the movie made right after the book?"

"Yes, it was."

"When we were seeing it, we had the feeling that these were real people, and that this was the real America."

Then it was time for the church service. The theme of the minister's sermon that Sunday was Christian love, the necessity of our forgiving other people, no exceptions allowed. I kept thinking what a strange thesis this idea of Christian love must seem to the Russians. I wondered how much of the service and the sermon they could grasp through the interpreter. But perhaps the Spirit of God was interpreting at a depth that no translator could.

After the service, the Russians questioned me further about the movie. Then one of them asked, "How old is your son?" And before I could answer, "Would you like to see pictures of my family?"

Several of the men began pulling pictures out of their wallets, and proceeded to tell me the precise ages of their children. "We leave for home tomorrow. Soon we shall be seeing our wives and children."

Mr. Izakov made a point of telling me, "Nikolai Gribachev here has—like you—written a book that has been made into a movie."

"I'm so interested. What kind of a book?"

"It's—well—like a Jack London story. . . ." He changed the subject quickly. "We must go now. We have to be on a television show. Mrs. Marshall, I'm an atheist, but I enjoyed coming here today. Attending this church has helped me to understand the American people better."

There was more bowing over my hand. . . . "Thank you, thank you. . . ." Then one man, looking right at me, said, "Mrs Marshall, you have lovely big blue eyes."

That's the only piece of Communist propaganda I ever enjoyed.

Preachers have traditionally been fond of telling the rest of us that fame and money do not bring happiness. Most of us only half believe this. Secretly we would be more than willing to try a little of the fame and security on for size.

Yet I know now that the preachers are right. I found out the hard way. For in the backwash of the movie of "A Man Called Peter" there was plenty of publicity. A portion of my life had been dramatized for all the world to see. My name had been on theater marquees from coast to coast. No escape was possible—up the back stairs or anywhere.

At first, it had been exhilarating to watch the ashes of grief turn into the fairy gold of success. There had been adventure in walking through doors that opened before me; satisfaction in knowing that I could earn my way when it was necessary; excitement in seeing how high the tower of success could be built. Still I tried never to forget whose Hand had unlocked the doors, whose direction and help had made possible the success.

Then in time my sense of mission was followed by a feeling of futility. The fame turned back to ashes; the glitter was not all gold. How can I explain what happened?

Success in our world panders to the human ego. In effect, the world says, "A laurel wreath for you! Your human powers have accomplished thus and so!" And the world's voice all but drowns out another Voice, that of a quiet Figure standing in the shadows saying, "Without Me, ye can do nothing."

We are helpless without the God who made us and whose Spirit animates us. Yet the cult of self-sufficiency is not yet dead. It beats daily at our eardrums. It encourages selfishness. It devaluates working for the joy of working instead of for the reward of money; it scorns living to serve other people.

I was well aware of the conflict of the voices. I knew that happiness flees when self takes the center of the stage. There was a period when I prayed daily, "Oh God, don't let me take any credit for the success of these books. Keep me simple, keep me humble, keep my vision clear."

Yet—did the ashes in my mouth mean that somehow I had taken my eyes off that quiet Figure in the shadows and focused them on myself? Perhaps. Admittedly, it's hard to be clear-eyed about oneself.

Perhaps on the plus side of the ledger was my negative reaction to publicity. This was a good sign. A little of it I had found heady wine; more than a little I found cloying.

This principle of moderation I had learned early through an unforgettable childhood lesson. In Mississippi, we had lived in a manse adjoining the church. On Communion Sundays, at the close of the service, the silver trays with their tiny glasses of grape juice—some empty, some untouched—were always left on our back porch until the glasses could be washed.

At age four, grape juice was my favorite beverage. One Sunday, disregarding the sacred use for which that particular grape juice was intended, I methodically drained glass after glass, dozens of them. My stomach promptly rebelled; I was a very sick little girl.

Since I belonged to a teasing family, it took the rest of my childhood for me to live down my indulgence. For years thereafter an uncle called me his "grape-juice girl."

At the beginning of my venture into the world of writing, I thought publicity as enjoyable as once I had thought grape juice. Then in the end, there was too much of it for my taste, and something in me violently rebelled.

Part of the rebellion was my reaction to those who tended to idealize me. With the release of the movie, Peter Marshall had become something of a legend, his memory placed on a pedestal. It was as if the public then insisted that I should share the pedestal.

In time, so much of this living in my husband's light became a problem to me. One era of my life was over—whether I liked it or not. Circumstances were forcing me to build a new life of my own. Yet I was haunted by the question . . . how could I find myself as a woman or as a writer, in order to make that new life—so long as so many people insisted on seeing me solely as Mrs. Peter Marshall?

I shall not soon forget an incident at a World Day of Prayer service where I had been asked to speak. A large crowd had gathered. Just before the service, as I tried to push my way through the crowd into the church, suddenly I felt someone tugging at my arm. I turned around questioningly and saw a nicely dressed woman just behind me. Very seriously she said, "Mrs. Marshall, I hope I didn't bruise your arm. I just wanted to be able to tell my friends that I had touched Peter Marshall's wife."

It was her lack of humor rather than her idealism that disturbed me. For weeks her words haunted me. Touch me? Why? She had meant it only in kindness. Perhaps she had thought that I would be flattered.

Yet idealizing can soon become idolizing, and no human being should idolize another. We open ourselves to inevitable disillusionment when we do. And we do the object of our idolizing an injustice, for pedestal-sitting can be a lonely business.

It is especially lonely when there is no one with whom to share what the world calls "success." A businessman whose wife had died expressed this to me in several poignant sentences. . . .

Since Jean died, my business has suddenly flourished and is now successful beyond my greatest hopes. . . . Yet I would gladly give up the success, if I could have Jean again.

What fun is it to get big orders when you have no one waiting at home to hear about them? What does money mean to me when I have no one I love on whom to spend it? In fact, my success now only highlights my loneliness. . . .

I understood only too well what this widower meant. No matter how full and friendly the outside world may be, the house stands quiet, the evenings empty. But there are additional complications for a woman caught in the same situation. The conflict in me that had been born that day of the autograph tea for *Mr. Jones, Meet the Master* had built to a climax about the time of the movie.

Many women in our time know the same conflict, both those who have sought careers and those who have had careers thrust on them by necessity. The crux of the problem is . . . can a woman replace love with accomplishment, marriage with a career, or even combine a career with marriage, and find her life entirely satisfying?

Men usually accept at face value the estimate of themselves that society accords them because of the work they've done. Not so most women. Our values are usually rooted in relationships to others, not in personal accomplishment. As wives, we have not lived our own lives. We have lived through a man. As wives we must accept—grudgingly or delightedly—the place in society that our husband's work has won. The same is true of us as mothers. To one degree or another we live through our children.

But our most sensitive awareness of ourselves as a person has come through our relationship with one man. Soon after we met him, we found that in his presence we were aware of our femininity as never before—our dependence; our passivity; the way our emotions ruled our reason; our delight in people rather than in abstract ideas; our compassion; our preoccupation with the minutiae of living—a flower arrangement for a party, the next meeting of the PTA, the selection of new draperies for the living room, a missing button on a shirt.

With a new awareness, we understood that men and women were meant to be different. We reveled in our differentness.

Then life dealt us a blow; 7,595,000 of us in the United States have lost our husbands through death. Economic need has forced many of us to earn our own living. We who had known completeness only in our relationship with a man who loved us, were now asked to be complete within ourselves. In order to survive, we have had to do a hundred things we had never done before—handle money, sell and buy property, keep a man's working hours, try to be both father and mother to our children.

We managed all this by summoning up latent masculine qualities we did not know we possessed—the necessity of accepting responsibility, aggressiveness, competitiveness, drive, a partial submerging of feeling in favor of reason.

Even as this happened, we found treasured values slipping away. In the business world, we saw differences between the sexes blurred in a way we had not known in marriage. With the blurring, life lost something precious.

It made us stop and think, "What am I now—since my husband's death? Have I gotten off the track? Am I still a woman?" And that led inevitably to the questions asked by every widow: "What was I then—in marriage? What is a woman supposed to be?"

The attitude of our men friends made us question our new position even more sharply. For we found that even as they lauded us for carrying on so bravely as a widow, they did not personally like the changes they saw in us. They did not like women whose heads ruled their emotions, or aggressive women, or competitive women.

The dilemma went even deeper. A woman's need is to be loved for herself, not for any accomplishment. A true woman finds her reassurance, her reason for living, by looking into the eyes of a man who loves her. And when that is withdrawn from her—well—then what? She may achieve something that society recognizes as fine, only to find herself unable to accept society's new estimate of her.

Perhaps in my case this conflict was one reason for an agonizing period of profound self-doubt. I had performed a certain mission. The world said that it had helped many. But as a woman I was not impressed with any accomplishment of mine. As a woman I felt drained, empty.

I stood looking back over the way I had traveled since Peter's death and knew that my personal answer to whether or not a woman can replace marriage with a career and find it satisfying was—no, definitely not. The career left the woman still wanting to be—only a woman.

Fifteen
Dreams Do Come True

I WAS SITTING at the kitchen table preparing the vegetables for dinner. Since we had our usual quota of guests at Waverley, there was quite a pile of potatoes to be peeled, peas to be shelled. From where I sat, I could look through the windows into the back garden. Phlox, zinnias, and petunias were in bloom. A bird, with much fluttering of feathers, was giving himself a vigorous scrubbing in the birdbath. Even as I watched, a rabbit slipped under the picket fence and practiced small jumps across the grass.

It was a lazy afternoon and the potato peeling was relaxing. All at once a new idea appeared as if out of nowhere, fullblown in my mind. There had been no knocking for admittance; the idea dropped into my mind—kerplunk! Where are your father and mother going to live when your father retires from the ministry?

My mind roamed back over their lives. . . . How they had met at the Ebenezer Mission School in the Great Smoky Mountains of Tennessee. . . . Then, six pastorates in five states. . . . I thought of how they had lived in a procession of manses supplied by different churches. . . . Of how Father, who had always liked using tools and building things, was always making improvements in each successive house. . . . Of how Mother had planted and planted in each yard—and then always had to go off and leave her flowers.

I remembered the way they had given themselves so unstintingly to their church and to the community wherever they had been . . . Father with his love for people and his easy outgoingness . . . Mother in her more restrained way, counseling with many a young person, quietly encouraging a teen-ager's ambition to go to college or to find the right spot of service or the right person to marry.

And now that retirement was upon my parents—what? Immediately the idea came: Why not find a small farm within easy driving distance of Washington? Then let them dispense the hospitality to their city children and grandchildren. They would love that.

I sat there turning the new thought over and over as one would stare at a shining pebble. Entrancing, yes—but wasn't it impractical? Dad is scarcely the farmer type, I thought.

I decided not to mention the idea to anyone until it had been given the test of time. If this were just my own unsupported idea, it would evaporate as quickly as it had come. But if it was authentic, then it would persist.

Far from evaporating, the dream about the farm haunted me all summer. Many times during those weeks I pondered the intriguing fact that everything in the world starts with an idea or a picture in someone's mind. Some man, thousands of years ago, conceived the idea of a wheel. At that moment, the history of transportation entered a new phase. But the wheel had to be a picture in that unknown man's mind before it could be projected into wood. In the same way, the Wright brothers had to have an idea about heavier-than-air craft before they could translate that idea into wood, steel, canvas, and wire.

The architect has to have a blueprint; the dressmaker, a pattern. Even the cosmos—the Genesis account tells us—was an idea in the mind of God, before order could be created out of chaos, light out of darkness. . . .

It's because everything does start with an idea that dreaming, visualizing, is important. In fact it can be a way of prayer—a very effective way. When the farm idea persisted, I began to wonder if it might not be more than just a lovely daydream, the real thing—a God-inspired dream.

Not long before his death, Peter had given some thought to the problem of Dad's retirement, but had reached no solution. It was a problem, because ministers' salaries are notoriously meager, leaving little leeway for savings. And since church pensions were a relatively recent innovation, my father's would be small.

Finally I decided to give the farm-retirement plan the next test by mentioning it casually to Mother and Dad. I picked a leisurely moment just as we were finishing lunch one day. The family was around the umbrella table in the side yard, sipping the last of our iced tea and enjoying the sparkling sea air.

"You know, Dad," I began, "how Peter always thought maybe you and Mother would live here when you retired."

Father pushed back his chair. "I know. But it's too far away from the rest of the family. We'd never see enough of our grandchildren—"

"Well, I have another idea—" Then I told them. To my surprise they were immediately enthusiastic. My father stood up, his husky six-foot frame belying his years. He ran a hand through his full head of white hair, excitement in his every move. Behind glasses, Mother's blue eyes sparkled. And just so, the idea took root. From the outset, it seemed to transform their retirement from a dismal must at the end of life to an exciting adventure with all the flavor of a new beginning.

I had thought of the plan as primarily for my parents. But as with any of God's plans, it benefited all who touched it. It gave me a lot of satisfaction to be able to return in this way some of the love that they had always lavished on me. It also proved to be one of my last steps out of grief. The bereaved must find new and creative patterns for the rebuilding of their lives. For me the farm represented an important part of that new pattern.

The Leesburg real-estate agent was a patient man. He had shown me a new ranch-type house set in an open field. . . . "It's a lovely house— but too new—no trees—no shade. . . ." He had me inspect a renovated house, a hundred years old. . . . "Great charm—but there are six grandchildren in the family now . . . not enough room." Next I was taken to see a large stone house set on a hillside. . . . "Large enough, but much too expensive—couldn't touch it."

A year and a half had gone by since that afternoon at Waverley. We had investigated every area within sixty miles of Washington. It was the rolling, fertile countryside of Loudoun County, Virginia, ringed by the mountains of the Blue Ridge, that each member of our family found most appealing.

On the way back to Leesburg, we drove through a small settlement. Waving one arm out of the car window, the realtor explained: "This is the village of Lincoln, population 101, used to be called Goose Creek— settled by the Quakers about 1735. There—over there—is the Friends Meeting House."

All at once around the bend of the road, a white house set back in tall boxwood and rhododendron came into view.

"What about this place?" I asked.

The real-estate man slowed the car to a crawl. "Beautiful, all right. Well known in this section—been in the same family almost a century. Used to belong to the Hoges. He was a Quaker minister—now owned by Hoge's nephew, a Baltimore physician. I don't think it's for sale, though." With that the realtor speeded up and seemed to dismiss the subject.

Out of the back window of the car, I was still staring. The sign said "Evergreen Farm." Several of the tallest evergreens I had ever seen gave support to the name. At that moment something clicked in my mind. I had the strange feeling that the next step in the implementation of my dream had just come into view.

But then reality settled in like a heavy cloud. The grounds were like a living fairyland—surely completely out of my reach financially. And anyway the place wasn't even for sale.

But during the next few weeks, I was to realize all over again that God's dreams are usually more wonderful than ours. The problem for most of us is how to stretch ourselves enough to accept His munificence.

Ten months later in a lawyer's office in Leesburg, I—mentally pinching myself to be sure it was true—was signing in triplicate the papers that made me the mortgage-happy mistress of "Evergreen."

The farmhouse had stood unoccupied for over ten years except for brief visits from the owner. It was only because the house and the farm generally needed so much work that I was able to buy it.

There was still eight months to go before my father's retirement; I had until then to get the house ready. As a minimum, we were going to have to install a heating plant, all new plumbing, a new kitchen, bathrooms, overhaul the water system, put closets in each room, redecorate the interior.

The main part of the house had been built in 1816 by Yardley Taylor, a Quaker. Yardley, like most of the Friends, built his house according to a standard plan approved by William Penn himself—walls of field-stone, a foot-and-a-half thick, with little binding. The masons of that day built a dry wall, filling the wide hollow space with tightly packed stones and sand. Only after the house was finished did they point up the walls with lime and mud. The thick walls were designed to keep out the cold of winter and the heat of summer. Always there was a large basement, low ceilings, massive hand-hewn beams, deep window sills. The plan was such that rooms could be added as the family increased.

Penn, in a tract published in London in 1684, minutely described his standard plan:

> To build then, a house of thirty foot long and thirteen broad, with a partition near the middle and another to divide one end of the House into two small rooms. . . .

The two small rooms immediately to the left of the front door, were originally bedrooms. At Evergreen, they had later been used as a parlor and sitting room. Another Quaker architectural device heated the rooms —two fireplaces built back to back, at an angle in a V shape, with a single chimney flue serving both. Throwing the two rooms together would make the spacious living room that the house needed. But that would necessitate the major task of rebuilding most of the chimney.

Many of the small-paned windows were still of the old hand-blown glass. There was some of the original hardware, including the front-door key made of brass and 7½ inches long.

Just down the hill was a barn, a spring house, and a smoke house, also built in 1816 of massive magnificent stonework. The tenant house, only five years old, stood on the site of the original, which had burned down many years before.

The main house stood on a little knoll. A double avenue of English boxwood originally with a walk between (but long since grown together) ran from the front porch down the hill and then up another hill almost as far as the eye could see.

Over and over I had been warned about the hazards of renovating old houses. One friend who saw Evergreen said bluntly, "It would be much cheaper to raze it to the ground and start over. No contractor would touch it except on a cost-plus basis."

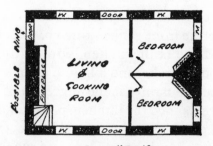

William Penn's standard house plan, London, 1684*

"But I couldn't bear to see this house demolished. It's been lived in and loved for over a hundred and fifty years. No new house could possibly have so much charm."

"Charm be hanged. You women! You're heading for trouble and more trouble. Don't say I didn't warn you!"

Later that week, a Washington architect went out to the house with me. His reaction had a little of the same dire foreboding as that of my pessimistic friend.

"It has possibilities, all right. So many, that as an architect, they intrigue me. But you know how old houses are. You never know what you'll run into. This two-faced fireplace situation, for instance. . . ."

"Do you think we would run into trouble rebuilding that chimney?"

"There's no telling. The whole house might collapse. But I don't think so. We might have to put a supporting steel beam across these two rooms though—"

"Would you be willing to take on this job?"

"I'm game, if you're prepared to stand the strain and the risks involved."

Thus—gingerly—I acquired an architect. His first task prior to making drawings, was to spend hours upon hours measuring. No two windows turned out to be the same size. No measurements could be taken for granted. Few lines were true. Often the tops of doors and windows were on such a slant that even the casual eye could see it.

When the architect's plans were completed, we poured over them. In addition to the living-room renovation, the dining-room fireplace—long

*Strong, Solange, *Old Stone Houses of Loudoun County, Virginia*, Loudon Times-Mirror Publishing Company, Leesberg, 1950.

closed—was to be reopened. The plans called for a picture window in the library facing on the front garden; three bathrooms, two of them on the second floor; a large farm kitchen, with a fireplace with a raised hearth, natural wood cabinets, and a Dutch door.

Each member of the family made suggestions. We took away and added, planned and replanned the kitchen, placed and replaced the downstairs powder room, closed up openings, added new windows. By February, four months before Mother and Dad were supposed to move in, the plans were complete on paper.

It took another six weeks to get bids. Finally the contract was let to a countryman, a local builder. I soon discovered why there is no high blood pressure in the country; it is because the pace is slow. It was the middle of May before any workmen appeared on the scene.

In the meantime, the gremlins designated to harass all new property owners descended on me in force. One day a neighbor's cattle got into the front lawn, soft from recent rains. Before the cattle were driven off, they had pockmarked the lawn with soggy hoof marks inches deep. We were months repairing the damage.

Then one night a drunken driver drove off the road over the embankment into the boxwood and rhododendron. The driver was not hurt but Evergreen's shrubbery was.

Meanwhile the grass was growing, the honeysuckle and the poison ivy were thriving, and the weeds on the hillsides were getting out of control. A power mower seemed indicated. Carefully I investigated the relative merits of various brands. The one I selected broke down the first day.

One night someone shattered several panes of glass in a front window. Heavy spring thundershowers forced water in under loosely hanging doors. Swallows came down the chimney into the house. All the mice and rats in the neighborhood were using the deserted building as a favorite rendezvous.

The lesson seemed to be that the gremlins needed an overseer. A young Negro applied for the job. In April, Earl and Flossie and their three children moved into the tenant house. Immediately the gremlins shifted the center of their activity to the interior. The contractor would set out to replace a square yard of plaster and an entire wall of plaster would fall. Window frames turned out to be rotten and had to be replaced. Often caulking would fall out the day after it was put in. It required some doing to chisel new openings in the thick stone walls. The termite man reported ominously that there was "termite activity underneath the house."

On the day after that, the county health authorities advised that a new drain field would have to be dug and a septic tank installed. The water people said that the spring would have to be cleaned and covered over, a new reservoir dug. They had a point, since a family of bats had taken up residence in the cool dampness of the spring house. I began to wonder if I'd made the worst mistake of my life the day I signed the paper for Evergreen.

The country contractor was afraid of rebuilding the living-room fireplace and had postponed it as long as possible. Finally, prodded by the architect, he started in. His plan was ingenious. He decided to leave the point of the two fireplaces as a supporting stone column and to rip out behind it. That done, he built the edges of the new fireplace to the second story level. He then let the newly laid brick harden over the weekend before tearing out the supporting column.

"First thing Monday morning, we'll know," he told me. He shook his head dismally. "If this side of the ceiling is gonna cave in, that will end it."

On Monday I received no message that the ceiling had collapsed. On Tuesday came a letter from the countryman. . . .

Dear Mrs. Marshall:

Since you have already noticed my worrying concern over the chimney and fireplace in the living room I can't help but to write and tell you it is up and safe. It is worked out to perfection in my book. If I stand alone in the job I think it is wonderful. And I am pleased to the limit. I have smiled as I have never smiled before. Hoping you find it the same, I am very truly yours . . .

Otto Kelley

I drove out as often as I could to see how the work was coming. With each trip I had to climb over more debris outside and in—tons of plaster, mountains of lath and ripped-out boards. The country workmen, always good-humored, would exchange banter and community gossip, spit tobacco, lounge on the front porch over their lunch pails, and allow that "It's comin'—ma'am—slow, but sure. We'll git there yet. Don't you worry none, ma'am."

It was slow all right. Two weeks before my father was due to give his valedictory sermon to mark the end of his forty-six years in the ministry, the plumbing was still incomplete, the kitchen was scarcely begun, the plasterer was still busy, no interior painting had been done.

Moving day came. The van Dad had hired appeared in the driveway, and there was no alternative but to carry the household possessions to the loft of an outbuilding. Mother and Father planned to stay in Washington until their home was ready.

The work dragged on through the summer. By September, Mother was unable to stand the delay a minute longer. Dad could do whatever he liked, but she was going to move in. If she had to cook on a Sterno or a campfire and have workmen appear in her bedroom every morning at dawn—well—enough was enough!

The workmen—marveling at her—good-humoredly swept out some of the debris and let her move. Then they went right on hammering and painting. It was October before the last workman, by then attached to us like brothers, bade us a reluctant farewell.

During all the months of the renovation, I had been accumulating things for the farmhouse. The antique shops of Cape Cod had yielded some furnishings. A coffee grinder and a plaster figurine would one day be lamps. Three captain's chairs had been real bargains. A New England craftsman made me a coffee table with ceramic tiles set in the top— perfect for the library. The Forgue at Sandwich Village supplied tiny colonial andiron reproductions just right for the kitchen fireplace. A ship's bell would make a resounding farm bell.

During the fall, the Georgetown shops and some country auctions added more. Our Washington basement looked like a combination used-furniture store and warehouse. It became a problem to keep a path open to the washing machine.

Then the question was . . . how were we going to get all of the furniture out to the farm? I decided that a U-Drive-It truck was the sensible solution. Peter John, who had just gotten his driver's license, said that he would be delighted to help. My brother-in-law planned to lend a hand loading the truck and driving it out to the farm.

Peter John and I appeared at the rental garage early the next Saturday morning. I told the young man behind the counter that I wanted to rent a truck.

"Yes, ma'am—what size?"

I turned to Peter for some help. He was thoughtful but silent. So I said, "I don't know exactly. What sizes do they come in?"

My tall son winced and gave me a withering look. Then he said knowingly, "We'll need about a ton and a half."

The man pulled a questionnaire form from under the counter.

"Okay—Now, madam, I'll have to ask you some questions. . . . Last name ?"

"Marshall."

"First name?"

"Catherine."

"State in which you have your driver's license?"

"District of Columbia."

"Married or single?"

"I'm a widow."

"By whom are you employed?"

"Well—I'm not exactly employed. I mean—I work for myself. What I mean is—well—I write books and things—sometimes."

"Mmm—seems a little odd. We don't usually—anyway, there isn't space here to put all that."

"Why not put the name of my publisher. That would look impressive—the McGraw-Hill Book Company."

"Okay—now—the name of your foreman?"

"Foreman? I've never had a foreman."

"No, I suppose not. Names of parents, if living?"

"Leonora Halestine Whitaker Wood and John Ambrose Wood."

That seemed to stop him cold. Suddenly the whole procedure seemed a little silly. . . . "Do you need the names of grandparents? Any genealogy? My great-grandparents came from—"

"No! No-o, but—color of eyes and hair?"

Peter John chimed in crisply, "Blue—brown."

"Height?"

"You know, it's a funny thing, but I always have trouble remembering that. I think it's five-six. No, five-six and a half."

"That will do. Weight?" Here the young man's eyes swept me up and down.

"Oh, about one hundred thirty-three."

Suddenly, I felt facetious. "Look, if I should try a getaway with this truck, I'm sure you could use my bust measurement. It's—"

Peter John reddened slightly. "Mother, pl-e-ase!"

The young man said, "Now, we require a deposit, a minimum of twenty dollars. If you'll sign right here, please, I'll bring the truck around. You can wait there by the front door." And he disappeared into the gloomy, gasoline-smelling garage.

As soon as the man was out of sight, Peter John whispered, "Mom, what are we gonna do? You can't drive a truck. And that man will be watching, so I can't drive it. That paper you signed said no one under twenty-one— Maybe we'd better call the whole deal off."

"Don't be silly." My tone carried more confidence than I felt. "Of course, I can drive it. A truck can't be so different from our Olds."

"But you're used to Hydra-Matic. It will be a gear-shift job and I—"

With a roar and an ear-piercing squeal of brakes, a monster of a truck appeared at the curb. Surely this couldn't be— But it was.

"Well, here she is, gassed up and ready to go. Now, if you'll just climb in the cab, I'll check you out."

Peter looked sheepish. "It *is* big—isn't it?"

"A ton and a half. That's what you said."

I climbed into the cab. It was like sitting halfway up the Washington monument. I could see over the top of every car on the street.

The young man began to explain the knobs, levers, and handles on the dash- and floorboard. In a bored monotone, he said that I should not pull this unless I wanted the truck to do so and so, and that I should turn this only after I had done something else. He mentioned something about a double clutch. I didn't know what a double clutch was. Finally he jumped down and, with a half-hearted wave of the hand, disappeared into the garage.

Peter John was still standing on the sidewalk. His face now wore a strained paternal expression. "I think, Mom, I'd better help you get this monster home. We can leave our car parked here awhile."

I tried not to show my relief. "I guess you're right."

So he climbed into the cab beside me and looked over the gadgets on the dash. "There's the starter, Mom—there. The clutch— Hey, don't forget the clutch."

The truck gave a lurch forward. "Easy, Mom, reach for the brake."

"I don't know where it is."

"Right there—*there!*"

We had several narrow escapes going down Sixteenth Street. I missed an Austin-Healey by a hair. The truck was so wide!

I noticed that Peter was biting his fingernails. "Man, would we have made mincemeat of that beautiful little car!"

A policeman at an intersection stared, but didn't blow his whistle. The driver of a Cadillac swore at me—in bellowing, stentorian tones. But fortune was with us. We made it back to our front door without passing any of our friends or acquaintances—we thought.

A month later a friend dropped by the house one afternoon. As she was leaving she said, "Apropos of nothing, awhile back I almost had an accident."

"You did? How was that?"

"One day I almost collided with a whopper of a truck weaving down Sixteenth Street. You know, it was the strangest thing—" here she looked at me curiously—"but I could have sworn that it was you driving that truck."

In one corner of the farmhouse attic, Mother found a pile of old books. Inside a nineteenth-century Latin grammar was a yellowed clipping. There was no date on it, but it described a party once held at Evergreen. The society-page columnist of another century had been strictly the poetic type and had liked flinging words around. . . .

. . . The house with every window ablaze threw out its beacon light far over the surrounding hills to greet the gathering guests, making their hearts to feel a genial warmth, which increasing, only reached the climacteric of fervor when they merged into the illumination of chandeliers and mellow tinted radiance of happy faces. . . .

The company consisted of about seventy-five guests, mostly young and susceptable, with a few couples of the younger married people of the vicinity. . . .

Supper was announced about eight o'clock. . . . We dare not attempt to describe the supper. . . . But this little secret we must tell. . . . We got it from the cook. More than a dozen turkeys and chickens were sacrificed and there was one cake for every four individuals. . . .

At a seasonable hour the guests departed and the dying echoes of joyful sounds, with the silvery moonbeams, wove into the silent night a mystical halo around the festal scene.

Long live the happy couple who treated us so well, and may their affectionate niece from the Buckeye State, visit them very frequently and occasionally between times.

Mother has always been the historian of our family. The clipping was her first intimation that there were happy ghosts at Evergreen. It gave her an insatiable curiosity to know more about them. Mother has always had her own techniques for historical research, which usually include visiting local cemeteries, along with leisurely conversation with local antiquarians.

Quakers from Bucks County, Pennsylvania, had settled two villages in Loudoun County—Waterford, about 1733, and Goose Creek (now Lincoln), two years later.

The Society of Friends, which from the beginning had granted equal rights to women, sometimes found themselves dominated by a woman. They might have known things would get out of hand!

Thus, for many years, Hannah Janney was the preacher of the Goose Creek meeting. In between having twelve children, she taught and preached, visited and settled disputes. Hers was the final word in the community.

The Friends advocated a strict, decorous life—no music, no levity, plain clothes—no bright colors or ornaments. But one member of the Goose Creek meeting had an irrepressible daughter. She loved music and gay colors. Her father cajoled and threatened, but it did no good. Still her feet tapped out rhythms, her laughter rang out, and her love for color went unabashed. Finally her father disinherited her. The next day he had a visit from Hannah Janney.

"Isaac, I have just heard that thee has made thy will and disinherited thy daughter, Mary. Is that true?"

"Yes, that I have."

"Why did thee do that, Isaac?"

"I can't do anything with Mary. She dances instead of walking. She goes about the house singing. She will not wear the plain clothes. Over and over she has broken the disciplines. She is stubborn and contrary, set in her evil ways."

"Isaac, thee knows she gets her stubbornness honestly—from thee. Thee knows that the Friends' discipline provides that all children shall share equally in their father's possessions. Thee knows well that two wrongs will never make a right. I am here to tell thee, Isaac, that thee must change thy will."

"I won't do it."

"Yes, thee will, Isaac."

Isaac didn't give in without a struggle, but he was no match for Hannah. The will was changed. Hannah lived to be ninety-three, a dominant figure in the community to the end. She is buried in the cemetery around the bend from Evergreen.*

Yardley Taylor, the first builder of Evergreen and another member of Hannah's flock, was the first surveyor and map-maker in Loudoun County. With only a compass and a viameter attached to his buggy, he roamed every road, plotted every stream and every house. In 1853 he published his *Memoirs of Loudoun County, Virginia*. His book was published by Robert Pearsall Smith in Philadelphia, another Quaker and the son of Hannah Whitall Smith, the author of one of my favorite books—*The Christian's Secret of a Happy Life*. So the strands twine and intertwine.

Yardley had three sons. One of them, Richard Henry, set up an iron foundry and grist mill on the bottom land at Evergreen. He made the "Taylor plow"—especially designed to keep to a straight furrow. His farm bells and a frog doorstop can still be picked up in antique shops in the Leesburg area.

Richard Henry's buildings have long since disappeared. But when we, out of curiosity, dug on the site, we unearthed a small iron pot and some pieces of a Taylor plow.

*Nichols, Joseph V., *Loudoun Valley Legends*, printed by Blue Ridge Herald, Purcallville, Va., 1955. Used by permission.

Another son, Oliver Taylor, had a green thumb. He turned part of Evergreen into the first nursery in the county. His boxwood—English and American—is now over a hundred years old. The trees he planted still stand—grafted walnut trees, from which the nutmeats come out whole; a row of red spruce to mark one boundary of the farm; the tall silver firs I had seen from the road that first day; rare Chinese cypress; chestnuts, Japanese maples, purple magnolias, and ginkgoes.

Local legend has it that, during an economic depression when Oliver was unable to sell his plants and shrubs, he set out all his left-over stock permanently on Evergreen land. It may be true because there is no end to the variety still there—forsythia, Japonica, arbor vitae, double-flowered Japanese cherry trees, mock orange, yucca, rhododendron, quince, bamboo.

Eventually the plants fell into other loving hands when Sarah and Howard Hoge bought the farm in 1894. Howard was the new preacher for the Society of Friends at Lincoln and also, like Oliver, a horticulturist. He developed a thriving business from fifty acres planted in apple trees and became the first county agricultural agent and the first president of the Virginia Apple Growers Association.

His wife Sarah was noted for at least two things—her interest in the Women's Christian Temperance Union and her caramel ice cream. She loved to entertain, and always when the rhododendron was in bloom, the Hoges kept open house.

I have tracked down the recipe and have tried it. No wonder it became famous . . . !

CARAMEL ICE CREAM

1 quart or 3 pints of new milk
1 egg
Scant ½ cup flour
1 heaping cup of sugar
1 quart cream

Boil the milk. Beat the egg and flour together and add to the boiling milk. Put the sugar in a hot skillet. Stir and shake frequently until the sugar gets brown and liquid. Then stir it into the custard. Cool the mixture thoroughly. Put through fine sieve. Add the cream and freeze.

The caramel mixture may be made the day before the cream is to be used.

In the 1890s when only hand separators were used, milk was very rich. "New milk" then would be about the equivalent of half milk, half cream, today. "Cream" then would be called whipping cream today. Therefore, Sarah's ice cream was rich—rich—rich.

This is a more economical adaptation of the recipe that I have worked out in my own kitchen:

CARAMEL ICE CREAM

1 pint half milk, half cream
4 eggs
½ cup flour
1½ cups sugar
1 can evaporated milk
1½ pints whipping cream
Pinch salt
1 teaspoon vanilla extract
⅔ cup water

Caramelize the sugar in a hot skillet, stirring constantly. Add the ⅔ cup water. Stir until sugar is dissolved and evaporated into a heavy syrup. Set aside to cool.

Separate the eggs. Beat the whites stiff, and set aside.

Add the flour and salt to the milk and evaporated milk. Beat in caramel mixture and beaten egg yolks. Cook mixture in top of double boiler, stirring constantly until custard begins to thicken and coats a silver spoon.

Fold in the egg whites. Cool, put through a fine sieve.

Whip the whipping cream and fold into custard mixture. Add vanilla. Freeze. This makes a gallon of ice cream.

One warning—this ice cream won't be as delicious as Sarah's unless it is made in a hand freezer. Old-fashioned ice creams have two characteristics not shared by most present-day ones—they are not slenderizing, and they will melt rapidly in the dish. This melting characteristic is not always true of some so-called ice creams today, to which gelatin, wax, or papier-mâché sometimes seem to have been added!

Since Sarah was once the president of the W.C.T.U., she might not like it that in Evergreen's new kitchen, the old bricks for the fireplace came out of a Winchester brewery that was being demolished. But then again, since the brewery was demolished, that should please her.

On a moonlit night anyone with any imagination can see Evergreen's happy ghosts—Yardley Taylor driving his two-wheeled gig with the viameter attached along the dusty roads; Hannah Janney with that certain glint in her eye, keeping the menfolk strictly in line; the spirited Mary, laughing and dancing; Richard Henry, wearing his leather apron, the sparks flying from the anvil of his forge; Oliver wandering among his cherished plants; Sarah at her stove, stirring the burnt sugar for her caramel ice cream; and of course, on a certain silvery night, that company of the young and "susceptable" entertaining the niece from the Buckeye State.

Once the moving was completed and some of the house in order, Mother turned to the task of cleaning up the yard. The project with top priority on her list was the elimination of the poison ivy that grew everywhere.

One morning she noticed big creepers on the trunk of the gigantic ginkgo tree. The vines had been there a long time. They were twined and intertwined, a many stranded rope.

After digging up the roots, she began pulling at the rope of vines, hand over hand. Suddenly, something came crashing out of the tree, struck her shoulder a glancing blow, and fell at her feet with a thud. A white-faced animal struggled to its feet, stood its ground, and snarled at her.

Mother took one look, opened her mouth, and gave a yell that could be heard all the way to the house. It was the biggest possum she had ever seen. I'll always regret that I was not there to see the expression on Mother's face at the moment that she grounded her first possum.

Poison ivy was not the only weed waiting to be eliminated. By early spring, the hillsides were knee-deep in them, choking out the gnarled apple trees, all but smothering the shrubbery. Since as yet we had no farm machinery, Dad decided to use some gadgets of his own.

Always my father has had a weakness for tools and gadgets; many times he has been tempted to spend too much of his ministerial salary for such things. Just after World War II, he had seen flame throwers advertised. It seemed that the War Department had been overzealous about flame throwers and had some extras. Father knew immediately that a flame thrower was just what he needed.

Mother was annoyed at the idea. "What on God's green earth do you want something like that for? You know perfectly well we haven't any money to spend on such silly things."

I remember that Father had looked wounded. He always looks wounded when any member of the family questions his judgment about buying gadgets.

"The flame thrower is exactly what I need to get rid of the tall weeds in the corners of the yard. And I *am* going to buy it." With that he strode off and slammed a door.

Buy it, he did. What Mother didn't know was that the old flame thrower had been transported to Evergreen along with the rest of the household possessions. So now, we had the rare treat of seeing the great warrior stalking around the yard spurting flame in all directions.

The only trouble was that one day Father singed a clump of box-wood along with the weeds. Mother, outraged, insisted that the flame thrower be retired from active duty.

Then Father had another idea. . . . A neighbor had told him that there was nothing like goats for getting rid of weeds.

Mother protested that too. "That's downright ridiculous. Besides, goats are smelly."

"I found out about that too. It's only the males. The females aren't—smelly."

"But goats aren't discriminating. They'll eat the flowers too."

"That can be controlled. You have to buy a chain and tether them where you want them to eat."

The goats—a big nanny goat and her kid—long-legged, wobbly, and shy, rode back to the farm in the open trunk of Dad's car.

So far they haven't eaten any boxwood. The grandchildren think they're wonderful—especially the baby goat. They like to see her shyly stick her head around the corner of the barn.

By now, other animals have been added to the menagerie—Mike, a thoroughbred collie; a pair of Easter ducklings; and Dad's chickens and turkeys.

Mother had scarcely finished unpacking the dishes before Father was in town pricing baby chickens and turkeys. What would a farm be without one's own poultry on the table? Still he had been told that turkeys were hard to raise, so he decided to be conservative in his poultry project—a hundred chicks and twelve turkeys would be a start.

Earl had the chicken house cleaned and ready. Dad reasoned that if he let the turkeys roam over Evergreen's steep hillsides, they would develop too much muscle. He took completely to heart the philosophy that, if you want tender turkeys, "a turkey's foot should never touch ground."

Seven chickens died, only one turkey. The growing birds were stuffed with all the corn and feed they could eat. The bills for poultry feed were appalling.

But it was not long before fried chicken and wondrously plump and tender turkeys began to grace the table at Evergreen. By Thanksgiving, Father had developed a pattern for his chatter as he carved—the life story and vital statistics of the bird on the platter, plus, of course, the fact that its feet had never touched ground.

My brother Bob had listened quietly to Dad's turkey-raising tales through Thanksgiving dinner. Finally, thoroughly saturated, he said mildly, "Dad, do you have a pencil?"

"Sure. Why?"

"Let's see if we can figure out what your turkey-feed bill has been to date."

"Sure, son—now let me see. It's been. . . ."

When Bob and father had finished their elaborate calculations, a conservative estimate was that the turkey we had just eaten had cost at least $1.75 a pound. The local grocery stores were selling turkeys at 59 cents a pound.

Father had other projects. I was continually finding old lists around the house, very impressive ones . . .

Prune and spray old apple trees
Deepen and widen the brook; plant willows, iris, mint,
    and watercress along its banks
Screen in the back porch
Build patio by kitchen door
Mend smokehouse roof
Build fences
Cut down locust tree

The locust tree was dead. Not only that, but its hollow trunk housed a hive of honeybees. Whenever Father ventured into the front yard, he was aggravated by the incessant buzzing of the bees around his head.

"We'd better put the tree cutting at the head of the list," Father told me. "The first strong wind will bring it down, and it might fall on the roof."

"Yes, but how are you going to do it?" I asked.

The problem was that there was only five feet between the tree and the front porch. On the other three sides were solid clumps of tall boxwood. Because that left nowhere for the tree to fall safely, felling it seemed to be a job for tree surgeons.

Father got estimates but whistled when he saw the figures. "It's outlandish! You'd think they planned to take that tree down an inch at a time. I'll show 'em! By golly, I'll do it myself!"

The first step was to get the bees out of the trunk. "Tomorrow morning we'll smoke 'em out," Father told Earl. "We can't work at getting the tree down with those infernal bees always in our hair."

Early the next morning a troubled Earl stuck his head in the kitchen door. "Missus Wood, de Rev'ent says we gotta smoke out dem bees. I's scairt of bees."

Mother thought fast. "Don't worry, Earl. I'll fix you up. I'll tell you what. You know that leftover wire screening in the corner of the tool house? Bring me a piece of that."

Earl produced the screening. Mother bent it in the shape of a helmet and put it over his head and face. Then she secured it around his neck with a long piece of cloth that terminated in a fetching bow in back.

"Now put on these canvas gloves, Earl. Then I'll tie your sleeves tight at the wrists with a string."

Earl went toward the scene of action with his dusky face grinning through the screening. Father, waiting at the foot of the tree, took one look at Earl, at the bow in back, and let out his most profane expressions. "Holy Jeehossifats, Earl! What happened to you?"

"Missus Wood, she fixed me up, Rev'ent. Dem bees—dey's daidly."

Father handed Earl a thick stick with some rags tied over it. "Now, let's start the rags smoking. Then you climb up the tree and hold the smoking rags inside the hollow."

Earl, looking like something left over from a Halloween party, struggled upward into the mighty locust. As he thrust the homemade torch inside the tree, the bees poured out in a torrent of angry buzzing. Helmet or not, Earl left the smoking rags in the hollow, slid down the tree trunk a lot faster than he had gone up, and made a dash for the safety of the porch.

Billows of black smoke were rolling out every opening in the rotten trunk. The tree warriors were just congratulating themselves that the bees must certainly have departed for calmer fields when Mother, who had appeared on the porch to watch, yelled, "Dad, look! The tree's on fire—"

She was right. Tongues of flames were lapping around the great trunk. Father and Earl ran to get the hose. They connected it to the nearest outlet only to find that it was too short.

By then the situation was serious. The fire was being sucked up the hollow tree, chimney fashion, with flames shooting out the top, dangerously close to the roof of the house.

But Mother had already gone to telephone the local fire department. Minutes later, the big trucks were clanging into the driveway, and the firemen soon had the flames extinguished.

That evening, Earl climbed the charred tree to scrape out handfuls of honey. "Rev'ent, it's de bes' honey I ever et," Earl said. "Dat smoke taste—dat's good."

Father looked gloomy. "I never ate smoked honey. You can have it. But I notice that the tree's still standing—and it has to come down."

A week went by. Daily Father grimaced at the blackened tree. Then Harlow, my brother-in-law, phoned and offered to help the following Saturday morning.

On the appointed day, I was there to watch. Father, Earl, and Harlow had gathered under the locust tree enough equipment to level all growing things in northern Virginia—a pile of rope, chairs, a crosscut saw, axes, whetstones, files, wedges, and a ladder.

As Harlow and Earl were busily engaged in hanging hand axes, saws, and lengths of rope to their belts, Father was giving them an unsolicited preflight briefing. "Now we'll do it this way—tie one end of the rope to the branch you're working on—just below the sawing point, of course. Then toss the other end over a limb above you, and one down to me here on the ground. I'll hold the rope taut. Then when you've sawed the limb through, I can let it down slowly—steering it clear of the boxwood and the porch roof."

It sounded good.

Earl and Harlow climbed aloft. Several of the smaller limbs were sawed off and successfully lowered to the ground. But then came a larger limb. As Harlow sawed, Father and I were getting increasingly uneasy.

Father yelled, "Hold up a minute, you two. That's a big one. I'm not sure I can hang onto it."

Harlow paused in his sawing and called down, "Why not find something to tie your end of the rope to?"

Immediately father had an idea. He looped the rope under his arms and tied it securely across his chest. Then he backed up until the rope was taut. He reasoned that his 200 pounds would be ample counterbalance for the weight of the limb.

"Okay, boys, everything under control now—go ahead—saw."

As Harlow's saw cut deepened, the large limb began to sag, then suddenly it cracked and broke loose. Father wasn't ready. He tried to brace himself, but instead he was propelled toward the tree. Then he was standing on tiptoe. Then he was being lifted off the ground in little jerks.

I stood there, not knowing what to do. "Help, Harlow—help—Dad, he's—"

Father's booming voice rang out . . . "Help! Earl! Harlow. . . ! Don't just sit up there— *Do* something . . . !"

Harlow and Earl started scrambling down. Father was dangling about four feet off the ground, fanning the air with his hands and feet. By then he had pulled out all the stops on his most unministerial vocabulary.

He was in no real danger, and the three of us were almost helpless with laughter. Finally Earl and Harlow got enough control of themselves to catch hold of Father's ankles. With much heaving and pulling, they got his 200 pounds back to earth.

Father, rubbing the rope burns on his chest and drawing himself up to his full six feet, said, "I fail to see what's so funny—"

I decided that it might be wise to ask for the services of the tree surgeon.

Bit by bit, step by step, project by project, the dream that I had that summer day in the Cape Cod kitchen is coming into being.

As I write, spring has come to Evergreen. Mike, the collie, roams the greening hillsides, sniffing the air. The baby goat is growing. The duck is sitting on fifteen eggs. The drake (typical male!) wanders around disconsolately, lonely, feeling sorry for himself. A few whitefaced Herefords now graze the bottom-land where once Henry Taylor's forge stood.

Last year's corn has been sold at a good price. There is freshly turned sod in some of the fields. The old apple trees have all been pruned. New strawberry plants are thriving. Father reports that the egg production for March was 809 eggs, and that he thinks he may try raising a few more turkeys.

The last time I drove out to Evergreen I found Father busy building fences. He paused in his hammering long enough to comment, "Three years of solid work may make a dent in my work list. . . . Nothing like retiring to go to work!"

It sounded like complaining. But there was contentment on his face.

That same afternoon Mother and I stood on the front porch looking out over the sweep of lawn and shrubbery. The sun was going down. The tall pines cast lengthening shadows across the grass. The forsythia was almost gone; the Japanese quince and the crab apple were coming into bud. Late daffodils still bloomed, punctuating the far hillsides with golden exclamation points. The two of us had been silent, our eyes absorbing the beauty.

"You know," I said to Mother, "when I was a little girl in Mississippi I dreamed of this. Remember? The *Little Colonel* series, the Southern mansion, and all. Only this is so much more beautiful than anything I imagined."

Mother said, "It's the realization of my dreams, too, only in a slightly different way. All my married life, Dad and I have moved from one manse to another, improving and planting; then we've had to move on, leaving our plants for the next family.

"Now at the end of our ministry, it's as if the Lord is saying to us . . . 'Here it all is with dividends—all you've invested in love and energy—filled up, pressed down, and running over. I had it in mind all the time.'"

Sixteen
You Can't Hold Back the Light

THE BACK OF the car was piled high with furnishings a boy would need for his room at prep school—a bookcase, a floor lamp, a desk light, sheets, blankets, towels, a cotton rug, some favorite pictures.

After we had crossed the Connecticut line into Massachusetts, the uneven contour of the land became rolling countryside, made lush by recent rains. Each mile was bringing us closer to the moment against which I had been steeling myself. Peter John was leaving home to take his last year in high school at the Mt. Hermon School in northwestern Massachusetts.

"Sons are different," my friends had often told me. "You may as well face it. Once they leave home, that's it. You get no more than glimpses of them after that."

The blond boy who was driving was entertaining no such serious thoughts. He was listening to a baseball game on the radio.

My mind kept wandering from the battle between the Braves and the Giants, or was it the Indians and the Yankees? Much to Peter John's disgust, I could never keep these intrepid warriors straight. Instead I was remembering something I had seen many years before—the last page of my Baby Book written in my mother's round feminine handwriting.

That morning years ago, she had combed my long curls more carefully than usual, brushing each one round and round her forefinger. Then she had walked to the iron grillwork gate with me, kissed me good-bye, and watched me skip gaily down the street to my first day in the first grade.

She must have stood at the gate a long time, thoughts stirring in her mind, as she watched that small retreating figure. Then she had turned back into the house and had written the thoughts down on the only blank page left in the Baby Book. . . .

Today our dear little girl starts to school—no longer a baby. Seven years of childish joy, blessings, and love—the sunshine of her father's and mother's heart. Mingled with the pride and thanksgiving that fill my heart, there is an undercurrent of sadness. The little life will no longer be wholly under the home influence. . . . My prayer is that my child may always bless and beautify everything that she touches. . . .

The lines written on this final page were unabashedly sentimental. But why not? I understood now what Mother had felt on that morning long ago. Each generation of womankind has the same set of feelings. Life asks women to give and to give and then to give up, and to do both with equanimity and courage.

When that certain moment was upon us in our rooms in the inn the next day, I was not big enough to take it alone. But I knew where to go for help. Besides, don't all such moments need the benison of a benediction?

I tried to keep my heart from showing—not because I was afraid of the heart, but because I didn't want to embarrass Peter John.

"We should be pushing off for school," I said. "But first, would you indulge me in something? This is a significant day for us both. Would you be willing for us to have a prayer together and ask God's blessing on it?"

Peter nodded a little impatiently, so I made the prayer brief. The moment hung in space—hung, and passed. But there was the unmistakable feeling in the prayer that we were not two, but three—united across barriers that were no barriers.

Silently, Peter picked up his suitcases.

I was a little disappointed in the room at school—circa 1890, golden oak woodwork, the floors well worn by generations of boys' feet, battered furniture, two small windows almost covered with a summer's growth of ivy.

But Peter didn't seem to mind. He had just met his roommate, Bruce, and liked him—as blond as he, also a senior. This room would be their digs—their very own. What did golden oak woodwork and worn floors matter?

Two other boys stuck their heads in the door and introduced themselves. "We thought you might like some help in unpacking the car—"

The five of us made a series of trips between the car and the room, back and forth, up and down the wooden steps—so uneven and worn down in the middle. Soon everything was deposited in a heap in the middle of the room.

Then Bruce's parents appeared. His mother was small and pretty, dainty and feminine. After the introductions, she said, "Mrs. Marshall, you and I are going to have to go into a huddle about curtains and scatter rugs for this room—"

"It's a warm day," Bruce's father interrupted. "Why don't the five of us go down to the school store? We can get something to drink and talk there."

So over sodas and Cokes, we had our impromptu conference. . . . "What do you boys want at the windows—curtains or short draperies . . . ? I wonder if we couldn't speak to someone about getting the ivy clipped off the windows to let in more light . . . ? What about bedspreads, scatter rugs . . . ? Your pictures will have to be hung from the molding. The rules say no nails in the walls. . . . You have no easy chair in the room. Won't you need one . . . ? So few clothes hangers—and no glasses in the bathroom. . . ."

As we walked back to the room, I noticed how Bruce's mother, all unconsciously, leaned on her husband's arm, smiling up into his face. "An intact family . . . ," I thought. "How wonderful it must be. . . ."

Back in their room Bruce's mother opened one of his suitcases and carried new shoes and galoshes to the closet, piles of new underwear and pajamas to his chest of drawers.

"I sat up till two last night sewing on name tags," she said. "Can you imagine these boys actually getting their own laundry together each week—and on time?"

"No—I can't. I suppose they'll learn."

She eyed the iron beds. "Bruce, can't I make your bed for you one last time? You never get it smooth."

"Never mind, Mom, I'll do it myself—later."

She was acting out what I was feeling . . . the apron strings almost severed, but the hands aching to perform a last chore or two. Yet she had three other sons, and Bruce was not the oldest. She had been through this before.

Peter looked at me. He knew too—knew beyond his years. He said with hesitant dismissal, as if uneasy to have me there longer, "I think you'd better go now, Mom."

So I shook hands with Bruce and his parents, stood on tiptoe to pat my tall son on his cheek, and walked out—down the worn, uneven steps.

As I drove through the winding avenue of trees to the highway, I thought of our home—now an empty house—waiting for me in Washington. I thought of it and turned aside from the thought. Not yet—not quite yet.

Besides, I wanted to see how Peter's and Bruce's room would look after they were unpacked and settled; then during the months to come, I would be able to picture Peter in that setting. But if I stayed a few more hours, I mustn't seem to hover; the boys would never stand for that.

The things they needed—that would be a handy excuse. When a woman is at loose ends, what does she do? She goes shopping for someone she loves. In my mind I was already making a list:

A lounge chair
More clothes hangers
Two plastic glasses for the bathroom

In the village of Northfield, I spied a sign "Furniture and Appliances." It turned out to be a combination store, quite a combination. The local mortician also sold electrical appliances and furniture. The hearse was parked in the driveway.

On the second floor of the store was a maple armchair. "That will do. It's for my son at the boys' school. You do deliver, don't you?"

"Sure—this afternoon, if you like. Which building?"

"Why don't I meet you there? Could you make it one-thirty?"

The man agreed and I left to search out the hangers and the glasses. That done, I still had several hours before one-thirty.

How could I fill the time? I must replace the loneliness—if that's what was welling up in me—with action. So I drove on through the village toward the New Hampshire border. Were the strands of my life suddenly unraveling? Then I would tie the strands together. . . . There must be someone else to shop for. . . . My sister Em had been wanting some antique bone dishes. Perhaps some shop had not yet closed for the season. . . . I would like to find some copper utensils for Mother's farm kitchen at Evergreen. . . . And some maple syrup for Father. . . .

I drove on, watching the hills of Massachusetts stretching themselves to become the mountains of New Hampshire. But across the border no antique shops were open. I turned down a side road, wanting to explore, yet half fearful that I might not be able to find my way back.

The road wound and twisted. I passed no other cars. After several miles I saw a sign "Maple Syrup" in front of a white farmhouse. As I drove into the yard, a little boy came running out to see who the visitor was.

"Do you still have any of that maple syrup for sale?"

"Come on in," he grinned. "I'll call Pop."

"I've sold almost all of this season's," the farmer said when he appeared. "But if you don't need too much—?"

"How about a half gallon? Could you spare that?"

"Sure could. Make yourself at home. Chair right there. I'll fix the syrup for you."

This was the family dining room. The round table in the center of the room was covered with pieces of tissue-paper dress pattern and cotton material. The two cupboards were filled with Early American pressed glass—a set of cranberry thumbprint tumblers and some ribbed opalescent like that Peter and I had once had so much fun collecting.

"The glass has probably been in the family always," I thought. "Antique dealers dream of finding places like this."

The farmer came back with the syrup in two shiny cans, bearing professional-looking labels. About him and his family there was an air of sturdy Americana. This was New England at its best. No wonder this man's ancestors had made things hard for King George III's troops!

The friendly New Hampshire farmhouse had warmed me; the strange road I'd traveled into the mountains had given me a sense of adventure. I could feel my old zest for living seeping back; not even my loneliness could extinguish it.

When I got back to the school, I found the mortician-furniture dealer waiting. I showed him the room and he carried up the chair. The boys were nowhere to be seen, and I made no effort to find them.

The heap was gone from the middle of the floor. The beds were made—bumpy, but made. A pair of pajamas was stuck under each pillow, half trailing out. Peter was using his bookcase as a bedside table. The mementos of home he had insisted on bringing with him—two Toby jugs, some model cars, some favorite pictures and pennants—were carefully arranged.

His new alarm clock was on top of the bookcase; the Toby jugs and model cars on the first shelf. From the molding his two favorite pictures had been hung by long wires—the wall plaque of Tam O'Shanter and Sauter Johnny he had bought in Scotland and an informal *Life* magazine photograph of his father.

I pinned a note on the new chair, put some hangers and a plastic cup on each bed, gave one long last lingering look, and tiptoed out. This time I resolutely turned the car toward home.

My thoughts leaped across the miles to Washington. It's odd, I thought, how each life seems to be divided into eras or chapters. That morning of Peter's death had been the closing of one chapter, the opening of another. And now, this day—in which I've parted with my son— is another ending, yet another beginning.

What did the new era hold? Who could tell? I had no more idea than I had had at that grim moment when I had walked out of the hospital room in which Peter's body lay, had heard the door click shut behind me, and had walked down the chilly corridor. But underneath all fear of an unknown future had been the faith that "Surely goodness and mercy would follow me all the days of my life."

The faith had become a fact. There had been the mercy of the God who had taken the unpromising raw materials of grief and smashed hopes and turned them into astonishing good; there had been the goodness of all the friends whom He had sent into my life.

Now, as I drove homeward, through my mind there trouped a procession of those friends . . . A. D. so wanting to be with me in my hour of grief, slipping into the little hospital room—"Catherine, it was in those moments that I learned what Christ's power over death is. Glory filled that room. . . ." That Chinese woman whose name I never knew, sitting beside me in church that first Sunday after Peter's death, her love flowing, flowing. . . . Anita, tall and imperious, standing in the middle of my bedroom, saying, "I'll be damned if I'll feel sorry for you. . . ." Rebecca Beard, folding me in her ample arms as she asked for the touch of the healing Christ for the stricken spirit of one woman. . . .

I thought of Tom Wharton, his face alight with conviction—"Catherine, you must insist that those sermons be printed in Peter's own style. Any other way would be unfair to him. . . ." I could hear again the ticking of the clock in my doctor's office, and his quiet reasoning voice, "You're flesh and blood, Catherine. Just thank God that you are . . . !"

I remembered that afternoon when I had stood in a New England village post office and eagerly ripped open a letter from a man I had yet to meet, Ed Aswell; of my astonishment at the words I was reading— "There is not the slightest doubt in our minds that this will be a good book and a deeply moving one. . . . We are now prepared to offer you a contract. . . ." Then Ruth Welty's face leapt into my mind. With her remarkable offer of editorial help, she had certainly added to my reservoir of good will. . . . And Jim Broadbent—that rugged Scot! I could see still the pipe smoke wreathing his head, hear him reminiscing in his buzz-saw accent about a boy with tousled hair who had carried in his heart the dream of becoming a minister. . . .

Still they came on—so many friends—all the soldiers who had written from Korea; the letters from Japan, Saipan, and Formosa; from the British Isles, from Australia and South Africa. . . . "Through the pages of this book, Christ walked right into my living room. . . ." "This book was like a shaft of brilliant sunlight on the dark path I was treading. Thank you, thank you. . . ."

They had come from other unexpected quarters—like Hollywood. There was Sam Engel. I could still see those brown eyes behind the spectacles looking at me so unblinkingly—"Sure, Catherine, we need to pray about the movie. You do it—now. . . ." And Marjorie Rambeau, hearing Peter's sermon with her heart instead of her ears, rising in faith to walk down that church aisle, not once, but fifteen times. . . .

I thought of the country contractor with his "worrying concern" over the chimney at Evergreen; of my Dad with the rope around his middle,

dangling four feet off the ground, yelling in his booming voice, "Help!
Earl! Harlow! *Do* something . . . !" And Mother standing on the porch
at Evergreen, a snared dream in her eyes, saying so joyously, "Toward
the end of our lives, here it all is with dividends—filled up, pressed down,
and running over—"

During those years since Peter's death, I had found that life *is*
people—wonderful people, dear people, God's people. Could it have been
that I—who had so valued solitude that I had fled up the back stairs to
find it—had had to be stripped, reduced to aloneness, to discover how
much I needed people, wanted them? Out of loneliness I had found love.
Out of the heart's need, I had crept humbly back to acknowledge that
need and to rejoin the human race.

As I drove, darkness began closing in—not night, but a sudden summer thunderstorm. The rain fell in sheets. The car's windshield wipers
struggled futilely to sweep away the torrents of water. Scissors of lightning slashed the sky with zigzag gashes. Then the storm was over as
quickly as it had come.

A question nagged at my mind, wouldn't let go. The future? To what
do you go home now?

At moments when the future is completely obscured, I thought, can
any one of us afford to go to meet our tomorrows with dragging feet?
God had been in the past. Then He would be in the future, too.

And with His presence had always come an end to tasteless living.
Always He had brought adventure—high hopes, unexpected friends, new
ventures that broke old patterns. Then out in my future must lie more
goodness, more mercy, more adventures, more friends.

Across the hills light was breaking through the storm clouds. Suddenly just ahead of the car an iridescent rainbow appeared—hung there—
shimmering. I hadn't seen a rainbow for a long time.

I drove steadily into the light.

BEYOND
OUR SELVES

To
Len

Acknowledgments

I WISH TO express my appreciation to Elizabeth Sherrill for her constructive criticism and wise counsel; to my husband, Leonard Earle LeSourd, who has assumed responsibility for my manuscript as though it were his own; to Dr. Dudley Zuver, who has checked the manuscript for biblical and theological accuracy; to Miss Patricia Harris, who has done a herculean job of typing and retyping manuscript; to the Fleming H. Revell Company for their generosity in loaning me Hannah Whitall Smith's out-of-print books; to the kind ladies at the Chappaqua Library; and to Mr. Robert F. Beach and his associates at the Union Theological Seminary Library; finally, my lasting gratitude to the friends who have been so gracious in allowing me to share their personal experiences with the readers of this book.

Contents

Foreword

BACK IN 1943, when illness hemmed me within the four walls of my bedroom certain questions presented themselves to me with terrible urgency:

Is it really possible for us to get in touch with the God who created our world?

Why does God allow evil, if He has the power to destroy it?

Can God heal where medicine fails?

Can prayer affect the outward circumstances of our lives?

Does God guide people today?

The search for the answers to these questions has brought adventure beyond anything I could have imagined. *Beyond Our Selves* is the story of that search.

Many others have shared in the explorations that made this book possible. Three persons especially have had a part in it, the first being a woman who died before I was born. I first met her in the pages of one of her own books.

It was in the fall of 1944 that a copy of Hannah Whitall Smith's *The Christian's Secret of a Happy Life* fell into my hands. Superficially the volume was anything but inviting. The print was small and cramped, the language quaint, the writing style outdated. All of this was understandable, as the book had been written in 1870. Since then—with almost no advertising—this little volume had sold about three million copies. I wondered why.

I soon found out. Here was a practical how-to book written in the days before there was any such thing. The chapter headings read like a table of contents still damp with printer's ink: "How to Enter In" (that is, into the Christian life); "Difficulties Concerning Guidance"; "Difficulties Concerning Doubts"; "Difficulties Concerning Faith" . . . .

The zest and decisiveness of her writing revealed Hannah Smith as a woman who knew what she believed and why she believed it. In her day, hell and damnation were still major emphases across Christendom.

Instead, her emphasis was that the Christian life is the happiest of all lives. Yet hers was no easy cult-of-happiness teaching, for she insisted that Christian joy could not be bought cheaply. There was no evading the total surrender of one's life and resources, no avoiding the giving up of doubt and the giving in to a costly obedience.

I read the book through, then read it again. Certain chapters I returned to, over and over. If I had a spiritual problem puzzling me, I could always find an answer in *The Christian's Secret,* provided—provided I meant business about getting straightened out. Someday, I told myself, I would like to write the same kind of helping book for my time. In it I would want to share, as Hannah Smith had, the discoveries—great and small—which had been of value to me in my Christian walk.

The second person whose mark is indelibly on *Beyond Our Selves* is Peter Marshall. When I was a college girl in Atlanta, Peter first caught my attention by the recurring note in his preaching of conviction based on personal experience. In a hundred different ways he said, "I know this is so, because I have experienced it."

He talked often of God's guidance, since he was an example of one whom the Lord had guided. He spoke ringing words about God's ability to provide material needs; God had provided his needs.

He had much to say about Christianity being a joyous life. Those who bowled with him or accompanied him on fishing trips or to baseball games saw the joy firsthand. He insisted that a man need not be a sissy to love the Lord. Other men listened to him, because he was walking proof.

To us college girls, the surety of his conviction and firsthand faith was more fresh and more impressive than any preaching we had ever heard.

Then after he became my husband, he continued to mold me. Here was the love of God pouring through as warm and vivid a personality as I have ever known. Through Peter I saw that our love for God should involve the emotions. Why not? For emotion need not be maudlin. It can also have a virile strength.

He taught me, and many another, the difference between going through the mechanical motions of a church service and the art of corporate worship. Through him I learned what worship is.

Peter imparted to me his knowledge of immortality. His sureness about it was a trumpet call of faith. He was certain of the continuation of a life beyond this one, certain in a way that few persons ever are.

He took my tendency toward snap judgments of people and situations and taught me that "there, but for the grace of God, go I."

And I can never forget his insistence that women should be women, that in our femininity is our glory.

All of this Peter did for me. Not often is there such a combination of husband and teacher. So far as Christianity is concerned, I sat at his feet as did thousands of others. I find now that his ideas, his convictions, even his word-pictures, have become a part of me, tissue and sinew. That is why any book I write is Peter's book too.

I also owe to Peter, in a strange sort of way, my present happiness. For he engrafted into me the truth that in God's scheme of things there is no place for rivalry or jealousy. Each beloved person's place is secure, his own for this life and for eternity. No one can take it from him, nor does it impinge on anyone else's place. That is why Peter is and always will be a part of my life. It is also why Leonard LeSourd, whom I married in 1959, can share him with me and is as grateful as I for Peter's influence on our life together.

I find that having an editor in the family has many compensations, along with a few drawbacks. As the executive editor of *Guideposts* and a writer himself, Len understands the hours that every writer must keep, the needed isolation. He is patient with me when I fall into a black mood because ideas are not flowing, sentences are wooden, and what I am turning out is just plain terrible. Always he gives me unstintingly of his fine editorial judgment.

There are times, however, when I want to slam the office door on my manuscript and not think or speak of it until the next day.

But ideas do not keep hours for Len. "Now, Catherine, if you shifted this section from the middle of Chapter Six to the end—" Or, "I hate to mention it, but the material slows down here. " Once he even telephoned me from a tollbooth along the New Jersey Turnpike: "I've been thinking about that chapter on forgiveness all the way down here. The opening paragraph still isn't quite right—" Then of course, like all editors, he is ruthless with the blue pencil.

But somehow he always knows when I need to shut the door on my writing for longer periods of time. "I want you to write FUN on your calendar for x number of days," he will say every so often. "See what you think of this plan for a trip."

Someday perhaps I shall write about the adventure of rearing a second family. Just at the point when I thought child-rearing was over, Len's three children have joined Peter John in calling me *Mother*.

There is Jeffrey, mischievous and lovable. Standing beside Peter John's six feet, four-and-a-half inches, Jeff appears even tinier than he is. Chester, quiet and sensitive, has enormous deep brown eyes and a well-developed passion for baseball. Peter John has earned his adoration by coaching him for Little League. Then there is Linda, who has always wanted a big brother, and looks on the one she acquired as a dispensation straight from heaven. Linda is also ecstatic over having a writer "for a mommy." She will be even more ecstatic, I hope, when she finds something about herself in this book.

Many experiences have tested me in my lifetime, but none more than this one. And none has made me happier. But writing about it must come later. A man swimming a horse across a turbulent stream does not stop to take a picture of the experience. I'll get my colts across the stream, see them thoroughly dried off, well fed, and on their way—then perhaps, the picture.

Thus, with these three people—Peter, Len, and Hannah—always at my shoulder, *Beyond Our Selves* has been written. Though so different, each of them has one characteristic in common: enthusiastic delight in what Peter Marshall liked to call "spiritual research unlimited." All too often this enthusiasm is the missing ingredient in Christian circles. So if I have succeeded in transferring to the pages that follow one onehundredth part of the excitement that I feel about Christianity, I shall have achieved my purpose.

C.M.

One
Something More

IF YOU ARE satisfied with your life and feel no need for any help outside yourself, this book is not for you. The search for God begins at the point of need.

Most of us feel this need either because of some problem for which we have no answer or because of a nagging consciousness that we should be getting more out of life or putting more into it. There is the realization that we are going through but the motions of living. Surely our half-somnolent existence is not living as it was meant to be! We yearn for something more.

I first felt this need for something more during my college days. Recently I came across these comments, written in a journal that I began about the middle of my freshman year:

> People bustle and strive and hurry. Their eyes are mostly on material considerations. They die, and apparently it's all over. What are we here for anyway? There must be some purpose in living, but I haven't found it yet.
>
> All of my life I've thought that I was possessed with a wanderlust. Now I know that the trouble lies within myself, and I cannot escape myself. I'm restless and unhappy.

Some of the restlessness may have been typical of late adolescence. But not all, for this search for something that I had not yet experienced lasted for ten years or more—into my late twenties.

297

I think of many of all ages who are on the same search. For example, a man named Alex. He is tall and lean, with the high forehead of the intellectual, the eyes of a thoughtful man. Alex is the product of one of the best of the Ivy League colleges and is now a successful free-lance writer.

Where religion was concerned, until a few years ago Alex was an agnostic—and proud of it. With a mind trained in materialism and rationalism, he suspected in all religion a form of elaborate self-deception.

"The truth is that my god has been reason," Alex told me recently. "And reason seemed a god worth worshiping until—"

Until Alex came squarely up against problems in his family life that no amount of reasoning could solve.

"It was hard for me to admit that there are areas in life for which reason has no answers—like man's emotional life and the knotty problem of human relationships. Realizing that shook me," he said. For the first time, he was encountering the indisputable truth that there must be something more.

And I think of Sheila Goshen, a housewife in Birmingham, Alabama, who asked for my help in her search:

> ... After ignoring God for fifty years, I recently got a new look at myself and believe me, I did not like what I saw. So now I've been trying to change myself into what I want to be, but I find that I can't make myself over.
>
> For the first time I know that I need God and faith. So now the question is, how does an ordinary person like me go about gaining an "intimacy" with God?

This is an easy question to ask, a hard one to answer. I puzzled for weeks, then months over it. In a way, this book is my answer.

There is abundant proof that vocational and material success fail utterly to satisfy the inner hunger. The famous Hollywood actress, Mary Astor, has known the fairy-tale magic of movie stardom. An Academy Award, glamorous marriages, two children, several Beverly Hills mansions, furs, jewels, publicity—what more could any woman want?

Yet Mary Astor admitted in print that "for years—even in the midst of fame and glamor—I yearned for contentment, happiness. It took me almost twenty years to go from idle curiosity about religion ... to meeting God as a Person and a Father, and knowing that walking in faith meant growing up."

I have seen this search in college students, especially during their senior year. One such incident happened during one of my weekend visits to Yale University to see my son, Peter John. Three of Peter's friends and I had been chatting over lunch in the cafeteria. The tall, dark-haired boy directly across from me rose. "Sorry to have to rush like this, but I have a one o'clock class. This has been an interesting conversation—"

An odd look, one that I could not interpret, crossed his face, and he hesitated before he spoke again. "Now that I'm a senior, I'm spending quite a lot of time these days trying to figure out what life is all about. Isn't it queer that we get so little help with this in college? I mean why we're here and how to handle life and all that. Well— g'bye, all."

Often the inner hunger catches up with those most immersed in materialism. One day I was talking with a man in the investment business: "During the last year," he told me, "I've experienced a kind of restlessness that baffles me. I've tried working late at the office, even plunged in the stock market so that I won't have time to think about myself. I've gone out on the town more, trying to have some fun. Even tried drinking more than usual. Nothing is ever as gratifying to the taste, sight and touch as I hope it will be. I've tried to find some satisfaction in new sports equipment, two expensive cars. Nothing helps.

"What I'm about to ask may sound strange—especially from a Wall Street broker who spends his time thinking about Dow-Jones averages rather than religion. But I wonder—could this gnawing inside be . . . well, my inner spirit crying out for its Maker and refusing to be satisfied with anything less? If this is a possible explanation, what can I do about it? How does one go about finding God?"

In every community, in every land, at every social and economic level, are individuals just as eager as the investment broker to find their way to God, though many are too shy to voice it as he did. They have questions to ask, problems to solve. They wonder if Christianity really does have answers for them.

To know where answers cannot be found is at least a step in the right direction. Until the first World War, many people were certain that the *something more* was right here on earth. Of course, we thought it wise to give lip-service to a Higher Power. *In God We Trust* was stamped on our coins. A sentence or two mentioning a Supreme Being appeared in most political speeches, rather like a sprig of parsley for garnish. But through all this there was the tacit understanding that we could work out our destinies, both personal and national, by ourselves. We did not really need God.

In fact, as the twentieth century dawned Americans were probably the most optimistic people on earth. Industry, stimulated by mass production and distribution, made the end of poverty seem in sight. Eventually all the inhabitants of earth could be provided with at least minimum requirements of food, clothing, and shelter. Given time, medicine would virtually stamp out disease. More inventions and gadgets would give us leisure time for fun and culture, perhaps even a little self-examination.

Best of all, education would finally convince men that war was folly. During the late 1920s, in high schools across the United States, boys and girls were studying about the League of Nations. I know, because I spent many a winter evening curled up in an easy chair near a gas heater, preparing for a stiff examination on the subject. The prize (which I did not win) was a trip to Geneva, Switzerland, to see the League in action. My generation was confident that intelligent arbitration guided by the League and the World Court would soon replace the senseless outrage of war. It was all a part of the doctrine of inevitable progress.

Without realizing what was happening, most of us gradually came to take for granted the premises underlying this philosophy of optimism. We proceeded to live these propositions, though we would not have stated them as blandly as I set them forth here:

Man is inherently good.

Individual man can carve out his own salvation with the help of education and society through progressively better government.

Reality and the values worth searching for lie in the material world that science is steadily teaching us to analyze, catalogue, and measure. While we would not deny the existence of inner values, we relegate them to second place.

The purpose of life is happiness. And happiness we define in terms of enjoyable activity, friends, and the accumulation of material objects.

The pain and evil of life—such as ignorance, poverty, selfishness, hatred, greed, lust for power—are caused by factors in the external world. Therefore the cure lies in the reforming of human institutions and the bettering of environmental conditions.

As science and technology remove poverty and lift from us the burden of physical existence, we shall automatically become finer persons, seeing for ourselves the value of living by the Golden Rule.

In time, the rest of the world will appreciate our demonstration that the American way of life is best. They will then seek for themselves the good life of freedom and prosperity. This will be the greatest impetus toward an end of global conflict.

The way to get along with people is to beware of religious dictums and dogma. The ideal is to be a nice person and to live by the Creed of Tolerance. Thus we offend few people. We live and let live. This is the American way.

So we believed. So we acted.

Then came the first World War and its hideous aftermath. In Europe and the British Isles, the disillusionment was deep and real. Europeans were no longer convinced of the inherent goodness of man.

But in the Western Hemisphere we had had no cities shelled, no countryside devastated. The ink was scarcely dry on the Versailles Treaty before our philosophy of optimism reasserted itself. The trouble that caused the 1914–1918 war, we assured ourselves, was not unredeemed human nature but the munitions-makers and kindred institutions inherited from an unenlightened nineteenth century. On college campuses, lecture platforms, and in church groups our indignation was loud and vociferous. I remember taking part in intercollegiate debates—some of them with international teams from Oxford, Cambridge, and the University of London—in which we aired our loathing for the armament-makers and the peddlers of war propaganda.

The fault was never in ourselves. No, this had nothing to do with man and his God. It was just a matter of ironing the kinks out of our society. Meanwhile technological developments rose to ever greater heights. The Golden Twenties gave certitude to the doctrine of inevitable progress. And while the Depression that struck in late October 1929 was, for a time, a shattering experience, once again most people felt that the trouble was not in man but in his institutions—in this case, monopolies, the stock market, buying on margin, greedy big business. Franklin Delano Roosevelt's New Deal with its relief, recovery, and reform would take care of all that.

Suspicions that mankind might not be working out salvation for our world came with Adolf Hitler. Czechoslovakia, Poland, Denmark, Norway, the Netherlands, Belgium, France—one by one they fell before the tide of Nazism. But it was not so much the war itself as the Nazi atrocities that finally shattered our philosophical optimism about man. These shocked us to our depths, destroying once and for all the pretty picture of man as inherently good. Certain pictures can never be erased. . . .

The year was 1941. The scene a Polish village called Minsk. Adolph Eichmann, Hitler's specialist for Jewish Affairs for the Third Reich, had been sent to witness the extermination of five thousand Jews.

The morning was cold. The condemned men, women and children undressed down to their underwear or their shirts. They walked the last hundred yards and jumped into a pit that had been prepared for them. Eichmann was impressed by the fact that they offered no resistance, apparently by this time reconciled to death.

Then the rifles and machine pistols opened fire. Children in the pit were crying, clinging to their parents. Eichmann saw one woman hold her baby high above her head, pleading, "Shoot me, but please let my baby live. Take my baby. Please take my baby—"

Eichmann had children of his own. For a moment he felt a twinge of compassion. He almost opened his mouth to order, "Don't shoot. Hand over the child." Then the baby was hit.

"I scarcely spoke a word to the chauffeur on the trip back," he reported later. "I was thinking. I was reflecting about the meaning of life in general. . . ."

What conclusions did Eichmann reach? Years later he summarized how he felt about the mass-execution program that destroyed some six million Jews. "I was a little cog in the machinery of the Reich. I merely carried out orders. Where would we have been if everyone had thought things out in those days?

"After all, the people who were loaded on trains and buses [for extermination] meant nothing to me. It was really none of my business."[1]

What had happened to the German people? Americans who had traveled in Germany between the two world wars remembered the charm of the tidy countryside, the friendliness of the people on the city streets and in the shops, the love of music, the gaiety. We had acquired a healthy respect for the typical German businessman; his approach seemed so akin to ours. And as more and more Americans had roamed the globe, one conclusion had seemed paramount: surely men everywhere are much the same.

So it was not only the enormity of the Nazi cruelties that appalled us but the ugly suspicion that imperfect man might commit other brutalities—anywhere, at any time. Was it really true that man was innately good, that education, science, technology, and a better environment would ultimately perfect him? The German people had had all those advantages.

But there was still one corner in which we as Americans might hide from the truth about human nature, so we fled to it. It was undeniable that evil things had happened in the rest of the world. But Americans, we reasoned, were different. We were people of good will. We hated war. We coveted no empire. Our intentions were of the best. We were a generous people.

And then, just at the close of the second World War, a bomb was dropped on Hiroshima. It made dubious our carefully drawn distinction between us and the evil of the rest of the world. It had not been merely German evil that had been responsible for unspeakable brutalities: it was human evil. And we, too, were a part of that humanity.

Some occurrences during the Korean conflict threw further light on man's potential for weakness, evil, even depravity. There were events involving Americans. Take, for example, an incident that took place in February 1951, just ten years after the mass murders of the Minsk pit. It happened in the mountains of North Korea, near Pyoktong. Forty-three American prisoners were huddled in a hut trying to keep warm. Two of the men had severe cases of diarrhea, not pleasant in the close quarters.

In the course of the evening, an American corporal suddenly got to his feet, picked up one of his sick comrades and dumped him outside. Then he came back and threw the other sick soldier out. Not a man stirred, not a voice was raised in protest. It was thirty degrees below zero outside; the exposed men were dead within minutes.

The merciless corporal who was thus responsible for the death of two fellow countrymen was tried after the war, convicted of manslaughter, and sentenced to life imprisonment.

But what of the forty witnesses? All of these were questioned about
the incident by Army psychiatrists. The typical interview, as reported
by the psychiatrists, went something like this:

"Soldier, did you see that man throw the two sick soldiers out of
the hut?"

"Oh, yes sir."

"What were you doing at the time?"

"Oh, I was just huddling together with the rest of the guys, trying
to keep warm. That's the only way you could stay alive."

"Then you knew that it would destroy these men to be exposed?"

"Well—sure."

"But what were you doing about it?"

"I wasn't doing anything—except trying to keep warm."

"Why *didn't* you do something about it, soldier?"

"Because," the reply came, "it wasn't any of my business."

The words echo strangely: "It was really none of my business."

To be sure, there were many examples of American self-sacrifice
and heroism in the Korean war, as in every war in which Americans have
been involved. Yet something about the attitudes and conduct of a percentage of men in the Korean conflict has seriously disturbed our leaders. These were American boys from all across the nation—a nation
presumed to be "under God." They had come up through our public
school system, a percentage of them also through our Sunday schools.
Since childhood they had heard about the worth of the individual, about
liberty and human rights, and "loving thy neighbor." How was it that
these values had not become a part of them?

Obviously something had happened back home, something that had
allowed them to grow up insecure children of an age of anxiety, with a
sense of isolation and a desperate need to make contact with other human
beings. As prisoners in the cold wasteland of North Korea, they found
that the Something More was not where they had thought it. Materialism had provided them pleasure, but it had given them no answers about
the meaning of life.

These boys were no better, no worse than the rest of us Americans.
For the raw drama of the Korean hut has been repeated often in the years
since then . . . Bystanders along the shore watched while an elderly man
drowned a hundred feet from shore; no one tried to save him. A man

attacked a woman during daylight in an apartment courtyard. Though her screams were heard by dozens of people, no one rushed to her aid. A twenty-six-year-old father, his hair burned from his head, stood naked in front of his burning home screaming for help from passing motorists for his wife and six children trapped inside. The cars sped by him; his wife and children—seven to six months old—were burned to death. And the words echo back, "It's really none of my business."

Though the lack of personal involvement was still with us, as the sixties progressed, a creeping national frustration was added to it. The "course of human events" was not going well. In spite of our much-vaunted military might, the war in Vietnam dragged on and on. Terror in the once-peaceful streets of American cities, riots in the ghettos, the assassination of leaders, ever-rising inflation—all fed this frustration. There was the terrifying feeling that the control of our national destiny was slipping from our grasp and that perhaps no leader could be found to help us rediscover the American Dream.

Yet still we cling to our philosophy of materialism, though we have had abundant evidence that this ideology which ignores the spirit has failed time and again. "Happiness is . . . the accumulation of things" our television commercials keep reassuring us. Then the Great Society, we assume, must be a bigger and better handout to more citizens, so minority groups march and camp and riot for their rightful share.

But man—where is man in all this? Jammed into our cities of concrete and steel and glass, crowded and threatened by our fellows, the air polluted, the soil and water poisoned, so much of the countryside and farmland desecrated, our lives dictated increasingly by centralized government—where are we, the people, now?

What we write and say about ourselves reveals that we believe ourselves not so much citizens of a republic, but a body of consumers. The difference is significant. As citizens of a republic we would still be concerned with the national destiny, with our individual creativity, with what we could contribute to our time. As consumers we have become a nation of takers, frantically scrambling to get ours while there is anything left to take. Instinctively we know that this is a diminishing proposition: "out there" somewhere is point zero, extermination—unless—

Unless we can find a way for man once again to control his own science and technology. But that brings us back full circle to man. Why

is man on earth? What are his goals? How can we handle the evil intertwined in human nature so that the golden age can come? Force does
not achieve it. Wars solve nothing. Atomic weapons in the hands of
unredeemed human nature bequeath us the ultimate in fear.

And so our only hope lies in a change inside man. Are we finally to
the place where we know that only with the help of a power greater than
ourselves can any man, can any nation be redeemed?

Is this too slow a way, now that civilization has arrived at the elev-
enth hour? No, for we have tried all other ways. And the influence that
can be wielded by a single great man in the grip of a spiritual passion
can never be measured. Even as a handful of leaders in the grip of evil
have wrecked the lives of millions, so other leaders who are willing to
put themselves into the mainstream of God's power may yet be able to
grant us a reprieve.

The stakes are higher than they have ever been. For the first time
mankind faces the possibility of self-extermination. But in these stakes
there is challenge and high adventure, along with the danger.

A few years ago, there were those who said that the atom could not
be split. The atom has been split. Why should we not go forward in the
same spirit to explore the spiritual world where lies the answer to a greater
riddle—the riddle of the nature of man and his relation to the universe?

This spiritual world is a real world. Of that some of us have abundant evidence. There is terrain still to be discovered; peaks yet to be
scaled; new truth to be mined; in short, the spiritual atom to be split.

We can learn much from the spiritual explorers who have sought and
found some of that truth. They can lead us at least a part of the way, to
the foothills beyond which rise the mountains that challenge our time.
Some of them, like Hannah Whitall Smith, lived in other centuries, and
we have the privilege of sharing their discoveries through the written word.
Many are contemporaries. A number are friends whom I have found eager to share anything that they have learned, so that others can go on to
further discoveries. Some of their stories are in the pages that follow.

This book, then, is the story of a pilgrimage. The end has not yet
been written. In a sense, you and I will be doing that in the days and
years ahead. What I have written here is for anyone who longs for Something More and who wants to be a part of the quest.

Two
The Unselfishness
of God

I KNOW A young scientist who admits he does not believe in God. He is warm-hearted and likable, is good to his family, but has a restless uncertainty about the meaning of life.

From talking to him I know that at intervals he goes through a certain cycle. Some experience or reasoning process will bring him to the conclusion that there has to be "something more" in life than birth, struggle, death, nothingness. He will thirst for things of the spirit, hunger to believe in God. Then just at the point where there could be a spiritual breakthrough, he encounters tragedy somewhere—possibly the death of a child, the disfigurement of a beautiful girl, cancer in someone well known and well loved.

"How can a good and loving God permit this, if He made and runs the world?" he asks then. Rather than seek an explanation, he shrugs off religion as something too baffling to comprehend.

If there is a Creator, what could His nature be? That is what the scientist wants to know. It is a question over which many would-be believers stumble. It is the question with which all of us who want the adventure of exploring the spiritual world must begin. Its answer is pertinent to our happiness. Unless each of us can find answers that satisfy, we cannot trust that Creator with our dearest hopes, and so we shall have no basis for faith in God.

All of us have had contradictory experiences of the nature of God. I know I have. They run like threads through my childhood. In the very beginning, the love of my father and mother taught me of the fatherliness of God lying at the heart of the universe. Looking back at that childhood, feelings of glorious freedom and of rushing joy rise even now to meet me. Safe and loved we were, in God's world.

My brother, Bob, and sister, Emmy, and I used to roam the woods and mountains that surrounded our small West Virginia town. We waded mountain streams to pick mint and watercress and violets on far banks. We skipped smooth stones across the water, dared one another to run across swinging bridges. There is the memory of struggling up a mountainside, gulping deep drafts of the cool air, all of the aching effort worth that moment when we would stand on the summit to survey the world we knew so well lying at our feet, with more mountains beyond pushing back the horizon.

There was the exhilaration of lying on our stomachs, coasting down long, snow-packed hills in the winter; skimming down the same hills on our bicycles in the summer, the wind in our faces. There was the way we would stand and "pump" in our swing: Begin slowly. Bend the knees in rhythm with the swinging. Make it go higher . . . higher . . . up and down. Now again, swishing through the air, until finally the jerk of the chains told us that the swing had gone as high as it could. Then "let the cat die . . ."

There were the twilight hours of long summer evenings when all the children of the neighborhood gathered to play "Kick the Can . . ." The breathless dash out of hiding to give the can a swift kick and listen to the music of its careening, crashing, clinking progress down the street.

This was the freedom of the child who is loved and knows that he is loved. It was not that we children were free to disobey or to do as we pleased. But neither did we have to strain to earn love by being good. For we had constant evidence that Mother and Father would keep on loving us even when they disapproved our actions.

How well I recall one spring day when an irate neighbor called upon Father to inform him that a portion of the wall in his back yard had collapsed. The neighbor was sure that this was no act of God; the Wood children were mixed up in it somewhere.

Father's investigation proved that the man was right. We had been using a coal house behind the neighbor's property as a clubhouse. All our spare time for several weeks had been used in digging a secret tunnel. Soon, our toy wagon had hauled out quite a mound of dirt. As a result the tunnel which had begun underneath the coal house had veered too close to the neighbor's stone wall.

At such times the parental temper could flare. Em and I, being girls, knew better than Bob how to placate this one weakness of Father's. What usually developed was a highly dramatic scene with Bob and Father in the leading roles, Em and I standing by trying to give Bob support.

"You know perfectly well," Father would begin in that strong booming voice he had developed in seminary, "that you had no business doing all that digging in someone else's yard. The mere fact that you kept it a secret proves that————"

Already Bob was in tears, his cowlick jerking. "But—we *had* to keep it secret. All three of us had signed a pledge in blood————"

"In *what?* Never mind—I don't care *what you* signed the pledge in. I have warned you over and over————"

By now, Em was behind Mother's back, signaling to Bob. All of us were a captive audience for Father's eloquent oration. Like his well-organized sermons, the oration had several clear points: first, reminder of previous warnings; second, our total lack of respect for parental authority; third, the uncertain destiny of the younger generation; fourth, the futility of trying to raise good, obedient children; fifth, this time was the last straw.

By the time the rising crescendo of the fifth point had been reached, Mother was saying, "Pl-lease-e, John, *lower* your voice. Must we tell all the neighbors?"

Father's mien was that of a wounded lion. "Leonora, it *so* happens that in this case, the neighbors already know *only* too well." Then, with giant stride, the great man would storm out of the back door, decisively snap a small switch off the privet hedge, re-slam the back door, and stalk back in.

This was the cue for Bob to increase the anguish of his wails: "I'm sorry, Dad, I'll never do it again—never—never—" And for me to try to make myself heard: "Father, Bob wasn't the only one Em and I————"

And for Em to burst into tears: "Don't switch Bob, Dad. I dug the tunnel too———"

But after the tempest had subsided and peace was restored, it was Father who patiently helped us rebuild the stone wall. Through his lecture and even the punishment that followed, his love (which was God's love to us then) shone through. Thus even in our wrongdoing we discovered that our father and mother would always be beside us in the midst of trouble, still loving us.

As a younger child, I can remember the warmth and strength of Father's arms as I nestled there, content to sit silently while he carried on leisurely conversations with grown-ups. Just as clearly I can remember Mother's firm hand on my forehead when I was sick, the deliciousness of ice-cold apple scraped with a silver spoon for a fevered tongue, the stories she read aloud during bouts with the measles or chicken pox. I learned early that stories were experiences, entrancing lands to which the gates were always invitingly open.

In the same awareness of God's love at its simplest and most profound, I remember the fragrance of the first hyacinths in the spring and of the reddish-brown blossoms of the sweet scrub. . . . The feel of bare feet on moss under our giant oak trees. . . . The luxuriance of the purple wisteria that made beautiful even the old coal house. . . . The way we children would bite off the tip of a honeysuckle blossom and suck out the honey. . . . And, toward the turn of the year, the smell of balsam Christmas trees, of candle wax and wood smoke.

One day my mother and I stood at a window watching the fury of a thunderstorm of near-hurricane strength. It seemed drama on a cosmic scale—the clash of cymbals in the sky, the rolling of drums, fireworks of lightning. Rather than being afraid, I felt like shouting and applauding as the ferocious wind shook the great trees backward and forward as though they had been twigs clenched in the jaws of a dog. All the while, my mother's arm lay protectively around my shoulders.

Only in retrospect would I one day see the connection between these childhood experiences and my understanding of the nature of God. Then I would know that it made no sense at all that God would create my parents with a greater capacity for loving than He has Himself.

At the same time, there was another strand of experience in my childhood. As I grew up, I could not but become aware of the evil and suffering in the world. In any clergyman's home, as in any physician's, the raw drama of life passes steadily before the eyes.

I vividly recall my first encounter with suffering—the winter's night Father was called to the local hospital to minister to a woman who was dying of first-degree burns over most of her body. A stove had exploded when she had tried to start a fire with kerosene. When, after a vigil of many hours, Father wearily returned home, we children found ourselves backing away from him. The odor of burned flesh clung to his clothes. For days Father was so haunted by what he had seen that he had difficulty eating.

Then there was the night the mayor of our town banged on our door at three A.M. to tell Father that the body of our friend and neighbor, Mr. Fisher, had been discovered on the Baltimore and Ohio railroad tracks near Harpers Ferry. Apparently he had lost his balance and had fallen off the rear platform of the Capitol Limited.

"I just can't bear to be the one to break this awful news to Mrs. Fisher," the mayor said. "You're a minister. You'll know what to say."

But Father was also a human being. His family knew that he found it just as hard as anyone to be the bearer of such tidings.

In a sense, Mother was as much a minister as Father. She had been appointed by the mayor to serve on the Board for County Relief because she had a reputation for always being on the side of the down-and-outers. Every Christmas she supervised the assembling of a hundred-odd baskets of food, clothes, and toys for the poor. And a spot like Radical Hill— the chief slum district of our town, where most of the baskets were taken—lay heavily on her conscience. There many families lived in shacks with no plumbing and little heat.

Then came the afternoon when Mother's deep conviction that something must be done spilled over into action. She spent the day tramping over Radical Hill surveying the situation. When she returned home, we children were awed to see her weep at the remembrance of what she had seen. Then she gingerly stripped herself of every garment, dumped her clothes in the washing machine, took a bath, even washed her hair.

Later, during my undergraduate days at Agnes Scott College, I was to have an experience reminiscent of Mother's. A group of college men and women were asked to give an afternoon to the Syrian Mission in Atlanta, Georgia. I was among the volunteers.

The mission was in the heart of Atlanta's worst slum district, close to the state capitol building, as is often the case. The afternoon was to include a short service at the mission and visiting afterward—two by two—in some of the homes. It was the visiting that brought the revelation. I had dimly realized that such squalid, dirty places did exist, but I had never been personally exposed to them.

Pictures still come back: Men around a fireplace, slinking away as we went in. . . . Broken window panes stuffed with rags and paper. . . . A sick child doubled up on a dirty bed in a corner. . . . Air so stale that we felt polluted to breathe it. . . . An absurdly young mother wearing ankle socks, nursing her baby before us. . . . In another room an old woman who had been ill, she told us, for six months, her yellow skin stretched tight over gaunt cheekbones. . . . A lamp on an old-fashioned dresser made grotesque shadows on flyspecked walls.

I wanted to flee. But even as we headed back toward college, I wondered—was this, too, God's world?

It was sometime during my teens that I received my first clear shaft of light on the riddle of evil. There was growing larger and larger in my mind the contrast between my loving, compassionate parents and a God who allowed such terrible things. One day I took this puzzling question to a woman who had become a very special friend.

Mrs. MacDonald was one of those remarkable people who love all young people. Because she never talked down to teenagers, many of us gave her our complete confidence. She was married to a Scotsman, a successful lawyer. On occasions when he had to be away from home on law cases, I would spend the night with her. Those evenings were talkfests.

The flavor of Mrs. Mac's life was reflected in her home. Windows were filled with African violets. On the stair landing stood a grandfather clock whose musical chimes marked the quarter-hours. There were current books of history and travel lying about. Just before bedtime Mrs. Mac and I would always have heaping bowls of ice cream,—more ice cream than I could eat. Then she would tuck me under an eiderdown in a mahogany bed with tall pineapple posts.

On one of these evenings I found myself spilling out my inner rebellion against a God Who permitted suffering and evil when He had the power to stop it.

"Catherine," she said thoughtfully, "you know how often I speak of Kenneth?"

I nodded. Quickly my mind reviewed what I knew about Kenneth. He had been the MacDonalds' only son, had died of diabetes as a teenager. It had compounded their sorrow that insulin had been discovered just a few months too late to save their boy. Here then, close at home, was an example of the kind of tragedy that made me question the love of God.

"Well," my friend went on, "if I had reasoned as you suggest, I could have railed bitterly against God for allowing Kenneth's death. God has power. He could have prevented it, so why didn't He?

"Even now, I can't give you a complete answer to that. But I can't be bitter either, because during Kenneth's long illness, I had so many examples of God's tender father-love. Like that time soon after Kenneth himself suspected that he was going to die and asked me, 'Mother, what is it like to die? Mother, does it hurt?'"

Even as Mrs. Mac repeated the questions, tears sprang to my eyes. "How—did you answer him?"

The white-haired woman seemed to be seeing into the past. "I remember that I fled to the kitchen, supposedly to attend to something on the stove. I leaned against the kitchen cabinet. Queer, I'll never forget certain tiny details, like the feel of my knuckles pressed hard against the smooth, cold surface. And I asked God how to answer my boy.

"God did tell me. Only He could have given me the answer to the hardest question that a mother can ever be asked. I knew—just knew how to explain death to him. 'Kenneth,' I remember saying, 'you know how when you were a tiny boy, you used to play so hard all day that when night came, you would be too tired to undress—so you would tumble into Mother's bed and fall asleep?

"'That was not your bed. It was not where you belonged. And you would only stay there a little while. In the morning—to your surprise— you would wake up and find yourself in your own bed in your own room. You were there because someone had loved you and had taken care of you. Your father had come—with his great strong arms—and carried you away.'

"So I told Kenneth that death is like that. We just wake up some morning to find ourselves in another room—our own room, where we belong. We shall be there, because God loves us even more than our human fathers and takes care of us just as tenderly."

We were both silent for a moment. Then Mrs. Mac said softly, "Kenneth never had any fear of dying after that. If—for some reason that I still don't understand—he could not be healed, then this taking away of all fear was the next greatest gift God could give us. And in the end, Kenneth went on into the next life exactly as God had told me he would—gently, sweetly." There was the look of profound peace on my friend's face as she spoke.

After Mrs. Mac tucked me in that night, I lay in the mahogany bed under the eiderdown, pondering her words. What she had really been telling me was that those on the inside of tragedy are often initiated into something that outsiders may not experience at all: the love of God—instant, continuous, real—in the midst of their trouble. With the presence of the Giver, they have something more precious than any gift He might bestow.

Not until years later, after my marriage to Peter Marshall, did I experience this for myself. During our first happy year in Atlanta, we had a close friend who had known much trouble—the death of children, financial reverses, the misunderstanding of friends. She used to look quizzically at us—young, so in love, fresh in our faith in the goodness of God.

"Neither of you has really had any trouble," she would say. "You're bound to have some sooner or later. Everyone does. When trouble comes to you, I wonder if you will feel as you do now?"

The friend's prediction was right. We did have trouble—much illness, and finally Peter Marshall's death at forty-six. So now I am in a better position to answer the friend's question. The answer is yes, I still believe in God's love, believe more firmly than ever, because my faith has stood trial.

A few hours before Peter's death I found out what the Hebrew poet meant when he wrote about "the everlasting arms."[1] I experienced the comfort of those arms. It happened in the early morning hours after Peter had been taken by ambulance to the hospital. I was forced to stay behind, so that our young son Peter John would not be in the house alone.

There was no doubt that Peter's life hung in the balance. I sank to the floor by the bed, put my head in my arms, pondering how should I pray. Suddenly there was the feeling of being surrounded by the love of God the Father—enveloped in it, cradled with infinite gentleness.

Awe swept through me, followed by the conviction that it was not necessary to *ask* for anything. All I had to do was to commit Peter and me and our future to this great love. At the time I thought this meant that Peter's heart would be healed.

Much later—when I had trodden the long way through the Valley of the Shadow—I realized that God had given me this experience in the hours preceding Peter's death so that I might have absolute assurance that He was beside Peter and me every minute, loving us, sharing Peter's glory and my grief.

That is how I came to know personally that the Apostle Paul's glowing assertion is literally true that nothing—neither death, nor life, nor tribulation, nor peril of any sort shall be able to separate us from the love of God. . . .[2]

Then, in the years that followed Peter Marshall's death, I thought I glimpsed another shaft of light illuminating the dark night of human sorrow. Not only is God always beside us in trouble, identified with our suffering, but He can also make everything—even our troubles and sorrows—"work together for good."[3]

How many times I have received letters from readers whom I have never met, who marveled at how God accomplished this in our case . . . "How I wish that I might have heard Dr. Marshall preach! But so far away here in New Zealand, I would never have known about him at all, had it not been for *A Man Called Peter*. And now, to think that he is preaching to more people than ever today."

This is not to say that God willed Peter's death in order that He might bring about a widened ministry. Rather that given his death, God could turn even that to good.

I remember a poignant letter I received from a reader posing a difficult question—why small children must be taken:

Our little boy was hit last spring in the street in front of our home by a truck. He died a week later. Billy was our only child. He had seemed like a gift from God, because we had hoped and prayed for a baby for two years. . . .

Then was it God's will that this little boy die such an unnecessary death? In trying to bring themselves to say with honesty, "Thy will be done," these parents found themselves confused. For along with the best physicians and surgeons they could find, they tried everything medical science knew to save their child. Then had they been working during those days against the will of God?

I understood the questions of this mother, because I had faced them all when death had invaded my life. Surely there is a difference (and it is not just a quibble) between God's ideal will and His permissive will. Thus, in my case, I cannot believe that it was God's ideal will that Peter Marshall die at forty-six. But given a certain set of circumstances—among them Peter's inherited physique, so fine that he was inclined to overtax it—God had an alternate plan by which He could bring unimagined good even out of early death.

In the same way I could not believe that it was God's ideal will that three-year-old Billy die in such a cruel way. But given a motorized society, given our congested cities, given human free will that resulted in a driver's and a child's carelessness, God would still not suspend the operation of His universe to violate the free will that conspired to bring about this tragedy.

And so illumination came to me. By giving humans freedom of will, the Creator has chosen to limit His own power. He risked the daring experiment of giving us the freedom to make good or bad decisions, to live decent or evil lives, because God does not want the forced obedience of slaves. Instead, he covets the voluntary love and obedience of sons who love Him for Himself.

This, then, is a large portion of the answer to my early question: Why does not a compassionate God hasten to remedy every wrong? I remember the way Peter Marshall answered this in a memorable sermon, "God Still Reigns," preached in Washington during the second world war:

> There is no use trying to evade the issue.
> There are times when God does not intervene—
> The fact that He does nothing is one of the most
>   baffling mysteries in the Christian life.
>
> It was H. G. Wells who voiced the dilemma
> that many troubled hearts have faced in war-time:

"Either God has the power to stop all this
carnage and killing and He doesn't care,
or else He does care, and He doesn't have the
power to stop it."

But that is not the answer . . .
As long as there is sin in the world.
As long as there is greed
                    selfishness
                        hate in the hearts of men
there will be war. . . .

It is only because God is God that He is reckless
enough to allow human beings such free will as has led
the world into this present catastrophe.

God could have prevented the war!
Do you doubt for a moment that God has not the
power?
But suppose He had used it?
Men would then have lost their free agency . . .
They would no longer be souls endowed with the
ability to choose . . .

They would then become puppets
                        robots
                        machines
                    toy soldiers instead.

No, God is playing a much bigger game.
He is still awaiting an awakened sense of the
responsibility of brotherhood in the hearts of
men and women everywhere.
He will not do for us the things that we can do
for ourselves. . . .

A few years ago I was asked to conduct a Sunday-evening seminar
at an exclusive girls' boarding school in the Virginia countryside outside Washington, D.C. When I arrived I found the high school sophomores grouped informally around a large living room, some sitting on
the Oriental rugs before a blazing fire.

The students had been told that they might ask any questions they wished. After the first few minutes it became obvious that while these were intelligent girls, their questions uncovered the most basic misunderstanding of God. One girl voiced the query that is always asked at every church young-people's conference: "What about people in remote parts of Africa or certain jungles of South America who have never heard of Jesus Christ? Will they be condemned to eternal torment? What would be fair about that?"

Another girl, who had obviously been studying sociology, chimed in, "Let's bring the question closer home. What about individuals who become criminals because they were born into slums or other terrible surroundings where they had no chance from the beginning? How could God be just and blame them?"

A beautiful fifteen-year-old posed the one that really tugged at my heart: "There's something that really bothers me. . . ." I saw that she had tears in her eyes as she tried not to make obvious what she most wanted to ask: "My mother and father seldom go near any church. Will God condemn them to eternal damnation for that?"

I was shocked at the terrifying illusion of God that those questions revealed. The mother and father of the fifteen-year-old were dear to her. Did God love them less than she? And how would she ever be able to trust her Creator with her own happiness so long as her only emotion toward Him was terror?

The family love that was so implicit in this girl's questioning reminded me of what my own joyous childhood had taught me: God would scarcely give fathers and mothers a greater capacity for loving their children than God Himself has for loving all His children. I suggested to the girls that God would not have bothered to create father-love and mother-love in the first place, if He Himself did not have it in great abundance.

Then as I told them of my own gropings toward this answer, I thought of how grieved God must be that any of His children should cower before Him in fright. And I realized how often we attribute emotions and deeds to God that we would ascribe only to the most depraved of human minds. Probably no personality in the universe is so maligned as that of the Creator.

Soon after the evening at the girls' school, I came across this same thought in one of Hannah Whitall Smith's books:

... The amazing thing is that all sort of travesties on the character of God and libels on His goodness can find a welcome entrance into Christian hearts. ... Nothing else matters as much as this, for all our salvation depends wholly and entirely upon what God is; and unless He can be proved to be absolutely good, and absolutely unselfish, our case is hopeless. ....[4]

Then Hannah Smith relates how she discovered for herself the unselfishness of God. Between the ages of sixteen and twenty-six, she had passed through a period of skepticism. During this period God had seemed far-off, an unapproachable Being, a stern and selfish Taskmaster, an Autocrat. She asked exactly the same questions that the sophomores in the girls' school asked me that Sunday evening: What about those born into circumstances for which they are not responsible and from which they cannot escape? Would vast numbers of fellow human beings therefore be doomed to eternal punishment for what they cannot help? Most of the church groups of her day taught that they would be. But, Mrs. Smith wondered, would that be justice from a Creator whose tender mercies were said to be "over *all* His works?"[5]

Hannah Smith began to see in every face the anguish which resulted from sin's entrance into the world. She came to be grateful that the fashion of her day dictated veils for women in public; at least the faces before her would be blurred.

One day she was riding in a tram-car along Market Street in Philadelphia. Two men came in and sat down opposite her on the straw seat. When the conductor came for the fare, she was forced to raise her veil to count out change.

She looked up and saw clearly the faces of the two men opposite her. They were lost, debauched-looking. Not only that, but one of them was blind. A new flood of emotion rose to engulf her. In her thoughts she railed against God: "How can You bear it? You might have prevented all this misery, but You did not. Even now You might change it, but You do not. How can You go on living and endure it?"

Suddenly, there in the tram car, God seemed to answer her. The word *lost* blazed with a tremendous illumination: nothing can be lost that is not first owned. Just as a parent is compelled by civil law to be responsible for his family and property, so the Creator—by His own divine law—is compelled to take care of the children He has created. And that means not only caring for the good children, but for the bad ones and the lost ones as well.

So the word *lost* came to be for Mrs. Smith a term of greatest comfort. If a person is a "lost sinner," it only means that he is temporarily separated from the Good Shepherd who owns him. The Shepherd is bound by all duties of ownership to go after all those who are lost until they are found. For Hannah Smith the question about the plight of individuals who have had little chance in life was forever answered. "Who can imagine a mother ever dropping a search so long as there is the least chance of finding a lost child?" Mrs. Smith wrote. "Then would God be more indifferent than a mother? Since I had this sight of the mother-heart of God, I have never been able to feel the slightest anxiety for any of His children. We can trust Him . . . trust Him.

In my dealings with people I have been surprised to find that so many honestly do not believe that God wants our happiness and fulfillment. We have heard all of our lives that God is Love, but we insist on "spiritualizing" this. Many Christians have been taught that God's love is different from ours—not the kind His creatures understand. Deeply imbedded in our consciousness is the idea that God is primarily interested in our spiritual and moral rectitude; that, therefore, most of what He requires of us will be about as welcome as castor oil.

Of course God is concerned about our growing into mature spirits. And the God I know sometimes asks difficult things of us, it is true. But His will also includes a happiness here on earth abundant enough to float every difficulty.

But when men persist in these mistaken and tragic ideas of the Creator, how can God show us what He is really like? This is the problem that He had with men. And He solved it in the Incarnation. If God were to break into the stream of history—come to earth as a man and demonstrate that He loved people, weep with them when they suffered, rejoice with them in moments of gladness—then there might be a closer relationship between God and His children.

A story that I first read in my late twenties helped me see why the Incarnation had to be:

One day a British scientist discovered a large anthill in his kitchen garden. These were different from any ants he had observed before, so he was eager to study them. But each time his shadow fell across the anthill, the terrified ants scurried off in terror.

"I stepped back," the scientist wrote in his diary, "and sat down on the grass to think out the situation. I had only good will for the ants, did not wish to harm one of them. But how could I make the ants aware of my good will?

"My imagination played with the problem. To those tiny ants, I was an all-powerful creature 'somewhere up there,' whose thoughts they could not guess, whose ways and intentions they could not know.

"If only I could communicate," the scientist wrote. "But even that wouldn't be enough. Even then, I would be a gigantic being to the ants, and they would never believe that I understood their problems—the minute organization of the hill, their struggles for food, their battles with other ants.

"Only one thing could give them complete confidence. That is, if by some alchemy, I could—for a time—become an ant————"

The gap between our understanding of the nature and the intentions of the Creator is far wider than the gap between that of ant and man. Only as much of God as could be contained in human flesh would suffice to demonstrate to us what the Father is like. That was why the Incarnation was necessary.

That was why Jesus insisted, "I have come down from heaven not to carry out my own will but the will of him who sent me. . . ."[6] and that "He who has seen me has seen the Father."[7]

Then in watching Jesus, what did His disciples learn about God?

The most obvious thing they observed was the daily intimacy of Jesus' relationship with His Father. At first this must have puzzled them. For always He appeared to be listening to a Voice beyond Himself. There is no record of His ever having argued with anyone about the existence of God; this was fact. Also there was no doubt that God was always present to help, to guide, to succor.

Jesus acted as if there was never any question of the Father's willingness to supply all needs—even such material ones as appeasing hunger. God was concerned about men's bodies along with their souls: Divine love delighted in dispelling pain, in restoring sanity, in straightening crooked limbs and opening blind eyes, even in banishing premature death. Jesus said that in heaven there was an instant readiness to for-give and great joy over finding the lost. And are not these the things that ordinary human father-love or mother-love would delight in doing, if it could?

At every turn, Christ Himself made the comparison between human families and the Fatherhood of God. There is the unforgettable story of the universal Father dealing with the prodigal son.[8] And in the Sermon on the Mount, Jesus asked:

> Why, which of you, when asked by his son for a loaf,
>   will hand him a stone?
> Or, if he asks a fish, will you hand him a serpent?
> Well, if for all your evil you know to give your
>   children what is good,
> how much more will your Father in heaven give good
>   to those who ask him?[9]

The gospels make it clear that to Jesus the Father is all loving, is of the essence of love, cannot help loving. Moreover, this love includes the attributes of love known to all of us—good will, unselfishness, considera-tion, justice, wanting only good things for us, desiring our happiness. It is not a love dependent on our earning it. God is "for us" first, last, and always. By every word and action, by all the force of His personality, Christ sought to tell us that the Father is always nearer, mightier, freer to help us than we can imagine.

There were those who said that any man who held such ideas must be mad. But the disciples who tramped the dusty roads with Jesus day after day, who witnessed His decisiveness in dealing with people, His fearlessness of criticism, His sense of the sacredness of human per-sonality, the realism with which He faced evil, knew that this One was not mad. Indeed He was more beautifully sane than anyone they had ever known.

And so the central issue became sharper and sharper. As the late D. S. Cairns has put it so memorably in his book, *The Faith That Rebels*, "Either Jesus Christ was a dreamer about God. . . . or they and all men were dreamers, walking in the darkness and deeming it to be light. Either He alone was awake to reality . . . in His incessant summons to faith and the staking of everything upon God and His purpose of good for all mankind . . . ,"[10] or else Jesus was a liar, a madman, a charlatan. There was no alternative. And the disciples were right in concluding that this was the all-important question which they and all men have to resolve.

The issue is as sharp today as it was then. I have come to believe that only if we can depend upon the Creator as a God of love (not an obscure, ethereal love, but love as you and I know it) shall we have the courage and confidence to turn our life and affairs over to Him. Hannah Smith once wrote this pithy sentence: "Perfect obedience would be perfect happiness, if only we had perfect confidence in the power we were obeying."

What builds trust like that in the Creator? Only knowing Him so well—His motives, His complete good will—being certain that no pressures will make Him change, knowing Him for a long enough time to be sure of these things.

There are many persons who claim that they have broken through to that kind of knowing—from the Apostle Paul down through spiritual adventurers in every century, even to our day. "I know whom [not *what*] I have trusted," is Paul's ringing assertion, "and I am certain that he is able to keep what I have put into his hands. . . ."[11]

And we who long for an equally confident and solid base to life, how do we go about entering into that kind of relationship with God?

Three
How to Enter In

SOMETIME BEFORE I was ten, evangelist Gypsy Smith, Junior, came
to hold revival services in our town—Canton, Mississippi. A large tent
was pitched on a vacant lot near the town limits. It did not prove large
enough to hold the crowds that flocked there. On a platform of raw wood,
from which the rezin still oozed, sat the massed choirs gathered from
all the churches. Their favorite anthem was "Awakening Chorus":

> The Lord Jehovah reigns, and sin is backward hurled!
> Rejoice! Rejoice! Rejoice! . . .

The "Rejoicings" reverberated so shrilly that they always raised goose-
bumps along my spine. As the congregation sang, the waving arms of
the music director would beat out the rhythms of hymns like

> *Stan*-ding on the *prom*-i-ses of *Christ* my *king*—

> or

> *Sing* them *o*-ver a-*gain* to me,
> *Won*-der-ful *words* of *Life*. . . .

Each time we collectively took a breath, the pianist would run in scales,
chords, and flourishes marvelous to my childish ears.

Then would come the preaching. Gypsy Smith would lean far over the crude pulpit, pausing from time to time to whip out a handkerchief and wipe his flushed, perspiring face or to take a drink of water. His was a sincere testimony. The emotion in his preaching would steadily mount, transferring itself to the congregation. And finally a hush would fall over the tent, as the choir sang almost in a whisper,

> Softly and tenderly Jesus is calling,
> Calling for you and me. . . .

"Believe on the Lord Jesus Christ, and thou shalt be saved," the evangelist would thunder. "That's all you have to do. Accept the Lord Jesus as your personal Saviour."

Soon at the far edge of the tent someone would rise and slowly make his way down the aisle toward the front. Then another person—and another—and another—and another.

From those evangelistic meetings of my childhood, I thought that "believing on the Lord Jesus Christ" simply meant being fully persuaded that what the church believed about Christ's divinity was true.

This did not seem difficult. In fact, it was not long after the revival tent had been packed up and moved to another town that I decided to join the church. One Sunday at the close of the regular morning service in our church, my preacher-father issued "the invitation." On an impulse, I rose, marched down the aisle, and so became a member of the First Presbyterian Church of Canton. Because I had marched spontaneously, I remember my father was so moved that he stood in front of the altar and looked at me through eyes swimming with tears behind his spectacles.

Years passed. Not until my college days did I recognize that something was missing in this inherited Christianity based on an untested assent. By that time I had acquired a parallel King James–Moffatt New Testament. Moffatt's translation brought the ancient words alive for me.

I found that the evangelist of my childhood had been right in insisting that the only way we can really know God is by looking at Jesus Christ. Christ is the center of Christianity. To pretend anything else—that we need think of Him only as a good man who was also a great teacher, for instance—is not Christianity, whatever else it may be.

But I was also astonished to discover that no mere intellectual acceptance of Christ's divinity would have satisfied Jesus as a way of entrance into His kingdom. He will settle for nothing less than making Him the ruler of one's life, with the inevitable result of a practical day-by-day obedience: "Why call ye me Lord, Lord, and do not the things which I say?"[1] No wonder marching down the church aisle had not changed me one whit.

> I feel that I have come to a crisis in my life [I wrote in the journal I was keeping during these college years]. It's very easy for me to see how people can lose their so-called religion when they have gotten enough education to make them think at all. That is very likely to happen to anyone whose religion is simply an inheritance or a habit. Unless something intervenes, it could happen to me.
>
> My religion is not on a very firm basis, I'm afraid. I have had no vital experience. God doesn't seem real to me. I believe now—because of people I know who do have something vital and real, like Peter Marshall. But I can't go on like this. What are we here in this world for anyway?

This questioning may have seemed like a prelude to change, but the fact is that I did "go on that way" for many years, even after my graduation and marriage to the young preacher, Peter Marshall.

During those years I was an active, interested minister's wife. In addition to my homemaking, I attended women's meetings, led Bible studies, made talks, called on parishioners, and took part in program-committee meetings. Obviously most of this work was on the organizational level. Even when I led Bible studies for small groups of women or gave a talk or book review, I was still relying mostly on other people's ideas about the Christian life. Those who listened carefully must have missed the authentic note of personal experience.

During all this time, I never stopped struggling to find the way to God for myself. Peter's preaching was a never-ending challenge to me:

> The Christian Church in its early days grew in numbers and in influence because God used the testimonies of men and women who had something to say about Jesus. What they had to say was that this Jesus, who had died on a cross, was alive and spiritually present every day to the disciples. And they proclaimed everywhere they went, with enthusiasm and conviction, the good news of the gospel.

It was to them the thrilling and exciting story
of how life had been changed for them,
   and how they had been changed for life.
They could no more keep silent than a flower can withhold its fragrance
or the sun keep back its light. This power that had made them different,
they said, was available to anyone who would believe . . .
Sins could be forgiven; Christ could come into human
life to change natures and dispositions
   to change moods and temperaments
     to banish fear and worry
     to remove shame and guilt
   to provide a new dynamic, a new purpose in life,
a new joy and a peace that nothing could destroy.
The early disciples were thrown into prison.
They were persecuted
       boycotted
       hounded from place to place.
Yet thousands joined their fellowship and discovered the truth they were
proclaiming, and found life becoming a new and thrilling experience. . . .

Why—under preaching like that, and especially when the preacher
was so close at hand to answer my questions and to help—could I not
make contact with the Christ whom Peter knew so well? Perhaps I was
still not ready. So often this personal encounter with God comes through
crisis. Peter's had been a vocational crisis, when he had had to decide
whether or not he would leave his native Scotland to enter the ministry. So far my life had been protected, serene, free of urgent need. There
was only that deep gnawing ache for Something More that I had known
since college days.

Then, in March 1943, came the event that was to change my life. A
routine physical check-up brought bad news. Chest X rays showed a soft
spotting over both lungs. Specialists were unable to make a conclusive
diagnosis, but the trouble appeared to be tuberculosis. *Tuberculosis!*
Hated word, hated disease. I was ordered to bed twenty-four hours a day
for an indefinite period.

Fifteen months later I had gained some fifteen pounds; otherwise
nothing was changed. The area of infection was as widespread as at the
beginning. When other specialists were consulted, they rejected the usual

pneumothorax treatment, as well as surgery, or even the use of the drugs that were then beginning to be used in TB cases. Their only advice was "More bed rest." When we asked "How long?" they said frankly they had no idea.

Despair settled in. After almost a year and a half in bed, I could see few gains. My husband and four-year-old son needed me. Our household situation was becoming more difficult with every month that passed.

Often during those discouraging days there was a vivid picture in my mind: I was groping my way along a pitch-black tunnel. There were passages, twistings and turnings off the main tunnel. I tried this way and that. Repeatedly I found only dead ends and was forced to grope my way back to the black center shaft. I clung to the hope that somehow, sometime, I would emerge from darkness into the sunlight again. But in order to get there, I had to proceed resolutely straight ahead. I knew by now that there were no short cuts. Did this mean that I had to deal directly with God, who was insisting through circumstances that He alone knew the shortest way to the sunlight of His presence?

There was in me a desire for an all-out effort to reach Him, born of desperation. Sloughed off now were all the trappings of religion, most of them concerned with the ceremonial or organizational aspects of churches that so often confuse the central issue. I began to see wholeness as more than the search for physical health. As I understood the viewpoint of Jesus, it was that physical soundness is merely part of a more profound wholeness. In this sense, wholeness can only come about as inner cleavages are healed, as man is joined to the Source of his being. Thus, for me, the search for health became the search for a relationship with God. The question was, what was blocking that relationship?

I stood before my Maker starkly, stripped of pretenses. My unworthiness shrieked at me. My tendency to overcriticalness, to harsh, hasty judgments. My little jealousies, the self-centeredness that had made me a poor one for teamwork of any kind. Lying in bed I summoned up the dishonesties of my past. Once in high school I had cheated on an algebra test. Another time, when I had been treasurer of a school organization, I had "borrowed" some money from the fund and then paid it back ten days later.

There were dishonesties of a different sort: I had not always been candid with my husband. I saw in myself a streak of secretiveness, a tendency to bar him from a corner of my mind and heart. I well knew that this was no way to build a solid marriage.

Through agonizing days I made methodical notes on these ignoble traits and deeds. Then I asked Peter to hear me out on the ones that affected him. He listened, looking pained, not so much at what I was confessing as at the spiritual anguish he saw in me.

I then felt it necessary to write two letters—one to the high school principal who had taught algebra, the other to the teacher who had been faculty adviser to the school organization. Since the last thing I wanted was to be considered a religious crackpot, I labored over the wording of the letters. In each case, as matter-of-factly as I could, I told why I felt it necessary to write the letter: that this was one of the steps which would help me to enter into a new and total Christian experience. Three days passed before I could muster enough courage to mail those letters. In the end, I posted them only because I knew that my relationship with God now meant more to me than the reputation that I had once thought all important.

Both recipients of the letters turned out to be as generous and forgiving as people usually are when confronted with honest confession.

Then Peter, through his preaching, taught me the next step to God. Facing up to ourselves in confession is therapeutic, provided we move on to forgiveness and do not wallow in our wrongdoing. It is possible to overemphasize the self-centeredness, the me-first angle, even in relation to our sins: "Look at me, what a great sinner I've been. My case is worse than most. God is going to have to do a special job on me . . . *I* . . . *I* . . . *I*. . . ."

Having confessed every wrong that had surfaced to my conscious mind, I then specifically claimed God's promise of I John 1:9: "If we confess our sins, He is faithful and just to forgive us our sins, and to cleanse us from all unrighteousness." Then I proceeded to burn the list and the notes I had made as a symbol that everything was, from that moment, forgiven—forgotten—gone forever.

No doubt the burning was a childish procedure. Yet in this way I stumbled on the value of dramatizing and thus making more real—that is, more real for myself—a definite transaction with God.

So now the housecleaning was over—except for one thing. I was aware that a psychiatrist would scarcely regard my amateur self-probing as a thorough enough job of analysis. So I prayed that God would see to it that any residue of debris in the subconscious would eventually come to light, or that He would deal with anything left by pouring His cleansing and healing Spirit into those subterranean levels.

In subsequent months more of the debris did come into my consciousness. For instance, I became aware of a compartment in my being in which I had locked certain persons whom I disliked. They could go their way; I would go mine. But now Christ seemed to be standing by the locked door saying, "That isn't forgiveness. It won't do. No closed doors are allowed. The Kingdom of God is the kingdom of right relationships. Remember what I said—'If ye forgive no men their trespasses, neither will your Father forgive your trespasses?' If you cannot forgive, you cannot enter the kingdom. This unforgiveness grieves me more than any cheating on an algebra test."

By the time I had faced up to this, it was the summer of 1944, time for our annual trek back to the Cape Cod cottage. I got there only by Peter's special arrangements—a compartment on the train and an ambulance to meet me at the station.

Later that June, early one morning I was reading Jesus' parable about the cleansed house:

> When an unclean spirit leaves a man, it roams through dry places in search of refreshment and finds none. Then it says "I will go back to the house I left," and when it comes it finds the house vacant, clean and all in order. Then it goes off to find seven other spirits worse than itself; they go in and dwell there, and the last state of that man is worse than the first. . . .[2]

There was danger, then, in my attempts to clean house unless the Spirit of God took over the house. The keys and the management of my house had to be turned over to Christ. For how could I ask Him to heal me until He was completely in charge? Any human physician requires the surrender of a given case into his care; he can do nothing unless the patient agrees to follow his orders. Common sense told me that exactly the same was true of the Great Physician.

So that sunshiny June morning, I got out of bed and stood at the bedroom window looking out at the garden that Peter had so lovingly planted . . . Roses and white hollyhocks, yellow day lilies, zinnias, all a

riot of color . . . A blue, blue sky above . . . The sea just over the brow of
the hill. There I stood and took the plunge. It amounted to a quiet pledge
to God, the promise of a blank check with my life:

"It is ten-twelve A.M. on the twenty-second of June 1944," I said.
"From this moment I promise that I'll try to do whatever You tell me
for the rest of my life, insofar as You'll make it clear to me what Your
wishes are. I'm weak and many times I'll probably want to renege on
this. But Lord, You'll have to help me with that too."

I took a deep breath; I was trembling. I had entered in. Yet nothing
seemed different. The hollyhock faces still nodded at the window. Fluffy
clouds still floated in that blue, blue sky. I turned and noted in my journal the date and the hour of the promise 1 had just made. There would
be moments in the future when this pledge would not seem real to me.
But it was real, and writing it down would help to remind me.

I felt no emotion other than the relief of knowing that I had completed my part, so far as I knew it. This brought me a peace of mind I
had not known during the tortuous days of self-probing and writing the
letters of confession.

The proof of the reality of the pledge I had made began coming during the next six weeks. My physical condition was improving. Each
morning I would lie in the yard, soaking up sunshine. Next I tried join-
ing the family for dinner each night. That did not tire me over much.
Then I began taking short walks some afternoons with Jeffrey, our cocker
spaniel, trotting beside me. It was a joy to stand at the top of the rise in
the road and see the sea again, feel the tangy salt air on my cheeks, laugh
at the sea-wind blowing back Jeffrey's floppy ears as he stood poised,
watching the circling gulls. It was even good to feel sand in my shoes.
As of old, I began taking an interest in the garden and the kitchen. Perhaps I could take it as my job to arrange some flowers each day for the
house. And would it be possible for the family to gather some beach
plums for jelly? I could not help much with the jelly-making, but perhaps a little. It was like coming to life again. And life was good, so good.
The speck of light at the other end of the tunnel was becoming a steady
beam.

God deals differently with each of us. He knows no "typical" case.
He seeks us out at a point in our own need and longing and runs down

the road to meet us. This individualized treatment should delight rather than confuse us, because it so clearly reveals the highly personal quality of God's love and concern.

At the same time, there is one central core of the entering-in or commitment experience that is common to everyone who undergoes it. It is the act of putting oneself—past, present, and future—into God's hands to do with as He pleases.

A girl once asked me, "But isn't that a terrible risk?"

Yes, it certainly would be, if we had a God who wanted to deprive us of joy rather than add joy to our lives, if He were not a God who cares supremely for us and our welfare. But what He wants for us is exactly what every thoughtful parent wants for his child—that pure, deep-flowing joy that springs out of maturity and fulfillment.

That God is like this, each of us must discover for ourselves. There is only one difficulty. The discovery comes second, the act of will first. The order of events can never be reversed: action on our part, that is, the decision to hand our life over to God and the promising of obedience; then, and only then, comes understanding and the unfolding knowledge of the character of God.

This decision need not be dramatic nor emotional. It is just as real, though it be but a quiet assent without any emotion whatsoever. This has been vividly demonstrated to me recently by John Sherrill, now a dear friend.

As with most of us, it was personal need that brought John to the point of commitment. My need had been a long illness. John's was a more immediate physical crisis. Three years before he had had a malignant mole removed from his ear which had been diagnosed as melanoma, one of the most vicious killers of all types of cancer. Miraculously—everyone felt—it had been caught in time. But now the doctor had discovered a small lump on John's neck that was suspect.

The details of the physical problems and the prayers for healing are not the point that I want to make here. Suffice it to say that as soon as I heard about the situation, I knew that John's crisis was also my crisis—part of "my bundle" of responsibility, as the Quakers express it so vividly. Then—how were we who were so concerned to pray about John?

A series of thoughts kept pounding at me and would not be put aside: healing is not an end in itself; it is a dividend of the gospel. Physical health is but one part of total wholeness. Then came the inevitable question: had John ever made an act of turning his whole being over to God?

Who was I to ask John a question like that? He was an intellectual—an editor and successful writer. Any emotional approach to Christianity, as well as the usual religious cliches and shibboleths, were repugnant to him. Considering all this, would not any question about his relationship to God be gross presumption on my part and anathema to him?

Still, time was running out. Only twenty-four hours remained until John would enter New York's Memorial Hospital for surgery. After all, what he thought of me did not matter at a time like this. The fact that a life was at stake gave me the courage to telephone John and tell him that I had to see him.

His wife, Tibby, came with him. The three of us found a quiet room and shut ourselves in. There was no attempt at a subtle approach. I explained what had led up to my telephone call, what I had learned about the process of entering in, and why this seemed important as a foundation for any prayer for healing. My heart was in what I was saying, so that several times my voice broke.

When I had finished, John asked wonderingly, "Do you mean that I can just decide that I am willing for God to take over my life, and tell Him so—as blandly and as matter-of-factly as that—and have it work?"

"That's right," was my reply. "Do it as matter-of-factly as you please. You do not have to have all your theological beliefs sorted out either. Nor do you have to understand everything. You just come to Christ as you are—questions, complexes, contradictions, doubts, everything. After all, how else can any of us come? You make a definite movement of your will toward God. After that, the next move is up to Him. The feelings, the proof that He has heard and has taken you on, even the understanding will come later."

At that point John and Tib had to rush away for their last hasty preparations for the hospital. It was not until later that I found out what happened immediately after they left me.

"After we told you good-by and backed out of your driveway," John told me. "I did the simple thing you had suggested—just said 'Yes' to God while driving the car. I can show you the exact spot on Millwood Road where it happened, right by a certain telephone pole.

"Then because it had been such a quiet, interior thing, I felt that I ought to go on record by telling someone. So I said to Tib, I suppose a bit ruefully, 'Well I'm a Christian now.'

"And she asked curiously, 'Do you feel any different?'

"'Not a bit different,' I told her."

Yet John is different now—so different. The quiet transaction at that certain spot on Millwood Road was real enough because never have I seen so much action on God's part in the life of one man in one short year. That too, is another story—an exciting one which is his to tell, not mine. Someday I hope he will. But I can at least add that when the famous New York specialist operated, all he could find was a dried-up *nodule,* easy to remove. There was no malignancy.

Church folk often give the impression that there are only two ways of entering into the Christian life: being born into a Christian family or stumbling into a dramatic religious experience as an adult. Either approach to Christianity seems to have two unfortunate factors in common: the initiative was apparently not with the individual and the way to God was clouded in vagueness.

I am convinced that God never meant for anything about the Christian life to be vague, least of all the steps by which we enter into a meaningful relationship with Him. The obscurity must surely be on our side, not God's.

Growing up in a believing family is not to be undervalued. It is still the ideal beginning, because it is the foundation of the happiest possible childhood. Yet I know now that something more is needed: each human being must enter into Life for himself. There is, therefore, no such thing as inheriting Christianity.

David duPlessis, a minister from South Africa and a new friend, recently told me a fascinating story about himself and this matter of an inherited Christianity.

"It happened one cold January night, really cold—in fact five degrees below zero. I had been sleeping soundly, then woke suddenly about four in the morning. I thought that a voice had wakened me. But as I lay there listening, there was no sound except the creak of snow-laden branches outside the bedroom window and the measured breathing of the children in the adjoining room.

"Then the voice came again. This sounds peculiar, I realize, but I don't honestly know whether it was an audible voice or not. At any rate, the words were clear enough, though they seemed nonsensical: 'God has no grandsons.' Just that—nothing more.

"Well, I snapped on my bedside light and reached for a Bible with a concordance in the back. I looked up the word *grandson*. No such reference anywhere in the Scriptures. Then I looked up *grandfather*. Not there.

"Sons? Yes, lots of references. 'Behold what manner of love the Father hath bestowed on us, that we should be called the sons of God. . . .' 'For as many as are led by the Spirit of God, they are the sons of God.' And lots more, a long list of them.

"But," I wondered, "what did these references have to do with God having no grandsons? Yet this one sentence had been clearly imprinted on my consciousness. More puzzled than ever, I finally turned off the light and went back to sleep.

"I didn't find out myself until ten days after the sentence was first given to me," he said. "I was aboard a plane, en route from Milwaukee to Chicago—when suddenly I knew.

"When Christ's apostles first started preaching, they insisted that every individual had to have a personal encounter with Christ and make the decision to accept His way—for himself. Judging from history, there must have been plenty of vitality in that first-century church—enough to shake the sophisticated Roman world to its depths.

"Well, the years passed. After a while those first followers of Christ began to reason, 'These children of ours were born into a Christian family. They have grown up in the church and have been instructed in the faith. They were born Christians. Surely they don't need any special experience of repentance as we did.'

"The church pews were soon filled with the sons and daughters of those first followers. But since the children had inherited their belief in Christ, they knew Him only secondhand.

"Perhaps it was not surprising that by the second century the vitality of the church had begun to decline. Proofs of God's power, like healing through faith, became the exception rather than the rule.

"Sure, in every century, there are always some who have had a personal confrontation with Christ. During revival periods—like the time of Luther in Germany, or the Wesleyan Revival in England—large numbers have had the personal experience of being truly born again to become sons of God.

"But then in the following generation, the same sad process starts over. And soon the pews are filled again largely with secondhand believers —grandsons and granddaughters."

My friend had unintentionally stated what had been my own case. I understood why my inherited faith had not been enough. I had been a prime example of a "granddaughter." *And God has no grandsons or granddaughters.*

I wonder how many others there are who have thought of formal church membership as a substitute for that direct Father-child relationship that God really wants of us? No wonder much of our religious life today is plagued by vagueness. Let us not mistake it: Entering in does take childlikeness. The door through which we enter into Life is a low door. And sometimes it is the humble and the needy who can show the rest of us the way.

So a group of ministers recently discovered. One of them, Bruce Larson of *Faith at Work* magazine, told me this story. They had gathered for a two-day retreat at a church in New Jersey to discuss mutual problems and to pray about them. As so often happens, the discussion part predominated. It was late afternoon of the final day when a startling event occurred.

Suddenly the door of their meeting-room opened and a stranger walked in. The minister of the host church knew him, had seen him often around the neighborhood. Self-consciously the man seated himself at the fringe of the circle. Though there was no more than a momentary pause in the discussion, the experienced eyes of the other clergymen present took in the situation—the watery eyes, the sagging shoulders, the seedy clothing. Obviously the man was an alcoholic.

The discussion continued, while the stranger listened. "It seems to me," a crisp voice said, "that all we have been talking about these two days can be summed up in our need for God's power—the kind of power that changes lives, heals, restores, that———"

He stopped, his attention arrested by the agitated movements of the stranger.

"That's it! That's what I need. I could use some of that."

There was sudden silence. While everyone watched, his bleary eyes filled a bit more and the quavering voice continued.

"My name is Ernie. I drink too much. People have tried to help me ... doctors, hospitals, clinics, missions, and all that. But I ... I can't seem to stop. How do I get this power you're talking about?"

The question hung, quivering in the silence. Despite the fact that these men were experienced in dealing with people in need, the intrusion was embarrassing. There was a time schedule for the meeting, trains and planes to be caught, families to get back to, next Sunday's sermons to think about. Closing time was at hand.

Finally, a white-haired man spoke up. "Ernie, all of us have problems too. It's a problem-filled world. . . . " The voice of the elderly minister was gentle, suave, as he sought to identify with the stranger. All of the men knew that the pastor who was speaking had had professional training in counseling.

"As to how we can get God's help. Well, that isn't always too easy. It takes patience, time. There are many roads to God, many avenues by which—"

"Damn!" The interruption was explosive, passionate.

"Damn . . . Damn . . . Damn . . . Damn!"

The quiet of the room was suddenly being blasted by Ted, a young minister and a former businessman, anger and impatience written clearly on his face. Again and again he beat his fist down on the seat of the empty chair beside him.

"This man doesn't want to hear about our problems," Ted said vehemently. "He's asked us a question—how can he get God's help to stop drinking? We haven't answered him. If we don't know the answer, then let's adjourn this meeting, stop our endless talking, go home and tell our people that the church hasn't any answers for today. In that case, we'd better stop being hypocrites and shut the church doors for good."

There was a shocked silence, but the impassioned words had cleared the air. Almost simultaneously, five or six men—including the angry young preacher and the white-haired minister—rose and walked over to Ernie.

Ted knelt in front of the alcoholic. "Ernie, do you believe that Jesus Christ can come into your life and change it?"

The watery eyes looked down, childlike. "Yes . . . Yes, I do."

"Then we're going to pray right now, Ernie, that He will do this for you."

The young minister took both of Ernie's hands in his. The white-haired preacher stood behind, placed both hands gently on top of the alcoholic's head. The others stood around in a semicircle, each one with his hands on the stranger.

Ted's prayer was short, hard-hitting, impassioned. He asked for Christ's healing power for Ernie, for the forgiveness of sins, for the beginning of a new life.

"Now, Ernie," Ted said, "you pray too. Just thank God that He has heard you and healed you."

"I hope so," Ernie quavered.

"Not hope so. He *has!*"

"I——Well, I'd like to believe that."

The answer was gentle, but firm. "Ernie, thank Jesus that He has already come into your life."

The room became completely still. And then in wavery sentences Ernie's voice reached up to God. "God, I'm a tired, weak old man. I don't see what use I am to anyone. But I'd like to find the new life they talk about. Please help me."

It was real. It was vital. Every man in the room knew it, felt it. They had been talking about power. This *was* power.

Forgotten were train schedules, plane reservations, other obligations. For the first time in two days, real contact had been made with God through one of the least likely of persons. The air was charged with emotion. Out from the depths came some of the deep needs of the ministers themselves.

A pastor from New England began it. At first his words seemed unrelated—"I was driving down here several days ago, feeling lonely and apart from God. While crossing over Bear Mountain Bridge, I looked in the ice-clogged river and saw a small boat locked in the ice some distance off shore.

"That boat fascinated me. For my life has been like that. Frozen, isolated, shut within myself. I'm frozen with the fear of other people's opinions, the fear of not being a success, the fear of not pleasing people."

Suddenly his eyes filled with tears. "Would you pray for me, that I'll get thawed out so I can really help people again?"

There was no hesitation now. The men quickly gathered around him. All but Ernie, who hung back, shyly. But the young minister walked over to him.

"Ernie, come on over and pray with the rest of us."

"Oh no! I couldn't do *that*. . . ."

The minister took him by the hand. "Look, Ernie, you've received; now you must give. And *we* need *you* now."

So Ernie knelt beside the minister and prayed with the others. The prayer was very simple. And in this room miraculously filled with power, every one of the ministers made his way back to God with a childlike renewal of commitment.

Later the minister from New England was marveling to the young preacher at the turn of events. "As long as I live, I'll never get over it," he said. "What had happened to Ernie minutes before was the real thing. The proof was that it was Ernie, with his winy breath in my face, who was God's channel for transmitting the power. It was like electricity flowing through him to me." And he added with awe in his voice, "Except ye become as little children, ye shall not enter into the kingdom of heaven. . . ."

And so we enter in, each of us, up our own secret stairs into the most joyous and rewarding relationship of our lives. The good news is that this is no experience meant just for the saints. God welcomes us no matter what our lives have been, no matter what we have done or have failed to do, whether we feel adequate or broken or merely empty.

And the rest of the good news is that the way into the Christian life need not be vague. Sometimes laymen who approach Christianity with few preconceived ideas can be surprisingly specific and helpful. A case in point are the twelve steps toward God outlined by Alcoholics Anonymous. Out of great need and hard experience, the men who were the founders of this movement hammered out the steps. When I first read them, years after my own entering-in experience, I was astonished to find that this path to sobriety was precisely the road I had traveled on my way to a personal commitment to Christ. I have changed only a few words:

1. We admit helplessness in one or more specific areas of our lives.
2. We believe that there is a Power greater than ourselves.

3. We make a decision to turn our lives over to the care of God as we understand Him.
4. We make a searching and fearless inventory of ourselves.
5. We admit to God, to ourselves, and to another human being the exact nature of our wrongs.
6. We are ready for God to change us, to remove these defects of character.
7. Humbly we ask Him to do so.
8. We make a list of all the people we have harmed, and we become willing to make amends to them all.
9. We make direct amends to such people when possible, when to do so would not injure them or others.
10. At intervals we continue to take personal inventory, and when we are wrong, promptly admit it.
11. Through daily prayer and meditation, we seek to improve our conscious contact with God as we understand Him, praying only for the knowledge of His will for us and for the power to carry it out.
12. We try to carry this message to others and to practice these principles in all our affairs.

The way to God is a clearly marked, well-traveled road. Only one question remains to us: Do we really want to find our way down that road?

Do we really want to enter in?

Four

The Secret
of the Will

SOME YEARS BEFORE Peter Marshall's death, a man approached him on the sidewalk outside the church following a Sunday-morning service. The stranger introduced himself as a visitor to Washington, a used-car dealer from St. Paul, Minnesota. He had a direct, blunt manner. What he had to say so impressed Peter that he told me about their conversation as we were driving home.

As I remember, the point that the man was making went something like this: "Dr. Marshall, you challenged me this morning to want to apply Jesus' teachings to life. But as a businessman, I'm puzzled by what appears to be a lack of realism in what Christ told us to do—such as in the Sermon On the Mount. Have you ever known anyone who loved his neighbor as much as himself? Or who's willing to turn the other cheek all the time? Or who never has a lustful thought? I'll even make a special trip back to Washington to hear you, if you'll promise to preach a sermon telling *how* we can do what Christ asked."

Like the used-car dealer, many of us are puzzled about the *hows* of Christianity. For some years, I too wondered if there were some principle involved here, some secret that I had somehow missed.

The day that I found the answer—in the book mentioned so often in these pages, *The Christian's Secret of a Happy Life*—I felt like someone who had stumbled on buried treasure. Hannah Smith, in turn, had

341

learned the secret from a book called *Spiritual Progress*, written by the Frenchman, François Fénelon, who lived during the seventeenth century. Fénelon was a cleric with an extraordinary insight into human nature. He was spiritual advisor to the lowly and the great, including Madame de Maintenon and the Duke of Burgandy, heir to the throne of France.

Where Fénelon and others learned the secret, stretching back to the New Testament writers, I do not know. But this I do know: in my life this formula has been the answer to the how.

The secret is simply this: that the Christian life must be lived in the will, not in the emotions; that God regards the decisions and choices of a man's will as the decisions and choices of the man himself—no matter how contrary his emotions may be. Moreover, when this principle is applied, the emotions must always capitulate to the will.

At birth, as I have pointed out, God gives each human being the gift of freedom of will. Under no circumstances will God ever violate this central citadel of man's being. The picture in the book of Revelation of Christ standing, knocking, outside the closed door of the human heart, I believe to be a literal picture:

> . . . if any man hear my voice, and open the door,
> I will come in to him, and will sup with him,
> and he with me.[1]

But the latch of the door is on the inside. It is our hand that must open the door. It is our voice that must invite Christ in. Genuine freedom of will permits no door-crashing, not even from the Lord of glory!

Before the entering-in decision, we have probably thought that we belonged to ourselves, that what we did with ourself was our business. We reasoned that since God gave us intelligence, He intended that we use it for all those decisions that go to make up a life—a career, whom we shall marry, where we will live, how we shall rear our children. Self-interest, what the self thought it wanted, what seemed best to the self—these have been the deciding factors.

But if the man is to enter in, he must decide that while this intelligent self-interest may seem good, there is a better way. A man must will that self abdicate its throne; that henceforth Christ's will determines action. And this movement of the will—that decision-making part of man—must be made without paying any attention to the emotions.

It is important that we not gauge the reality of spiritual experience by our feelings. A sixteen-year-old girl posed this question to me in a letter: "How can one be sure he is a Christian? If a person has asked Christ with sincerity to come into his heart, but still doesn't feel any different, well—how can he know whether He has or not?"

The key to her quandary, it seemed to me, was the word *feel*. We petition, we pray, we wait, but we do not "feel" any different. Feelings are at the bottom of most of our Christian difficulties. Our emotions are often painfully misleading, and at best we have imperfect control over them. This should come as no surprise, for psychology tells us that these emotions often rise up out of the depths of the subconscious, even out of the emotional set of ancestors long dead, out of the race consciousness. Our feelings can be affected by such irrelevant matters as the mood of those around us, by whether we had a good night's sleep, by hunger or indigestion, or by a morning in which the rain blew through the open window, spattered the wallpaper, and the neighborhood dogs turned over the garbage pail. "I don't feel God's presence today," we wail.

What is the remedy? It is simplicity itself: Our emotions are not the real us. The motivating force at the center of our physical being is our will. The dictionary describes *will* as "the power of conscious deliberate action." The will is the governing power in us, the rudder, the spring of all our actions. Before God we are responsible only for the set of that will—whether we decide for God's will or insist on self-will. Our Maker knows that our feelings are unruly, unreliable gauges. So if we see to it that our intentions (our motives) are right, we can trust God to see to the results.

If the girl who is not sure that she is a Christian will make a definite act of giving her will to God, even though she feels nothing at all, in God's eyes that is a real transaction—done, finished. As soon as she accepts the truth of this, God will handle her emotions. Eventually she *will feel* different. Eventually she *will feel* God's presence. The emotions trail behind the will. In the interval, she must not be led astray by ephemeral emotional responses to a date that turns out badly or ants that invade the picnic basket.

Does this sound too simple? Actually, I believe it to be the only principle that makes entering the Christian life possible.

It is a theory that works in real life. I think of what happened in the case of the late Fulton Oursler—for years editor of *Liberty* magazine and senior editor of *Reader's Digest* at the time of his death. Perhaps best known for his *The Greatest Story Ever Told*, Oursler was for years a close friend and associate of my husband Len.

At thirty Mr. Oursler was a self-styled agnostic. He believed in no absolutes of right and wrong, certainly not in anything approaching the supernatural. As he described himself, he was "genially loyal to ethical standards when they did not interfere too much with what I wanted to do. But I sneered at God as an elaborate self-deception and did all that I could to tear down the faith of those close to me."[2]

Then trouble surrounded Fulton Oursler in all phases of his life. *Liberty* went under, so he was out of a job. At the same time there were health and marriage difficulties. There came the day when he realized that he was absolutely helpless to do one thing for himself.

What happened then is vividly described by Oursler himself in a book he later wrote, *Why I Know There Is a God*. On a blustery day with dark clouds lowering, the distraught man wandered down Fifth Avenue in New York City. He stopped in front of a church—self-conscious, filled with conflicting emotions, but knowing that unless he got help he had come to the end of the way. For the first time in years, he ventured inside a church. Let him tell the rest of it in his own words:

"In ten minutes or less I may change my mind," he prayed. "I may scoff at this—and love error again. Pay no attention to me then. For this little time I am in right mind and heart. This is my best. Take it and forget the rest; and if You are really there, help me."

What Mr. Oursler did in the quiet church was what Hannah Smith meant by setting the rudder of the will and disregarding everything else—conflicting thoughts, contrary feelings. And God must have accepted this as the real decision of the real man, exactly as Hannah insisted that He always does. Within two weeks Fulton Oursler's problems began to resolve.

"Only chance would explain it to the unbelieving," he said later, "because nothing either I or anyone else did contrived the events. The complications dissolved . . . by what the rationalist would call a series of beautiful coincidences God literally took over my life, took it out of my hands."

The more impressive proof that God accepted Fulton Oursler's gift of his will that day in the church is the massive contribution to the religious life of the nation that Mr. Oursler made during the remainder of his life. A knowing, spirited faith replaced his former agnosticism. Lost in emptiness, he found direction. His enthusiasms, his intensity, his insatiable love of a good story that had once poured into murder mysteries, plays, and movie scripts he now dedicated to the building up of faith in others. Since that experience his work includes some eighteen books, an endless succession of articles, and his column "Modern Parables," syndicated in about a hundred newspapers. When he was stricken with a heart attack on May 23, 1952, his *The Greatest Faith Ever Known* was interrupted in mid-sentence.

The principle of the will has the most practical sort of application to numerous everyday difficulties. At the moment we have a home-grown illustration of it with our twelve-year-old daughter, Linda. She is having corrective dentistry to straighten her teeth. After she wore braces for a year, the dentist fitted her with a retainer, a complicated and expensive plastic device to correct the bite. The trouble is that the retainer is removable.

On too many evenings we have had a scene like this:

"Linda, where is your retainer?"

Silence. Then a slightly bewildered expression on her pretty freckled face. "I don't know."

"Did you wear it to school this morning?"

"Yes—but I took it out during lunch."

"And then?"

"Some of the girls started passing it around from hand to hand under the table . . . just in fun, of course."

We give her a glassy stare. "Fun? But not very sanitary! Don't you know that————"

Linda, sensing that a real outburst is coming, adds quickly, "It's in my purse. I'm sure it is. Pretty sure, that is."

"Would you mind looking?"

Linda soon returns, holding the troublesome item aloft. There is a mild note of triumph in her voice. "See—all safe. It wasn't in the purse though. It was in the glove compartment of the car."

We bite our lips helplessly, make no comment. Then—"Linda, how *are* we going to get you to wear it regularly?"

"I don't know" (the stock answer for everything).

More months pass. More hairbreadth rescues of retainer from cars, a doctor's office, the front lawn. Once it had to be mailed back from her grandmother's. Then one day Linda bequeathed it to the Pennsylvania Railroad by leaving it in a ladies' room on one of their trains. She remembered it hours later, after the train was hundreds of miles away. Correspondence with the railroad revealed that my English—even with a thesaurus—was not up to an adequate description of a retainer. Anyway they had not seen it. So back Linda went to the dentist to be fitted for a new one, while her Daddy ground his own teeth thinking about the bill.

The dentist warned Linda that if she kept forgetting, she would undo his two years of work. Neither warnings nor naggings helped. Finally, I decided to try out on her the principle about the will.

One night before her prayers I suggested that because the retainer was clumsy and uncomfortable, something deep inside her had decided "I don't want to wear it, so I won't remember."

"Do you know what it is to have will-power, Linda?" I asked.

"Yes, I think so."

"What does it mean to you?"

"To do something I don't want to do," she answered after some hesitation.

"That's pretty good. You remember that we have told you that all through your life you will have to do certain things that you may not enjoy doing. You can try to make yourself do these hateful things by will-power. But Linda, there's a much better way. If you tell God that you're willing to have Him change you, so that you'll like doing what you must do, then He will. It really works!"

That night Linda added to her bedtime prayers, "God, I hate the old retainer. But I know that if I don't wear it, I won't have pretty teeth. So I'm willing to have You change me on the inside, so that I *want* to wear, want to remember—and then I will."

After praying this way several nights in a row, the problem of the retainer was on its way to being solved. When Linda set the rudder of her will in the right direction, so that God's will became her will, then she no longer had trouble remembering, and she was no longer miserable wearing it.

Remembering a retainer may seem unimportant beside the big issues of life. Yet I have seen this principle of the will operate just as successfully in some of the knottiest, most soul-rending situations life can hand us.

Several years ago a veteran pilot was forced to land a passenger plane in a dense fog in California. The instructions from the tower were apparently not clear to him. To the horror of all who were there to meet the plane—mostly wives and children—the plane crashed at the edge of the landing field and burned. All aboard were killed.

The Civil Aeronautics Board's investigation and findings fixed the blame on the pilot. Many who knew the circumstances felt that this was unfair. In any case, it compounded the widow's grief. It was devastating enough to lose her husband, but it seemed more than she could bear to have him blamed for the death of twenty-three other human beings.

I am acquainted with the pilot's widow and her three daughters. The problem she posed to me was: "How *can* I let go my resentment at the unfairness of this and find peace again?"

Nothing in my experience approached the bitterness of this woman's problem. I pondered it and then wrote her about what had helped me to handle smaller resentments. . . . Grudges or resentments are emotions. We cannot get rid of them by saying, "I will no longer feel that way. I shall now love this person who harmed me."

Recognizing the principle of the will, I pray something like this: "Lord, You have plainly told me that all vengeance is thine, not my business at all. You have said that I must forgive. I am willing to, but I've tried over and over, and the resentments keep surging back. Now I *will* this bitterness over to You. Here—I hold it out to You in my open hand. I promise only that I will not again close my fist and reclaim the resentment. Now I ask You to take it and handle these emotions that I cannot handle."

There I leave the matter. When thoughts return to it, there is the quiet inner assertion that it has been turned over to God, and that He is taking care of it. Always for me, in a matter of hours or days, I find the resentment has evaporated and in its place has come peace. The pilot's widow had a long struggle, but she wrote me that eventually she did find a peace of mind that led her into a creative new life.

I once had success in applying this secret of the will to a neighbor who invariably irritated me. Ann Sheldon (not her real name, of course) had not wronged me. Indeed, any reasons I could have given for not liking her were not reasons at all . . . such things as her ceaseless chatter, and that habit of asking you a direct question and then never pausing to hear the answer. Her personality affected me like scratching fingernails across a blackboard. My human inclination was to avoid her. Let Ann Sheldon go her way, and I'd go mine, I told myself. The world was plenty big enough for the two of us.

But then a curious thing happened. Each time I tried to pray, the thought of this woman popped into my mind. About the fourth time it happened, I concluded that God was trying to tell me something. With a sinking heart, I was afraid I knew only too well what the message was. "Avoiding Ann will not do. It is not good enough. Have you forgotten that we are to love one another?"

Love Ann Sheldon? The idea seemed ludicrous. Nevertheless I knew 1 had to try. First, 1 recognized that it would have been most unlike Jesus Christ if by "love" He had meant billowing waves of gushing sentimentality. By love He meant something more substantial—respect for another human being, caring about him and his problems, being sensitive to his needs, wanting him to prosper and to be happy.

As soon as I faced up to my defective relationship with Ann, I saw that everything turned on my will. I had to be *willing* to like this woman. Suppose that by some miracle God could replace my irritation with congeniality, even affection? (That *would* be a miracle, I thought glumly.) But all that God was asking of me was a shift in consciousness at the center of my will to include this possibility.

For help I went back to Hannah Smith's illustration in which she compared the will to a wise mother in a nursery and the feelings to clamoring, crying children. "The mother makes up her mind to a certain course of action which she knows to be best. The children rebel, declare they will not obey. But the mother, knowing that she is mistress and not they, pursues her course lovingly, firmly, never giving in for a moment to their contrariness. Eventually the clamoring ceases; the children do what they're told. All is harmony in the nursery."

So, in essence, my prayer was, "Lord, let me admit that my every clamoring emotion rebels at the thought of liking Ann Sheldon! But I put my will over on the side of what is best. So I ask You to handle my feelings."

The first result of my prayer was that I stopped avoiding Ann. On closer contact, I began to realize that her chatter was a camouflage for a desperate unsureness about herself. Ann had always seemed to me a hopeless sentimentalist—witness the way she kept a memory book on the level of a teen-ager. She even pasted into it paper cocktail napkins and poetry clipped out of women's magazines! Then I saw the reason. She and her husband had always wanted children and had had none. Her affectionate nature had never had enough of an outlet. Soon I had evidence that underneath the sentimentality was a rare capacity for staunch friendship. Then one day I was astonished to realize that Ann Sheldon no longer irritated me.

She never got over her habit of asking questions and interrupting the answer. But there came the time when without malice I could say freely, "Ann, do you want me to answer that—or don't you?" And we would laugh about it together.

Ann died at forty-three—suddenly—of a brain hemorrhage. I had seen her only two days before her death, and we had parted with real affection.

The secret of the will is particularly effective in those areas where emotionally we are divided personalities. We know perfectly well what we should do. We want to do it; at the same time we do not want to.

The tangled emotions of grief often accentuate this divided self. This is the way one widow from a small town in Arkansas analyzed it in a letter to me:

It is five years since my husband died at the age of forty-nine, just half an hour after the doctor told him he would recommend him for insurance any time.

For months, I was so numbed and crushed with grief that I couldn't even realize what had happened to me. Yet in my heart I knew that a big part of this was feeling sorry for myself.

*My husband had always praised me for being a sensible person in what-
ever situation I had to face, and in time I came to know that if I persisted
in this self-pity I would be failing him in the worst kind of way. So—how
can I handle this?*

I think there are several reasons why, in grief, the will is so stubbornly
at odds with itself. In the first place, the ego is deeply involved. Love has
been wounded, and in the process part of us has died too. Also, like Queen
Victoria who made a production of mourning for forty years for her Albert,
most of us have a lingering pagan suspicion that those who do not exhibit
strong and continuing sorrow are dishonoring the dead.

We take a long time to face up to the fact that no amount of grieving will bring the one we love back to our side. And since life must go
on, we are faced with simple alternatives: will it be a good life or a miserable, sniveling existence? At this juncture the secret of the will can
take over and steer us down the right road.

After the publication of my book *To Live Again*, which was about
my own experience of grief at my husband's death and my subsequent
recovery, letters poured in from the bereaved—both men and women.
Often the letters were disconcerting, for in effect many of them said, "I
have read your book. But let me tell you the peculiarities of *my* case.
Do you have something more to say to me?"

Since I had poured myself out in *To Live Again*, I thought I had
shared everything that might be helpful. But now I find there is something more. The secret—Hannah Smith's secret—is simple recognition
of the fact that sorrow is an emotion and that you have little control
over it. You know that God loves your loved one, who is now with Him,
and that He loves you. You know that God has a plan for your life. So
you admit to God that you are divided. One part of you is clinging to
grief almost as an indulgence; another part knows well that until you
are willing to let grief go, happiness and a good life cannot be yours
again.

The principle of the will can handle this division, though we have
to begin farther back. Our prayer here must be, "Lord, I am willing to be
made willing."

And there one lets the matter rest for days or weeks, doing no forcing or straining, giving God time to change the emotional climate at deep
levels in the personality.

A clergyman friend of mine from St. Louis once told me how he had applied this same principle to a broken marriage. The young woman, Marty, who came to see him at his church office, began by saying that she no longer loved her husband, Bill. He had been unfaithful and had lost her respect.

"Did you love him once?" the minister asked.

"Yes, I did."

"And how does your husband feel now? Is he unchanged, or contrite—or what?"

"We've been separated for a year. Two months ago Bill came to me. He said he'd been a fool, that the affair was all over, and asked my forgiveness. Now he's pleading for a reconciliation."

"Well, can you forgive him?"

The woman hesitated. "I've heard you say often enough from the pulpit that we have to forgive, no matter what. But that isn't my worst problem. When respect goes, love goes. What I really came to ask is: Is it right, even fair to Bill for me to live with him again when I don't love him?"

"Marty, what do you think God's will is for you and Bill?"

She thought for a while. "I suppose that in God's sight Bill *is* my husband. I took him 'for better or for worse.' Then it must be God's will for me to love my husband."

The counselor smiled at her. "But your difficulty, Marty, is that love can't be summoned like whistling for one's dog. Is that it?"

"Yes, that's it."

"There is an answer, Marty. If you are willing to do what you deeply feel God wants you to do, then He will attend to your emotions, give you back your love for Bill."

"How can you be so sure of that?"

"I can guarantee it, if you'll fulfill certain conditions." Then the minister explained to the young woman the principle of the will. As he talked, he shoved across his desk a crude diagram. "This is not original with me," he explained. "I got the idea from Dr. Glenn Clark."

I will . . .   to will . . .   the will of God.
↓   ↓   ↓
Man's will   the will   God's will
                     in
                     action

Marty studied the diagram. When she finally looked up, her eyes were hopeful. "I begin to see a way out of my box! You mean that love is an emotion, and I can't control *that*, but I can control my will. And if I set my will right, then the emotions *have* to come right too. Is that it?"

"That's it."

"Then," Marty continued, "my part is to decide to go back to him."

"A little more than that," the clergyman corrected. "You have to go back, not reluctantly or half-heartedly, but willing to find joy and a new love for Bill. You can supply the willingness; God will do the rest."

That was five years ago. The marriage has not only lasted, but according to this minister Bill and Marty—now more mature and tested— are happier than they ever were before.

Surely we have misunderstood Christianity if we think God wants us to obey Him reluctantly—resisting, bucking, hating every step of the way. In fact the New Testament tells us that this reluctant obedience growing out of fear of punishment was the old way, the Old Covenant. Jesus came to show us a new way by which God promises to work in us "both to will and to do of His good pleasure."[3] This means that God will bring about such a change in us that His plans and desires for us will be our delight.

God's will gets written in our hearts by the simple application of the principle of the will to each life situation as we meet it. Christ would indeed be unrealistic if He asked us to do the impossible. He does not. His "secret?" not only tells us how, but speeds us on our way with joy.

Five
Dare to Trust God

"Now don't push the term *faith* at me," a lawyer told me bluntly at a dinner party recently. "The word is like a red flag."

"Why such a violent reaction?" I asked.

"Well, because I object to the way Christianity uses faith as a theological gimmick to duck all rational problems. At every point where a man wants to understand, they say, 'You just have to have faith,' or 'Reason can only go so far.' I resent it! I see nothing wrong with 'Prove it to me first, then I'll believe.'"

As we talked, I realized that it had never occurred to this intelligent, well-educated man that in his everyday life he often follows the reverse order—belief and acceptance first, then action. Every day he lives, he acts on faith many times with little proof or none at all, and he does not feel that he is being impractical.

He demonstrates an act of faith each time he boards a plane. He believes that it will take him to his destination, but he has no proof of it. He entrusts life itself to several unknown mechanics who have serviced the plane, as well as to a pilot about whom he knows nothing.

Each time he eats a meal in a restaurant he trusts some unknown cook behind the scenes and eats the food on faith, faith that it is not contaminated. He enters a hospital for an operation and signs a release giving permission for surgery. This is an act of faith in an anesthetist

353

whose name he may not even know and a surgeon who holds in his hands the power of life or death.

He accepts a prescription from a doctor and takes it to a druggist, thus acting his faith that the pharmacist will fill the prescription accurately. The use of the wrong drug might be deadly, but he is not equipped to analyze the contents before swallowing the pill.

It is obvious that were we to insist on the "proof first, then faith" order in our daily lives, organized life as we know it would grind to a screeching halt. And since life together among men is possible only by faith, as we act our trust in other people, it should not seem odd that the same law applies to our life with God.

The New Testament makes it clear that in the spiritual realm, when for some reason or other we refuse to act by faith, all activity stops just as completely as it does in the secular realm. There is no way for us even to take the first steps toward the Christian life except by faith, any more than a baby can get launched on his earthly life without blind baby-trust in his parents and other adults. We have to accept the fact of a personal relationship with Jesus Christ by faith, even as our young children accept the fact of parental love. For the child, as for the new Christian, understanding and proof come later.

In the same way, every step in our Christian walk has to be by faith.

In Jesus' ministry of healing the spirit, the mind, and the body, faith seems to have been necessary before the divine act, not (as logic would have it) afterward. The gospels are studded with statements of this:

And he said to the woman, Thy faith hath saved thee, go in peace.[1]
Then touched he their eyes, saying, According to your faith be it unto you.[2]

. . . Jesus said . . . all things are possible to him that believeth.[3]
All that ever you ask in prayer, you shall have, if you believe.[4]

Much of my own problem with faith arose from an early misunderstanding of what faith is. First of all, I used to believe that faith had something to do with feeling. For example, when I had messed up some situation and had asked God for forgiveness, then I would peer inside myself to see if I *felt* forgiven. If I could locate such feelings, then I was sure that God had heard and had forgiven me. Now I know that this is an altogether false test of faith.

We would not be so foolish as to go to a railroad station, board the first car we saw, then sit down and try to feel whether or not this was the train that would take us where we wanted to go. Our feeling would obviously have no bearing on the facts. Yet I know now that at times my actions in the spiritual realm have been just that foolish.

Another misconception I once had was that faith is trying to believe something one is fairly certain is not true. But faith is not hocus-pocus, opposed to knowledge and reality. In fact, faith does not go against experience at all; rather it appeals to experience, just as science does. The difference is that it appeals to experience in a realm where our five senses are not supreme rulers.

Nor is faith a kind of spiritual coin which you and I can exchange for heaven's blessings. Nor is it simply believing doggedly in some particular doctrine. One can believe in the divinity of Jesus Christ and feel no personal loyalty to Him at all; indeed, pay no attention whatever to His commandments and His will for one's life. One can believe intellectually in the efficacy of prayer and never do any praying.

Perhaps one reason that the real meaning of faith eluded me personally for so many years was that it is so surprisingly simple, so practical. Faith in God is simply trusting Him enough to step out on that trust.

My first lesson in stepping out on trust came in connection with the problem of financing a college education. We were then living in a little railroad town in the eastern Panhandle of West Virginia. By the time I reached my senior year in high school, the town had for some years been struggling through the long aftermath of the 1929 crash. Its only industry—the Baltimore and Ohio railroad shops—were all but shut down. The church my father served as minister was suffering along with everything else. Father had voluntarily taken several cuts in his already meager salary. Even grocery money was scarce. It was fortunate that Mother knew how to prepare fried mush in a way that made it seem like a rare delicacy.

Something I had dreamed of as far back as I could remember—a college education—now seemed out of the question. The dream even included a particular college—Agnes Scott in Decatur, Georgia.

Agnes Scott accepted me. Although the school was accustomed to ministers' and missionaries' daughters whose ambitions outstripped their pocketbooks, the financial burden nevertheless looked hopelessly heavy. Even with the promise of a small work scholarship and the $125 I had saved from high school essay and debating prizes, we were several hundred dollars short.

It was frightening to see that my parents were helpless in this situation. It was in their faces, in their voices. Through all my growing-up years, in every childish emergency they had been equal to anything. What now? Did this mean that I was going to have to relinquish my heart's desire?

One evening Mother found me lying across my bed, sobbing. She sat down beside me, put her cool hand on my forehead. No words were needed. She knew what the trouble was.

Presently she said quietly, "You and I are going to pray about this. Let's go into the guest room where we won't be disturbed." And she took me firmly by the hand.

We sat down on the old-fashioned golden-oak bed, the one that Mother and Father had bought for their first home. "Let's talk about this a minute before we pray," Mother said slowly. "I believe that it is God's will for you to go to college, or else He would not have given you the mental equipment. Furthermore, all resources are at God's disposal. Do you believe that, Catherine?"

"Yes—yes—I think I do."

"All right. Now here's another fact I want you to think about. Everybody has faith. We're born with it. Much of what happens to us in life depends on where we place our faith. If we deposit it in God, then we're on sure ground. If we place our trust in poverty or failure or fear, then we're investing it poorly. So keep that in mind while I read something to you." She opened a Moffatt Bible to I John 5:14, 15:

> Now the confidence we have in him is this,
> that he listens to us whenever we ask anything
> in accordance with His will; and if we know that he
> listens to whatever we ask, we know that we obtain the
> requests we have made to him.

"Note how the thought goes in that promise, Catherine. Whenever we ask God for something that is His will, He hears us. If He hears us, then He grants the request we have made. So you and I can rest on that promise. Let's claim it right now for the resources for your college." And so we knelt by the bed and prayed about it.

I shall never forget that evening. During those quiet moments in the bedroom, I was learning what faith is and how it works. It is true that my faith was immature and weak, but the strength of Mother's was contagious. She had helped me take my first step in faith. The answer would come. We knew it would, though neither of us had any idea how.

When it came, it was the offer of a job for Mother with the Federal Writer's Project. Would she be willing to write the history of the county? Would she! Her salary would cover the amount needed for my college expenses with a little to spare. Since history has always been one of Mother's loves, no job could have been more to her liking. Moreover, she could work at home and, along with her writing, keep a hand on all of the family projects.

That was the way I learned that we must have faith *before* the fact, not after, if we are to function as human beings at all. The only question is—faith in whom? Faith in what?

God challenges us to place it in Him rather than in fallible human beings: "Taste and see that the Lord is good."[5] In my experience this is not an ivory-tower approach. It is the only effectual one.

I have seen faith in God vindicated many times in stirring ways. No story ever captured my imagination so much as George Müller's. My children will read it and—if I have anything to say about it—my grandchildren.

In the year 1828 a man sat in a room in Teignmouth, England, struggling with a problem. A German, George Müller was then twenty-three years old. His father was a collector of excise taxes in Prussia, and the son had inherited the father's preoccupation with figures, his adding-machine mind, his astute business sense. During this period in England the Industrial Revolution was well under way. George Müller felt he could become a successful industrialist. Yet he hesitated.

Only three years out of the University at Halle, George had been mostly preoccupied with taverns, women, cards, and occasional study. He certainly had not been at all interested in religion. Then there had come a turning point. It had come through Müller's unexpected discovery one night at a friend's party that he could have fun in a Christian group—a different, deeper kind of pleasure than he found in his favorite tavern.

To his own surprise, George Müller began to think about the meaning of life. Often he pondered the fact that all through the Gospels there kept recurring Jesus' plea for us to have faith, to ask . . . ask . . . ask:

> Hitherto you have asked nothing in my name;
> ask and you will receive, that your joy may be full.[6]

> If for all your evil you know to give your
> children what is good, how much more will
> your Father in heaven give good to
> those who ask him?[7]

Had Christ meant those words literally? If so, then why—generation after generation—did mankind continue to ignore them or water them down?

Müller thought of several individuals he had recently met. One was a man who had to work at his trade fourteen to sixteen hours a day. He had no time for his family, no time to enjoy life. Concerned, Müller had spoken to him only a week before: "Henry, you simply have to work less. Your family needs something more of you than your pay. Your body's suffering and your soul is starving."

But the reply had been, "But if I work less, I won't earn enough for the support of my family."

When Müller had quoted him the promise, "Seek ye first the Kingdom of God, and His righteousness, and all these things shall be added unto you,"[8] Henry had said with a wry grimace, "I wish I could believe that applies to my situation, George. Guess I just need more faith."

Müller now sat chin in hand, staring out the second-story window over the chimney pots of the town to the sea in the distance, foaming and curling at the base of the red cliffs of Parson Rock. But he was not seeing the beauty of a sunset on Teignmouth's coast now. Instead he was thinking of an old woman, Marie, so frightened of old age without a pension, so terrified of the poorhouse waiting for her at the end of the road. Where was her faith in God's ability to take care of her? And then he was thinking of Lawrence, a man now in his early thirties and in a business he hated. But he dared not switch to where his heart was— medicine. "How would I take care of my family while I complete my studies?" He too had merely shrugged when Müller had mentioned faith in God as the solution.

So what could he—George Müller—do about it? How could he define this matter of faith and prove to these people that Jesus had meant it when He bade us *ask*.

At that moment he saw out the window two ragged little girls on the cobblestone walk. He had seen them before. Their father was a merchant seaman whose ship had been lost last year off Desolation Island in the Magellan Straits. Two weeks ago their mother had died of tuberculosis. Müller recalled the pathetic funeral, the raw pine casket, the lost look on the faces of the children. He knew that the eleven- and thirteen-year-old girls were trying to take care of three younger children. And these were not the only destitute children in the town, either. There seemed to be no institutions for needy children in England. He wondered why not.

The thoughts went round and round. And then he noticed his Bible open on the table beside him. It was open to the Psalms: suddenly he was reading a verse he had never noticed before: "Open thy mouth wide, and I will fill it."[9] Müller suddenly found himself quietly praying, "All right, I'm opening my mouth to ask. If You want me to do something about all this, you'll have to show me how and where to begin."

George Müller began by offering his services to a local mission. His drive and imagination soon revitalized it. The records show that he met and married Mary Groves in 1830. The two of them consecrated their marriage vows with a rather remarkable demonstration of Jesus' words . . . "Sell what you possess and give it away in alms. . . ."[10] Just so, did George and Mary part with their household goods. Like many daring experimenters, Müller wanted to go all the way. His desire was to make himself and his wife dependent for everything on God alone. Their motive was sincere, above all suspicion. At the time he and his wife kept the act of giving away their possessions a secret from all who knew them.

The next step was even more daring. Müller refused all regular salary from the people of the small mission he had been serving. He and his wife would henceforth tell their needs to God alone in prayer. Theirs would be a test case for the world to see.

Then George found his thoughts centering on the idea of founding an orphan's home. It would not be just a place to care for a few homeless children, but a vast institution—built and operated on faith. He would make it too a pure example of trust in God.

On April 21, 1836, the first Orphan Home was dedicated in a rented building. Within a matter of days there were forty-three children to be cared for. Müller and his co-workers decided that the controlled experiment would be set up along these lines:

1. No funds would ever be solicited. No facts or figures concerning needs were to be revealed by the workers in the orphanage to anyone, except to God in prayer.
2. No debts would ever be incurred. The burden of experiment would therefore not be on local shopkeepers or suppliers.
3. No money contributed for a specific purpose could ever be used for any other purpose.
4. All accounts would be audited annually by professional auditors.
5. No ego-pandering by publication of donors' names with the amount of their gifts; each donor would be thanked privately.
6. No "names" of prominent or titled persons would be sought for the board or to advertise the institution.
7. The success of the institution would be measured not by the numbers served or by the amounts of money taken in, but by God's blessing on the work, which Müller expected to be in proportion to the time spent in prayer.

When the first building was opened, George Müller and his associates stuck to their principles, spending time in prayer that ordinarily would have gone to fund-raising. An unbelieving public was amazed when a second building was opened six months after the first. Müller concentrated on prayer, and the money kept coming in. Eventually, there were five new buildings, with 110 helpers taking care of 2050 orphans.

Before opening his first orphanage Müller had said that he would consider the experiment a failure if ever the orphans had to go for a single day without food. They never did. Nor were these children taken care of in minimal fashion. Part of George Müller's conviction was that God not only provides, but that He provides bountifully. For their time, his orphanage buildings were constructed with remarkable details—built-in cupboards with a large pigeonhole for each child's clothes; sunny playrooms with shelves and cupboards for the toys that were not yet there. Each child must always have not one but three pairs of shoes. Each boy, three suits; each girl, five dresses. There must always be white tablecloths for the evening meal and flowers whenever possible. Behind the scenes were the latest laborsaving devices available: one of the first American washing machines in England and an early type of centrifugal dryer.

After each year's audit a detailed report was made public showing how the Lord had provided for that year. Soon it became apparent that all around the world people were watching this experiment with fascination. Businessmen were particularly interested. One executive traveled a considerable distance for an interview with Müller. His firm was threatened with bankruptcy. In his methodical manner, Müller wrote out for his visitor a prescription of five parts—advice as applicable today as it was then:

1. Each day you and your wife are to spread your business difficulties before the Lord.
2. You are then to watch for answers to prayer and expect them.
3. Absolute honesty necessary; avoid all business trickeries.
4. Beginning immediately, a certain proportion of your income must be given to God.
5. Keep a record—month by month—how the Lord is dealing with you, what's happening.

The man did keep a record; in fact he sent a monthly report to Müller, and in his journal Müller recorded that during the first year the man's business came out of the red and up some three thousand pounds over the previous year. For as long as George Müller recorded the figures, the businessman's profits continued to mount.

The results of his amazing orphanage experiment have been published in detail in the four volumes of George Müller's *Journals*. For more than sixty years he recorded every specific prayer request and the result. His mathematical mind kept meticulous books on every penny received and all money expended.

So great did public interest in the orphanage become that when Müller was seventy, he felt that the time had come to tell the story himself. So over a number of years he traveled 200,000 miles, lecturing in forty-two countries. For hundreds of thousands of people he became a living demonstration of the fact that faith is nothing more or less than believing God, not just intellectually but actually.

Faith is only worthy of the name when it erupts into action. Unlike George Müller, most of us can show few trophies won through faith.

Were we to use the muscles of our legs as little as we do the muscles of our faith, most of us would be unable to stand.

Then what can we do to strengthen them?

First, we cannot trust God until we know something about Him. The way to begin is by reading His word and thinking about it. The Bible acquaints us with the nature and character of God: His power; His unselfish, unchangeable love; His infinite wisdom. We read instance after instance in which God has exercised His power and wisdom in helping and delivering His people.

Second, faith is strengthened only as we ourselves exercise it. We have to apply it to our problems: poverty, bodily ills, bereavement, job troubles, tangled human relationships.

Third, faith has to be in the present tense—now. A vague prospect that what we want will transpire in the future is not faith, but hope.

Fourth, absolute honesty is necessary. We cannot have faith and a guilty conscience at the same time. Every time faith will fade away.

Fifth, the strengthening of faith comes through staying with it in the hour of trial. We should not shrink from tests of our faith. Only when we are depending on God alone are we in a position to see God's help and deliverance, and thus have our faith strengthened for the next time.

This means that we must let Him do the work. Almost always it takes longer than we think it should. When we grow impatient and try a deliverance of our own, through friends or circumstances, we are taking God's work out of His hands.

George Müller was faithfully reflecting the New Testament in his blunt, realistic insistence in depending on God alone. The Epistle of James declared that "faith, unless it has deeds, is dead in itself."[11] And John added more bluntly still, "He who will not believe God, has made God a liar. . . ."[12]

Believe what? Believe the consistent testimony in Scripture of the unfailing love and good will of our God, of His ability to help us, and of His willingness—indeed eagerness—to do so.

The adventure of living has not really begun until we begin to stand on our faith legs and claim—for ourselves, for our homes, for the rearing of our children, for our health problems, for our business affairs, and for our world—the resources of our God.

Six
The Prayer
of Relinquishment

AFTER THE DISCOVERY that faith in God can make life an adventure, comes the desire to experiment with prayer. Like most people, I was full of questions, such as why are some agonizingly sincere prayers granted while others are not?

Many years later I still have questions. Mysteries about prayer are always out ahead of present knowledge—luring, beckoning on to further experimentation.

But one thing I do know; I learned it through hard experience. It is a way of prayer that has consistently resulted in a glorious answer, glorious because each time power beyond human reckoning has been released. This is the Prayer of Relinquishment.

I got my first glimpse of it in the fall of 1943. The illness that I have mentioned before in these pages had kept me in bed for many months. A bevy of specialists seemed unable to help. Persistent prayer, using all the faith I could muster, had resulted in—nothing.

One afternoon a pamphlet was put in my hand. It was the story of a missionary who had been an invalid for eight years. Constantly she had prayed that God would make her well, so that she might do His work. Finally, worn out with futile petition, she prayed, "All right. I give up. If You want me to be an invalid for the rest of my days, that's Your business. Anyway, I've discovered that I want You even more than I want health. You decide." The pamphlet said that within two weeks the woman was out of bed, completely well.

This made no sense to me. It seemed too pat. Yet I could not forget the story. On the morning of September fourteenth (how can I ever forget the date?) I came to the same point of abject acceptance. "I'm tired of asking" was the burden of my prayer. "I'm beaten, finished. God, You decide what you want for me for the rest of my life. . . ." Tears flowed. I had no faith as I understood faith. I expected nothing. The gift of my sick self was made with no trace of graciousness.

The result was as if windows had opened in heaven; as if some dynamo of heavenly power had begun flowing, flowing into me. From that moment my recovery began.

Through this incident and others that followed, some of which I want to tell later, God was trying to teach me something important about prayer. Still I got only part of the message. I saw that the demanding spirit—"God, I must have thus and so; God, this is what I want you to do for me—" is not real prayer and hence receives no answer. I understood that the reason for this is that God absolutely refuses to violate our free will and that therefore, unless self-will is voluntarily given up, even God cannot move to answer prayer. But it was going to take more time and more experience for me to begin to understand the Prayer of Relinquishment.

Part of that understanding has come through learning of other people's experiences with this type of prayer. It has been exciting to uncover in contemporary life, in the Bible, and scattered through the writings of men in other centuries the infallible power of this prayer technique.

Some years ago, I stumbled across one example in the life of the New England writer, Nathaniel Hawthorne. In 1853 Hawthorne had decided to take his family abroad for an extended stay. He wanted a broadening of his horizons, contact with other writers in England and Italy. By then he was already recognized as a master of the craft of the short story through his *Twice-Told Tales* and was famous as the author of the successful novel *The Scarlet Letter*.

In late 1858, the Hawthornes were settled in a villa in Rome. February 1860 found them in the midst of a grave crisis. Una, their eldest daughter, was dying of a virulent form of malaria. The attending physician, Dr. Franco, had that afternoon warned the distraught parents that unless the young girl's fever abated before morning she would die.

As Sophia Hawthorne sat by her daughter's bed, her thoughts went to her handsome husband in the adjoining room. She could picture him—his troubled blue eyes, that splendid head with its mop of dark hair, bowed in grief. She recalled what he had said earlier that day, "I cannot endure the alternations of hope and fear, and therefore I have settled with myself not to hope at all."

But Sophia could not share Nathaniel's hopelessness. Una could not, must not die. This daughter strongly resembled her father, had the finest mind, the most complex character of all the Hawthorne children. Why should a capricious Providence demand that they give her up?

Moreover, Una had been delirious for several days and had recognized no one. Were she to die this night, there would not even be the solace of farewells.

As the night deepened, the young girl ceased her incoherent mutterings and lay so still that she seemed to be in the anteroom of death. The mother went to the window and looked out on the piazza. There was no moonlight; heavy clouds scudded across a dark and silent sky.

"I cannot bear this loss—cannot—cannot." Then suddenly, unaccountably, another thought took over. "Why should I doubt the goodness of God? Let Him take Una, if He sees best. I can give her to Him. No, I won't fight against Him any more."

Then an even stranger thing happened. Having made the great sacrifice in her mind, Sophia expected to feel sadder. Instead she felt lighter, happier than at any time since Una's long illness had begun.

Some minutes later she walked back to the girl's bedside and felt her daughter's forehead. It was moist and cool. The pulse was slow and regular. Una was sleeping naturally. Sophia rushed into the next room to tell her husband that the crisis seemed to be past. She was right. Though Una was months getting the malaria out of her system, she did recover completely.

A contemporary answer to prayer reminiscent of the Hawthornes' experience was related to me by a friend in a letter:

. . . Three years ago our son was born. At first he seemed a normal, healthy baby. But when he was not quite twelve hours old, while I was holding

him in my arms, he had a convulsion. More convulsions followed the next few days.

The only explanation the doctors had was that he must have suffered a brain injury of some kind at birth. This only added to my terror. . . . If he lived, perhaps he would be blind, deaf, dumb, or a cripple, or with his mind affected.

I've never felt so alone as during the time that followed. I prayed, but I couldn't feel that God cared about me any more. Why had this had to happen to my baby?

I know now that my prayers were not prayers at all, but accusations. I was demanding that God heal my child.

Then out of sheer exhaustion of body and soul, I stopped commanding God and gave in to Him completely. I just said, "Take him if that's what You want. Anything You decide will be all right with me. Even if You want him to be a cripple or deaf, then I will just have to learn to accept it and live with it." I put myself and the baby entirely in His hands.

From that instant, not only did Larry begin to improve, but suddenly my tears left, and my fears went with them. An inexplicable peace filled my heart, and I knew, just knew that Larry would not only live but would have a normal, useful life. . . .

Well, the end of the story is that Larry is now as normal and healthy as any little boy. He's very very intelligent, and if he were any more active, well I'd be the one to be a cripple.

Larry's story and Una's have several points in common. In each case, the mother wanted the same thing desperately—life and health for her child. Each mother commanded God to answer her prayer. While the demanding spirit had the upper hand, God seemed remote, unapproachable.

Then, through a combination of the obvious futility of the demanding prayer plus weariness of body and spirit, the mother surrendered to the possibility of what she feared most. At that instant there came a turning point. Suddenly and inexplicably fear left and the feeling of soul-strain with it. Peace crept into the heart. There followed a feeling of lightness and joy that had nothing to do with outer circumstances. This marked the turning point. From that moment the prayer began to be answered.

The intriguing question is: What is the spiritual law implicit in this Prayer of Relinquishment? I think I know at least part of it. . . . We know that fear blocks prayer. Fear is a barrier erected between us and God, so that His power cannot get through to us. So—how does one get rid of fear?

This is not easy when the life of someone dear hangs in the balance, or when what we want most in all the world seems to be slipping away. At such times, every emotion, every passion, is tied up in the dread that what we fear most is about to come upon us. Obviously only strong measures can deal with such a powerful fear. My experience has been that trying to overcome it by turning one's thoughts to the positive or by repeating affirmations is not potent enough.

It is then that we are squarely up against the law of relinquishment. Was Jesus showing us how to use this law when He said, "Resist not evil?" In God's eyes, fear is evil because it is acting out of lack of trust in Him. So Jesus is advising "Resist not fear."

In other words, Jesus is saying: "Admit the possibility of what you fear most. And lo, as you stop fleeing, as you force yourself to walk up to the fear, as you look it full in the face, never forgetting that God and His power are still the supreme reality, the fear evaporates." Drastic? Yes. But effective.

One point about the Prayer of Relinquishment puzzled me for many years. There seemed to be a contradiction between the Prayer of Faith and that of relinquishment. If relinquishment is real, the one praying must be willing to receive or not receive his heart's desire. But that state of mind scarcely seems to exhibit the faith that knows that one's request will be granted. And as I read the gospels, Jesus placed far greater stress on the Prayer of Faith than on the Prayer of Relinquishment.

Now I believe I have the explanation. The fact is that I went through a period of misunderstanding faith. Once I thought that faith was believing this or that specific thing in my mind with never a doubt. Now I know that faith is nothing more or less than actively trusting God.

Peter Marshall liked to illustrate what such active trust means by a homely example:

> Suppose a child has a broken toy.
> He brings the toy to his father, saying that he
>   himself has tried to fix it and has failed.
> He asks his father to do it for him.
>
> The father gladly agrees . . .
>   takes the toy . . .
>   and begins to work.

Now obviously the father can do his work most quickly and easily if the child makes no attempt to interfere, simply sits quietly watching, or even goes about other business, with never a doubt that the toy is being successfully mended.

> But what do most of God's children do in such a situation?
> Often we stand by offering a lot of meaningless advice
> and some rather silly criticism.

> We even get impatient and try to help,
> and so get our hands in the Father's way,
> generally hindering the work . . .

Finally, in our desperation, we may even grab the toy out of the Father's hands entirely, saying rather bitterly that we hadn't really thought He could fix it anyway . . . that we'd given Him a chance and He had failed us.

Grabbing the toy away is certainly not trust. But what does demonstrate trust is to put the thing or the person one loves best into the Father's hands to do with as He pleases. Thus faith is by no means absent in the Prayer of Relinquishment. In fact this prayer is faith in action.

And that is why this prayer is answered, even when the one making the relinquishment has little hope that what he fears most can be avoided. For I have always felt that God is not half so concerned about our having a few negative thoughts as He is concerned with what we do. And the act of placing what we cherish most in His hands is to Him the sweet music of the essence of faith.

This kind of faith can be used to solve any type of problem. I remember an attractive young girl, Sara Bradford, who sat in my living room and shared with me her doubts about her engagement.

"I love Jeb," she said, and there was deep feeling in her words. "And Jeb loves me. But there are problems. He had an unhappy childhood. His mother and father were divorced when he was ten. His mother was a great beauty. She's still a beautiful woman at sixty-two. She married again, and that marriage was unhappy too. Jeb is most defensive of her."

"Does this make you feel that Jeb is a poor risk for marriage?"

Sara hesitated. "Well, it's left a lot of marks. There are other problems too. At twenty-four, Jeb is still restless———"

"You mean he hasn't settled on a career?"

"No, he hasn't. Then too, it bothers me that religion doesn't mean much to him. Oh, a few times he's gone to church with me. But his heart isn't in it. I don't really want to establish the kind of a home in which God will be left out. And then there is his drinking . . . What should I do? Do all these doubts mean that God is trying to tell me to give Jeb up?"

As she talked on and on, Sara reached her own conclusion. It was that she would lose something infinitely precious if she did not follow the highest and the best that she knew. Her voice broke as she said, "I'm going to have to break the engagement. Then if God wants me to marry Jeb, He will find some way of showing me."

Right then, simply and poignantly, she told God her decision. Her prayer was a true relinquishment. She was putting her broken dreams and her now-unknown future into God's hands.

I remained interested in Sara and in knowing how her future turned out. Jeb did not change, so Sara did not marry him. But a year later Sara wrote me an ecstatic letter. "Something wonderful happened that afternoon in your living room. It nearly killed me to give Jeb up. Yet God knew that he wasn't the one for me. Now I've met The Man. He's terrific and we're to be married in October. Now I *really* have something to say about trusting God."

The Prayer of Relinquishment also helps us in small matters. A friend confided that she had been suffering from insomnia. Her doctor had prescribed sleeping pills.

"I've been reading so much lately about how the sales of sleeping pills rise and rise. Are we becoming a nation of addicts?"

"Not you, certainly," I reassured her.

"Thanks. But the principle of this bothers me. I'm not sure I want this crutch."

Later we met again and she told me what happened.

"I decided nix on the pills. So that night I lay and prayed, 'All right, God, I put myself and my sleep into Your hands. If You want me to stay awake most of the night, fine. You decide'."

"And did you stay awake?"

There was a sheepish look on her face. "No, I slept like a baby."

No doubt psychologists, as well as the sleep experts, could comment knowingly on this incident. But I relate it here only because it illustrates the Law of Relinquishment not in a dramatic crisis but in an ordinary situation.

My own latest adventure with the Prayer of Relinquishment came in connection with the mundane problem of household help. In the weeks prior to my marriage to Leonard LeSourd, I was happily excited but at the same time panicky at the thought of taking on three young children. After all, I had thought myself finished with child-rearing. Peter John had then been out of the home nest for three years, away at school. At the same time I wanted to keep on with my writing. What if I was not adequate to the situation?

In his efforts to reassure me, Len made solemn promises of household help. But after our marriage, the help was slow in materializing. Three months passed, four. One maid stayed for three weeks, then decided to go back to her home in North Carolina. Then a cleaning woman who was helping me one day a week had to stop when she fell and injured her leg.

Many a morning Len and I prayed about it. Soon after our marriage, we had hit upon a pleasant way to begin our day with quietness and prayer. An automatic coffee pot attached to a clock would waken us with the fragrance of percolating coffee. Then we would sit propped up in bed, sipping coffee, reading a portion of Scripture together, thinking through the day ahead.

One morning I was particularly discouraged. I was caught between all my blessings—a wonderful husband, three lovely children at home and a fourth in and out, a big new house, and my daily writing. I was, quite frankly, exhausted. We had tried everything we knew: agencies, the suggestions of friends and relatives, the Help Wanted columns in the local and New York newspapers. Just the evening before a promising candidate from Boston with whom we had been corresponding had telephoned that she could not come.

So once more we took the situation to God. . . . "Lord, we've tried everything we can think of. Every road has seemed a dead end. Doors have been so consistently shut in our faces that You must be trying to teach us something. Tell us what it is———"

There followed the illumination that prayer often brings. In this case, it was not pleasant. I had been trying to dictate the terms of my life to God—what I wanted: help in the home so that I could get on with my writing. A thought stabbed me. What if—for this period of my life—I was supposed to give up the writing? Immediately this possibility brought tears. Why should I have to relinquish something which I had from the beginning dedicated to God—and something from which I also got such intense satisfaction? Still it was obvious that our home and the children had to come first. So, knowing that I would get no answer from God until I was willing to surrender the writing, I set myself to the task.

At that point, Hannah Whitall Smith's practicable principle of the will came to my rescue. Resolutely I set my will to accept what had to be accepted. Though my emotions were in stark rebellion, I knew that sooner or later they would fall into line.

I plunged into homemaking, completing the furnishing and decorating of the house . . . meals . . . laundry . . . groceries . . . creating an atmosphere of security for children who badly needed it.

Then I realized that, beyond the writing, there had been another reason why I had wanted help. It was the haunting fear that I would be physically and emotionally unable to handle all the housework, take care of the children, be a good wife to my husband—all at one time. But now I was learning that I could cope with it. With that knowledge came the self-assurance that washed away all fears. And I would never have had this sense of security and confidence if we had started our marriage with domestic help.

When the relinquishment was complete, the breakthrough occurred. Unexpectedly a letter came from Boston. The woman who had refused us before said that she was now available. Lucy Arsenault came to us. Lucy—settled, reliable, a superb cook, a rare person. As always, a loving God had planned so much better than we ever could have.

The morning mail frequently holds surprises for me. On one particular morning a few months ago I noticed that the tissue-thin air mail letter was postmarked Quito, Ecuador. After glancing over the first two paragraphs, I turned to the second sheet to see the signature—and gasped. Betty Elliot! Only a few days before I had been reading about her in *Life* magazine. Her husband had been one of the five missionaries brutally massacred by the Auca Indians on January 8, 1956. I was curious to know why she should be writing to me.

I have just spent Christmas alone here in an Auca Indian settlement reading your book, To Live Again. *Though my present circumstances could*

hardly be more remote from those you describe, I responded deeply to
much of your message, and I felt I wanted to thank you. . . .

Then she went on to tell me what her circumstances were. Betty
and her small blonde daughter, Valerie, together with Rachel, the sister
of Nate Saint (another of the murdered men) are now living in the midst
of the South American Auca tribe. The two women and the tiny girl are
altogether at the mercy of the same men who killed their husband and
brother. They have no weapons; there are no other white people within
miles of jungle, inaccessible except on foot or by airlift. How did such
circumstances come about? "God led us here, opened the way through
Dayuma, an escaped Auca woman. . . ." Betty explains simply.

Yet Betty Elliot is a realist. "It is possible for us to lose our lives
any day. The Aucas are still savages, who do not even think of killing as
wrong. Fear can drive them to kill in a twinkling. What the future holds
for Rachel and Valerie and me is God's business. . . ."

I found my imagination straining as I thought of how the pages I
held in my hand had been written. She had penned them seated in the
doorway of the palm-thatched hut that Betty calls home. The muddy
Tewaenon River flows nearby. Her husband's body, a broken spear still
imbedded in it, had been found three years before floating face down in
the same river. And closer, the lush green jungle forever impinges on
the natives' clearing.

All around her as she wrote those words were the short savages with
their tea-colored skins and straight black hair. Both men and women go
naked except for the vines tied tightly around waists, ankles, and wrists.
Valerie nearby chattered animatedly with a pet parrot. . . .

I was awed at the evidence of such a love for God as these two women
were demonstrating. Then my eye fell on the last paragraph of the letter:

Your solution to grief is just another way of giving the same answer that
God gave me in the first empty days—Accept this. Only in acceptance
lies peace—not in forgetting nor in resignations nor in busy-ness. His will
is good and acceptable and perfect. . . .

So this woman, in the midst of such cruel events, had discovered
the secret too: there is a difference between acceptance and resignation.
One is positive; the other negative. Acceptance is creative, resignation
sterile.

Resignation is barren of faith in the love of God. It says, "Grievous circumstances have come to me. There is no escaping them. I am only one creature, an alien in a vast unknowable creation. I have no heart left even to rebel. So I'll just resign myself to what apparently is the will of God; I'll even try to make a virtue out of patient submission." So resignation lies down quietly in the dust of a universe from which God seems to have fled, and the door of Hope swings shut.

But turn the coin over. Acceptance says, "I trust the good will, the love of my God. I'll open my arms and my understanding to what He has allowed to come to me. Since I know that He means to make all things work together for good, I consent to this present situation with hope for what the future will bring." Thus acceptance leaves the door of Hope wide open to God's creative plan. This difference between acceptance and resignation is the key to an understanding of the Prayer of Relinquishment.

Obviously Betty Elliot's acceptance left the door open to a creative plan daring enough that only God could have conceived it. Can two women and a tiny girl succeed in taking Christianity to Stone-age savages where many men have failed? For other white men died violently at the hands of the Aucas before the five missionaries. In 1942 the Shell Oil Company lost three men by Auca spears, in 1943 eight more. Since then the tribe has repaid with death any invasion of their territory by white men.

So now the world watches while an adventure story unfolds. In the plan that God gave Betty Elliot, I have never seen a better example of the "foolishness" of God being wiser than men, and the "weakness" of God being stronger than men.[1]

To the disciples of Jesus Christ, His actions during the last week of His life on earth must have seemed equally nonsensical. Their Master had a great following among the common people. His disciples were hoping that He would use this following to overthrow the Roman grip on their little country and move, at last, to establish His earthly kingdom.

Instead He deliberately set His feet on the path that would lead inescapably to the cross. For let us not mistake it. Christ could have avoided that cross. He did not have to go up to Jerusalem that last time. He could have compromised with the priests, bargained with Caiaphas. The disciples were probably right in thinking that He could have capitalized on His following, appeased Judas, and set up the beginning of an earthly empire. Later Pilate would all but beg Him to say the right words so that he might release Him.[2] Even in the Garden of Gethsamane on the night of betrayal, Christ had plenty of time and opportunity to flee.

But He would not flee. Instead He knelt to pray in the shadowy Garden under the gray-green leaves of the olive trees. And in His prayer that night, Jesus gave us, for all time, the perfect pattern for the Prayer of Relinquishment.

Jesus had been given genuine humanity, as well as divinity. Part of that humanity was His free will. He chose to use His free will to leave the decision to His Father as to whether He must die by execution.

It was agony, such agony that as He knelt there He could not have been aware of the beauty all around Him. The valley under the brow of the hill was washed in moonlight. Below Him the brook Kedron rippled and sang over stones and through rushes. Around Him were the myrtle trees, palms, and fig trees that melted into the olive groves. And in the enclosed Garden of Gethsemane, all around His prostrate figure were the leaves and trunks of the olive trees silvered by filtering moonlight. . . . This was not a world that Christ, the man, wanted to leave.

Was there a moment when He wondered *how* to pray about the terrible alternatives before Him? If so, in the end He knew that only one prayer could release the power that was needed to lift a sin-ridden world:

"Dear Father, all things are possible to You. Please—let me not have to drink this cup. Yet it is not what I want, but what You want."[3]

In these words Jesus deliberately set himself to make His will and God's will the same. The prayer was not answered as the human Jesus wished. Yet power has been flowing from His cross ever since.

God has given you and me free will too. And the voluntary giving up of our self-will always has a cross at the center of it. It is the hardest thing human beings are called on to do.

When we come right down to it, how can we make obedience real, except as we give over that self-will in reference to each of life's episodes as they unfold? That is why it should not surprise us that at the center of answered prayer lies the Law of Relinquishment.

Seven
Forgive Us Our Sins . . .

AT THE HEART of the Christian gospel lies forgiveness, the greatest miracle of all. Only as each of us opens himself to receive this most wondrous of gifts, can the inner self deep within us be freed to become the happier, finer person we are meant to be. Whenever I think of our desperate need for forgiveness and of how difficult it is for some of us to accept it, my thoughts go back to Margaret Stanley—Meg, as some of us call her.

It is a long story covering some four years. It begins in the drab living room in a government housing project called Lillypond in Washington, D.C. Meg was musing, letting her mind roam over the previous evening. Every detail remained vivid. From the street the building had looked like a Victorian stone mansion. Only the polished brass plate beside the door had revealed that this was a church. Meg had not been near a church in years. She had let her sister, Alice, talk her into going this Wednesday night only because she had been assured that she would meet some interesting people.

She recalled the moment when they had pushed open the green door and a turbulence of voices, humming and buzzing, rising and falling, had beat upon them. She shut her eyes to recapture her first impression of the large entrance hall. There were stairs, with curving arches above them forming a backdrop. The bare parquet floor had been polished to

375

mirror brightness. A square, old-fashioned grand piano stood to one side. People had been clustered in little groups talking animatedly. Alice had linked an arm through hers and had taken her from group to group. Names . . . so many names. There had been an obvious affection for Alice, a warmth that had flowed from her and back to her. Meg thought of that now with envy. She wondered if anyone had ever really loved *her?*

Then there had been dinner at small candlelit tables, with music in the background; afterward they had assembled in the little chapel to the left of the hallway. The chapel must have been made, Meg thought, by forming together two rooms of the old mansion.

Alice had tried to reassure her that this was not a church service. "Just a class," she had said lightly. "Meets every Wednesday. Arnold teaches it. He's the minister."

But he had not been Meg's idea of what a minister should look like. He was young, with a crew cut. His clear blue eyes had laughter crinkles at the corners. His clothes were preposterously casual. He even wore loafers.

If Meg had known that the class was called "What Christians Believe and Do" she probably would have fled before it started. As it was, the young minister had startled her into listening. "Christ requires a toughness to follow Him that frightens us," he began. "He asks that we deal decisively with all the things that keep us petty and make us ineffective.

"This is not just 'religious stuff.' It is practical. It works. In fact, if you are willing to try Christ for even six months, I'll guarantee that your life will be changed."

Back in her drab housing-project living room, Meg grimaced as she thought back to those words. Then she lifted one foot, kicked disgustedly at the ridiculous-looking coal stove in the center of the living room. Changed? Maybe some people, but not *her*. If those people at the church knew about her past, they would never let her set foot in the place!

She and her sister had come from a broken home. After years of dissension, their parents had been divorced. As a little girl Meg had been so unhappy that she had been unable to adjust to any school. There had been eighteen of them in all. After her second year in high school, she quit school and found a job.

Her need for affection drew her to friendships with men. Many of them were nice enough fellows and they had needs too. If she could give them a little pleasure, why not? Then she discovered that liquor helped to dull the feelings of guilt that always went with the affairs. There were a succession of men, then an illegitimate baby.

The Florence Crittenton home placed the baby for adoption, and a few months later she met Maynard. He seemed even nicer than the other men she had known. So she married him, because she thought marriage would change her. It had not.

Maynard had gone into the service and was sent to the West Coast. For Meg back home there began again the round of parties, heavy drinking, and now extra-marital affairs. A psychiatrist later analyzed her behavior not so much as wanton depravity but as a type of "sloppy kindness" brought on by her desire to please. Without a spiritual morality it quickly got out of hand.

Eventually Meg began spending every Saturday night at a down-at-the-heel dance hall. She found the young men there quick to take advantage of her weakness. Almost always there would be a drunken brawl; most Saturday nights the patrol wagon had to be called. Though Meg was disgusted by the brawls and managed to stay out of them, the police in the vicinity came to know her well.

Tales of what was going on at home got to Maynard. By this time, 1944, he was in a psychiatric ward in a veteran's hospital in Texas. There he tried to commit suicide. Hearing of this, Meg had been jolted enough to try and pull herself together. Eventually Maynard came home and fourteen months later a daughter was born to the couple. But their marriage was in no better shape. Finally Maynard asked Meg for a divorce.

The young minister's words rang now in her mind: "If you are willing to try Christ for six months, I'll guarantee that your life will be changed." Guarantee! How could he guarantee? One part of Meg's mind said, "Better not go near that group again, if you want to hang on to the old life." But another part of her wanted to see those people again. There were things she wanted to figure out. For instance, what was the vitality that flowed from them? Why did they get so excited about ideas? Why did she feel a warmth—yes, that was it, warmth—in their presence? Suddenly Meg realized how starved she was for love. Love! All her affairs and her attempts at love had not touched the aching need that gnawed at her.

So on other Wednesday nights Meg did go back to "the church in the house," as she came to call it. After several dinners with the group, she decided that hypocrisy must be lurking somewhere: nobody could be *that* nice. But how could she accuse the folks at the church of hypocrisy when they kept saying that the church was meant for sinners, that those who thought themselves good were not yet ready for a church.

Moreover, there was a closeness in their relationships that Meg had never seen before. It was more than friendship. For instance, she marveled at the way Steve, once a seemingly hopeless alcoholic and now a successful piano salesman, was helping Phil, a painfully shy man who worked in the Interior Department. Ben, who drove a bread truck, would at times minister to Betts, an interior decorator. There was Martha, a secretary; Sam, an oceanographer; Jane, a beautician; Bill, a former Harvard professor; Estelle, a publicity girl; Karl, who had spent forty years as a sailor—drunk most of the time. All saw a great deal of one another and shared each other's problems. Their lives were transparently open to the fellowship. In this transparency it seemed the natural thing to reveal their faults freely and to ask for help.

Nevertheless Meg was sure that she had a margin on all of them when it came to sin. She went through a period of trying to shock them. Over the years she had developed a hard line of talk. Increasingly she tried it out at the church. Once she let out some oaths in the chapel. No one batted an eyelash.

Then she had a conference with the minister, Arnold, and tried out on him raw statements of disbelief liberally sprinkled with profanity. She was dismayed to find him shockproof. He seemed neither surprised nor impressed by anything she said.

"Why should any of us be startled," he commented to her one afternoon, "to find out that human nature is capable of anything? There aren't any new sins, Meg. Just variations on old ones. Besides, the sort of thing you've been telling me is pale stuff compared to the adventure that Christ brings into life." He grinned at her discomfiture, and it was a disarming grin.

"Christ doesn't want to condemn you. He didn't come to earth to deepen our sense of moral defeat. He came to deliver us from what defeats us. All He wants, Meg, is to lift the weight of your past from you, so that you'll be free—really free. It's His love that makes that possible, Meg, His love———"

Meg burst into tears and fled from the office.

There were times when Meg was sure that Arnold and all the people at the church were crazy. Then there was a period when she thought they were rich—how else could they give so much money to the church? Finally there came the time when Meg did not care what they were. She knew only that she wanted what they had. She needed their love, needed to know that she belonged. Still—how could they love *her?*

Meanwhile Meg had asked Maynard to delay the divorce. She was now actively enrolled in a course called "Christian Growth" and there was the outside chance that she might get some help toward saving their marriage. Maynard was distant and unimpressed, but agreed to postpone divorce action for a few weeks. He even began dropping in at the church to see what it was all about.

One evening Arnold was talking about sin. "Sin is not simply the violation of a code," he told the class. "Sin is an affront by one spirit against another—an outrage of love.

"That's bad enough, but it's even worse when we try to deny our sin to God and ourselves. Because that shuts off forgiveness and the peace that comes with a reconciliation with the God of love.

"Why does the Bible tell us that sin is so deadly?" As Arnold talked on, Meg began taking notes:

1. Our sins come between us and God and make it difficult to feel His presence. They are like mud and dirt thrown up on a window pane, shutting out the sunlight.
2. Even small sins narrow down the channel by which life and vitality flow to us, thus choking off creativity. But often we don't understand the connection between our lack of productivity and sin.
3. Sin divides us on the inside, splits us asunder. It separates conscious mind from subconscious, so that we are a personality in conflict with ourselves.
4. Our wrongdoings cut us off from other human beings. God reaches down to hold my hand. With my other hand I touch the lives of fellow human beings. Only as both connections are made can the power flow. And sin will break the connection every time. Isn't that why Jesus warned us that if we want forgiveness for ourselves, we'd better forgive others?

Outside the classroom a bell rang. The young minister picked up his notes, put them in the pocket of his coat. "Now that we are all aware,

I hope, of our need for forgiveness, next Wednesday we'll try to answer the question how can we go about getting it."

Meg sat there for a moment staring at him. That was what she most wanted to know.

The following Wednesday, Meg had her notebook out and her attention riveted on getting down the steps in forgiveness as Arnold outlined them:

1. We have to be honest—candid and above board with God about all our sins and failures.
   Drop all excuses and explanations; these are not important.
   Be as specific as possible in confession.
2. We claim for ourselves one of God's promises of forgiveness.
   Here are some to choose among:
   "If we confess our sins, he is faithful and just to forgive us our sins, and to cleanse us from all unrighteousness."[1]
   "Him that cometh to me I will in no wise cast out."[2]
   "Come now, and let us reason together, saith the Lord:
   though your sins be as scarlet, they shall be as white as snow;
   though they be like crimson, they shall be as wool."[3]
   "For Thou, Lord, art good, and ready to forgive; and plenteous in mercy unto all them that call upon thee."[4]
3. We accept Christ's forgiveness *right now*, by faith—even though we feel no different yet.
   We also accept an initial entering into a personal relationship with Him, or an instantaneous return to fellowship with Him, as the case may be.
4. God may ask you to make some restitution. (This is not always possible. Some wrongs can never be righted by us.) If He does ask restitution, obey—no matter what the cost to your pride.
5. Now turn from the past to face the future. No more wallowing in remorse. God has forgiven you and wiped out your sins. Now you must forgive yourself. "Forgetting those things that are behind" is the only healthy way.

"When you've gone through these five steps," Arnold continued, "you're ready to begin living. Remember that it's everyday life that Christ wants to sanctify. Sometimes a new Christian makes the mistake of thinking he ought to be mystical, of wanting a sort of ivory-tower faith.

Believe me, when you let Christ order your days, you won't spend your time reading spiritual books while your children are on the street and your house in disorder————"

Meg raised her hand. Her face was flushed, her voice trembling a little. "I've taken notes on all this, but there's still something I don't understand."

"Ask any question you'd like," Arnold encouraged.

"Well, Maynard and I have a coal stove in our living room. It's the bane of my life. Shake it down once and coal dust covers the whole house. Talk about disorder! I hate it almost as much as I hate myself." Meg hesitated, then blurted out, "How in th' hell can you sanctify a coal stove?"

When the friendly laughter had subsided, Arnold's answer seemed inspired: "In other words, the hated stove has become a sort of symbol to you. Think of it like this, Meg. When the coal is placed in the stove to come in contact with the flames, there's always an initial burning off of surface dust, gases, the superficial debris. The coal is not yet united with the flame. We are the coal. The flame is God's love.

"Once the superficial things are burned off, then a more fundamental change takes place. The coal itself catches fire. Finally it glows red-hot, even at its heart. This is a depth transmutation in which the coal and the flame are fused————"

"What about all the ashes which I have to dust and which Maynard has to keep carting away?" Meg asked.

"The ashes, Meg? All during your lifetime ashes will be sifting off. . . ."

On Good Friday of that year Meg and Maynard slipped into the back of the chapel to find a play going on. During their drive to the church, Meg had been talking about how stupid Good Friday seemed to her. Why did the churches make such a commotion about it? What did Jesus' death and resurrection have to do with them?

There was little space at the front of the chapel, so the stage set had to be simple. The play had been written by Elizabeth Ann Campagna, one of the group. It consisted of a conversation between two middle-aged women about their sons, their hopes for them, the trials and joys of raising children. In the end it turned out that one woman was the

mother of Judas, the other the mother of Christ. It was direct and powerful. And something profound got through to Meg. When she left the
chapel an hour and a quarter later, for her Jesus Christ had passed from
a historic figure who had lived and died long ago to a Person alive now.

Meg described later how she felt after that performance. She saw
that she had a choice. She could say to Him, "Yes I will let You live in
my heart." This would be disturbing, unsettling to her existence. Or she
could say, "No, I will not let You into my life." In that case, she felt she
would be a part of the mass of people who crucified Him. She would, in
effect, be pounding in some nails herself. And far as she was concerned,
Christ's agony would have been for nothing.

As she walked down the stone steps into the Washington spring,
she whispered an interior "Yes" to this Christ of whom she was now
acutely aware. All along Massachusetts Avenue the trees were a delicate chartreuse lacework of green. Azaleas flamed here and there in the
yards—fuchsia and coral and magenta. She sniffed the fragrant air. Soon
all across Haines Point and the Tidal Basin the Japanese cherry trees
would be budding—rose and pink, flesh and white. Meg tried to let the
spring seep into her spirit.

But something was wrong. Even the "Yes" she had whispered had
left her no feeling of relief—only the dead weight of wrong, so much wrong.

Late that spring Meg became pregnant again. During the previous
two years she had had two miscarriages. The doctors at the George
Washington University Hospital could find no physical cause for her
problem.

After talking with Meg at length and after several examinations, one
of the gynecologists summed up their findings for her: "Our conclusions
will probably surprise you. We believe that on occasion a deep-seated
sense of guilt can bring about a spontaneous abortion. Let me explain
that a woman's emotions are a powerful factor, especially in the first
months of pregnancy.

"You've been amazingly frank with us about your past. Because of
certain actions resulting in guilt, your subconscious mind has persuaded
you that you aren't fit to be a mother. Understand, I'm not saying that
is true. That's your verdict about yourself. But the result is that each
time you become pregnant, you abort the fetus."

Meg, abrupt as usual, merely asked, "So what can I do about it?"

"This is where medicine has to join hands with psychiatry or religion—maybe both. There are several possible approaches," the doctor answered cautiously. "I'm going to stick my neck out here a bit because your situation is unusual. Psychoanalysis might help. Or if you're a Catholic, the confessional might do it. If you're a Protestant, you could seek out a minister. But if you are intent on bringing this baby to term, we do urge something in addition to the drugs and the help we're going to give you."

The doctor stood up and held out his hand. "Good luck. You know we will do everything we can here at the clinic."

Now that it was imperative that she find the way to accept forgiveness, Meg felt desperate. The baby's life depended on it. Apparently guilt could kill. But she and Arnold had talked so often about getting rid of guilt. What more could he tell her? Nevertheless she set up a conference with him for the first afternoon he had some free time.

"The problem as the doctor analyzed it," Arnold reflected, "is how to persuade yourself at deep levels of consciousness that God has forgiven you. This may take time, Meg. What I suggest now is that you try the game of 'acting as if———'"

"I don't understand—"

Arnold rose and stood in front of the fireplace, his hands behind his back. "Meg, do you believe that God is so eager to have us as His children that He accepts us the minute we come asking for forgiveness?"

"Yes, I think I can believe that."

"All right, then. You have asked, and He has forgiven. But there is something in you that dies hard, that refuses to feel clean. So from now on, try disregarding that soiled feeling. Act the truth—that the past is wiped out. And if that sometimes seems like hypocrisy, like acting a lie, tell yourself you're playing the game of 'acting as if.'"

"All right, I'll do it. I'll try anything. I've got to have this baby! I've got to!"

In the days that followed Meg found a technique that helped her with the 'act as if' game. Each time a self-despising thought assaulted her, she would counter by reading over one of the Scripture verses she had typed on cards. Some of the friends at the church who were more familiar with the Bible than she had helped her cull them:

Now ye are clean through the word which I have spoken unto you.[5]

We know that we belong to God. . . . We reassure ourselves whenever our heart may condemn us; for God is greater than our heart, and he knows all.[6]

We do know, we have believed, the love God has for us. . . .

Love has no dread in it. . . .

So you must consider yourselves dead to sin and alive to God. . . .

Let us enjoy the peace we have with God through our Lord Jesus Christ.

There were more verses. Meg found them living words, weapons against the still-lurking shadows. After a time she scarcely had to glance at the cards. Her hope was that as she memorized the words, spoke them over and over, that stubborn core inside would finally yield to the love of Christ.

The nine months of her pregnancy seemed endless. On two occasions when self-loathing rose strongly to haunt her, she came close to losing the baby. Each time she took a firmer grip on 'acting as if' and on the healing words of Scripture. Even so, final victory was to come only after the baby's birth.

It happened in the hospital, three nights after Jacqueline was born. Meg awoke about midnight. The room looked as it had a few minutes before—pale moonlight streaming across the polished linoleum floor. Scrim curtains billowed gently into the room on an evening breeze. Three pink roses drooped in a vase on the dresser, yet there was a Presence in the room. Meg felt it, knew it. This was Christ, and He had come to take her on a journey.

The journey took her back to her childhood. All that long night Christ helped her emotionally to relive episode after episode from her past. Through part of this she appeared to be dreaming. Then she would emerge into consciousness and would cringe and weep over the vivid pictures that had risen to haunt her, the faces of those whose lives she had soiled—no detail too tiny to recall.

Yet she was aware that something wonderful was happening. Into each painful memory there was flowing the healing of the Spirit of God. Then she would sink again into the dreaming state, and she and Christ would move on to the next episode—and the next. It was a falling and rising, a falling and rising, and in the process the recalcitrant subconscious was being healed and made of one piece with the conscious.

She knew now that Christ did not minimize her sins. He loathed the deeds that had soiled and betrayed her. Yet how tenderly He loved her!

As light flooded the hospital room Meg knew that she would never again see a sunrise so beautiful. She wept once more, this time not from shame, but to think that Christ had cared enough about her—after all she had done and been—to seek her out and to make complete the forgiveness she and Arnold had begun by faith. For the first time in her life Meg felt clean.

One of the fascinating sidelights of her experience was that although on that memorable night the name and face of every man with whom she had been sexually involved were vividly remembered, she was to discover a few years later that she could not recall a single name. Thus it was literally true that her transgressions were wiped out, removed from her.

Almost immediately her friends saw the transformation. Meg's hardness and profanity died in her. The expression on her face was different; her manner altered. Even her taste in clothes changed.

And how she looked forward to seeing her friends at church and to listening to Arnold's teaching! Step by step she moved ahead. "If we don't keep our window panes clean," Arnold told her and the others one night, "the excitement that we feel when we first enter the Christian life will fade. Even an accumulation of small sins can make life seem like a bottle of ginger ale from which all the fizz is gone. So here are some hints.

"Discouragement about our failures and stumblings is never the way to handle them. In an old book I found this statement, 'All discouragement is from the devil.' Whether you believe in the devil as a personality of evil in the world or not, ponder that one.

"Some kind of methodical cleaning out at intervals is necessary if we are to have an uninterrupted fellowship with God. We in the Protestant churches don't make enough provision for this, though certain high Episcopal churches do offer the Confessional.

"In trying to keep cleaned out, beware of things that you have an instinctive desire to keep hidden—no matter how insignificant these may seem to you.

"In this connection, I want to read to you a paragraph from Carl Jung's *Modern Man in Search of a Soul:*

"To cherish secrets and to restrain emotions are psychic misdemeanors for which nature finally visits us with sickness. . . . It is as if man had an inalienable right to behold all that is dark, imperfect, stupid and guilty in his fellow beings—for such of course are the things that we keep private to protect ourselves. It seems to be a sin in the eyes of nature to hide our insufficiency—just as much as to live entirely on our inferior side. There appears to be a conscience in mankind which severely punishes the man who does not somehow and at some time, whatever cost to his pride, cease to defend and assert himself, and instead confess himself fallible and human. Until he can do this, an impenetrable wall shuts him out from the living experience of feeling himself a man amongst men. . . ."[7]

For Meg came the final step toward forgiveness that Christ sometimes requires—restitution. She knew that she could never undo all the wrong she had wrought. Yet now that Christ had offered her the love that would never let go, He was making it clear to her that neither would that love let her off.

"Christ told me," Meg said later, "to go back to the spot where I'd shared degradation with so many youngsters and show them some real fun. It was a case of 'Go home to thy friends.'"

So each Saturday night she went. About the fifth week a burly Irish cop met her at the door of the dance hall. "Lady, it's wonderful what you're doing for these kids," he confided. "You know, there used to be the most awful woman down here————"

"My head went down and I stared at my shoes," she recalls. "I breathed a quick little prayer, 'God, when you gave me a new life, I hope that you gave me a new face. Please don't let him recognize me. I couldn't take that—yet!'

"I guess that there wasn't much danger that the cop would recognize me. Already God had done a pretty thorough job. The man just patted my hand in a fatherly way and said, 'Lady, the police force is sure glad you're here!'"

The new person that is Meg became an integral part of the small church that had lured her away from the old life. It was there that I came to know her. Of course, Margaret Stanley is not her real name. I have cherished her friendship for something over ten years. I have marveled at her ceaseless striving for growth in her new life, have been astonished at the flashes of insight that come to her.

Often as I have witnessed her unwavering compassion for the failures and foibles of all human beings, I have remembered that nameless woman of long ago. Out of her shame a group of Scribes and Pharisees had dragged her before Christ. For me, the scene is forever etched as Peter Marshall's words painted it:

> . . . The woman lies before Christ in a huddled heap,
>   sobbing bitterly. . . .
>   shivering as she listens to the indictment.
> The penalty for adultery is stoning.
>
> Jesus' steady eyes take in the situation at a glance.
> He sees what they try to hide from Him—
>   the hard faces that have no mercy or pity.
> Every hand holds a stone and clutching fingers run
> along the sharp edges with malicious satisfaction.
>
> They have brought the woman to Christ as a vindictive
> afterthought, not for formal trial,
>   (for they have already tried her)
> but in a bold effort to trap Him.
> Either He will have to set aside the plain commandment
> of the law, or tacitly consent to a public execution. . . .
> And has He not said often, "Be ye therefore merciful"
> How can He condemn the woman and still be merciful?
> The circle of bearded men wait impatiently for His
> answer. . . .
> Christ looks into the faces of the men before Him, and
> steadily—with eyes that never blink—he speaks to
> them:
>   "He that is without sin among you,
>   let him first cast a stone at her."
>
> His keen glance rests upon the woman's accusers one
> by one. . . .
> There is the thud of stone after stone falling on the
> pavement.

Not many of the Pharisees are left now.
Looking into their faces Christ sees into the yesterdays
that lie deep in the pools of memory and conscience.
He sees into their very hearts . . .
                              Idolater . . .
                    Liar . . .
                 Drunkard . . .
               Murderer . . .
               Adulterer . . .

One by one, they creep away—like animals—slinking
into the shadows . . .
     Shuffling off into the crowded streets to lose
     themselves in the multitudes.

"He that is without sin among you, let him cast the first stone at her."

But no stones have been thrown.
They lie around the woman on the pavement.
She alone is left at the feet of Christ.

The stillness is broken only by her sobbing.
She still has not lifted her head. . . .
And now Christ looks at her.
He does not speak for a long moment.

Then, with eyes full of understanding, He says softly:
     "Woman, where are those thine accusers?
     Hath no man condemned thee?"
And she answers,
     "No man, Lord."
That is all the woman says from beginning to end.
She has no excuse for her conduct.
She makes no attempt to justify what she has done.
And Christ looking at her, seeing the tear-stained cheeks,
                         seeing further into her heart,
                    seeing the contrition there,
says to her, "Neither do I condemn thee:
                         go, and sin no more . . ."

And His voice is like a candle at twilight,
     like a soft angelus at the close of the day. . . .
          like the singing of a bird after the storm. . . .
It is healing music for the sin-sick heart.

All is quiet for a while.
If she breathes her gratitude, it is so soft that only
He hears it.
Perhaps He smiles upon her, as she slowly raises her
eyes,
    a slow, sad smile of one who knows that He Himself
    has to pay the price for that absolution. . . .

She has looked into the eyes of Christ.
She has seen God.
She has been accused
                convicted
            judged but not condemned.
She has been forgiven!

And now her head is up.
Her eyes are shining like stars, for has she not seen
the greatest miracle of all?

It is more wonderful than the miracles of creation. . . .
    more mysterious than the stars. . . .
        more melodious than any symphony. . . .
            more wonderful than life itself. . . .
that God is willing, for Christ's sake, to forgive sinners
like you and me. . . .[8]

And that is the miracle that came to Meg.

Eight
... As We Forgive Those Who
Sin Against Us

FORGIVENESS HAS TWO sides that are inseparably joined: the forgiveness each of us needs from God, and the forgiveness we owe to other human beings. Most of us prefer not to face up to the fact that God's forgiveness and man's are forever linked.

Jesus warned us that if we want the Father's forgiveness, there is only one way to get it: Start the flow of forgiveness between heaven to earth by forgiving our brother from the heart. The story of Harvey Smith, a friend of my husband Len, is an extraordinary example of man's need to forgive those who have wronged him.

This young minister recently wrote Len that he would soon be passing through New York. "I'm resigning my pastorate in Danielsville, Georgia, to move to Boston for some graduate work. With a wife and four children, you can imagine that this has been a hard decision. I could come out to Chappaqua to see you late Saturday afternoon." So it was arranged.

When our guest arrived, I found him as curious about me as I was about him. At first, I put this down to his interest in how I might be adjusting to my new situation: a husband, a new household, and three young children in addition to Peter John. But as Harvey Smith shook my hand firmly and looked me straight in the eyes searchingly, he said, "Before I leave, I want to tell you the main reason that I've been so eager to meet you."

"Then that makes two stories for me to hear," I told him.

Harvey and Len had been friends in 1950 when they were both attending the Marble Collegiate Church in New York. Len had told me the bare outlines of Harvey Smith's story—his experience with forgiveness—but I wanted to hear it directly from him.

Our guest settled himself in a lounge chair and crossed his long legs. He had an easy manner and soft speech of the Southerner. "Forgiveness? I used to think I knew a lot about that subject." Suddenly Harvey Smith's thoughts seemed far away.

"Every time my congregation repeats that one sentence in the Lord's Prayer, I stand there in the pulpit wondering if they realize the terrible condition of forgiveness that they are acknowledging."

"How do you mean?" I asked.

"The sentence 'Forgive us our trespasses as—that is, in proportion as—we forgive those who trespass against us.' "

"Christ was even more specific after He had finished teaching them the prayer," Len added, "when He says that if we do not forgive other men, God will not forgive us.[1] That seems rugged."

"I've had good reason to ponder that teaching," Harvey continued. "It certainly doesn't mean that God is threatening to punish us by paying us back in kind."

"But Jesus must have meant what He said," I added. "He could not have been more clear-cut or emphatic about it."

As the three of us discussed the sentence in the Lord's Prayer, we came to the conclusion that the terrible condition is there, not because Jesus willed it but because it states an inescapable fact, a law. When we hold unforgiveness or malice in our hearts, then we cannot possibly have our hearts open to the love of God. We are the ones who have shut the door, not God.

And then Harvey Smith spoke several memorable sentences which I hope I can quote accurately:

"In forgiveness, there has to be a flow. It is the law of the tides; the law of seedtime and harvest. No receiving without giving; no dead-sea hearts are possible. As we give, it is given unto us—in money, in health, in love, in forgiveness. We just cannot have forgiveness in any other way, because that is the way life works."

And then Harvey told us his story.

In the autumn of 1950 Harvey Smith had come to New York City from La Grange, Georgia, to attend Columbia University. Soon after arriving, he had met a boy named Jack in one of his classes. Jack was a young man with an unhappy background, reared in a broken home. He had just done a miserable stint in the Navy, and now was confused about his future. He seemed to need a friend, so Harvey let him share his apartment. It was a basement apartment in the shadow of the Cathedral of St. John the Divine.

What the Southerner did not know was that Jack had always been an emotionally disturbed person. This unhappy truth came out soon enough. Periods of seeming normalcy would be followed by uncontrollable temper tantrums. As these became more frequent and Jack's drinking bouts grew heavier, Harvey realized that he was in a situation he could not handle. Moreover, his unhappy friend refused to go to a counselor.

Finally Harvey knew what he had to do. He would move out and leave the apartment to Jack. His plan was to find a room nearby, so that they could still be friends. Perhaps then he could be more objective and so be of more help.

It was on a Thursday morning just as he was about to leave for school that Harvey told his apartment-mate of his decision. It was only later that he realized how shattering this was to the distraught man. Apparently he had become Jack's only security. Now love was being withdrawn, and his whole world was collapsing.

The agitated Jack pleaded at first. Then rage took over. He struck out at Harvey, who protected himself from the flailing arms and held them until the other boy quieted down.

When the anger seemed to be spent, Harvey went over to the mirror to tend to a cut on his nose. At that moment he heard a noise like a snarl behind him. As he wheeled, Jack shoved the door to with one foot. In one hand he was brandishing a hammer.

Harvey was not frightened. He was a larger man than his apartment-mate; he was sure he could disarm him easily. But as he grabbed for the hammer and kicked it under the dresser, he felt a heavy blow in the back. Then as the two men grappled, there were two more sharp thrusts in Harvey's back.

This was the worst tantrum yet. He must get Jack out of the room. He shoved his antagonist back to the door, then held him with one hand, while with the other he turned the latch. Suddenly there were two more lunges at him, one to the abdomen and one to the chest. And at that moment Harvey's eyes caught the flash of a knife.

Summoning all his strength, he shoved Jack into the hall, threw the latch, and stood leaning against the door, trying to understand why he could not get his breath.

Through the closed door, he called for help. Mr. Rogers, the building superintendent, had a workshop just down the hall. Perhaps he would hear. Then Harvey realized that his voice did not sound right. Feeling something sticky on his sweater, he looked down. Red-tinged bubbles were seeping through the sweater from his chest. A sickening realization swept him. "I've been stabbed. My lungs are punctured." He swayed, then steadied himself against the door.

Immediately there was a knock. *Must be Mr. Rogers.* The wounded man managed to open the door, then collapsed in a heap on the floor.

The superintendent took one horrified look. Blood-specks had spattered the young man's face and sweater. A red stain was spreading across his chest. Color was draining from Harvey's face, his eyes were glazing.

Fear gripped Mr. Rogers. Without realizing what he was doing, he left Harvey where he was and ran to get the police, leaving the apartment door open.

Jack appeared again in the doorway. He stood over his helpless victim, the bloody knife still in his hand. Lying there, Harvey knew that there was nothing he could do to prevent Jack from finishing the job. One more stab would probably be enough.

Instead, Jack half-lifted, half-dragged Harvey to the bed. From far away, his assailant's voice came to him, "Harvey, can you forgive me?"

Harvey tried to open his eyes. Jack's face swam hazily above him. *Jack was sorry.* The haze cleared a bit. He saw Jack raise the knife to plunge it into his own chest. *Must stop him—must.* With his last strength, Harvey half-raised himself, grabbed the knife, and dropped it behind the bed.

Now the blackness began to close in. But Jack's request for forgiveness lay like a stone on Harvey's mind. He heard his own voice from a great distance, "Yes, Jack, I forgive you."

Mind and spirit seemed to be separating from body. *That's not me, the natural man speaking. That came as a response from all the things I've ever learned in my Christian faith. . . .*

There were no more thoughts.

In the operating theatre of Knickerbocker Hospital on New York's West Side, Dr. Ruth Selznick was examining Harvey Smith's multiple chest wounds. This skilled physician, a specialist in chest surgery, had never seen a worse case. Five deep knife wounds . . . lungs rapidly filling with blood . . . patient in a state of deep shock . . .

She set to work. Hours went by. Then suddenly there was a new crisis. The patient's breathing stopped. A split-second decision required a new incision, then alternate pressure and suction on the lungs. No response from the inert form on the table. Minutes passed . . . four . . . six. Suddenly a tremor went through the patient's body. Harvey began to breathe again.

Seven hours and fifty minutes after having been placed on the table, Harvey was wheeled from the operating room. But the struggle to live had only begun. The doctor sat by his bed and labored over him all that night.

For a week Harvey hung between life and death. Most of the time he was conscious and thinking clearly, but he had to lie still. With both lungs punctured and collapsed, the least movement might cause hemorrhaging.

There was pain too—much pain, and at moments, self-pity. *Do I really know the meaning of forgiveness? I told Jack I had forgiven him. I gave it all I had. And it wasn't enough, because I still feel resentful.*

Harvey lay very still, thinking. His thoughts roamed over the weeks prior to the stabbing. Then an idea came to him. Are any of us ever blameless? Maybe it had been out of pride and not a little self-righteousness that he had been trying to help Jack. Perhaps his "goodness" had actually been a stumbling block to Jack.

Then the pain would come back again. Harvey would gasp for a breath that was slow in coming. Nothing but a gurgling sound deep in his chest. And in his heart, fear.

This isn't easy. Forgiveness is costly. Am I really willing to *pay the price? Do I* really forgive *him?*

It seemed even more costly that day when Harvey heard that Jack was building his testimony on the basis of self-defence. Harvey's fingerprints were on the hammer. Of course they were! So Jack had decided to plead that he had been attacked first, had struck with the knife only to protect himself. Grimly Harvey pondered the irony of it. *Forgiveness is costly. . . .*

He thought back to that moment when he had lain on the bed with Jack standing over him brandishing the bloody Knife. "Yes, Jack, I forgive you. . . ." The instinct that had told him that this was not really him speaking had been right.

He had not the ability to get rid of the surging resentments, the bitterness, the self-pity, the temptation to compare Jack's conduct to his. He could not cleanse himself of those emotions, but the One who had spoken those words of forgiveness for him that day in the apartment could complete the job for him now. All he had to do was to be willing to let the resentment go and to set his will toward forgiveness. Christ would do the rest. *But forgiveness is costly: it cost Christ a great deal.*

As he lay in his hospital bed, near death, Harvey found the meaning of life. Out of new understanding, once more from the depths of his being, came the words "Jack, I forgive you." And at last there was peace in his heart.

Meanwhile, during those weeks in the hospital, Harvey's friends at the Young Adult Group of the Marble Collegiate Church were donating blood—a great deal of it. Over and over they met to pray for Harvey and for Jack. One member of the group was Ann Hougasian, whom Harvey had met some months before.

Quietly the young people raised the money to pay all of Harvey's hospital expenses. Daily they inquired about him, sent flowers, fruit, showered small kindnesses on him. Through them Christ's love was flowing to him. He dared not dam up any of that love and prevent it from flowing to the one who needed it most—Jack.

Then Harvey learned something else about forgiveness. It was his red-haired doctor who taught him.

"You're going to get well," she told him one morning.

The patient smiled at her. "I've known that for several days. It's mostly thanks to you, too."

"No–o. There's another reason. Your condition has been so precarious that anything could have tipped the scales."

"What do you mean?"

"I've watched you closely. You've been at peace with yourself, especially the last ten days. If you had held on to any hate at all, that negative emotion would have sapped so much of your energy that you probably would not have pulled through."

Throughout the rest of the day, Harvey pondered the doctor's words. In this case, hateful unforgiving thoughts would literally have destroyed him.

The doctor was right. Her patient eventually did make a complete recovery. And Harvey, convinced that his life had been spared for some purpose, became intent on finding that purpose.

It was more than three years before he knew. In the meantime, he had taken a full-time job with the Boy Scouts of America. On Christmas Day 1952 he and Ann Hougasian were married in a quiet ceremony in La Grange, Georgia.

Len and I had listened to this gripping story through part of the morning and during lunch. Immediately after lunch our twelve-year-old Linda appeared in the doorway. "Daddy, I've spilled something on the rug by my bed and need to use the vacuum sweeper. But it won't work. Something's wrong. Will you———?"

"I'll have a look at it," Len said. Soon he and Harvey were down on hands and knees taking the plug apart. In the end, it was Harvey who found the loose wire and reconnected it. I remember this little incident because what to some might have been an annoying interruption was to Harvey Smith a pleasure: he was helping someone.

After that, Harvey told us the second part of his story, "This is the part I really came here to tell you," he said to me. "It happened one Saturday night in mid-April 1955. I was then completing my third year as a district Boy Scout executive in New York City. Ann and I and another couple had gone to the Roxy to see the movie of your book, *A Man Called Peter.*

"I sat there completely absorbed in the story. There came that scene at the Naval Academy in Annapolis where Dr. Marshall had decided at the last minute to change his sermon and preach about death. He didn't know why; it seemed an odd topic for the young cadets. But that same afternoon he discovered why. Over the car radio came the news that Pearl Harbor had been bombed. We were at war.

"In that scene God got through to me. Nothing spectacular—no visions, mind you. Just a simple message to heart and brain, 'Harvey, I want you to give up Boy Scout work. I led Peter Marshall. I can lead you. You're to go back to school and prepare for the ministry.'

"My response was immediate. No struggle, in spite of the fact that I loved Scout work. No indecision, though going back to school would mean a financial struggle. By then, Ann and I had a year-old son.

"I just said to myself, 'All right, Lord, if that's what you want for me.' I remember trying to hold back the tears. Ann sensed my emotion because she reached for my hand.

"The rest of the movie was lost to me. I had to go back a few weeks later to see how it ended.

"Later that evening, when I told Ann what had happened in the theatre and asked her how she would feel about being the wife of a minister, she was jubilant. 'Why, darling, now I can tell you. I thought you were studying to be a preacher when I first met you. Be a minister's wife? Nothing could please me more.'

"The decision had to go through a time-testing period to make certain that this was no ephemeral emotionalism. But months later I was as sure as ever, the call as clear, my enthusiasm just as great. So I entered seminary in the fall. You know the rest of the story."

The three of us marveled at the events that had dovetailed and conspired to bring Harvey to the place where God wanted him.

Then I asked, "But what happened to Jack?"

"He was sentenced to several years' treatment in a corrective institution. I understand that now he is out again." Harvey was silent a moment. "There is so much to learn the hard way about forgiveness."

Then he repeated again the steps.

"First, came the realization that I was not without blame, that none of us ever are. Second, that forgiveness isn't easy—it's costly. And then

I learned that from God's point of view, forgiveness isn't complete until a severed relationship has been mended. It took me a while to see that this is the point of that Scripture verse, 'If thou bring thy gift to the altar, and there rememberest that thy brother hath aught against thee; Leave there thy gift before the altar . . . . first be reconciled to thy brother, and then come and offer thy gift.'[2]

"This means that we won't feel that our prayers are getting through, or our gifts being accepted, until we have done something to try to heal the broken relationship. So you see, actually the forgiveness process between Jack and me is not finished yet."

"But Harvey," Len interrupted, "after all that has happened and considering Jack's emotional situation, do you really think a constructive relationship could be established now?"

"It takes faith to think so," Harvey answered slowly. "I can't honestly say I relish trying it. But it's unfinished business, so only God can tell me how to finish it."

I have a feeling that Harvey will get back to Jack. Someday I shall learn the final chapter of this extraordinary story.

Jesus had a great deal to say about forgiveness. Take the scene recorded by Matthew in which the subject is under discussion: The disciples know that according to old Jewish law, one must forgive three times. After that, a man can be as hostile to another as he wishes.

But impetuous Peter is feeling expansive. He draws his striped robe about him and asks, "Lord, how oft shall my brother sin against me and I forgive him?" A smug look creeps across the disciple's face. He will be overly generous in answering his own question and so win a word of approval from the Master: "Until *seven* times?"

Christ looks at His disciple, His eyes showing amusement. Peter is so transparent, always ready to talk. "Your arithmetic is all wrong, Simon, as wrong as that of the Scribes and Pharisees. Forgive seven times? Nay—seventy times seven."

Then seeing Peter's face screwed up, obviously working on the sum in his head, the Master says, "Let me tell you a story:

"A certain King had a servant who owed him ten thousand talents—"

Immediately Matthew, the former customs collector with the mathematician's brain, exclaimed, "Ten thousand talents! Why, the total annual taxes of all five provinces of our land are but eight hundred talents. That's—that's twelve and a half times that much!"*

Jesus continued. "Of course the king knew that a debt like that was impossible of repayment, so he ordered the servant, his wife, and children sold into slavery.

"But the miserable servant prostrated himself, bowing his head in the dust before the king. 'Lord, have patience with me. I will pay thee all.'

"It was so preposterous as to be touching. The King's amusement was tinged with pity. This servant had many lovable qualities. With sudden compassion, he said, 'All right, I release you from the debt. Rise up. Be gone!'

"The servant leapt to his feet, rejoicing. He would have kissed his master, had he dared. He was free—free!

"Later on the same day, the servant went to the bazaar to purchase fresh pike for the master's household. Suddenly down the street, opposite the linen draper's shop, he spied Nahum's retreating back. Nahum had owed him a hundred shillings for half a moon. Was the rascal trying to avoid him?

"The servant drew his robe about him and ran down the cobblestone street, ducking women with baskets and pails, sidestepping donkeys and asses. He caught up with Nahum at the dove stall. Roughly he reached for his throat. 'You've been running from me long enough! You'll pay what you owe me right now.'

"Nahum fell at his feet. 'Look, I'll pay. I promise. Just have patience. If you'll give me till the sun goes down tomorrow————'

"'Patience, indeed! I will not! I've caught you now, and I'm not going to let you go again or else it will be another moon. A few days in jail may sharpen your conscience.' And he summoned the magistrate, who had no choice but to throw the debtor into jail.

"Soon word of the episode got back to the King. His own generous forgiveness had wrought no gratitude after all! He summoned his servant to him. 'Thou wicked servant! I forgave thee all that great debt.

---

*About two million dollars in our money; the purchasing power of that sum was many times what it would be today.

Could you not have had like mercy on your fellow servant? Your heart is hard, incapable of receiving forgiveness. Torment is always the end of the hard heart. Torment will be yours until you learn that only as you forgive, shall it be forgiven you.' "

The Master finished. His penetrating eyes circled the group, looked into each man's face in turn. For once even Peter was silent. The message of the story was sinking into their hearts: Our debt to the Heavenly Father is inordinate, unpayable, so we are at the mercy of the Father's compassion. In comparison with our debt to Him, the most any human being can owe another is trifling.

Every one of us is guilty before God. There are sins of the mind and the spirit as well as of the body. There are unworthy motives. There are all the opportunities that have gone begging away. There are all the times we have chosen second best. Yet God is willing freely to forgive us, no matter what we have done, *provided* we are willing to be "kind one to another, tenderhearted, forgiving one another, even as God for Christ's sake hath forgiven you."[3]

Today our civilization cries out for forgiveness. Husbands and wives need it . . . Parents and children . . . Friends . . . Statesmen. Businessmen and labor leaders need it.

Yes, and nations. Jesus would tell us that we Americans must forgive the Japanese for Pearl Harbor, just as the Japanese must forgive us for Hiroshima. The Jews have so much for which to forgive the Germans. And the Germans have much to forgive the Russians; and the Russians the Germans. Have the Ethiopians forgiven the Italians? And what about the Israelis and the Arabs with so much bitterness on both sides. If the wounds of millions are to be healed, what other way is there except through forgiveness?

Jesus, at least, gives us no alternative. The command is stern. The terms are set. "But if ye forgive not men their trespasses, neither will your Father forgive your trespasses."[4]

God's forgiveness and man's are one.

Nine
How to Find
God's Guidance

IN A POPULAR magazine some years ago, I read a story whose broad outlines have haunted me ever since. The author followed a man through one day of his life. First we saw him on a May morning, walking down the tree-shaded Main Street of his home town. He passed children on their way to school. Already some of the housewives were busy with their spring cleaning.

Up ahead on the left was the white frame cottage of a girl he knew well. All at once, he longed to push open the iron gate and stroll up the uneven brick walk for a chat with her.

For a moment he hesitated. The upstairs shades had been raised; she must be up. But no—he really should get on down to the bank. So he walked on.

Then the author interrupted his own story to show us how different the rest of this man's life would have been had he followed that impulse to push open the iron gate and walk through.

Ah—but that was not the way he decided it. And so the story went on through the trivia of the rest of the man's day.

It is a parable of our lives. At the time of each choice, we stand at one of life's crossroads. How many examples each of us could cite of seemingly insignificant decisions that changed the course of a life! The plane reservation canceled a few hours before the plane crashed. . . .

The strange timing that led to meeting the man one later married . . . and so on.

Then, if decisions—large and small—can be so important, on what basis shall we make them? Without God, most of us muddle through somehow, often with better hindsight than foresight, and sometimes with poor to disastrous consequences. To make decisions, we employ a potpourri of common sense, what we have learned through past experience, immediate circumstances, the weighing of factors for and against, the advice of others—all with a dash of emotion and another of prejudice.

Christianity from the first has taught that a better way for making decisions is available: the direct guidance of God to the individual. The promise that God can guide us is the clear teaching of Scripture, both in its total sweep and in its specific promises.

This Scriptural teaching rests on three pillars: (1) that God has all wisdom, hence knows the past and the future and what is best for His children; (2) that He is a God of love who cares about the individual enough to want to direct him right; (3) that He can communicate with men. As Abraham Lincoln once commented, "I am satisfied that when the Almighty wants me to do, or not to do any particular thing, He finds a way of letting me know it."

As for specific promises, there are many in the Bible, among them:

In all thy ways acknowledge Him and He shall direct thy paths.[1]

He calleth his own sheep by name, and leadeth them out. . . . He goeth before them, and the sheep follow him: for they know his voice.[2]

If any of you lack wisdom, let him ask of God, that giveth to all men liberally, and upbraideth not; and it shall be given him.[3]

Howbeit when he, the Spirit of truth is come, he will guide you into all truth . . . and he will show you things to come.[4]

Then the Bible goes on to show us how these promises were fulfilled in the lives of men and women. Take, for example, the incident concerning Paul and Ananias, as told in the ninth chapter of Acts. Let me put the story in modern language. . . .

One morning in the city of Damascus about the year A.D. 34, God spoke to a man named Ananias. "I want you to get up and go to number

38 Straight Street. That is the home of one Judas. There you are to ask for a man named Saul—"

"But Lord—"

"This Saul has lost his sight. You will know why later. I want you to lay your hands on him, and he will recover his sight."

Suddenly a thought stabbed Ananias. "Lord, you can't be sending me to Saul of Tarsus! Appalling reports are abroad about that man. He's a murderer! He stood by and watched Stephen's death and did not lift a finger to save him. He's even had men and women who claim to be Your disciples put in chains. Why Lord, he's one of your worst enemies—"

So Ananias, wondering if he had heard God aright, tortured with the thought that his mind might be playing tricks on him, started out for Straight Street. He found that number 38 was indeed the home of Judas and that a man named Saul was there.

But the moment he walked into the room where Saul sat, all doubts and fears left him. Whatever this Saul had been before, he was now a broken man—stunned, bewildered, lost. In a wave of compassion and confidence which Ananias scarcely understood himself, he heard himself saying, "Saul, my brother, I have been sent by the Lord to let you regain your sight and to tell you the next step—"

What if Ananias had refused to follow God's directions that day? Was this one of those hinges upon which history turns? For Saul was to become Paul, saying "I have been wrong," one of the most dramatic turnabouts any man has ever made. He was to become Paul of the towering mind, of the blazing convictions, giant of an apostle to the Roman empire, impelling advocate of Christianity to the Western world.

There are many such instances of direct guidance in Scripture. Apparently the first-century Christians expected to receive their marching orders from God, regarded this kind of inner guidance as the rule rather than the exception.

But what about today? Can we expect the same sort of direct word from God?

It would seem so, for the New Testament attaches no time tags to its promises of guidance. When I first became interested in this subject, I could not ignore Peter Marshall's oft-reiterated conviction that God can and does communicate His will to modern men and women just as He did to those in Biblical times. In his life, Peter had not often had the guidance of the inner Voice. More frequently his direction had come through providential circumstances plus a strong inner feeling of rightness about a particular decision. He had thus been led from Scotland to the United States to enter the ministry when he had thought he wanted to go to China. When the door to China had been shut in his face, he had tried for home-mission work in Scotland. That door closed too. Through a series of remarkable circumstances, the way to the United States then opened. Certainly this was God's guidance to an extraordinarily fruitful life.

I too knew more of this type of guidance by circumstance than that of the inner Voice. But it was of inner guidance that Peter and I both longed to know more.

About two years after we moved to Washington, the matter was further brought to our attention by a certain group of friends in the old Oxford Group, which was the forerunner of Moral Rearmament. They believed that quietness, a receptive mind, and a pad and pencil would result in God's Voice speaking to the inner man. Since this technique was obviously meaningful to some people, I decided to try it.

Each morning after Peter left for the church office, I would shut the bedroom door and sit quietly, trying to still my churning thoughts. My thoughts were usually unruly: those two thank-you notes that should be written . . . Don't forget to telephone for the pick-up of the dry cleaning . . . What are we going to have for dinner tonight?

Impatiently I would break away from such trivialities, trying to make my mind a blank again. No use! Morning after morning no mighty inspiration came, no inner Voice made itself heard. The notebook on my lap had little written on it other than lists of household tasks.

Peter and I had close friends, however, who often experienced inner direction. Sometimes the guidance they received was of quite a dramatic nature.

For instance, we had two women friends who customarily spent their winters together in Florida. On Sunday they went to separate churches, because Tay is a Catholic and Fern is an Episcopalian. On one particular Sunday, after Mass in Palm Beach was over, Tay picked up Fern on the corner nearest her church. As Fern got in the car, Tay said, "I've got news for you. We're going to run down to see Grace." Whereupon she started backing into a driveway to turn around.

"You mean now? Before lunch?" They both knew that Grace's home was in Delray Beach, twenty-two miles away.

Tay nodded. "I know it's an odd time to go visiting. I may as well tell you the truth, Fern. During Mass it came to me strongly that Grace needs us desperately, right away."

"I—see. Well I'm not going to argue with that." Fern sensed an authority behind her friend's words. There had been a long series of similar guidances in the past, most of them uncannily correct. And Fern herself had often experienced a similar sort of inner direction.

As the women drove into their friend's yard, the screen door of the house burst open, and Grace came to meet them. "Am I glad to see you! I've been trying to reach you for hours by phone."

Then she told them of the emergency. During the night her husband had suffered a stroke. Already the doctor had warned her that the sick man could not possibly recover. His distraught wife was anxious to get him home to Akron, Ohio, where their married children and their families were. If the doctor's prediction was correct, then above all else her husband would want this final reunion with his family. But it was now a race against time. Tay and Fern spent the rest of the day making the arrangements.

Not until a month later, after Grace and her husband had gotten safely home and the dying man had had six days of joyful reunion with his children and grandchildren before the end, did Grace think to ask Fern how it was that she and Tay had driven by her house that Sunday.

At the time I wondered how to analyze such a dramatic happening. Some might call the direction Tay received in church that Sunday an example of extrasensory perception. I suspected that the first Christians would have said, "There is more to it than that."

It is true, of course, that as the church grew and spread across the centuries, some of the ideas that had meant most to those first-century disciples were almost forgotten—sturdy practical beliefs like the communion of the saints, healing, and God's direct leading. As often in the history of Christendom, it is the rebellion of small segments or fringe groups that points unerringly to the dead spots in the organized church.

Thus it was in the England of 1647 that George Fox, the son of a weaver of Drayton-in-the-Clay, conceived some strong convictions about the formalism and deadness of the churches of his day. Fox had no thought of forming a separate religious sect; he simply wanted to see the church revivified. He and his cohorts called themselves the society of friends (not even with capital letters) and among other convictions they held strongly to the "perceptible guidance of the Holy Spirit," "the inward light," meaning the distinct and conscious voice of God in the heart and mind.

During this period of my searching out the question of guidance I became especially interested in the experiences of the Society of Friends, since this is one of their strongest teachings. One memorable story of a visiting Friend, a woman who was talking to a weekday meeting in a suburb of Philadelphia, appeared in one of Hannah Whitall Smith's books.[5] The visitor knew no one in the room except those to whom she had been introduced a few minutes before.

Suddenly she interrupted her talk to say, "A young man has come into this room who has in his pocket some papers by which he's about to commit a great sin. If he will come and see me this afternoon (and she told where she was staying) I have a message from the Lord for him that will show him a way out of his trouble." Then the woman resumed her sermon.

Hannah Smith, who was present that day, followed up this case. A strange young man did call that afternoon at the house where the woman preacher was stopping. He had a forged check in his pocket. He was on his way to cash it when something made him stop and slip into a seat in the back of the meeting house. His name was not asked for nor given, but he tore up the check in the presence of the woman. Later it was discovered that he had been so impressed with this message from God that, from that hour, he determined never to attempt such a dishonesty again.

On another occasion the same woman preacher was staying with a cousin of Mrs. Smith. The guest came down to breakfast one morning saying that during the night God had told her to take a message to a man living some miles away. She had been given neither name nor directions. Yet her faith was such that she asked the cousin to get out his carriage and take her. "God will show us the way," she insisted.

At each crossroad the woman would point the direction they were to go. Finally, after about six miles in countryside which neither of them knew, she pointed to a farmhouse in the distance. "That is the house, and when we get there, I'll find the man in the garden. Thee may wait for me at the gate."

It was as she said. She delivered her message to the man in the garden: "Thee art contemplating a wrong action that will bring great trouble on thee and thy family. The Lord so wants to deliver thee that He told me to come and try to open thy eyes to the danger."

At first the man was too startled to reply. Then he haltingly admitted that what his strange guest had said was true. This was the day on which the plan was to have been carried out. Now he dared not go on with it. If God had cared that much about him, then surely He could be trusted to work out the problem. And subsequently this man's problem was resolved in a much simpler way than he had thought possible.

I could have no reasonable doubt as to the authenticity of these stories because I appreciated Hannah Smith's Yankee hard-headedness. In fact, so clear-eyed was she that throughout her work, she warns against the dangers of delusion and fanaticism if one does not apply certain commonsense checks to these inner impressions.

It was not until after my entering-in experience in 1944 that the inner Voice became a reality to me. Apparently this surrender of self is necessary groundwork, since not even God can lead us until we want to be led. It is as if we are given an inner receiving set at birth, but the set is not tuned in until we actively turn our lives over to God.

Then too, most of us think of our lives in compartmentalized fashion—home life, business life, social life. Actually the various aspects of a truly creative life must dovetail. God will not direct a man's business life, for example, when the man insists on running his family life his own way. Any such partial surrender or halfway commitment will not work.

Next I discovered that for a beginner like me, it was important that I concentrate on one or two questions on which I needed light, and ask God for directions on those. This selectivity proved more effective than trying to make my mind blank, ready to receive any message on any subject.

Also, I found that I had to be willing to obey—no matter what. Otherwise no directions would be forthcoming. Receiving guidance is definitely not a matter of telling God what we want and hoping that He will approve.

A further finding was that the inner Voice was more likely to speak to me at the first moment of consciousness upon awakening, or during some odd moment of the day as I went about routine tasks, than while I waited expectantly with pad and pencil in hand.

I experienced this one day when I was working on a curtain for our kitchen door. In a woman's magazine I had seen a picture of an hourglass-shape curtain, so attractive that I decided to copy it. It looked easy, but I soon discovered that when I pulled the curtain together in the middle, the rods bowed at top and bottom.

I worked and struggled, trying without any success to figure it out. Some sort of mathematical problem seemed to be involved, and I am not good at mathematics! I grew more and more exasperated at my own stupidity. How silly to be nonplused by such a small problem!

Then I called a friend in, but she could not solve it either. Finally, in great disgust, I gave up, went upstairs and flopped down on a bed. After I had been lying there a few minutes, the inner Voice said very quietly, "You do it this way." There followed a set of simple directions involving graduated tucks. The directions worked easily, perfectly.

Does this seem trivial? Of course it is. Moreover, it might be argued that it is not unusual for a solution to be served up *in toto* from the subconscious when the mind is relaxed. People experience this constantly. Then how can I justify connecting God with it?

In the first place, I think it a mistake to think of God's intervention only in terms of great events and dramatic circumstances—a sudden healing, or the saving of a life in jeopardy. After all, most of our days are full of ordinary events and common experiences. Are we to believe that God has no interest in these?

Secondly, who knows what the subconscious, or the unconscious, really is? Psychologists admit that they do not. For example, here is what the late Carl Gustav Jung had to say on the subject:

. . . . in so far as anything is unconscious it is not definable. Since we cannot possibly know the limitations of something unknown to us, it follows that we are not in a position to set any limits to the self. . . .

Since a scientific man like Jung admits that we cannot set limits to the self, the Christian may be permitted to wonder whether somewhere in the deeps of personality—still beyond the reach of our scientific probing and measuring—there is not a place where the Spirit that is God can impress upon the spirit that is man a thought, a direction, a solution. Certainly it is neither plausible nor scientific to say that such things "just happen." Or if so, then many things have "just happened" to me during the course of my ordinary days.

One Sunday, our whole family (including a small guest of Peter John's), went to a Washington Hotel for Sunday dinner. After dinner, Dr. Marshall lingered in the lobby of the hotel to talk to an acquaintance. Since the grown-up talk went on for some time and the two little boys got restless, they asked to go out and play. The hotel was set safely back from the street in wide lawns, so I let them go.

Minutes passed. Then, gently but clearly, that still small Voice gave me a message, "The boys need you. Better go out to them immediately."

I excused myself and went. The two boys were standing hand in hand on the curbing just ready to try to cross 16th Street—one of Washington's busiest and most dangerous thoroughfares.

Such happenings make me wonder whether God does not try more often than we know to save His children from the accidents and disasters of our lives on this earth. But many of us do not practice the art of listening to the inner Voice with regard to small everyday matters. Because we are not tuned in, He cannot get His message through to us even in emergencies.

Sometimes these emergencies are a matter of life and death. On the evening of December 7, 1946, a businessman, Stuart Luhan (he prefers that his real name not be used), checked into the Winecoff Hotel in Atlanta, Georgia. He asked for and got a room on the tenth floor above the city's traffic.

Sometime after retiring, Mr. Luhan was wakened by noise in the corridor. A strange red glow was reflected in the sky outside his window. *Fire!* Heart pounding, he opened his bedroom door into the corridor only to have billowing clouds of suffocating smoke all but engulf him. Backing into the room, he hastily shut the door and the transom and rushed to the window to fill his lungs with air.

What he saw there was even more terrifying. Ten stories below a crowd was gathering, milling around fire trucks. Behind him, he could hear screams and cries for help.

Fear so consumed him that it was like a weight on his chest. But years before he had formed the habit of setting aside a time each morning for prayer and practice in listening to the Voice inside. From long experience, he knew that he could rely on God in any emergency, even in a burning building.

He retreated to the center of the room and forced himself to begin speaking slowly the Ninety-first Psalm: "Because thou hast made the Lord, which is my refuge, even the most High, thy habitation, there shall no evil befall thee. . . ."

No evil befall thee? In this situation? How could he claim that for himself?

As he repeated this verse, suddenly his thoughts cleared. God is my very life, he reasoned. Therefore that life is eternal. "I hereby put myself in Your care and keeping," he prayed. "Let Your presence be my fortress. I await Your instructions as to the way out of this crisis."

"The first sure sign that God was with me in that fire-surrounded room was that after this prayer my fear just left me, siphoned off like poison," Mr. Luhan wrote me later. "Judging from the sounds around me and the increasing heat in the room, the situation was getting worse by the minute. Yet on the inside was a center of calm, such calmness that I really could hear that inner Voice."

The first instruction was that he should pull on his clothes. The next clear suggestion was to make a rope of the sheets, all blankets, even the bedspread. As he tied the knots, he knew that the rope would not reach more than a third of the way to the street. But he followed instructions, sure he would be told what to do next.

As he put the rope out the window, he heard the Voice say, "No—not yet, Trust Me—"

It seemed as if the delay might be fatal. Again the man started to throw the rope out the window. Again the clear order came, "Not yet. . . . Wait."

It took will power to obey, because now black smoke was seeping into the room. But long ago he had learned to trust the Voice of God; it had led him out of other predicaments. Finally the Voice said, "Now is the time. Put the rope out the window. Tie it around the center part of the window frame and climb out."

As Mr. Luhan climbed over the sill, the wood was getting hot. In his mind rang the words, "God is my life and my salvation. . . . I shall not fear. . . . God is my life—"

Down the twenty feet he slid, but his rope reached only to the eighth-floor level. What could he do now? Once again he deliberately turned his thought to God, his fortress. "God is my life. . . . My life. . . . God is my life. . . ."

Across the face of the building he saw a fireman extending a ladder to the eighth floor. That was as far as the ladder would reach. Even so it was still too far away, one room to the right.

Suddenly the fireman saw Mr. Luhan hanging there. He signaled him and swung a rope hanging from a window above toward him. The first time the rope came close; the next time not so close. How could he grasp the swinging rope and still cling to the knotted bedclothes? Once again the rope hurtled through the air. This time Mr. Luhan caught it.

He took a deep breath, twisted the rope around his right hand, let go the knotted bedclothes, and swung in a wide arc across the burning wall. The fireman at the top of the ladder leaned over as far as he dared, caught the end of the rope on which the man dangled, pulled it over. For a moment both men balanced precariously on the slender ladder. Then Stuart Luhan climbed down to safety.

He looked up. His improvised rope was already burning. Flames billowed from the window of the room he had just left. Yet here he was, safe on the ground with no injuries except some rope burns on the palms of his hands. God's timing had been perfect.

The next day the nation's newspapers carried ghastly pictures of the disaster and its victims, calling it one of the nation's worst fires. One hundred twenty-seven people lost their lives; many more were injured. The details that I have put down here have been checked in correspondence with Mr. Luhan.

Why was one man saved by such split-second timing when so many others died? Did God love them less? Not at all. A loving God plays no favorites, is "no respecter of persons." Could it not be that God was unable to get through, to make His voice heard and His help tangible to those who lost their lives? On the other hand, Mr. Luhan was one of those rare individuals who was not only aware of the inner Voice, but had practiced using his "receiving set" in tranquil days—before crisis struck.

The guidance Stuart Luhan received, as well as most of the other instances I have mentioned, came to the individual concerned at the psychic level. Or, expressed in theological terms, these people are what the New Testament calls "the sons of God . . . . who are guided by the Spirit of God."[6]

There is, however, a warning or corollary teaching to be seen in the New Testament. I have already mentioned it in passing: the guidance or inspiration that reaches us via the unconscious should be subjected to certain tests.

The reason that guidance must be tested is one that many find difficult to believe. The writers of Scripture insist that at the unconscious level, we are open to influences not alone from the Holy Spirit but also from perverse and evil spirits. Even those who cannot credit this in the Bible have no trouble accepting the same point when a psychological interpretation is put on it. Everyone has experienced thoughts and impulses rising out of the subconscious that are selfish rationalizations or so wrongly motivated as to be evil. The end result is the same, to whatever source we credit the evil.

What are these tests to which we should subject inner messages? There are at least four of them: that of Scripture, the advice of trusted friends who are also seeking God's leading, providential circumstances, and the application of our judgment and what we might call sanctified common sense.

Testing our inner impressions by Scripture is important. Our generation is rediscovering the Bible. Modern translations, many making use of newly discovered ancient manuscripts, have made the Scriptures more readable and understandable. Anyone who means business about God's leading will need to turn again and again to the Bible as a textbook. There are several reasons why this is important. We cannot really know what God is like until we know how God incarnate in human flesh acted, what Jesus' attitude was and is with regard to every facet of the human experience—sin, sickness, disasters, and so on. For this we have to study the Bible intelligently, not as if the Scriptures were a sort of holy rabbit's foot, but for its wisdom in the broad sweep of its teaching about the nature of God and of man.

Then too the Bible has more explicit guidance for us than most of us are willing to obey. It gives clear directions about money, lawsuits, racial prejudice and social snobbery, marriage and divorce, the discipline of children, how to treat servants, advice about avenging injuries, about scruples, and much more.

Especially important, God's voice will never contradict itself. That is, He will not give us a direction through the inner Voice that will ever contradict His voice in the Scriptures.

Hannah Smith once cited a humorous example of this. A Quaker, actually a woman of integrity, stole some money because she had opened her Bible at random and put her finger on I Corinthians 3:21: ". . . For all things are yours. . . ." Obviously the woman would have done better to have considered the consistent voice of Scripture on the side of total honesty, and its thundering "Thou shalt not steal."

The point is that, in the main, the Bible deals in principles—not disjointed aphorisms or superficial rules of conduct. These principles are valid checks: God is love, so He will not tell us to do anything unloving. God cares about other people as much as about us, so He will not tell us to do something selfish or harmful to others. His true guidance works for the benefit of all persons concerned. God is righteous, so He will not guide us to any impure act or dishonest act.

The check of a close fellowship is the next most important one. Christianity was never meant to be a lone-sheep experience. One reason the first Christians received so much guidance was that they had the *koinonia,* a corporate fellowship which made them "of one heart and soul." It was in this setting that illumination, inspiration, and guidance flourished.

Every one of us needs as much of the *koinonia* as he can find. We must seek out mature Christian friends with whom we can share questions, problems, and the joys of discovery. Ideas will often come to our corporate mind that would not come to us in isolation. And sometimes God does speak directly through these friends. At the very least, their love, perspective, and common sense will help to steer us clear of wild tangents.

Then there is the check of providential circumstances. We are most fortunate in having this test. When we have asked God to guide us, we have to accept by faith the fact that He is doing so. This means that when He closes a door in our faces (as when Peter Marshall wanted to go to

China and was turned down by the London Missionary Society), then we do well not to try to crash that door.

Sensitivity is needed here. When God is guiding us, we need not ride roughshod over other people's viewpoints, lives, and affairs. The promise is that the Shepherd will go ahead of the sheep; His method is to clear the way for us.

Fourth, there is the check of our judgment and common sense. It is true that sometimes God asks us to do something the reason for which we cannot understand at the time—as in the case of Ananias in the Bible or my friend in Florida. On the other hand, neither individual was being asked to do anything that violated basic principles of right and wrong, or indeed that violated anything except personal convenience. God does not ask us to cancel out the minds or ignore the common sense He has given us, except in most unusual circumstances.

In relation to the matter of inner judgment, the Quakers were fond of saying, "Mind the checks." They meant that when we feel a strong doubt that a particular course is right, then wait. Don't move on it. Or to put it positively, we should always move forward in faith—never out of fear.

If a strong inner suggestion is from God, it will strengthen with the passing of time. If it is not from Him, in a few days or weeks it will fade or disappear entirely.

In addition to these four checks, there are other truths about guidance that have accumulated through the centuries. Here are a few time-tested suggestions I have found useful:

Obey one step at a time, then the next step will come into view. God will not give us a blueprint of the future; He still insists that our walk be step by step in faith.

As we practice obedience, the Voice becomes clearer, the instructions more definite. Perhaps it should not surprise us that with guidance, as with anything else, we learn through practice.

That is why it is wise to give God a chance to speak to us each day, perhaps the first thing in the morning when the mind is freshest. A few minutes of quietness helps us focus on the areas where we most need God's help. And we need to remember that even God cannot get His word through to us when our prayers are limited to self-centered monologues.

Do not rule out God's help with the small details of life. After all, details make up the totality of life. If we do not let God into our every-day lives, He may not be able to intervene in the crises.

Finally, if you are one of those individuals who does not believe that the Creator can possibly be interested in your little affairs, then you are just the person to experiment with guidance. A few personal experiences of finding God's wisdom (a wisdom easily recognized as beyond your own), a few proofs of His personal solicitude; and your doubts too will melt away.

But you will never know until you try.

Ten

The Power
of Helplessness

WHEN I LIVED in the nation's capital, I used to notice how often the Washington papers reported suicide leaps from the Calvert Street Bridge over Rock Creek Park. In fact, this happens so repeatedly that the site is often called "suicide bridge."

It was easy to sense the human tragedy behind these brief notices— the plunge of the young wife of an Air Force major who had learned that she had an inoperable cancer, or that of the elderly man whose wife had just died. These were people in the grip of circumstances which they felt helpless to change. They saw no way out of their predicaments except the way that lay over the bridge.

Helplessness is a terrifying thing to most of us. We resist it, deny it, and when we are finally face to face with it, a few of us find that we are unable to endure it.

Yet I often thought that if I could speak with such persons at the zero hour, I would use one thought to try to stop them in their mad race toward death. That thought would be that helplessness is actually one of the greatest assets a human being can have. In clichés like "God helps those who help themselves" there is but half truth. Of course, if there were no God and if we could expect no help outside ourselves, then naturally we would do well to work up all the self-confidence and self-sufficiency possible. When we could no longer muster it, we would react as did those people who took their last walk to the Calvert Street Bridge.

416

But since God does exist, then the cult of self-sufficiency is mistaken—tragically so in some instances, misleading in all. In my case, the most spectacular answers to prayer have come following a period when I could do nothing for myself at all.

The Psalmist says, "When I was hemmed in, thou hast freed me often."[1] Gradually I have come to recognize this hemming-in process as one of God's most loving and effective devices for teaching us that He is gloriously adequate for our problems.

This was first brought home to me at the time of Peter Marshall's death. On that chilly January morning in 1949—as I looked at my husband's face for the last time, then turned to leave the bare little hospital room—it seemed like whistling in the dark to believe that God could bring good out of such tragic loss. For to me and others in Washington and across the nation, the stilling of this effective, prophetic voice at forty-six seemed tragic waste indeed.

Here was the ultimate in helplessness—death. Sometimes life finds us powerless before facts that cannot be changed. Then we can only stand still at the bottom of the pit and claim for our particular trouble that best of all promises, that God will make even this to "work together for good to them that love God."[2] So that is what I did, and the Great Alchemist set to work.

I, who was a novice at writing and editing, put some of Peter's sermons together to form the book, *Mr. Jones, Meet the Master.* From the work I got immense satisfaction and some assuagement for my sore heart. Then there came the thought of a book I might write myself. Bit by bit my childhood dream of becoming a writer seemed to be coming true. This only began to happen after God had underscored for me again—so that I would never forget it—the creative power that can begin at the point of helplessness.

It happened about halfway through the writing of *A Man Called Peter.* While I had always had a penchant for writing, I had had no training except in college English courses. I knew nothing about the technique of putting a book together. I was also on shaky economic ground because I had resigned a teaching position in order to give full time to the book.

Events reached a climax on the day that I received devastating criticism from a man whose judgment I trusted: "The manuscript lacks warmth, emotion. The facts are here—" my critic thumped the pile of pages in his lap "—but not the heart. You haven't even begun to get inside the man Peter Marshall."

Back in the apartment Peter John and I shared in Washington, the gravity of this criticism shattered what little self-confidence I had. Yet I knew that my friend had spoken the unvarnished truth. I remember standing at the bedroom window looking out through a blur of tears at a group of children playing in the courtyard, then throwing myself across the bed to cry it out.

What I did not realize then was that this was the crucial point at which the book and my future could have gone either way. Every human inclination was pulling me toward the trap of self-pity.

And why not? It is easy to rationalize self-pity. How much can one person take? My husband was gone at the prime of his career, leaving me with a small boy to rear alone. There was no overabundance of money. And what made me think that I could write anyway? I had no training except as a preacher's wife.

My thoughts went back to lines from one of Edna St. Vincent Millay's poems that I had been fond of in college:

> My spirit sore from marching
> Toward that receding west
> Where Pity shall be governor. . . .

What does one do when the spirit is sore from marching? Give up? Let Pity be governor? Yet I knew that this kind of thinking was self-indulgence. It was settling down to a self-centeredness that shuts God out, blocks His power, cuts the nerve of creativity.

And so I faced my crossroads. Perhaps I should put the manuscript aside for a while. That would give my thoughts time to jell, I would tell myself. Meanwhile, the practical solution was a job that would provide a steady income for Peter John and me. Looking back now I wonder whether, if I had yielded to this urge, I would ever have gotten back to the writing.

Sometime during the next hour, out of some dusty pigeonhole of my mind, rose words to haunt me from Brother Lawrence, a seventeenth-century French Carmelite monk. I had read his tiny *Practice of the Pres-*

ence of God so often that many of the archaic sentences were forever mine.

> . . . . When an occasion of practising some virtue offered, he addressed himself to God saying, "Lord, I cannot do this unless Thou enablest me.
> . . . . When he had failed in his duty, he simply confessed his fault, saying to God, "I shall never do otherwise if Thou leavest me to myself; it is Thou who must hinder my falling, and mend what is amiss."

"It is Thou who must mend what is amiss. . . ." For me, a great deal was amiss. Odd that I should think of those words now! Yet not so odd, because it was Brother Lawrence who had first called my attention to the power of helplessness. He, like so many other seekers through the centuries, had finally seen his human helplessness as the crucible out of which victory could rise.

And so I was able to turn from my sense of failure enough to put the writing project into God's hands. I was inadequate, but God was adequate. He knew the secret of successful creative effort. I did not. Without realizing what I was doing, I prayed the Prayer of Helplessness. I asked that God should guide the creation of *A Man Called Peter* and that the results should be His too.

And they were. I still regard as incredible the fact that from time to time I hear of lives changed by that book, of men entering the ministry because of the inspiration of Peter Marshall's life, and of Peter's voice reaching now to a world-wide audience. And significantly, in the years since, no one has ever commented to me about *A Man Called Peter* without mentioning—often ruefully, referring to their own involuntary tears—a quality in the book that irresistibly reached in to touch their emotions.

Out of this experience I learned that when achievement has come because of our helplessness linked to God's power, it has a rightness about it that no amount of self-inspired striving can have. Furthermore, when achievement comes this way, it does not bear in it the seeds of increasing egocentricity that success sometimes brings. Because we know that ideas and the ability to implement them flowed into us from somewhere beyond our selves, we can be objective about our good fortune. We know, too, that if, in the future, the connection with the Source of creativity is broken, there will not be success the next time.

Since then God has never allowed me the fulfillment of a soul's sincere desire without first putting me through an acute realization of my inadequacy and my need for help.

It should not surprise us that creativity arises out of the pit of life rather than the high places. For creativity is the ability to put old material into new form. And it is only when old molds and old ways of doing things are forcibly broken up by need or suffering, compelling us to regroup, to rethink, to begin again, that the creative process starts to flow.

Fritz Künkel, German physician-psychiatrist noted among other things for his attempts to unify the findings of Freud, Adler, and Jung, puts it this way: "The way to real creativeness is through danger and suffering. Thus we see that each creative act must be preceded by a certain time of need, distress, or even despair. . . . Nor should anyone say, 'I am clever enough to overcome all the difficulties of my crises. I can bring myself through all their changes.' Such statements reflect egocentric thinking. . . . He who relies upon his own small private consciousness must fail, for the source of creativity is not the individual but the We, or to state it another way, not the individual but God who manifests Himself in the We, of which the Self is a part. . . ."[3]

Crisis brings us face to face with our inadequacy and our inadequacy in turn leads us to the inexhaustible sufficiency of God. This is the power of helplessness, a principle written into the fabric of life.

At this point some realist will surely say, "I cannot accept this helplessness theory. It goes against everything I have been taught about rugged individualism. Where would our nation be now, if it were not for the pioneer spirit of our forefathers who refused to admit defeat in the face of tremendous odds? America was built by men who scorned weakness and helplessness."

It is precisely here that the realist misses the point about this principle. For the realization of helplessness in no sense precludes a courageous pioneer independence. Being adventuresome does not mean that we cannot admit our need for God. To be sure, if by a rugged individualist one means a man who says, "I can by myself do all things," then he violates the principle. But as I read American history, our nation was not built by men who denied their dependence on their Creator.

Preachers and patriotic speakers mention glibly "the faith of the Founding Fathers." How much do most of us really know about their faith? Anyone who has stood on the deck of the *Mayflower II* (the modern replica of the tiny original) has some inkling of what a terrifying voyage it was to America in the seventeenth century. Those who sailed on the first *Mayflower*, or any other sailing ship, had to want to come in the most ardent way. Powerful motives beyond self-gain must have been involved. The settlers' trepidation and awe, along with their spirit of adventure, are reflected in such documents as the Mayflower Compact, the Fundamental Orders of Connecticut (1639), the Rhode Island Colonial Charter, the Articles agreed on at Jamestown in 1651, and other ringing statements of purpose.

In the summer of 1787 in Philadelphia, the Constitutional Convention was in full swing. The sessions were long and wearying. May and a part of June had come and gone. There were marked differences and long debates. At a critical point, Benjamin Franklin, the oldest delegate in the assembly, rose and made a daring and impassioned speech:

> Mr. President: The small progress we have made after four or five weeks close attendance . . . is, methinks a melancholy proof of the imperfection of human understanding. We indeed seem to feel our want of political wisdom, since we have been running about in search of it. . . .
>
> In this situation . . . how has it happened, Sir, that we have not hitherto once thought of humbly applying to the Father of Lights to illumine our understanding? In the beginning of the contest with Great Britain, when we were sensible of danger, we had daily prayer in this room. Our prayers, Sir . . . were graciously answered. . . . And have we now forgotten that powerful Friend? Or do we imagine we no longer need His assistance?

Thereupon the Constitutional Convention waited upon God in prayer—with results that have stood the test of time.

It was George Washington's habit to begin and close each day with a time of prayer, alone in his room. How important this was to him is reflected in statement after statement of his public speeches: "No people can be bound to knowledge and adore the Invisible Hand which conducts the affairs of men more than those of the United States. Every step by which they have advanced to the character of an independent nation seems to have been distinguished by some token of providential agency. . . ."

Abraham Lincoln is considered the classic example of the rugged individualist, the frontiersman, the rail-splitter who went from log cabin to the White House by the most prodigious feats of energy and application.

Yet this is the same man who prowled the White House corridors at night, pleading for direction from God for a nation in mortal struggle. This is the same man who went on record as saying, "I should be the veriest shallow and conceited blockhead . . . if I should hope to get along without the wisdom that comes from God and not from man."

Thus through hard experience Americans have learned the truth of that towering Biblical statement, "Apart from me, ye can do nothing."[4]

Nothing? That seems a trifle sweeping. Perhaps Jesus meant simply that we shall be more effective with His help than without it.

But when we go back to the context in which the statement is made, we find that Jesus meant precisely what He said. This is the allegory of the vine and the branches: "I am the vine, you are the branches." The point is not that the branches will do better when they are attached to the vine. Unless attached, the branches must wither and die.

Dr. Arthur Gossip, famous Scottish theologian who wrote the exposition on John for the *Interpreter's Bible*, calls the statement "Apart from me, ye can do nothing" the *most hopeful words in Scripture*. "For it is on the basis of that frank recognition of our utter fecklessness apart from Him that Christ enters into His covenant with us, and gives us His tremendous promises. . . ."[5]

In the complex world of today, just how self-sufficient are we? We had nothing to do with our being born—no control over whether we were male or female, Japanese, or Russian, or British, or American, white or yellow or black. We did not control our ancestry or the basic mental or physical equipment with which we started life.

Even after birth an autonomic nervous system controls the vital processes of life. A power that no one understands keeps our hearts beating, our lungs taking in air, our blood circulating, our body temperature up.

A surgeon can cut human tissue, but he is helpless to make the severed tissue heal. We grow old relentlessly and automatically. In the end, despite all the so-called miracles of modern medicine, every one of us must die.

Self-sufficient? Hardly!

The planet on which we live rotates on an axis tipped at the angle of 23½ degrees, the necessary angle for the climatic conditions that support life. Were the earth not tilted, continents of ice would lie at the poles and probably deserts between them. Moreover, the earth is exactly the right distance, some ninety-two million miles, from the sun. Any nearer, we would be consumed with solar radiation; any farther away, we would be frozen to death. Were this angle and this distance somehow to change, we would all be instantly destroyed.

The natural balance of oxygen and nitrogen in the air we breathe is exactly right for men and animals. The law of gravity which holds the world together operates independently of us. And is man—little man who struts and fumes upon the earth—self-sufficient? Not at all . . .

The Scriptures say that you and I are helpless even in relation to our own spiritual lives. We want to feel that God is real. We think that we are reaching out for Him. This is an illusion. "No one," Jesus said, "is able to come to me unless he is drawn by the Father."[6] "Ye have not chosen me, but I have chosen you."[7]

We want salvation from our sins and we yearn for eternal life. We think that we can earn these things; Saul of Tarsus thought so too. Then we find out, as Paul did, that we cannot pile up enough good marks and merits to earn anything from God. No, salvation "is the *gift* of God: not of works, lest any man should boast."[8]

Indeed, not a single spiritual quality—faith, peace of mind, joy, patience, the ability to love the wretched and the unlovely—can we work up by self-effort. Anyone who has tried, knows that he cannot.

Moreover, Christ tells us that the same human dependence applied equally to Him while He wore His human flesh. "I can of mine own self do nothing," He told His apostles.[9]

I came across a dramatic example of this human helplessness of God several years ago in the writings of Dr. A. B. Simpson, a famous New York City clergyman. While in his twenties, Dr. Simpson had developed serious heart trouble. His preaching and pastoral work were done at great physical expense. Usually it took him until Wednesday to get over the effects of his Sunday sermons. Climbing stairs or even a slight elevation was suffocating agony.

Dr. Simpson was only thirty-seven when he was told by his physician that he might not have long to live. On his doctor's advice, he went for a long rest to the resort town of Old Orchard Beach, Maine. There he happened into an unusual religious meeting conducted by a Boston physician, Dr. Charles Cullis. Dr. Cullis was then having much success with treating tubercular patients through prayer and common sense health measures alone.

Several statements made in the meeting about healing through prayer sent Dr. Simpson back to the Bible to find out what Jesus had to say on the subject. He soon became convinced that Jesus had always meant for His gospel to include healing of the body along with healing of the mind and the spirit.

In the quiet of his room, Dr. Simpson reviewed his life. He was always struggling desperately for even his minimal needs—for enough health to keep going, for enough ideas and intellectual resources to write talks and sermons, for enough caring about other people. It was almost as if his creed was "Of myself I must do everything." But somehow he always fell short of his objectives. Was God now trying to reach him with a new idea? Had he ever really given God a chance to run his life?

One Friday afternoon shortly after that, Dr. Simpson went for a walk. Since he was always out of breath, he was forced to walk slowly. The path led into a pine wood, and he sat down on a fallen log to rest. All around him was that thick carpet of moss so often seen in the Maine woods. Sunlight filtered through the tall pines, laying striped patterns across the emerald green floor. Simpson pulled out his watch and saw that it was three o'clock.

"All things in my life looked dark and withered," Simpson wrote afterward. "The doctors had made it clear that they could do nothing for me. Intellectual life and spiritual life were also at a low ebb. So there in the woods I asked God to become my life for me, including physical life for all the needs of my body until my life work was done. And I solemnly promised to use His spiritual and physical strength in me for the good of others. God was there all right, because every fiber of my body was tingling with His Presence. He had come to meet me at the point of my helplessness."

A few days later, Simpson took a long hike and climbed a mountain three thousand feet high. "When I reached the mountaintop," he related joyously, "the world of weakness and fear was lying at my feet. From that time I literally had a new heart in my breast."[10]

He also had a new source of creativity. For the first three years after his heart was healed, he kept count and found that he had preached more than a thousand sermons, had held sometimes as many as twenty meetings in a week—and without exhaustion. Simpson's output of literary work was equally prodigious. He lived as vigorously as any man could and died at seventy-six. To this day much of his work, including the Christian and Missionary Alliance, is still a vital force.

An experience like Dr. Simpson's points up the other half of the Prayer of Helplessness. For in helplessness alone there would be no value, our situation would be intolerable if Jesus had left us there. But He went on to add, "With God all things are possible."

"All things!" This is as audacious a statement as the opposite was, "Apart from me, ye can do nothing." Jesus must be saying that there is nothing in heaven or in earth over which God does not have control.

Most of us can believe that God can control us, provided we are willing. Thus if we are in the hole because of our own foolishness, misjudgment, or sin, we can concede God's ability to help.

But there is another type of life situation at which faith often staggers. This is when heartbreak has come to us because of other peoples' sins and failures—what might be called "second causes."

The tragedies most difficult to take are those that come through the failures, ignorance, carelessness, or hatred of other human beings. These are times when men seem to be working havoc with God's plans. I had a friend, for instance, a well-known man in the District of Columbia, who died because of an error made by a pharmacist in filling a prescription. Another friend's husband is an alcoholic. No amount of institutional or religious help can seem to cure him. But it is my friend and the children who are the real victims.

It is important that we believe that God is adequate even for these situations. Otherwise the Prayer of Helplessness will fall to the ground. In order to fly, the bird must have two wings. One wing is the realization of our human helplessness, the other is the realization of God's power. Our faith in God's ability to handle our particular situation is the connecting link.

What the Bible says about this is worth listening to, if we are to find a creative way out of the holes into which life so often throws us. For if we cannot believe that God can help us recover from troubles shaped by human beings as well as those we bring upon ourselves, then we have a narrow basis indeed for our faith in Him.

The Old Testament story of Joseph illustrates perfectly how God can operate in and around and in spite of the sins and shortcomings of men. When Joseph was a seventeen-year-old boy, he was literally at the bottom of a pit. He had been thrown there by his own brothers. Their act was the climax of years of hostility arising out of envy.

Joseph was the favorite child of their father's old age. To his brothers, the boy seemed overprotected and spoiled, a threat to their futures. So they bargained with some Ishmaelite traders and sold him into slavery for twenty pieces of silver.

A bewildered boy found himself being carried to the slave market of Egypt's capital. He was forced to stand, stripped, on the slave block, while he was measured and scrutinized. He was finally bought by Potiphar, one of the Pharoah's officials.

The years went by swiftly. Transplanted from his simple nomad world, the boy adjusted to the sophistication of Egypt. For him it was a new world of city streets and chariots, of pleasure barges on the Nile, of elaborate tombs and great granaries, of clean-shaven men in white pleated garments and women with painted eyes and heavy jewels.

The boy made the adjustment by coming to terms with himself. Since his fate was to be a slave and he was helpless to change it, he determined to be the best slave Potiphar had ever had. Thus the Israelite soon found himself chief steward, in charge of his master's house.

Adversity had changed a spoiled boy into a mature man. And Potiphar's wife found the man attractive. Undoubtedly a sensualist and a woman with too much leisure and too much luxury, she propositioned the slave.

Joseph could have reasoned that when in Egypt, he might as well do as the Egyptians. Their flexible standards knew few scruples and little morality. But since his master had trusted him so completely, the Israelite could not bring himself to betray that trust. Day after day he turned away from her allurements so brazenly displayed.

Joseph did not reckon with the fury of a woman scorned. Unable to seduce the handsome young slave, Potiphar's wife turned violently against him. One day she caught and tore a piece of the slave's garment, made a scene, and then cried out to her husband, "The Hebrew servant . . . came in to mock me: and . . . as I lifted up my voice and cried, he left his garment with me, and fled out."

Potiphar believed his wife and promptly had Joseph thrown into prison. Egypt's prisons were terrible beyond belief. In the midst of filth and despair, Joseph must have faced his supreme moment of truth.

He had lived up to the best he knew. He had resisted temptation when giving in to it would have been easy. Goodness had not been rewarded. Bitterness and self-pity must have clamored for possession of him. Betrayed by his own kinsmen, now he languished in prison, not through any sin he had committed, but because he had refused to commit one. He remained in prison for more than two years.

How many times during those years Joseph must have prayed the Prayer of Helplessness and by so doing, overcame the bitterness and self-pity. The captain of the guard found something about the young man's spirit so appealing that he put Joseph in charge of some of the other prisoners.

When the answer to Joseph's prayer finally came, it was marvelous beyond belief. Through a talent he had possessed from childhood—the gift of dream-interpretation—he caught the attention of the Pharoah. Then through a series of remarkable events, Joseph at thirty suddenly found himself prime minister of Egypt.

The suffering through which he had passed reaped its harvest in a burst of creativity. Joseph conceived a workable plan by which the Land of the Nile piled up a crop surplus while neighboring countries run by less imaginative men were in the grip of famine.

The final testing of Joseph's character came when his own brothers came from the land of Canaan and stood before him, begging to buy grain. They could not possibly have recognized the strong-jawed, bronzed Egyptian as their kinsman.

But the fires of despair had done their work well. Joseph had no thought of vengeance. When he finally revealed his identity, it was in words that could only have been spoken by one whose eyes had so often been washed with tears that now they saw clearly. "Now therefore be not grieved, nor angry with yourselves, that ye sold me hither: for God did send me before you to preserve life. So now it was not you that sent me hither, but God. . . ."[11] And a little later he reassured them with the unforgettable words, "But as for you, ye thought evil against me; but God meant it unto good. . . ."[12]

Joseph was saying that his brothers had only *thought* that they were in control of the situation. As long as Joseph maintained his dependence on God, He was able to take all these evils that had befallen Joseph and weave them into His master plan. Thus an omnipotent God could make even "the wrath of man to praise Him." He can take any sins, any evil, any calamity—no matter where it originated—and make it "work together for good to them that love God." This practical omnipotence of God is the consistent cry of all of Scripture, written by a variety of men over a period of some thirteen hundred years.

It was also the viewpoint of Jesus. That black moment in the Garden under the olive trees when Judas betrayed his Master with a kiss appeared to be the opening scene in a drama written, staged, and directed by the powers of evil. It would seem to us that if ever the free will of wicked men—sundered from and at cross-purpose with the will of God— was in control, it was at the execution of Jesus Christ by crucifixion.

"Not so," was Jesus' assertion. Never for an instant during the acting out of that drama did God abdicate as sovereign ruler. Christ made this point over and over. In the Garden, when impetuous Peter whipped out his sword, Jesus ordered, "Put your sword back into its place. . . . Do you think I cannot appeal to my Father to furnish me at this moment with over twelve legions of angels?"[13]

To Pilate, as the Roman governor boasted to the Nazarene of his power of life and death over Him, Christ retorted bluntly, "You would have no power over me, unless it had been granted you from above."[14]

The powers of darkness in control? It only appeared so. Long before Passion week, Jesus was explaining, "Therefore doth my Father love me, because I lay down my life, that I might take it again. *No man taketh it from me,* but I lay it down of myself."[15]

Thus even the events that swept Christ toward the cross had been woven into a plan for the greatest good of mankind.

Ever afterward there would be men who would glory in that cross "towering o'er the wrecks of time"—the wrecks that we always manage to make in every century. They would glory because the cross stands as the final symbol that no evil exists that God cannot turn into a blessing. He is the living Alchemist who can take the dregs from the slagheaps of life—disappointment, frustration, sorrow, disease, death, economic loss, heartache—and transform the dregs into gold.

This is the hope and the promise that I claimed for myself that long-ago day and that I yearn to pass on to everyone whom life has hemmed in; to the would-be suicide, and to the merely discouraged who do not consider suicide but who also will not consider God.

So sure am I of this alchemy by which all things can be made to "work together for good to them that love God" that I would stake my life on it. This means that no sinner is hopeless; no situation is irretrievable. No case is past redeeming. That is why Jesus' insistence on our helplessness is the most hopeful note in Scripture. That is why every one of us—imperfect as we are—can take heart and thank God for the power of helplessness.

Eleven
The Prayer That Makes Dreams
Come True

ONE OF THE most provocative facts I know is that every man-made object, as well as every event in anyone's life, starts with an idea or a picture in the mind. It was my mother who first taught me this, as over and over she demonstrated to me the prayer that helps our dreams come true.

Mother always believed in action; she was certain that idle children—hers or anyone else's—were headed for trouble. It was she who suggested that my brother and sister and I make a collection of butterflies and moths, plant a wild-flower garden, build a treehouse in the cherry tree.

Mother also headed the Girl Scout program for our West Virginia town—all six troops of us. She persuaded my good-natured father to go on camping expeditions (which he loathed), made him sleep on canvas cots in tents that often leaked, wade through mud, endure mosquitoes, warmed-over hot dogs and canned beans, and (what was worst of all to him) breathe the fumes of citronella. Father made endless jokes through it all.

Idle? Not a chance for any of us. Beyond all our family projects and the Scout program, Mother devoted even more energy to her one-woman crusade for the individual and civic rehabilitation of Radical Hill.

This slum district was located in what should have been the town's most beautiful residential section on the side farthest removed from the railroad tracks. There unbelievable filth was surrounded by gently rolling hills, and beyond them, towering mountains.

Mother stood one day in the midst of it and envisioned what Radical Hill would be like with clean, newly painted houses, with tidy yards filled with flowers, with running water, plumbing, garbage disposal. And there would be a small white church. Her first move in the direction of her dream was to rename the district "Potomac Heights."

Next she started taking a personal census of the area. This involved calling on every shack. Some of the young people from our church helped. I have already described how awed we children were when Mother came back from her first afternoon of visiting and wept at what she had seen.

She and her young helpers found that, of some five hundred families in Potomac Heights, only eighty had even a nebulous connection with any church. So Mother and her group rented a building, cleaned it, painted it, crudely furnished it, and began holding a Sunday school on Sunday afternoons.

There Mother met a boy, Raymond Thomas, who had no idea who his real parents were. He lived with foster parents in a small, clean house set in the midst of the dirt.

Dressed in working clothes and clodhoppers that seemed to reach up to his knees, Raymond came often to our home to talk with Mother. He was always clean, but he did not even own a suit of clothes. Despite a slight speech impediment that made him self-conscious, he would sit on the top step of our vine-shaded front porch on a summer afternoon talking . . . talking . . . while Mother sat in a wooden rocker shelling peas or stringing beans or darning socks. Mother soon saw that this boy had boundless energy and a fine mind.

During one of these talks there emerged one clear-cut idea—the dream of Raymond going to college. Once the dream was out in the open, standing there shimmering, poised in the air, Mother was delighted to see the wistfulness in Ray's brown eyes replaced by kindling hope.

"But how can I manage it?" the boy asked. "I've been working on the state roads, but I've been turning over my paycheck to my folks. I've nothing saved."

There was another obstacle, too: His foster parents had not gone to college; why should Ray? They thought the idea so foolish that they actively opposed it.

Mother quietly encouraged and prodded. "Raymond, whatever you need, God has a supply of it ready for you, provided you're ready to receive it. What seems impossible for you is entirely possible for God. Ours is still a land of opportunity, Ray. The sky is the limit! Money—what's money? Money should be the slave, not the master, of every dream that's right for you, every dream for which you're willing to work."

For a preacher's wife who had little enough herself, this was a doughty philosophy, but Mother believed it and had often proved it so. And these ideas took root in Raymond.

There came the day when Ray accepted Mother's philosophy so completely that she could lead him in the prayer that releases dreams to make them come true. On so many occasions in my own life has she prayed the dreaming prayer for me that I can easily imagine how it was for Ray: "Father, you've given Ray a fine mind. We believe You want that mind to be developed, sharpened, to know some of the wisdom of other men through the ages. You want Ray's potential to be used to help You lift and lighten some portion of our world. All resources are Yours. So will You please make it possible for Ray to receive what he needs for an education?

"And, Father, I believe that You have big plans for Ray. Unshackle him from all thoughts of lack. Let him know that there are no limitations to what You can do. Plant in his mind and heart the vivid pictures, the specific dreams that reflect Your plans for him. And, oh, give him joy in dreaming—great joy."

Raymond never forgot that prayer. A decade later he was recalling to me the fragrance of the clematis vines on the porch that afternoon, a fragrance that even now can recreate the moment for him. Long afterward he would be saying with awe in his voice, "To one woman I owe the key to life."

Even while Mother was praying the dreaming prayer with Ray, the name of a certain wealthy woman friend had slipped into her mind. So without telling Ray, she wrote the friend about him and his yearning for more education: "All this boy needs is a chance. If it should seem right to you to help him, you will find that every dollar invested in his education will pay big dividends."

The reply came within a week. It would give her real pleasure to help a young man like this one. She agreed to underwrite a portion of Ray's expenses for the first year.

When Raymond read this letter, he stood speechless, looking at Mother, shaking his head. Finally he said, "Pinch me . . . I can't believe this is really happening to me."

When Ray's friends at our church heard what was going on, they wanted to have a part too. A group of men bought him a suit and some other clothes. The women bought luggage and even packed for him. They thought of everything—even items like buttons, needles, thread. And Ray, his dream brighter than ever, climbed on a bus and went off to college at Davidson, North Carolina.

He insisted on repaying the woman who wanted to be his benefactress and who lived in the college community by mowing her lawn, scrubbing her floors, firing her furnace—anything she would let him do.

Soon Ray was sending Mother the schedule he had worked out. She was astonished at how he was budgeting his time as well as his money: a certain number of hours for study, for classes, for work, for church services, for recreation.

At Christmas he hitch-hiked home. His foster parents had softened and were glad to see him. The following summer he worked for the Celanese Corporation in Cumberland, Maryland. That enabled him to return to college in the fall with enough money saved for the first semester. From then on he made ends meet through some twelve jobs—waiting on tables, baby-sitting for the faculty, repairing typewriters, typing papers for other students. It was hard going sometimes, but Mother kept encouraging him with a letter a week. It was as proud a day for her as for Ray when he received his Bachelor of Science degree, *cum laude*.

Then during the second world war and afterward, I lost touch with Raymond. I had heard that his ship had been sunk under him in the South Pacific, and that in the explosion he had lost all but five per cent of his hearing. Sometime after that mother told me that he was living in Vienna.

In the summer of 1958, I was in Europe and wrote Raymond that Vienna was on my itinerary. His response was immediate and enthusiastic.

In Rome, I found a glowing letter from him, listing for me the sights that I should see. Then when I checked into the hotel in Florence, the mail clerk handed me another letter from Ray:

When you see the high dome of the Duomo, remember that it took Brunelleschi fourteen years to build it. Last winter I climbed to the highest balcony right at the top of the dome and crawled all around it. . . .

The letters kept coming: Venice . . . "I've written to my friend at the Salviati Glass works and asked him to send a gondola for you. You must see the master glass-blowers at work. . . ."

Bad Gastein . . . "You'll find it rugged. I've skied quite a lot near there. . . ."

By now I was very curious. This man bore no resemblance to the underprivileged boy from Radical Hill. Obviously he knew Europe as few Americans do. And the drive and indefatigable zeal in his letters intrigued me.

Ray met me at the airport, a bouquet of flowers in hand. "Flowers and music are a part of Vienna," he explained. He had changed little, except that his hairline had receded. He was tall and spare and still had the trace of the speech impediment.

Later, over *Sachertorte* and coffee, I asked Ray about his life since graduating from college. He had absorbed European ways and would not be rushed. "After I learned from experience that what your mother had said was true—and had graduated from college, I knew that any right dream can be realized. Material resources *are* at the beck and call of the dream. There are no ceilings to dreaming."

Then he described his war experience. He was one of a handful of survivors of a torpedoed destroyer. During convalescence he had dreamed up a plan for the rest of his life.

"At that time my dreams were three," he went on. "I wanted to be a world citizen. That meant traveling extensively. I put no limits on that. But I knew I couldn't be a world citizen without mastering several languages. Tied with that, I wanted to get my Ph.D. preferably from a fine European university. After all, why stop with a B.S.? Then out of gratitude for all that America means to me, I wanted to serve my country somehow in peacetime."

"I'm amazed that your dreams were that specific," I interposed.

He seemed lost in thought as he stared out the window at the lights of Vienna. "I've come to feel that this dreaming process won't work unless we are specific. That's because a big part of the power to make the dream come true arises from a mental picture. And for a mental image, you need specifics."

"Ray, you astonish me! From Radical Hill—excuse me, Potomac Heights—to Vienna. Who would have thought it? Now tell me how these three dreams have come out."

"Well, so far I've traveled in sixty countries. I still haven't gotten to Australia, New Zealand, South America, or the southern half of Africa. I'm working on that! Every vacation I strike out for some new spot."

"And your studies?"

"I got my Ph.D. in physics from the University of Vienna."

"But Ray, how did you manage the lectures with your hearing problem?" I asked.

"I found a girl who would take the lectures down in shorthand. That meant that I had to learn shorthand too. Work on the Ph.D. also meant mastering German. I can speak Spanish now, passable French, some Italian, Dutch, and Swedish, a little Russian."

And the dream of serving his country was coming true through his job with the United States Atomic Energy Agency here in Europe. "Ray, what does your foster mother back in West Virginia think of all this?"

"She couldn't be more proud. To hear her brag you'd think it was all her idea. I manage to fly home to see her once a year."

"So now you've achieved all these dreams, what next?"

Ray laughed. "One of the pitfalls of middle age is that we stop dreaming—especially dreaming big. But I'm working on one—"

In the spring of 1946 a friend, Anita Ritter, asked me to join her for a few days rest at a little inn in the Valley of Virginia. Her invitation came at a welcome time. Peter and I had then been living in the city of Washington for nine years. The upheaval of the second world war was over. Both in church life and in private life, we were feeling the need of rethinking our situation to chart a clear course.

I took with me to the inn a religious book which someone had sent me.[1] One section charted a procedure aimed at helping an individual discover himself and what he wanted out of life. I decided to take this program seriously—a minimum of an hour a day at the task. I took along a notebook and a dozen pencils, ignoring no technique that the author suggested as too infantile.

One of the first suggestions was that the reader retrace his steps to childhood to remember what his ambitions were then. Of what did the child dream before the adult world muddied the waters with its false values?

Thinking back to my childhood immediately conjured up two pictures. The setting for both was the same West Virginia town in which Raymond had grown up. First, I saw a girl sitting with her back against an ancient locust tree, gazing dreamily out over a panorama of valley and mountains.

The grove of locust trees—grotesquely stark in the winter, fragrant with white blossoms in the spring—was at the back of our large manse yard. Out beyond the locusts were granite ledges which we children called "The Rocks." They formed a sheer drop of some two hundred feet from the back of our yard to a dirt road winding around the base of the cliff. Ferns and rare Scottish bluebells grew out of the rock crevices.

From atop The Rocks we could see for miles up the narrow green valley hemmed in on two sides by the rugged Appalachians. This world of far horizons fed imagination and spirit and was the scene for much of my adolescent daydreaming. There I conceived the idea of being a writer, in fact made first attempts at putting ideas, conversations, and descriptions on paper.

The second remembered scene was that of a girl sitting at the kitchen table by a window. Sheets of paper were spread out all over the oilcloth cover. One day I was writing a story with the unimaginative title, "Virginia Dare and What Happened to Her." On another occasion I began a "novel". It never progressed beyond the second chapter.

So definitely did the flavor of those childhood moments return to me that I could recollect the exact form of the little-girl ambitions I had put alongside the writing. . . . I had wanted to be "a pretty lady with plenty of perfume—and also a writer!" At age—what? I've no idea. Remembering that the perfume had been just as important to me then as the writing, I laughed at myself. Still, deeply entrenched desires were there.

The self-analysis went on. There were areas other than the childhood one to search out. What capacities did I desire for myself? . . . A better sense of humor? The ability to speak in public? Social graces? . . . What things, what possessions, did I want? . . . What kinds of ideas interested me? . . . What persons in my life? What kinds of friends? Suddenly I realized how important friends could be as a part of this dreaming. Is not aloneness every man's problem? And what can any one of us achieve apart from other human beings?

It was suggested that in all of these areas, we make the wishing as specific as possible.

After the desires were down on paper, then they were to be submitted to a series of hurdles to test whether or not they were dreams true to one's own nature and therefore requests that one had a right to make in prayer. Would the dreams fulfill the particular talents, temperament, and emotional needs that God had planted in one's being?

These are not easy questions to answer. But they are so important that any degree of probing or length of time required to answer them is worth the effort.

In the beginning I had wondered why the author of the book had implied a connection between constructive daydreaming and prayer. Psychologists tell us that no creativity is possible unless the subconscious and the conscious are both brought into play and working together and that the subconscious responds only to suggestion through visualization. Thinking along the same line, the author suggested that praying can take the form of visualization—which is dreaming in specifics. Jesus often insisted that people not only ask but be definite about what they wanted. There was a blind man who kept calling after Jesus, "Have pity on me! Jesus, have pity on me!" The man's chief problem—blindness—must have been obvious to Christ. Yet He required that the man make his request specific by asking the leading question, "What do you want me to do for you?"[2]

As I pondered it, it seemed to me that guided day dreaming also lays a solid base for prayer, because it is certainly the Creator's will that the desires and talents that He Himself has planted in us be realized. God is supremely concerned about the fulfillment and productivity of the potentially fine person He envisions in each of us.

How foolish it would have been for Fritz Kreisler to dream of becoming a world-known labor leader. What wasted effort for Einstein to have dreamed of being a movie star!

On the other hand, would not Fritz Kreisler actually be committing a "sin of omission" if his whole life were not a prayer aimed at making a contribution to the world through his music? Knowing that, he has the strongest foundation possible for answered prayer. His music, written into his being, is "the will of God" and he can pray with absolute confidence for the overcoming of every obstacle in the way of its fulfillment.

Since those days at the little inn thinking about the Dreaming Prayer, I have discovered that there are those who are wary of the prayer that makes dreams come true on two counts: they have doubts about the rightness of praying for material needs; and they are cautious—correctly—about trying to use God and spiritual principles for selfish ends.

Both are valid objections that need to be considered. As for whether God means for us to include material needs in our petitions, one answer would be that Christ was interested in the bodies of men along with their souls. He was concerned about their health and their physical hunger.

Christianity acknowledges material things—bread and wine, water, good and bad soil, the lilies of the fields, the birds, men's bodies; it seeks to lift all these material objects to serve man's spirit and God's purposes. I believe that is why the Scriptures make no distinction between the secular and the sacred, the everyday and the religious. The ideal is that all of life, every vocation and profession, is to be used to glorify God.

As for the danger that our heart's desire may be our selfish human will rather than God's, there are ways by which we can test this. Only when a dream has passed these two tests (so that we are certain that our wish is also God's dream) can we pray the Dreaming Prayer with faith and thus with effectiveness.

The first hurdle is simply our recognition that God's laws are in operation in our universe. Does our dream involve taking anything or any person belonging to someone else? Would the fulfillment of it hurt any other human being? If so, then we can be sure that this particular dream is not God's will for us.

Are we willing to make all our relationships with other people right? If we hold resentments, grudges, bitterness—no matter how justified we think they are—these wrong emotions will cut us off from God, the source of creativity. After all, no dream can be achieved in a vacuum of human relationships. Even one such wrong relationship can cut the channel of power.

Do we want our dream with our whole heart? Dreams are not usually brought to fruition in divided personalities. Only the whole heart will be willing to do its part toward implementing the dream.

Are we willing to wait patiently for God's timing?

Are we dreaming big? The bigger the dream and the more persons it will benefit, the greater will be God's blessing on it.

If our heart's desire can pass this first series of tests, then we are ready for an even greater hurdle. My experience has been that the last necessary step in the Dreaming Prayer sequence is that we hand our dream over to God to fulfill or not, as He wishes, and then go off and leave it with Him. This is where the prayer that makes dreams come true must also include the Prayer of Relinquishment. With this final test available to us, we need have no fear of trying to use God for selfish ends. We are asking only that His will be fulfilled in us.

One day soon after I returned from Europe in 1958, a close friend and I were discussing Raymond's story. Tessie is an attractive, lively brunette whose husband, Phil, had died suddenly at thirty-two, leaving her with three small children. She had loved Phil with all her being and, so far as I could tell, there had been a fine relationship.

Tessie's widowhood and mine had drawn us together. We had formed the habit of eating dinner together regularly. One of Tessie's deepest desires, which she had confided to me, was for remarriage.

"You know," she said one evening, "it's funny how our society is about courtship and marriage—that is, as far as women are concerned. It's all right for men to be frank about what they want and go after it. But we women have to be hush-hush and hole-in-corner. We have to sit and wait.

"So here I am, lonely, needing help with my children, and needing love—physical love, too, why not admit it? What am I supposed to do? Go around keeping up the false front that all is well? Everyone says that if we women appear too eager, *that* drives men away. . . . Where and how do we meet eligible men, anyway?"

As we talked it over, the story of Raymond and my mother and Radical Hill prompted Tessie and me to try the Dreaming Prayer for her problem. I pledged myself to work with her on it for as long as necessary. As I considered my lively friend and her three children, it seemed highly probable to me that happiness and fulfillment through a second marriage were God's will for her. Yet neither of us dared assume that. The last word would have to be God's.

Tessie's first steps were practical ones toward self-improvement. In her grief over Phil's death and her battle to be both mother and father to her children with no household help, she had neglected her appearance. She heard of a Charm School and managed the money to enroll.

The results—psychological as well as physical—were well worth the effort. After that came some new clothes. Tessie joined an informal dance group that met once a week and consented to her first dates since Phil's death. Yet she found many of these men unexciting, some even boring. It seemed to be a constant effort for her.

After talking that over, she and I decided on several other steps. It was time for Tessie to begin thinking specifically about what she wanted in a husband and in a marriage. This did not mean that she must decide on a man over five-eight tall, a blond with blue eyes, between thirty-five and forty-five who did not wear glasses. It was rather a question of the character of her man and the values she wanted in marriage.

The second step was that Tessie decided to stop thinking of dates simply in terms of having fun herself. She began concentrating more on the art of *giving*, for instance working hard on an occasional home-cooked meal for a date rather than always expecting him to take her to an expensive glamour spot.

These efforts led Tessie to a deeper realization. One evening she confronted me with a surprising confession: "Remarriage may be God's will for me, but I'm not sure it's Tessie's will for Tessie."

"What on earth do you mean?"

"I've wanted the icing on the cake—the romance, the ego satisfaction of being sought after by men. But lately something inside me has been asking questions, and they're making me squirm. Such as, do I realize that love isn't getting but giving? And what do I have to give to some man with deep needs? What qualities can I contribute to a new marriage? And am I willing to pay the price of the adjustment that will be necessary? Or suppose a man with some handicap fell in love with me, or one without much of an income, or a widower with children of his own? ... See what I mean about the questions being disturbing?"

I saw, all right. I also recognized in this incisive realism the Spirit of God hard at work on Tessie and her dream. "I suppose all those questions point to the fact that it's dangerous to have any inner division about your heart's desire," I commented. "You have to want your dream with your whole heart."

My friend had a rueful look on her face. "Right! So this is as far as I've gotten. I've admitted to God that I *am* divided. For instance, at the moment I don't feel a bit enthusiastic about taking on a widower with children. So since I am divided—what's the next step?"

She and I pondered that one for a while. "You're being honest, Tessie," I said finally. "That's a big step in itself. Why don't we try asking God to mend those inner cleavages, make you completely willing for His will."

And both of us were silent, startled by the revelation that we are the ones—not God—who have to be persuaded to be stretched enough to receive from Him the realization of our dreams.

The next bit of progress did not come until three months later. It amounted to Tessie's realization that falling in love is more than a spontaneous burst of sentiment, through happenstance. She finally saw that it would be her capacity for love that would draw love to her.

We spent many evenings trying to think through how one can develop this capacity to love. I wanted the answer for myself as well as for my friend. We concluded that the ability to love is not limited to sexual or romantic love. If one cannot be loving in all areas of life, he or she is not capable of enduring love for the opposite sex either. So there is nothing for it but the hard assignment of giving love and being lovable in every area of life with people of both sexes, of all ages, shapes and sizes.

We tried to think through some of the qualities wrapped up in that word *loveableness*. This was a start on the list that we made together.

Outgoingness
Interest in other people
Vitality—physical, intellectual, and spiritual
Joy and a sense of humor
Sex appeal (the kind that's unself-conscious, not artificial)
Femininity

In the midst of this, Tessie and I were learning that the Dreaming Prayer, like all serious prayer, can be a difficult business, difficult in the sense that God can ask for many changes in the one praying, and changes are never easy.

One year and four months after my friend and I had embarked on the prayer-project, Tessie met a crisis. A married man with four children fell in love with her. There was a great physical pull between them, and some undesirable circumstances in the man's marriage provided the rationale: he suggested a quick Mexican divorce in order to marry Tessie.

This period was painful. Tessie felt cut off from God. "I used to have a sense of adventure about this Dreaming Prayer, the feel of getting somewhere, no matter how slowly," she told me. "Now I've hit a dead spot." Then she was defensive. "But I do love this man, and our love is a beautiful thing. So—What's wrong?"

In the end, Tessie answered her own question. I had admiration for the courage of her conclusion that this friend was not the answer for her, because the situation could not pass one of the acid tests for any right dream: the fulfillment of our heart's desire cannot take anything or anybody belonging to someone else. In spite of the rapport and the physical attraction between them, this man was an essential part of someone else's life pattern—not Tessie's. So with anguish and tears, Tessie sent him back to his wife to make a new beginning in his own marriage.

For a while, my friend was disconsolate. Then she concluded that since she had been "a good girl" God would surely reward her by sending her dream man quickly. It was a nice thought, only we found out that God does not work that way. We cannot bargain with God and buy His blessings by being good. Another year and a half passed, and Tessie was still a widow.

This dramatized for us the fact that the Dreaming Prayer can require patience. God's perfect timing oftener than not seems slow—slow—slow to us.

In the meantime, the changes in Tessie were more apparent to me than to her. After her relinquishment of the man who had wanted to marry her, the loveableness that she had wanted so much suddenly wrapped her round like a cloak. Perhaps the difficult experience had mellowed her. Undoubtedly untouched emotion potentials were now released. Whatever the reason, suddenly she seemed all woman, with a tenderness and an aliveness that had not been hers before. Looking at her, I knew that the fulfillment of her dream could not be far away.

As it turned out, only one more hurdle lay between her and her deepest wish. This was an important one, and it grew out of profound discouragement. More than three years had passed since that first evening when Tessie and I had discussed the Dreaming Prayer and had decided to try it for her problem. It had been three years of intense, sincere effort at self-evaluation, self-improvement, and cooperation with God. Yet the dream still remained unfulfilled. Was our joint effort at the prayer a failure, a mockery? For several weeks my friend thought so and went into a mental slump. She grew almost bitter as she talked about "prayer being just self-hypnosis anyway. Why do we bother? Why don't we just throw out the whole experiment as a bad job?"

Then one day we met over luncheon downtown, and I found Tessie's mood changed. In fact, she was impatient to get the ordering done so she could share what was on her mind.

"It's about six years now since I gave my life to God," she began. "Since then, He's had a stake in me. From His point of view, I'm His child—even though I'm inclined to forget it sometimes. I suppose there are certain lessons He must teach me."

The waitress came with our order, and Tessie was silent until we were alone again. "I've come to the reluctant conclusion that right now one of these lessons is that He wants me to stop running off in all directions, trying to force the fulfillment of my dream. I've tried Charm School, new clothes, the dance group, socializing, trying to be outgoing and thoughtful in dating, the art of listening—you know, a hundred things. Let's face it—these are all valuable, but they simply have not worked."

"So what's your idea of a solution?" I asked.

"Well—I think God is trying to tell me to relax and let Him take over now. If He wants me to remarry, somehow I think He's capable of arranging it."

"Tessie, you've just said 'if God wants me to remarry—' Does that mean that you're ready to let Him decide whether or not remarriage is in the picture for you?"

Tessie grimaced. "What alternative do I have? My best efforts have failed. At this point I feel defeated. So—either God does this for me, or it doesn't come off."

There it was again—relinquishment! When Tessie made that decision, a lot of tension drained out of her. There were some surprising psychological and social results. By some radar which I do not pretend to understand, Tessie's male friends sensed the new relaxation and inner freedom in her. Their response was immediate. Soon she was having a difficult time finding enough evenings.

Apparently when she had finally handed her problem over to God's management, she had also relinquished that overintensity that puts men on the defensive. The new contentment and poise that resulted seemed to disarm and attract them.

About three months after our luncheon talk, she met Van at a dinner party. He was a bachelor from Cleveland, in Washington on business. It turned out that six years before Van had been engaged to an Army nurse who had died of pneumonia while stationed in Germany. His reaction to Tessie was instantaneous, though he did not reveal it that night. But frequent long-distance calls from Cleveland were soon revealing a confident man who knew what he wanted and was going after it with every power he possessed.

Tessie had often commented to me that she was wary of all bachelors over thirty-five or so. "In my opinion," she had insisted, "they're usually warped in some way, else they'd be married. They're momma's boys or women haters or something. Anyway, I can't imagine any bachelor having the courage to take on a ready-made family of three squirming youngsters."

Van turned out to be an exception on both counts. The idea of assuming greatly increased responsibilities not only did not deter him but his masculinity responded to it. His proposal of marriage came just three weeks after they had met. Later Tessie confided to me, "Of course, my immediate reaction to his proposal was a sputtering 'Why, Van, you've lost your marbles! I scarcely know you at all.'"

I laughed. "And of course, that was true. You'd only had—what was it—three dates?"

"Four," corrected Tessie. "Van made it clear that he expected no answer right then. He wanted me to know how *he* felt, that he was positive in his own mind and determined. Then he added that if, at that moment, I was certain that he couldn't be a part of my future, he needed to know, so that he wouldn't go on hoping."

"That certainly is the direct road to courtship," I marveled.

"Yes, and what left me gasping," Tessie added, "was the way Van made himself so vulnerable, so naked to hurt. It was a kind of raw courage ready to risk the rejection of the life that he was offering me."

I saw that there were tears in Tessie's brown eyes. "After that I began to realize that here was a man with rare qualities. Then came the special moment when it seemed as if Christ was standing over our courtship saying, "This is My gift. Take it with joy and My blessing."

Van and Tessie were married that April.

And with the fulfillment of Tessie's dream, I saw all over again what Mother had taught me so many years before: when the dream in our heart is one that God has planted there, a strange happiness flows into us. At that moment all of the spiritual resources of the universe are released to help us. Our praying is then at one with the will of God and becomes a channel for the Creator's always joyous, triumphant purposes for us and our world.

Twelve
Ego-Slaying

I SHALL LONG remember a certain June day in 1955. It was spent with a group of thirteen Christian friends at a rustic lodge in the rolling Maryland countryside. This day in the woods was to be a time apart. The plan was to share portions of two books—C. S. Lewis' *Beyond Personality* and A. W. Tozer's *The Divine Conquest.* Then we would separate for some individual meditation on what had been read; after that lunch, more sharing, and some prayer. It was hoped that the day would end with some definite step forward toward Christian maturity.

Tozer's thoughts and Lewis' are now merged in my mind. But as I remember, what we were studying could be summarized this way: A misconception that many church people have is the theory that with Christ's help we can become "nice people." This teaches that the good in man can be separated from the bad, and the good developed. It says that education is the answer to most problems. It admonishes us to self-effort, human endeavor. Our lives are to be "man's best with God's help."

The main trouble with the "nice people" theory is that when we try living by it, we find ourselves getting nowhere. What is more, it is not Christianity. Nowhere do the Scriptures tell us that, with God's help, we can sort out the good and the evil in ourselves and cultivate the good. Rather, these writers insist that ever since the first man and woman were tempted to pull away from their Creator, hoping that they would be "as

446

gods," all men have been tainted with the same desire to bow the knee to no one but themselves. Our nature might be compared to an apple shot through with brown specks of imperfection. There is no way to cut out every brown speck and save the apple; the doom of decay is on the fruit.

Just so, each of us is tinctured with self-will; with self-ambitions; with the desire to be pampered, cushioned, and admired; with over-criticalness of everyone else and oversensitiveness about ourselves; with a drive to enlarge the self with an accumulation of things. Thus, try as we may to separate these self-centered qualities from the unselfish ones, the self keeps cropping up again and again, tripping us every time.

What is Christ's solution to our dilemma? It is recorded for us in the eighth chapter of Mark. "Whosoever will save his life shall lose it," He says, "but whosoever shall lose his life for my sake. . . . shall save it."[1] To put it another way, there is no solution apart from the painful, all-out one of handing over to Him all of our natural self to be destroyed (the good parts of the apple along with the brown specks) so that Christ can give us a new self, one born from above, one in which He will live at the center of our being.

If the idea of Christ living at the center of life frightens us, it may be because we fear that by handing over self-will we would then become spineless creatures, colorless carbon-copy personalities. We need not be afraid on either count. Actually, it's when selfishness and self-will pro-gressively take over in our society that we become carbon copies of one another. When an adolescent is still unsure of his selfhood, he has a horror of being in any way different from his friends. When adults are not in the least concerned about pleasing God, they are desperately con-cerned about pleasing each other. When we have few inner resources, we hold up masks to hide our poverty. And all the masks seem to be turned out by the same factory—suburbia, the "organization man," "the man in the gray flannel suit," all aided by mass advertising, extended by the media of mass communication.

Whenever we exchange self-will for God's will, we find greater strength, a finer quality of iron in the new will given us. And, by a strange paradox, we then become more individualistic, with more unique per-sonalities than we would have thought possible. That is because we have exchanged the mask for the real self.

On that day of retreat, I remember being impressed with how viv-idly C. S. Lewis expressed it. I copied several sentences in my notebook:

Christ says, "Give me *all*. I don't want so much of your money and so much of your work—I want *you*. I have not come to torment your natural self, but to kill it. No half-measures are any good. I don't want to cut off a branch here and a branch there, I want to have the whole tree down. I don't want to drill the tooth, or crown it, or stop it, but to have it out. Hand over the whole natural self, all the desires which you think innocent, as well as the ones you think wicked—the whole outfit. I will give you a new self instead. In fact I will give you myself, my own will shall become yours."[2]

To the Apostle Paul this matter of handing over the whole man to Christ to be annihilated was at the heart of Christianity. "For we know that our old self was crucified with Him (that is, with Christ) to do away with our sinful body, so that we might not be enslaved to sin any longer. . . ."[3]

To Paul the essence of sin lay in a man's life being ruled by "My will be done" rather than by God's will be done. There is, he was say-ing, a fundamental choice at the heart of life. It is simply "Who is going to be master?" And if we fail to make a conscious choice on this, then we make it by default. In that case, self will rule from the throne of our hearts.

As we sat in the living room of the rustic retreat lodge that day, some of us on cushions on the floor, Sheldon Turner, the lawyer and lay leader who was guiding the discussion, pointed out that the relatively new science of psychology has—independently of theology—arrived at the same conclusion: there is no maturity or fulfillment of man's personal-ity apart from the slaying of egocentricity. A psychiatrist put it this way:

Egocentricity in any form . . . always leads to difficult experiences which we call crises. . . . The more we are egocentric, and therefore rigid, the less we are able to bear life's burdens. . . . [Increasing egocentricity destroys itself! He who tries to save his life kills himself.] This is as it should be, since the breakdown of the Ego—the collapse of the system of mistaken ideas which like a shell encase the Self and limit the expression of its power—is one basic aim of human destiny. . . .[4]

Just before lunch that day, paper and pencils were handed around, and each of us tried putting down the characteristics of the self-centered person as opposed to the God-centered person. Combining the lists, they looked something like this:

THE EGOCENTRIC PERSONALITY	THE GOD-CENTERED PERSONALITY
"My will be done"	*"Thy will be done"*
Is intent on self-glory.	Has true humility.
Is concerned about other people's opinions of self; craves admiration and popularity.	Is increasingly free from the necessity for the approval or praise of others.
Is rigid, self-opinionated.	Is flexible.
Cannot stand criticism.	Handles criticism objectively; usually benefits from it.
Desires power over others, uses others for his own ends.	Is devoted to the common good.
Wants ease; is self-indulgent.	Ease given up when necessary; knows that many comforts precious to the self may have to go.
Holds self-preservation of supreme importance.	Is aware that you lose your life to find it.
Tries to be self-sufficient; has a practical atheism by which he feels he does not need God's help.	Is acutely aware of his need of God in everyday life.
Feels that life owes him certain things.	Realizes that life owes him nothing; that goodness can not earn him anything.
Is oversensitive; feelings easily hurt; nourishes resentments.	Readily forgives others.

THE EGOCENTRIC PERSONALITY	THE GOD-CENTERED PERSONALITY
"My will be done"	*"Thy will be done"*
Springs back slowly, painfully from disappointments.	Has capacity to rise above disappointments and use them creatively.
Trusts in material possessions for security.	Knows that security is in relationship to God, not in things.
Indulges in self-pity when things go wrong.	Has objective resiliency when things go wrong.
Needs praise and publicity for his good deeds.	Works well with others; can take second place.
Is tolerant of, even blind to, his own sins; appalled at the evil in others.	Understands the potential evil in himself and lays it before God; is not shocked at any evil possibility in self or others.
Is self-complacent; craves the peace of mind that relieves him of unwelcome responsibilities.	Knows that warfare between good and evil will not allow undisturbed peace.
Loves those who love him.	Can love the unlovely; has a feeling of oneness in God toward all humanity.

When the group gathered again after lunch, one girl asked immediately: "But *how* does one deal with the 'My will be done'? Who can ever get rid of self completely?"

"Perhaps not in this life," Sheldon said thoughtfully. "But no human progress could have been made in any field had we followed the line that if we can't do everything perfectly, we won't try. Remember—Christ promises us a miracle with this ego-slaying, a much bigger portion of self slain in this life than we think possible."

The girl repeated her question, "All right, how do you go about it?"

Sheldon then quoted Paul's words: "For you died, and your life is hidden with Christ in God."[5]

It was pointed out that the "have died" is the past perfect tense; it looks back to a definite point in the past. Therefore this matter of getting rid of the old tyrant self is a deliberate step, exactly as entering into the Christian life is a definite step.

We worked out a plan for ego-slaying which goes something like this:

1. We see the limitation of self-centered living and the danger of it in every area.
2. We pass sentence on the natural self by telling God that we are willing to have Him slay it. Our statement of willingness is a definite act at a given time.
3. We accept by faith the fact that God has heard us; that the next action will be His. We reckon by faith that He has indeed undertaken the execution.
4. There will be a crisis or series of crises. We live through them step by step. This is the overt evidence that the slaying of the self has been undertaken.
5. Every day of our lives we shall still have to choose between selfishness and unselfishness. But the big decision to let Christ rather than self rule makes all the smaller decisions easier. This is the "taking up the cross day after day" of which Jesus spoke.[6]

Sheldon warned the group that we had better not tell God that we desired ego-slaying unless we meant it. For no one can predict what painful experiences God will allow in order to make the experience real. After all, each man's self-will takes a different form, and God is going to touch self-interest at its most vulnerable spot.

Then he went on to add wryly, "But I don't want to sound too grim. Maybe this will be some comfort to you. For you who have already embarked on the Christian life, this execution of self is something that has to happen sooner or later, here or in the next life. So you may as well get on with it—get it over with, so that you can break through to real happiness now."

He grinned at us, and his blue eyes held a special light. We had known this remarkable layman for a long time. Somewhere back in his past he had left self behind to a degree that scarcely seemed possible.

Yet he had not only survived the experience, but became one of the most delightful personalities I know, successful in his profession, powerful in his way with other men.

What Sheldon called "the execution of self" is the great "crisis," or the series of smaller crises, of which the psychiatrist spoke in the quotation above. This is Paul's "old self" in the process of crucifixion—and it is only human to flee that. Christianity, most of us think, is fine up to a point, so long as we can make it serve us. So long as it gives us peace of mind, settles some of the dust of our inner conflicts, makes us more likable people—well, fine! But of course this is peripheral stuff. This is interpreting Christianity as a rosewater philosophy to make a comfortable atmosphere for nice people. But nice people have no cutting edge. Nor have they any answers for the problems that beset our world.

We begin to see that no man is worthy to rule until he has been ruled; no man can lead well until he has given himself to leadership greater than his own. Even Jesus Christ was no exception. Repeatedly He said that He was not carrying out His own will, but the will of the One who sent Him.

I found Sheldon Turner's thought disturbing: "The Christ of the cross isn't going to become real to you until you come to terms with this hard core of reality at the heart of Christianity. How could He be real to you when you—not He—are still at the center of your life?"

As the woods around the lodge grew dark and the retreat drew to a close, we had much to think about. Those of us who decided to take the plunge, did not do so lightly. In fact, we felt rather as if we were agreeing to a sort of spiritual Russian roulette.

Before parting and driving back to Washington, we agreed that we would check back with one another to find out what had happened to us following the retreat. In actual fact, how would God make real to us this slaying of self? Looking back now, I know that not one of us could have guessed.

It would take a book in itself to tell the details of what happened to the seven of us who said *yes* to the risky adventure of ego-slaying. For what I can tell here, I have changed names and a few details in order not to embarrass the friends concerned.

One businessman, Ed, was touched at two points—his masculinity and his professional reputation. He was the sort of married man who enjoyed flirting with women up to a point, especially with women much younger than he. He had told himself that the flirting game was harmless fun, so long as he always stopped short of actual affairs. I do not think it had occurred to him that in feeding his masculine ego with the adoration and flattery of young secretaries, he ran the risk of their falling in love with him and getting hurt.

It seems that for weeks he had been driving Isobel, the youngest girl in the office, home from work each afternoon. The attention of an older man, especially the boss, had been flattering. In her room at night, Isobel built dream-castles, romanticized every gesture, every remembered sentence. She even wrote the boss a series of love letters. She had no intention of mailing them, kept them locked in a leather jewelry case in her dressing-table drawer.

One night she forgot to lock the case.

In the process of cleaning her daughter's room the following day, Isobel's mother found the letters. From them she concluded that her daughter was having an affair with her boss. Incensed at the idea of an older man seducing an innocent girl, she decided on a course of action.

Soon Ed received an anonymous letter. It accused him of adultery and threatened to reveal the matter to his wife and to his board of directors. At first he regarded the letter as a joke. He was not guilty of adultery! No doubt the letter had been written by some crackpot. Contemptuously, he tore it into small bits and tossed the pieces in the wastebasket.

But by the time the second, the third, and the fourth letters arrived, each more violent than the last, and now threatening blackmail, Ed was in a fine state of nerves. The reiterated threat of the anonymous writer to go to his wife made him decide to tell her about it himself. In addition, he went to the District of Columbia Chief of Police with the letters in hand and told him the story.

Using the United States mails for attempted blackmail is a penal offense, so the officers went into action. Through clever detective work, the mother was apprehended. When the Chief of Police telephoned Ed to tell him that the anonymous writer was Isobel's mother, he was horrified. How could just driving a girl home from work a few times result in such serious misunderstanding?

Then he had a clear-eyed look at himself and his old habit of using women for what he had regarded as harmless ego satisfactions. With a new humility, he paid a call on Isobel and her terrified family. It must have been quite a scene in their family living room that evening. Ed said afterward that during those hours he became a man.

He assumed full responsibility for what had happened. He assured the girl's parents that there was no affair. Gently he tried to spell out to Isobel how much he loved his wife and valued his marriage, and he asked her forgiveness for what she had interpreted as unspoken promises.

Isobel's mother would actually have received a prison sentence had not Ed personally gone to court and pleaded for leniency. He knew the judge, having played golf with him at the Burning Tree Club. Realizing by now the connection between the sequence of events and the ego-slaying he had pledged, Ed felt that—pride or not—there was nothing for him to do but tell the whole story to the judge in his chambers. Surely, he told the judge, this woman had learned her lesson and would never repeat such an offence. It would be devastating to the family to have the mother taken away. And Isobel and her two younger brothers might never live down the stigma of their mother being sentenced to prison.

So, after a stern lecture to the mother, the judge suspended sentence and paroled her. But the detectives who had worked so hard to apprehend her at Ed's request felt that justice had not been done and made no attempt to hide their anger at Ed and his "softness." This was hard on his pride, too.

Thus the crisis ended. It had come only two weeks after Ed's decision at the retreat. Though the seven of us had known one another for a long time, we marveled that Ed wanted to share so intimate an experience with us. He insisted on doing so. "Telling it to this one group of close friends is part of the therapy, I guess. Besides it will make it harder for me ever to repeat such immature nonsense. Sheldon warned us all that this process would be painful. It sure was! Yet I'm grateful, ever so grateful, that it happened to me."

Out of Ed's experience, and those of others, we began to see some of the characteristic ways God handles the slaying of the old self. In one sense, the crisis is not sent by God—that is, imposed from above. In each instance, the emergency is the direct result of weakness, the rigidity, the lack of wisdom of one's own self-centered actions. However, the timing of the various crises in the weeks following the retreat seemed remarkable.

Another feature common to all the emergencies was that they never got so completely out of hand that permanent damage resulted to the individual involved or to other people. The dagger thrusts were against the false values, against the evil masquerading as good. The real self emerged unhurt, indeed stronger than ever, with a fresh ability to stand up to life's problems. As in Ed's experience, God seemed to keep His finger on the situation, directing it, stopping it short of disaster.

This seemed to us awe-inspiring proof of God's love for the individual—that Divine love that combines in such an inimitable way tenderness and the iron of discipline. Ed told us that he thought he understood now what the writer of Hebrews had meant when he wrote: "The Lord disciplines the man he loves. . . . God is treating you as sons. . . . Discipline always seems for the time to be a thing of pain, not of joy; but those who are trained by it reap the fruit of it afterwards. . . ."[7]

Included in the group of seven was one minister. Roger had an impelling personality and had been born with a gift for preaching. Some thirteen years out of seminary, he was then the popular pastor of a thriving Lutheran church in northern Virginia.

Roger's crisis was merely uncomfortable compared to the pain Ed suffered, probably because Roger had already dealt more forcibly with the old self-centered tendencies than the rest of us.

"In the last few years," Roger explained to us, "I've had several overtures from other churches about becoming their pastor. Some have been important churches in our Lutheran conference. It's quite flattering to be waited upon by a pulpit committee, to be asked to preach a trial sermon to a congregation in some distant city, to be dined and feted and wooed, to be offered all sorts of inducements to accept their call.

"I'd been telling myself that I had no way of knowing what God wanted me to do with each of these offers unless I investigated them. Sometimes that resulted in carrying the negotiations quite far. So the pulpit committees would be most hopeful that I would come. In the interim, my own church would plead with me not to go, sometimes offer inducements for me to stay. Then in the end I would know that I had to turn down the offer of the pulpit committee."

"But wasn't that a sort of ecclesiastical flirting?" someone asked.

Roger smiled. "I know that now. It was similar to the flirting Ed has told us about, and for the same reason. My ego got well fed every time by the process."

"What was the crisis?" I asked.

"Shortly after the retreat I received an overture from a church in Denver, Colorado. My wife and I went out there at the church's expense. Delightful trip!

"There were flowers in the hotel suite, corsages for Betty. There were newspaper stories with pictures of Betty and me. Headlines like VISITING PASTOR LIKES HOSPITALITY OF DENVER or VIRGINIA MINISTER TO PREACH AT 11 A.M. SERVICE TOMORROW; POSSIBLE SUCCESSOR TO DR.————.

"We found the church divided down the middle theologically. Their previous minister had been an arch-conservative who had split hairs about the second coming of Christ. It was unfortunate for me that my visit got newspaper publicity. Two days after we got home, I received a letter saying that the pulpit committee had recommended that the congregation call me, but that the congregational meeting had voted 608 to 462 not to. They didn't think me doctrinally sound—or something.

"I know this may seem trivial to the rest of you, but my pride smarted for days. Betty laughed and said it was good for me. She's right, of course! But that newspaper publicity! Especially the headline that read: DENVER CHURCH WON'T CALL PASTOR; VIEWS ON CHRIST GIVEN AS REASON. My views on Christ weren't the reason at all. That hurt, because Christ is everything to me. Don't think the whole story didn't filter back to Virginia, too! Well, as a result I've had to face up to the fact that trifling with the feelings of groups of people—like churches—just won't do. And I've been probing for my motives in what you've called my 'ecclesiastical flirting.'

"Mixed up in it is always the temptation to run away from problems in my own church. Then there's the flattery of being wanted by two congregations. But the worst part of it has been lack of strict honesty with myself and with everyone else. From now on," Roger concluded, "I've got to be honest, completely honest in the most transparent sort of way."

I lived through Beverley's crisis with her, since she and I were the closest of friends. We had the intimacy that comes through sharing the deeps of life together. At first, we had been drawn together because we were both widows with sons to rear. Beverley had two boys, Kenneth, a teen-ager, and his younger brother, Sam. Her husband had been lost in World War II in the New Guinea jungle. At first he had been declared missing in action. But as the months melted into years, Bev's initial hope died and was replaced by a conviction that Jim would never come back. Nor did he; his body was never found. All of this she had shared with me—and much more.

During one of the recesses at the retreat, Bev and I had been sitting out under the trees. "I certainly needed this retreat," she confided. "I've been so mixed up recently. There's a barrier between me and the boys, especially Kenneth. Can't seem to get through to him at all. No zest in my work. I don't even get my fun out of recreation these days. The other night a friend took me to the Blue Room of the Shoreham. Suddenly, right in the midst of dinner, it was as if some part of me had detached itself and was standing off to one side watching objectively."

"And what did you see?" I asked.

Bev leaned her brown curly hair back against the tree trunk. "Oh, a lot of people, including me, determinedly working at trying to have fun. There was pretense at the heart of our play. You know—a sort of attitude of 'this evening is costing me plenty. I've paid for it, so I'm going to have fun, if it kills me.'"

We both laughed. "I know what you mean."

"Well, anyway," Bev continued, "already today I've found out what's wrong with me."

My friend toyed with a piece of grass reflectively. "Right after Jim went away, I did ask God to take over my life, rule it. But self has crept back and has been doing a lot of ruling in God's place."

"Looking on from the outside, it doesn't strike me that way," I objected.

"It's true, though. I've been compromising in the matter of drinking, for instance, and that can't be best for my boys. I find myself taking a cocktail sometimes when I don't want one at all, just so folks won't think I'm different. That's caring far too much about other people's opinions of me and not enough about my own.

"Then there's the matter of selfish use of time. I haven't been putting myself out for the boys. Some of their interests, like baseball, I find beastly boring. But I'm not making enough effort to identify with them. There's more, too."

We were called back to the lodge then, but with this much new insight into herself, Bev was one of the seven who decided to take the plunge in ego-slaying.

Her crisis began on a certain Monday morning which was to hold heartache and drama for her. At seven-thirty the telephone rang. It was Detective C—— of the Sixth Precinct, Juvenile Squad. His voice was gentle. He well knew that what he was about to tell this young widow would be a blow. Her Kenneth and three other boys had gotten into trouble on Saturday night. They had taken some property from their school—two axes and a fire extinguisher—and had broken the headlights of two school buses. Bev told me later that she began trembling so violently that she could scarcely hold the telephone.

"You and your son will have to appear at the Sixth Precinct Station at three-thirty this afternoon," Detective C—— concluded.

Bev hung up and immediately dialed me. I was shocked for her but asked no questions over the phone. "I'll be over as soon as I can get dressed," I told her.

Her voice was quivering. "How on earth could Kenneth do something like that? I just don't understand?" She started crying, and we both hung up.

When I got to Bev's home, I found Kenneth with her in the den. She had kept him home from school, so that we could talk with him before the three-thirty hearing.

The boy was fourteen, tall, in the gawky stage. His face was alternately flushed and pale that morning, his features pinched beneath a reddish shock of hair. His mother kept insisting, "Kenneth, you've got to tell us everything. It would be awful if anything else were sprung on us this afternoon. It's time for honesty now—real honesty. Otherwise, how can we help you?"

But Kenneth had little to say, plead and probe as we would. He claimed that we knew everything there was to know. The barrier between him and his mother was there, all right.

Then the school principal telephoned. He wanted to see Kenneth later that morning. After the boy had gone, Bev and I prayed together. It was one of those real prayers—when two people mean business and get down to cases. Both of us wept.

That afternoon we spent three hours at the Precinct Station. Two men from the Juvenile Board were an hour and forty-five minutes late arriving. We waited with the other parents in the front room, watching the hands of the clock move with maddening slowness. I remember one father in particular—a man with black hair peppered with gray and large luminous brown eyes. He was wearing clothes that didn't match and tennis shoes in the middle of winter. And the sad shocked face of another father, his eyes with the look of a hurt animal's.

One mother with a lined, seamed face had brought along the little family dog. She held the little terrier close to her with a leash made from her son's tie. The parents of one boy were abroad and in their place had come a relative who was a psychiatrist, young and prematurely gray. I could almost see his trained mind wrestling with the question of what had happened to these boys from good families.

Finally the two officials arrived, and we were asked to go into a back room. Though it was informal, there was, nevertheless, a courtroom atmosphere. The Juvenile Board sat behind the one long table. There were several benches for the boys and their parents. I looked at Bev and knew that her head was throbbing, and that tears were close to the surface.

While we waited for the hearing to begin, one of the boys, the son of the man with the shocked, hurt eyes, put his head down on the table and began sobbing. He cried softly, not wanting to attract attention, trying to smother the sound with his arms. Later we found out that since early childhood the boy had wanted to go to West Point. If this incident went down on a police record, he would never achieve his heart's desire.

Through it all Kenneth seemed to have a permanent blush. He kept chewing on his fingernails long after there was no bit of surplus nail to chew. It came out in the questioning that he was the one who had bought beer for the other boys. How much had the beer been responsible for their conduct? Who could tell? I knew that Bev would be connecting her recent leniency on drinking with her son's buying the beer.

Kenneth stood straight and said, "Sir." I looked at him and suddenly felt sure that this boy would turn out all right. But that didn't lessen the agony I felt for Bev and Kenneth.

The men on the Juvenile Squad could not have been more compassionate and understanding in their handling of the situation. No word appeared in the Washington newspapers. Wisely, they strung the matter out enough so that Kenneth was badly frightened. A week after the first hearing, he and Bev had to go down to the Juvenile Court again. Of course, they were required to pay for the property damage. But in the end, convinced that these boys had learned their lesson, the Board dismissed their cases with no record against them.

Once again God had permitted circumstances to go only so far as severe discipline would dictate but not to permanent hurt.

A week later Bev was saying to me, "I didn't know a mother's pride of ownership in her children could make her so vulnerable. *My* sons . . . the fear that *my* reputation would be hurt . . . the possible reflection on *my* dead husband's good name . . . all self-pride!

"I know that my insistence on owning my children was the crux of my problem with Kenneth. Kenneth is an individual in his own right. He belongs to God, not to me; he's just been loaned to me for a few years.

"Since then I've been talking to my son, person-to-person. I've admitted some of my mistakes and fears and weaknesses, where I need his help. Catherine, this one week I've watched a miracle unfolding."

Bev's face glowed with her discovery. "That wall between us has come crashing down like the walls of Jericho." Once again quick tears swam in her eyes—this time tears of happiness, relief, gratitude.

One cannot live through experiences like the seven of us had and retain any doubts about the thrust of a living Lord into contemporary life. We learned much in a short time. The literalness of His standing outside the door of our hearts and never intruding until we invite Him in . . . The immediacy of His invasion of our lives when we do open the door. His overweening concern that we call a halt to our trifling with life and move on toward maturity and effectiveness. His incisive knowledge of the most vulnerable weaknesses in each of us. Who but Christ could know so unerringly that point of mutiny, so covertly hidden even from ourselves?

All this left us wondering, awestruck. Worship Him? Of course! How can we help it? For He is the only One worthy of worship, supremely worthy! And yet the first step in the direction of that great love must always be ours.

Thirteen
The Gospel of Healing

OUR SUNDAY-SCHOOL teacher was telling us the story of the man born blind who had received sight from Jesus. We were impressionable twelve-year-olds. I can remember hugging delightedly to myself the thought of the big commotion the healing must have caused. Surely everyone in the man's home village would have talked of little else. I imagined the conversation something like this:

"Isn't he the beggar, the one who's been blind all his life?"

"It looks like him!"

"It isn't possible. Who could cure a man who was born blind?"

"Let's ask his parents. They'll know. . . ."

And so they sought out the man's father and mother, who were noncommittal: "We don't know what happened. Why don't you ask our son about it?"

While people wrangled and talked excitedly, there stood the man saying over and over, "All I know is that I used to be blind; now I can see. Isn't it wonderful?"

"But what did he do to you—how did he make you see?" his questioners had persisted.

Then the man had grown impatient. "I've told you before. He put a paste on my eyes; I washed it off, just as He told me to in the Pool of Siloam. Now I can see. Don't you understand? I can *see!*"

461

But the elders of the church had not thought it wonderful at all, because the healing had upset their intellectual fruitcart, and the fruit was rolling helter-skelter in all directions.

A certain exuberant quality in the story appealed to the rebel in me. I wondered if Jesus had enjoyed the ruckus too. . . .

Then, a few Sundays later, I heard a sermon that seemed to contradict the wonderful story that we had heard in Sunday school. I cannot remember the precise words of the man in the pulpit, but the gist of it went something like this:

"We should not expect miracles in our day like those recorded in the Bible. After all, the New Testament miracles were for a particular time. They were a special dispensation from God needed to authenticate the fact Jesus had really been sent from God. Also they were needed to get the Christian movement started. Gradually the miraculous element in Christianity died out, because it was not needed any more, indeed might have been dangerous. Today God answers our prayers in other ways, through drugs and the skill of modern physicians and men of science. . . ."

I felt let down and indignant. If the preacher was right, then why had they bothered to tell us the story of the blind man in Sunday school? At the time I had not enough knowledge of the New Testament to know what the holes in this man's position were. Later I discovered that he was reflecting the popular eighteenth- and nineteenth-century Protestant position regarding miracles. To these men it seemed a safe middle position, because it effectively preserved the inspiration of the Scriptures, yet did not put the theologians in conflict with the new discoveries of science.

For the next fifteen years I was not at all concerned with whether healing came about through miracles or science. I took health for granted. College, romance, marriage, the birth of a son filled my days to the crowding point. The question of whether those New Testament stories of supernatural cures have relevance for our time touched my life not at all—until . . .

Until that afternoon in May 1943, when the illness I have already mentioned stalked into my life. Over in Baltimore, where I had gone for a physical check-up, Dr. Thomas Sprunt told me as gently as he could that I had an early case of tuberculosis in both lungs. I would have to go to bed full-time. It might take a long while to get well.

It did take a long while—three weary, endless years. Most of this time I spent in the big front bedroom of the manse with its five windows and five Peter Marshall seascapes on the walls. I traveled every tiny design in the pale yellow wallpaper with my eyes hundreds of times. I even remember two stains on the ceiling over my bed where Peter had swatted mosquitos the summer before.

How tired the muscles of one's back can become from too much lying in bed! What is there to fill the hours, the days, the weeks that stretch on and on? I could still work out the week's menus and make marketing lists. But as time went on, the kitchen seemed farther and farther away and food became of little interest. I would lie there, longing to know what was going on downstairs, hearing the hum of voices in the living room. If only I could listen in on the conversations and take an active part in something!

At the beginning of my illness, Peter John was three years old. I could tell him an occasional story and help him with a wooden puzzle, if he would perch on a stool by the bed. I had the late afternoon to look forward to, when Peter would come back from the church office. Through him, I could get glimpses of the world beyond the bedroom walls.

But there was never much for me to tell him. All too often he came home to my discouragement, even my tears of weariness and rebellion. He was patient with me, loving, wise. But not even Peter could answer my pleading questions: "Why—oh, why do I have to lie here month after month? Why can't the doctors do something?"

As it became increasingly apparent that they could not, my need sent me back to the New Testament in eager search for an answer to the question that had so troubled my child's mind: did Jesus mean for healing by faith to be limited to His days on earth?

I made an honest search. Neither self-deception nor wishful thinking about what the gospel narratives meant would help me. The shadows on the X rays of the lungs plus the weakness that chained me in bed were real enough. I was in search of truth as clearly as I could perceive it.

The results of several months of reading and pondering might be summarized like this: Jesus said that He had come to earth to reveal His Father's nature and will to man. Then what was God's attitude towards sickness and disease as reflected in Jesus? I found that He placed any deviation from health in the same category as sin: He saw both as the work of an evil force, both as intruders in his Father's world. Jesus consistently "rebuked" disease precisely as He did demons.[1] At the beginning of His ministry, He declared an all-out offensive against sin, disease, and death.[2] Practically speaking, that meant that Jesus' attitude toward sickness was exactly that of any doctor today: He fought it all the way.

Nowhere in the gospel could I discover any hint of retreat or compromise with this position against disease. Jesus never refused to heal anyone who came to Him for help. He reproved every question of His unwillingness or His inability to heal.[3] Never once did He say, as we so often do, "If it is God's will to heal. . . ." For Him there were no *ifs* about His Father's will for wholeness of body as well as of spirit and mind. In fact, roughly one third of Christ's public ministry was taken up with the healing of men's bodies.

He seems never to have suggested that any individual was unworthy of healing. Worthiness or unworthiness were not the condition of receiving God's gifts. The criterion was rather the most practical one imaginable—the individual's need. He "cured those who needed to be healed."[4]

I could find no record of Jesus implying that an individual's spiritual state or the Kingdom of God would be furthered by ill health. Not once did He say that sickness is a blessing. I was impressed with the fact that there is no beatitude for the sick or for those who suffer physically, while there is a beatitude for those who suffer persecution.[5]

Clearly it was Jesus' desire that we be rid of disease. What was his plan for achieving this? He said that faith in His Father's willingness and ability to give His children all good gifts is the key. In His eyes there was no evil that faith could not vanquish, no need that faith could not supply.

I had not gone far in my study before I discovered that there were some religious leaders in Jesus' day who tried to interpret His miracles exactly as had that preacher in my childhood: that God used the miracles to prove to us that Jesus was divine. This was what Jesus called wanting "a sign" and He had harsh words for it: "Only an evil generation would demand a sign. . . ."[6]

Jesus' chief motive in healing seems rather to have been nothing more or less than pure compassion. The word *compassion* is used over and over to describe His attitude toward the sick. That was why He often went out of His way to heal when the sufferer had neither asked for nor thought of His doing so.[7] He delighted in straightening a bent back.[8] He rejoiced in that moment when a man gleefully flings away his crutches. He was glad that He could break up a funeral and give a beloved son back to his mother.[9] It was a gratifying thing to Him to see the light of reason and sanity return to the eyes of a violent demoniac.[10] Jesus healed because the love of God flowing irresistibly through Him in a torrent of good will, simply swept evil away as the debris that it is.

Before Christ's crucifixion He commissioned His apostles to carry on His healing work and sent them out on several test missions.[11] When they returned, after having healed successfully, He rejoiced with them, "I watched Satan falling from heaven like a flash of lightning."[12] As restrained and stripped as the narrative usually is, a lilting, triumphant quality breaks through here. The physician-Apostle Luke says that Jesus "thrilled with joy at that hour," breathed a prayer of thanksgiving and then turned to his disciples, exulting, "All has been handed over to me by my Father . . ."[13]

But then the next question to which I sought an answer was this one: Did Jesus mean for His disciples to continue with their healing ministry after His ascension? I found no doubt that He assumed that they would. How else could we interpret the solemn words spoken on the night before his betrayal, "Truly, truly I tell you, he who believes in me will do the very deeds I do, and still greater deeds than these. . . ."

Moreover, after the resurrection, Jesus' commission to His followers for all ages contains the admonition: "Go ye into all the world, and preach the gospel to every creature. . . . and these signs shall follow them that believe; . . . they shall lay hands on the sick, and they shall recover."[14]

Matthew's version of the same great commission stresses the "teaching all nations . . . to observe all things whatsoever I have commanded you. . . ." The "all things" and the "whatsoever" are inclusive enough. Certainly Jesus meant that the whole gospel should be taught and practiced, not an effete, watered-down version of it.

The Acts of the Apostles leaves no doubt that Peter and Paul and the other apostles interpreted the whole gospel to include healing. For these men proceeded to heal on many occasions.

Going back to my original question, "Did Jesus mean for healing by faith to be limited to His days on earth?" I found that the New Testament cries a consistent, unequivocal, resounding *"No!"*

For me those were days of engrossing discovery. The four walls of my bedroom no longer confined mind or spirit. I was off adventuring in another realm, and I felt like a discoverer who had stumbled into a hidden valley rich with deposits of gold. Something of the pristine intoxication of those first followers of "the Way" winged out of the ancient records into my heart.

Obviously the next step was to appropriate what I had learned. My faith was simple, perhaps even naive. I reasoned that had I been living in Jesus' day, I would have been among those who sought Him out for healing. I knew that the Scriptures insist that nothing has changed about His compassion or His power, that He is "always the same, yesterday, today, and forever."[15] And we have His unequivocal promise, "Lo, I am with you always, even unto the end of the world."[16]

Then since He was with me—though I could not see Him or even feel His Presence—I pictured how the scene might be. I saw myself bowed before Him, looking up into His eyes, "Lord, I need Your help. You made my body. You can heal it. Will You do for me what You have for so many others?" He would have smiled at me, I thought, and stretched out His hand to lay it on my head. Then I proceeded in the simplest way to ask for His healing.

After that I waited impatiently for the next routine chest X rays.

Usually I received the doctor's telephone report several days after the X rays. The moment finally came; I found picking up the telephone by my bed for this particular call something of a traumatic experience. During the pause while the nurse transferred the call to the doctor's inner office, my heart began to race, my throat went dry. Every sense had its antennae out to catch the mood and timbre of the doctor's first words.

My imagination toyed with what I would say to him when he told me of his amazement in finding my chest healed. Would I tell him the truth? But what if—no, I wouldn't even admit the thought. I had read somewhere that real faith entertains no doubts. By a process of will power that I found somewhat wearying, I clung resolutely, desperately to the thought of complete health.

Finally at the other end of the phone there was a click and the doctor's voice came on. He sounded casual, "We find no increased density in either lung. The shadows and infiltration are just about the same. No real change . . . the sedimentation rate has gone down one point. Just carry on! I'll see you in a few days."

Slowly I rested the telephone back on its cradle. The doctor's words had already pricked and burst the self-inflated balloon that I had thought was faith. For that day and the next I was too numb, too stunned even to try to reason out what had happened. Then came rebellious tears, followed by a period of feeling sorry for myself and by hours of black depression. Finally my mind began to function again.

I knew that I had come to the boundaries of my human reason. I stood on the edge and stared off into an abyss of despair. Since medical skill was not solving my problem and my spiritual efforts—so far as I could evaluate them—had gotten me nowhere, what now?

Was it possible that Jesus Christ and Christianity were myths *in toto*, a carefully wrought system of nonsense? Or if God did exist, was He so bound by the natural law that He Himself had created that He was helpless too?

In that mood of near-despair, I went for a visit to my parents' home on the Eastern Shore of Virginia. My doctors still did not want me out of bed for more than thirty minutes at a time. The trip was made possible by my taking a boat to Norfolk. I remember that Peter actually picked me up in his arms and carried me up the gangplank to the bunk in my stateroom.

A few nights after my arrival—on September 14, 1943, to be exact—something happened to me that defies analysis. I have relived it in my mind hundreds of times since that night. All I can do is to describe it exactly as it happened. . . .

I awakened about 3:30 A.M. There was blackness all around me, not a sound. I had no idea what had awakened me. Nor did I understand why I had emerged suddenly from deep sleep into alertness with no interim drowsiness.

Then it happened, I was aware of a Presence, a Power, a Personality in my room. My physical eyes saw nothing, yet a new way of seeing was instantly available. My body tingled as with a shock of electricity.

The new set of senses which I had suddenly been given enabled me to perceive the vivid Personality who stood at the right side of my bed. There was in Him a curious combination of kingliness and tenderness.

Through His tenderness shone the fact that He looked upon me as a child, quite a foolish child at times. And He had a sense of humor—and the light touch. With my new eyes I saw that He smiled at me. His attitude was, "Why do you take yourself and your problems so seriously? Relax! There's nothing here l can't take care of."

I realized too that He knew every detail of my life and household. And with my new ears I heard Him speak in contemporary language. There was never a "thee" or a "thou."

"Go and tell your mother," He said. And then He smiled again. "That's simple enough isn't it?"

My humanness immediately asserted itself. "Go and tell my mother— what?" I thought. I wanted to argue, "It's the middle of the night, what will mother think?"

But again, I was conscious of that note of mastery in the One who had just spoken. And I understood something else: He was standing there waiting, leaving me entirely free to obey or to disobey. For an instant I wavered between my disinclination to obey and that compelling quality in Him, sensing that something terribly important—as important as my whole future—hung on my decision. Then resolution welled up in me. "I'll do it, if it kills me," I told Him as I threw off the bed covers.

And once again, He smiled at my intensity . . . and stood aside for me to pass.

Mother wakened immediately and sat up in bed. Father was still asleep. "What's happened?" There was alarm in her voice.

"Don't be frightened. Something wonderful has happened. I just want you to know that I'm going to be all right now. I'll tell you about it in the morning."

This was scarcely fair, since Mother must have been consumed with curiosity. Yet because she sensed the combination of excitement and restraint in me, she did not question me further.

A few minutes later when I returned to the bedroom, it was empty. I lay there wide awake until dawn marveling at what had happened. Now I knew what the New Testament writers meant when they spoke of Jesus "speaking with authority." I had felt His kingliness. I could understand how it was that the skeptic Thomas could in the same Presence pass in an instant from unbelief to worship before this Christ, saying "My Lord and my God."

In the morning I wondered if I was healed. Would the next X ray finally show healthy lung tissue? But something far more important even than healthy lungs and body tissue was now clear to me. I knew that

Christianity is no myth. I could understand why no intimidation, not even the threat of death, could shake Peter and James and John and the other apostles from their insistence that Jesus Christ was alive!

How was His resurrection possible? I had no idea. But suddenly all theological controversy as to *how* it had happened seemed unimportant in the face of the fact that it was so.

As for my health, I dared not assume that Christ had healed me. He had made no such statement!

As it turned out, this experience was the turning point in my illness. For the first time the next X ray showed progress, as did every X ray thereafter. Even so, months were to pass before I was pronounced well.

Why did it take so long? The tardiness was not God's will. Of that I am sure. Rather it was due to two deficiencies of mine. The first was an inner difficulty. As time went on, I began to realize that the psychologically penetrating question Jesus had once put to a man at the Pool of Bethesda—a man who had been ill for thirty-eight years—also applied to me: "Do you want your health restored?"[17]

This seems a ridiculous question. Who wouldn't want to get well? Yet many doctors today believe that one of the root causes of much illness is a deep-seated retreat from life. Psychosomatic medicine has much to say about the will to live and its converse, the subconscious death-wish. Apparently any interior division about this, any chronic state of indecision about facing some necessary adjustments to life, can directly contribute to illness.

So I had to ask myself, "Am I willing to go back into life ready to assume full responsibilities? Am I willing to make adult adjustments to whatever life hands me? Can I accept such robust health at Christ's hands that no one need ever feel sorry for me again, that I shall never again be able to use poor health as an excuse for avoiding some responsibility? This had to be a clear-cut decision of my will. I was aware of Christ standing aside for me to make it, even as He had stood aside that night of September fourteenth while I decided whether or not I would obey Him.

But the second reason for the delay in my convalescence was not so easily resolved. It was my inability to grasp an inviolable spiritual principle—one that is seen everywhere in the New Testament—that faith must always be in the present tense. The most succinct statement of the principle is in Mark: "So I tell you, whatever you pray for and ask, believe you have got it, and you shall have it."[18]

I puzzled for months over this one verse. The verb tenses seem contradictory. How can one believe that he already possesses health, for instance, at the same moment that he is being promised health in the future? Yet I wondered if that was not exactly what Christ had been asking me to believe that night of September fourteenth: that X rays and medical reports notwithstanding, I was healed right then.

Every time that Jesus forgave sins or healed, he demonstrated this principle. One could pick examples almost at random. Though Zacchaeus had spent a lifetime in sin, Jesus told him, "This day is salvation come to this house."[19] The woman in the synagogue who had been bowed over [with arthritis probably] for eighteen years was told, "Woman, you are released from your weakness"[20]—right now, at this moment.

About this time, I came across Hannah Whitall Smith's statement that God's inevitable order is Fact, then Faith, and last, Feeling. In relation to health, this order would mean that health would precede one's faith for it; that feeling well, the disappearance of symptoms, and the clinical proof of health would come last of all. This too substantiates the formula that Jesus gave us.

I came to realize that our mortality, which forces us to divide time into past, present, and future is probably the simplest key to the seeming contradiction in the verb tenses in the verse in question. In the world of spirit, there is only the eternal Now. But Jesus was trying to explain the principle to men still in the flesh. Even with this much understanding, the most my faith could grasp was that my healing was *in the process* of coming. I felt that this was scarcely good enough. No wonder my recovery was so slow.

There are those who are able to grip this principle of present-moment faith more firmly than I did, enough to act on it. In such cases, the healing process is accelerated accordingly. This was dramatized for me by what had happened to another tubercular patient. Her story was to be a decisive factor in my own recovery.

One afternoon in the late spring of 1945, during a period when my progress toward health seemed especially slow, a former college friend came to call. I had not seen her in years. Apart from her news of our classmates, one thing seemed uppermost in her mind—the story of Rosa Bell Montgomery. "She's just had a remarkable recovery from TB," the friend told me. "Her case was much worse than yours! In fact she was in a sanatorium in New Mexico and not expected to live out the month. Hers was a case of spiritual healing, pure and simple. She's fine now. In fact, she's getting married next month."

As I sat in bed propped up against pillows listening to this, I kept questioning, probing for more details.

My friend saw my eagerness. "I'll tell you what. I'll write Rosa and tell her about you. I think she'd be happy to write you herself and give you the story firsthand. Would you like that?"

Would I like it!

The promised letter, however, was slow in coming. When it finally arrived, I could understand why. It was a lengthy letter for a girl to write in longhand on her honeymoon. It was postmarked New York.

How sorry I am to have waited so long to write to you. My only excuse or reason for this delay is that the letter telling me about you reached me in Los Angeles just a few days after I was married, and I have been on a lovely but hectic honeymoon ever since. . . . Now that we are in New York, far from the sweet attentions of friends and family, I can chat with you undisturbed. . . .

It has been more than three years now since I turned my case over to the Lord and He really did a good piece of work on me. No one talked me into it—in fact no one talked to me about it at all—and I didn't read anything that influenced me. This is how it happened, and I shall be as brief as possible. . . .

Rosa had been a bed patient in a sanatorium in Albuquerque for almost ten months, a cavity in the left lung, fluid on the right, losing weight steadily. There came the night when Rosa took a long look at herself spiritually. She felt that her heart had been wayward and proud. In her mind she went over all the things that she had been hugging to herself. Suppose God should want her to give up these things? For example, her deep desire to find a husband. Perhaps marriage wasn't in God's plan for her because of her health problem. But how could she bear the thought of never marrying?

472 *Beyond Our Selves*

Then suddenly, none of these things seemed to matter any more. She decided that she wanted Christ more than she wanted anything else. Lying on her hospital bed, watching the shadows from the desert moonlight on the ceiling, her will bowed itself before Christ and called Him Master. Immediately there was a feeling of peace.

The next day she had the same keen desire I had to search the Scriptures on the subject of healing. Rosa had grown up in a physician's home. She had been taught all her life that God uses doctors and medicine to heal today. But she also knew that medicine still had no real cure for tuberculosis. The doctors could cooperate with nature to achieve an arrested case—and that was all. So she determined to drop all previous ideas and to find out for herself what the Scriptures had to say on the subject.

Her conclusions were just what mine had been from the same sort of search. So she turned her case over to God.

Jesus had talked about the agreement of like-minded people as being one prerequisite for answered prayer. "If two of you agree on earth about anything you pray for, it will be done for you by my Father in Heaven. For where two or three have gathered in My Name, I am there amongst them."[21]

So one March afternoon, a few friends met Rosa in the sanctuary of a local church. Rosa was too ill to get dressed, so she went in her bathrobe. There, before the altar, the group gathered around her and prayed. It was simple and direct. Yet when they prayed nothing dramatic happened. Rosa felt no different, except for an inner assurance that the answer was on the way.

That being so, she no longer asked for healing but began thanking God for it. Here Rosa was demonstrating that principle that had so puzzled me, "Believe you have got it and you shall have it." She decided that she would begin acting her faith by getting up and walking about, so far as her strength would permit.

The fact that faith has to be in the present then led her to a daring decision: she would permit no more pneumothorax treatments.

Rosa's doctor at the sanitorium was appalled. Dr. Werner cajoled and threatened. Once the lungs were collapsed, it was suicide to stop the pneumothorax before healing was complete! But his warnings were to no avail; Rosa quietly stood her ground. She knew how foolhardy her decision seemed to the medical men. Nor was she implying that others should act in so drastic a manner. But this, she felt, was what Jesus was telling *her* to do. She must obey. It was as simple as that. God would take care of the results.

Rosa found all the pressure harder to withstand than she would admit. Many symptoms of her disease were still bothering her—fever, a cough, the fluid in her left lung. Yet she knew that she had to keep her attention fixed on Christ, not on her symptoms; that she had to listen for His directions, not those of others, however well-meaning and loving they were.

Her doctor made one last desperate try. He asked that Rosa's father, Dr. Nelson Bell, in Montreat, North Carolina,[22] be appraised of the situation. "But I don't think it would do for me to talk to him just now," Dr. Werner told Rosa. "I'm too upset about this." So a friend at the sanitorium put the telephone call through.

Dr. Bell did some sharp questioning. When he had satisfied himself that Rosa was firm in her decision, and that she would agree to stay in the sanitorium where the doctors could keep an eye on her, he gave her his blessing.

After that, Dr. Werner battled Rosa no more, only watched her more closely than ever. By April she had begun to gain weight. Her pulse had gone down to normal. The afternoon fever was decreasing.

By June, Rosa was out of bed most of the time. By July she had formed the habit of walking sixteen blocks down the hill for an afternoon milkshake, then sixteen blocks back up the hill. In October she pleaded for and got a position in the institution's laboratory.

The following February—not quite a year since the little group of friends had gathered in her room for prayer—the leading radiologist of New Mexico compared a new set of X-ray plates with the old ones. He was dumfounded at the change.

In April the same technician found the cavity of her right lung "completely obliterated." At that time he also wrote Dr. Bell that Rosa's "explanation of her healing is the only adequate one."

Then Don Montgomery walked into her life, and God gave her the one joy she had thought He might ask her to relinquish—love and marriage.

I am still in touch with Rosa. She has never had any recurrence of her old trouble. Nor has health required her to live in the Southwest.

She is no fanatic on the subject of healing, but her experience has made her relationship with Christ an intensely personal one.

In all her letters to me she stressed Christ's individualized treatment of each case. "You must listen for His orders, not copy mine," she warned.

The first hint of my directions came in an odd way. I dreamed that the lung specialist said to me, "There are people who don't get well until they get up and go about their business. Of course, as a doctor I couldn't take the responsibility for telling you that, but—" and I woke up.

I mentioned the dream to my mother. "That's queer," she answered as a startled look crossed her face. "The same thought has been coming to me over and over."

Still I was cautious about acting on this. After all, perhaps the dream had been nothing more than wishful thinking in my sleep. But in time, my orders did come in an inner conviction that did not fade with the passing of days: *As you give strength to others, strength will be given to you. Stay under the doctor's care, but start getting out of bed.* And that is just what I did.

I began with a small chore, tidying up the linen closet once a week; I could sit down to do that. Then I assumed the responsibility and fun of dressing Peter John each morning. After that came a short afternoon walk with Jeffrey, our cocker. First, a half a block. Then to the corner. After a few weeks, we were circling the block. I was inching my way, but little by little vitality was flowing back to me.

Then came the day when the doctor's nurse telephoned to report that the sedimentation rate had returned to the normal range. This meant that there was no longer evidence of infection in the blood stream. So far, so good. But the X-ray pictures still showed trouble.

By now X rays were being taken three months apart. Two months after the good laboratory report, I went down to add the next routine chest film to the doctor's fat file. It was on a Tuesday morning that I was to telephone to hear the result.

The first time I called, the doctor was in the midst of a consultation. Would I please try again in about an hour?

During the hour, some of my old fears of those telephone reports came creeping back. *What if*—I thought—*No, "what ifs" are always silly, because they borrow trouble.* Nevertheless, when I dialed the number again it was with an unsteady hand.

The doctor's voice was as calm as always. "The appearance is that of perfectly healed lesions—"

"Perfectly healed!" I almost shouted at him. "You mean I'm well?"

There was a smile in his voice. "That's what I mean. But wouldn't you like to hear the remainder of the report?"

I listened impatiently to the droning technical language. How could he be so maddeningly placid about it? He was reading it as if this were a weather report! The first minute I could hang up, I dropped the telephone and rushed downstairs shouting the great news.

In a few hours when I could be calmer about it, gratitude of a deeper kind welled up. I was grateful not only because I was well again, but because of my personal encounter with Christ, which had settled certain questions forever. Inestimable blessings had come out of a difficult experience. I had discovered myself and what I wanted out of life. The woman who rose from bed and went out to meet life was a different woman.

After such an experience, I of all people should have been convinced for all time of God's power to heal. But there was still an area that continued to trouble me. I now had no doubt that an individual can open himself to the healing love of God. But can that love be sent winging to someone else? Can prayers affect another person's illness?

In the intervening years I have had this question answered for me again and again. The answer is definitely *Yes!*

I have chosen to use Karen Emmott's story out of many, because the medical facts are indisputable. Not only is the man who initiated the prayers for her a surgeon, but her father too, is a doctor. Karen is the eldest daughter of Dr. Ralph Emmott, a specialist in urology in Oklahoma City.

Her physical problem began soon after her fifteenth birthday in the spring of 1960. It was nothing serious—just an abscess which required a minor operation, incision, and drainage. Twenty-four hours in the hospital (the one where her father practices) seemed to clear everything up.

Karen plunged into a busy summer. Before me as I write this is a small picture of her as she was then. Yes, she was a charmer: short curly hair, sparkling eyes, a piquant quality about her. At the close of the school year she had been voted drum-majorette. Her five younger brothers and sisters were proud of her. She seemed to be following in the footsteps of their mother, who had been a campus beauty queen in Canada.

On July first, Karen noticed that another abscess was forming. Again her doctor recommended the minor operation and drainage. The operation was set for 1 P.M. on July fifth. It was such a routine matter that Karen's father went on to his regular afternoon clinic in the urology department.

As Karen was placed on the operating-room cart, she gave her mother a puckish kiss. It was to be her last volitional act for many months.

The first indication that Karen's father had that tragedy had struck came when the Operating Room Supervisor—a friend of the Emmott family—summoned him from the clinic. Hastening to the operating floor, he learned that toward the close of the ten-minute operation there had been sudden cardiac arrest. The chest had been incised. The heart had been massaged. Now it was beating again.

But during the emergency, no one in the operating room had paused to look at the clock. How long had it been from the cessation of heartbeat until circulation had been restored? Four minutes? Five? It was a question that was to haunt everyone concerned with Karen's case. For with cardiac arrest, time is of the essence. The sensitive brain tissues are damaged almost immediately when the constant supply of oxygen is cut off.

Karen's mother shut herself in her husband's office and tried to pray. In the recovery room, two doors away, everything that science knew was being done for Karen—a hypothemia blanket to keep body temperature at thirty-one degrees and prevent further swelling of the brain; a tracheotomy to help the paralyzed lungs to breathe.

Kneeling by a leather chair, Mrs. Emmott groped for a way to pray. "Oh God, let me have Karen back again. These fifteen years are so brief and unfinished. . . ." Then her thoughts would wander off. *Such a fine thread between this world and the life beyond. How can we be so indifferent to God when things are going well?* "God, will You take care of our girl? Oh, God. . . ." *This can't be real . . . Karen will wake up soon and this scare will be in the past.*

But by nine o'clock that night, it was apparent that Karen was not going to wake up.

Except for the beating of her heart, Karen was dead. On the morning of July sixth, those watching beside her bed saw one eyelid flicker. Weeks went by and there was no other sign of life. Then the convulsions began. Sudden seizures with bloody froth on her lips and soaring temperature alternated with deep coma.

By mid-August the convulsions were under control. But the consensus of all the specialists on the case was that the outlook was hopeless, the brain damage beyond repair.

Every body function had to be artificially maintained. The girl's mother could scarcely bear the sight . . . a tube in Karen's chest; cutdowns in her leg veins for some limited nutrition; the tracheotomy tube; a catheter, even needle electrodes stuck in her scalp and legs to monitor her heartbeat.

At last the doctors spoke the brutal truth. "Your daughter will always remain in a vegetative state," they told the Emmotts. "Alive, but unknowing. It is possible that we will be able to keep her alive for years. But we advise you to put her out of your minds and your lives. Forget she ever lived."

Forget? A mother and father forget part of their own hearts? Their lovely intelligent Karen alive, and yet not alive; dead and yet not dead. For Isabel and Ralph Emmott, horror closed in. There is no blackness like the eternal night of no hope. Isabel had long since stopped praying. Surely there could be no God of mercy, else He would not allow this to happen. Death could have no sting compared to this.

On August 16 to free a hospital bed for a patient whom the doctors could help, the girl was moved to a Children's Convalescent Home. A month passed. There was no change in her vegetative existence except a steady loss of weight.

On Thursday, September 28, Isabel Emmott was invited by a friend to hear a talk at a local church. She went only because the speaker was to be Dr. William Reed, Consulting Surgeon at Samaritan Hospital, Bay City, Michigan. Mrs. Emmott was mildly curious as to why a physician would be speaking in a church.

Dr. Reed was a tall, earnest young man in his late thirties. He told about the sequence of events by which he had learned that medicine plus prayer can bring about cures otherwise impossible.

"Science, mathematics, and physics, as a result of Einsteinian thought, have left the realm of the material and have in certain ways become mystical sciences. There is a sense in which medicine too must go beyond the material. The whole man must be treated. I am now convinced that neither medicine nor surgery can achieve maximum effectiveness—especially for the case which is beyond the scope of the physician to cure—so long as the body is treated to the exclusion of the spirit."

It was not the usual religious talk. Isabel Emmott was fascinated. In all her years of churchgoing she never heard anyone mention healing through prayer. Nor had she heard of a doctor who prayed in the presence of the operating room personnel before he began each operation. Mrs. Emmott smiled to herself as she thought of how he had put it. "I used to bow my head and pray silently. But then I thought the nurses might just think I had a headache. Now if I hesitate about the prayer, they remind me." And this was a doctor, not a minister!

At the conclusion of the talk, her friend told her, "I've done something without asking you. Hope you won't mind. I've already told Dr. Reed about Karen. If you'd like it, he has agreed to ride out with us to the Convalescent Home this afternoon." Her eyes searched Isabel's face.

Light sprang into the black eyes. "Like it? Of course!"

That afternoon at the door of the Convalescent Home Karen Emmott's father was waiting. Dr. Reed judged him to be about his own age. As the piercing brown eyes of the girl's father looked him over, the thought crossed his mind that probably Dr. Emmott had already looked him up in the American Medical Association's directory.

In dispassionate medical terms, Karen's father told Dr. Reed the history of her case. As the words of hopelessness poured out on him, Bill Reed was thinking, "Lord, you've handed me a tough one this time." He had never tried praying for such a difficult case. Yet he could not dislodge from his mind the words, "With God all things are possible . . . all things. . . ." Obviously his first task was to give hope back to Karen's parents. This would not be easy when one of them was a knowledgeable doctor.

Dr. Emmott's face was a study in skepticism. "I'd advise you not to form any opinion until after you've seen Karen," he said. "Come on in, my wife is waiting for us in the room."

The first glance was shocking. A once-beautiful girl, now emaciated, spastic, her black eyes so like her mother's—wildly staring, without recognition. Constantly there were aimless thrashing movements. The sides to her bed were high to keep her from falling out. Dr. Emmott was watching his face.

Cautiously Dr. Reed told how it had been shown by some men working in the field of hypnotism that the subconscious mind of a patient under anesthesia is aware of what goes on in the operating room. "And I believe that it may also be true in coma," he added.

Dr. Emmott seemed mildly interested in the thesis. As for Isabel Emmott, a faint light of hope flickered in her tired eyes.

"Now what I suggest," Dr. Reed said, "is that we begin to treat Karen as if she were spiritually awake and spiritually perceptive. Do you think you could do it?" Both parents nodded. They had nothing to lose. "Then shall we begin right now?"

So Bill Reed placed his hands on Karen's head and prayed, not about her, but with her, taking her situation to God, thanking Him for His loving care. Nothing happened. The violent jerking and twisting did not even momentarily subside.

"I haven't the least idea how God will answer this prayer," he admitted. "But we've got to keep reminding ourselves that in His eyes, there are no hopeless cases. Now let me explain what I think your role will be in getting Karen well again—"

Getting Karen well again? Mrs. Emmott could scarcely believe what she was hearing. In all the long months since the tragedy, no one—no one at all—had even mentioned the possibility of Karen getting well. And here was this stranger . . .

Dr. Reed outlined several steps: (1) Prayer continuous and confident; (2) Daily conversations with Karen, always assuring her of complete recovery; no negative words or even thoughts in her presence; (3) as soon as possible discontinuance of all artificial aids—sedation, catheter, breathing-tube, intravenous feeding, etc.

The following morning Mrs. Emmott drove to the Nursing Home and sat down beside her daughter. Karen was showing the same thrashing movements as before. Gently she placed her hand on Karen's forehead. "Karen," she said softly, "you are going to get well. Your friends have been asking about you. They're missing you at school and at majorette practice."

Did she imagine it? Were the movements a little less violent? Day after day Mrs. Emmott talked to Karen—about family activities, about Karen's friends, about what was happening at school. Always she would come back to the same persistent theme: "You are going to get well,

Karen. God loves you, Karen. We love you. Won't it be wonderful to be well again?"

After the first day there was a definite change; Karen's spastic contortions were less violent. Two days later her mother and the nurses were able to put her in a wheelchair and take her into the sunshine for the first time in three months. But still she showed no sign of awareness.

The next step—taken in faith—was the removal of the catheter. With that, the severe urinary infection began to subside.

Then came the matter of food. Isabel Emmott decided to try letting Karen eat in the normal way. Three friends took turns helping her. At first, chewing was impossible for Karen; even swallowing was hard. But gradually she learned to eat baby foods and mashed potatoes.

Slowly the miracle unfolded. One evening in mid-November Karen's father put a ball-point pen in her hand. She punched the release button and began to scribble on the blanket cover.

Almost frantic with joy, her parents began handing her other familiar objects—a stick of gum, a Chapstick, sunglasses. She put the sunglasses on upside down, then righted them.

That night they went home jubilant. Now they set themselves a new goal, to have Karen home for part of Christmas Day. And it happened as they pictured it: on Christmas afternoon the whole family was together. Around the table at Christmas dinner every one of her brothers and sisters thanked God that Karen could be with them for a few hours.

Back at the Convalescent Home, Karen began rebelling. She hated the tube feedings that still had to be used to supplement the baby foods. Unless her hands were tied, she would pull the tube out. Then she began refusing the baby foods too.

Her mother had an inspiration. She would prepare a tuna-fish sandwich. In the old days that had been one of Karen's favorites. She asked a group of friends to meet and pray for the little venture.

Karen gobbled the sandwich down with better coordination in chewing and swallowing than anyone had thought possible. In the next few days ice cream, French fries, and hamburgers met equal enthusiasm. Soon there were no more tube feedings, and Karen's weight at last started up.

Isabel and Ralph Emmott were learning. They would take a step at a time, each launched by hope, taken in faith. After this, they recognized rebellion in Karen as her readiness for another step.

December was drawing to a close. Still Karen had not spoken. Getting rid of the tracheotomy tube was next. During a ten-day period, successively smaller tubes were placed in the wound. On the tenth day, the tube was withdrawn entirely. The girl breathed normally but still seemed incapable of speech.

But with the tube out, now Karen could be brought home to stay. January fourth was a gala day for the Emmott family. Isabel could scarcely hold back tears of gladness over Karen's homecoming.

And then a few days later the girl began to whisper. Her first sentences in a low voice and with precise enunciation were a series of revelations. Her mother wrote them down, "I want to live my life in the old natural normal way." . . . "If heaven and hell are worlds, then I want to go to the heaven-world." . . . "I want to meet and greet the man Jesus." . . . "Please assure me that my life has been a successful thing. I need the reassurance if it has been."

Each evening as she tucked Karen in, Isabel would repeat the Lord's Prayer and the 23rd Psalm. On Easter Sunday, 1961, Karen repeated the Lord's Prayer by herself—with a few flourishes of her own: "Who art in heaven—way up in that world we call heaven. . . ."

Progress is slow, but progress there is. Karen now feeds herself, reads, walks unassisted. Last June she developed a new rebellion. Unless she is watched, she will slip out of the house and try to drive the family car.

Whenever Isabel Emmott needs more prayer-stamina and physical stamina for the long road ahead she gets down on her knees and thanks God for the long way Karen has already come from her vegetative state. Hopeless! No! The Emmotts know now that Bill Reed was right: in God's view there is no such term as *hopeless*.

Surely the preacher in my childhood was mistaken in thinking that the miraculous element in Christianity has died out because it is not needed any more. Not needed? When always there are so many—like Karen—for whom the doctors have no answer?

No, it is not the absence of need that has caused the sharp decline of the miraculous element in Christianity. Something has chilled and contracted our faith in God's love and in His freedom to stoop to our need and to heal our bodies. Healings through prayer are still the exception rather than the rule. Yet it takes just as much power to forgive sin or to release men and women from enslaving habits as it does to heal. And the truth is that these other miracles are just as rare in our day as are healings.

Still spiritual progress is being made, for in the last two decades there has been a groundswell of interest in spiritual healing among all religious denominations. The National Council of Churches recently surveyed a number of Protestant ministers to find out what they thought about healing through prayer. Thirty-four per cent of the clergymen answering the questionnaire said that they had attempted spiritual healing, in many cases with success astonishing even to them.

The new collaboration between ministers and physicians is also a sign that there is no longer an imagined conflict between religion and medicine. On the religious front, all those I know who are interested in healing believe that divine healing should always be undertaken in cooperation with doctors, never in competition with them.

On the side of medicine, every adequately trained modern doctor recognizes the connection between his patient's mind and spirit and the tissues of his body. Many hospitals (like St. Luke's in New York City) have full-time chaplains on their staffs.

Meanwhile, psychologists like Adler, Jung, and Fritz Künkel have steadily closed the lag in our understanding of how mind and spirit affect body. They are also bringing us closer and closer to Jesus' teaching that man's being is a whole, that he can in no way be separated into compartments.

Practically speaking, we shall have taken our greatest step forward in the realm of spiritual healing when the average Christian becomes as sure of God's will for health as he is of his doctor's. Only those who have settled this in their own minds, can press forward in the adventure of spiritual research. And press forward we must, for Christ has commanded us to do so.

Of course, we shall not always succeed; neither do the doctors. Jesus Himself had some failures in His home town of Nazareth "because of their unbelief."[23]

But above all, let us not be stopped by a particularly subtle roadblock. "Isn't it a dangerous thing to ask for healing through prayer?" this argument goes. "Suppose you pray for health and fail. . . . Mightn't you then lose your faith in God altogether?"

One minister who has had a healing service every week for twelve years answers this by saying, "In twelve years I have never had anyone come to me and say, 'I followed your suggestions. I went all out. It hasn't worked. I will have nothing more to do with religion and the church.' But I have had marvelous experiences with people who have received answers that are even better than what they asked for."

In my own case, it was precisely while my prayer was still unanswered that I received the most vivid assurances of God's reality.

What this comes down to is the simple but powerful truth that God can be trusted in this regard as in all others. Hope is always of God; hopelessness is always of evil. Faith is always right; fear and despair are always wrong.

We can rest on the love of God, knowing that His love for us boundlessly surpasses our own. Nothing can ever separate us from that love except our own blind unwillingness to receive.

Fourteen
Journey into Joy

SOME TIME DURING the second year after my entering-in experience, I found myself with a lively curiosity about what seemed an odd subject—the Holy Spirit. Like most people, I had thought of the Holy Spirit as a theological abstraction, a sort of ecclesiastical garnish for christenings, weddings, benedictions, and the like. As for the term *the Holy Ghost*—that I regarded as archaic, if not downright eerie.

However odd the subject seemed, the fact remained that this was no passing curiosity. As is often the case when something is brought sharply to one's attention, everywhere I turned during those months, I seemed to hear or read something about the Holy Spirit.

During our vacation at Cape Cod, the church that Peter and I attended with Peter John included a talk for children as part of its regular Sunday service. The first Sunday we were there, the guest preacher gave as his sermonette an object-lesson talk on the Holy Spirit as related to the Trinity.

Three glass containers had been placed on a table before the young preacher. One was filled with water, the second with ice, the third with what appeared to be steam, probably dry ice.

"Children," he began, "perhaps you've heard of 'The Trinity.' *Trinity* means 'three.' When we speak of the Trinity, we mean the three Persons that go to make up God: God, the Father; Jesus Christ, the Son; and the Holy Spirit.

"Now look at these three jars. This one has water. This one has ice, and that one, steam. They all look different, don't they?

"Yet you know that ice is only frozen water. And that when your mother boils water in a pan on the stove, steam rises from it.

"That means that water, ice, and steam are really the same thing.

"Now, the same thing is true of the Trinity . . . Jesus Christ, the water of Life, is different from the Father—yet the same too. The Holy Spirit, like the powerful steam that can drive an engine, is different from Christ and the Father, yet the same."

I listened, as interested as any of the children. What the young minister said that morning gave me a new concept and provided a background for approaching the subject that continued to occupy my mind.

Then about two months later something happened which took this interest out of the realm of theory and placed it on a personal basis. It was in the early fall of that year that my friends Tay and Fern told me of the experience of guidance that they had had in Florida the previous winter (pp. 404 ff.).

I had known Tay for a long time. Often she had inner nudges and proddings of the kind that had sent her out to help her friend Grace at a time of desperate emergency. Curiously I asked her, "How do you explain these intuitions—this—well, Voice on the inside?"

"Some people call them intuitions," Tay answered promptly. "But I would prefer to call the help I got at Delray Beach that morning the direction of the Holy Spirit."

So there it was again!

Tay was looking at me curiously. "What does the Holy Spirit mean to you?" she asked.

I remembered the sermonette at the Cape Cod church. "Oh—one of the three Persons of the Godhead—the third Person of the Trinity."

"But I sense something in the offhand way you say that—" she looked at me sharply. "Let me guess that in your mind the Spirit has an insignificant and unnecessary place. Isn't that right?"

I nodded. "That's right."

"But I know from personal experiences that the Holy Spirit is just as great, just as needed as the other two Persons of the Trinity. Anyway you still haven't answered my original question, what is He to you?"

Tay's intensity seemed to demand a candid reply. "I've got to be truthful, Tay," I replied. "He's nothing to me. I've had no contact with Him and could get along quite well without Him."

Although at the time I believed my own statement, I was soon to find out that it was not so. As a matter of fact, I could not get along at all well without the Holy Spirit. Some searching in the Bible told me why.

Using a concordance and a notebook, I began methodically looking up all the references I could find on the third Person of the Trinity. Gradually I worked the findings into a logical outline in the notebook.

I learned that the Holy Spirit is not "an influence" but a Person; not "a thing," an "it," but "He." In a sense, He is both the most basic and the most modest member of the Trinity, for His work is to reflect Christ and to glorify Him.

The obvious meaning of the word *glorify* is "to give homage to, as in worship." But there is a deeper meaning. Dr. Leslie Weatherhead, in a 1952 Lenten sermon in the City Temple, London, brought out this richer meaning: "I would define glory as that expression of the nature of a person or thing which, of itself, evokes our praise."

Then the "glory" of a sunrise must be in the beauty of its delicate pinks and oranges reflected in the sky just before the sun itself appears over the hills. In this sense the glory is in the qualities or characteristics of the sunrise which we can perceive.

The "glory" of Jesus Christ lies in the characteristics of His nature that makes us want to adore Him. These traits are not kingly trappings or the halo placed around His head by medieval painters. Far from it! Men saw His glory in His humanity—His instant compassion, tenderness, understanding, fearlessness, incisiveness, His refusal to compromise with evil, His selflessness which culminated in His ultimate self-giving on the cross.

The Apostle John puts it in unforgettable words: "And the Word was made flesh, and dwelt among us, (and we beheld his glory, the glory as of the only begotten of the Father) full of grace and truth."[1]

But then I found the New Testament declaring that these qualities of Jesus' nature are not apparent to us any more than a sunrise is apparent to a blind man. That is why we need the Holy Spirit to make Christ's glory perceptible to us. It is as if the Spirit gives us a new way of seeing, with which we can perceive spiritual truth where all has been darkness before.

I found that Jesus had his own preferred names for the Spirit. Christ spoke in Aramaic, the tongue of His own people. This was the dialect of the bazaars and the seaside, replete with colorful idioms, metaphors, and probably picturesque humor. There is good reason to believe that the tone of Jesus' speech was quite unlike the English of the King James' Version of the early seventeenth century. The King James' translators often rendered the Holy Spirit the "Holy Ghost." But Jesus liked to call Him "the Helper," "the Spirit of Truth," "the Teacher," "the Comforter," "the Counselor."

The gospel of John was especially helpful in giving me more understanding about the Holy Spirit. In His last talk with the eleven (Judas had already left the group), Christ made it clear that they were to experience Him through the Spirit. On that last night, He had important things to say to His apostles, most of them concerning the Comforter.

The disciples knew that their Master was in imminent danger. They were frightened, sorrowful men.

"Do not be frightened about my leaving you," Jesus told them, in effect. "It is actually to your advantage that I go away."

Then He outlined His plan:

When He could no longer be with them physically, Another would take His place. This One—the Helper—would be the continuation and extension of His [Christ's] life on earth.[2] All the wonders that the disciples had witnessed of teaching, preaching, forgiving, cleansing, healing would go right on. But even greater accomplishments would be possible through the Helper, ones that had not been possible during Jesus' earthly ministry.[3]

This had to be so, because there was more truth, much more, to be discovered. And it would be the Spirit of Truth that would lead men into these undreamed-of areas of exploration.[4]

This is the only plan by which men in all centuries could have fellowship with the risen Christ. Without the Spirit transmitting His continuing presence to us, we would have no more than the memory and recorded words and deeds of any good man, such as St. Francis of Assisi or Lincoln or Gandhi.

Jesus made a surprising statement that last night to His apostles: the plan was that this Spirit would dwell in men's bodies. We were being offered the privilege of presenting our bodies to the Helper, so that He could not only be with us, but *in* us. This would be God the Father coming closer to men than He had ever been before. This is expressed in a variety of ways in Scripture. It is "God tabernacling with men." Paul was later to cry: "I live; yet not I, but Christ liveth in me."[5] And, "Do you not know that your body is the temple of the holy Spirit within you— the Spirit you have received from God?"[6]

Christ promised His disciples that if they would thus offer their bodies as an abiding place for the Helper, the Father's power and wisdom, as well as His [Christ's] would be theirs.[7]

He also warned that people in the world would think all of this odd, and could not possibly see or recognize the Spirit until they too had experienced Him.[8]

Then He instructed the eleven what to do in order to receive the Spirit.[9] And He admonished each of them not even to try to be His witness until *after* the Spirit had come to Him.[10]

Probably the apostles understood little of this at the time. Even so, it must have been obvious to them that Jesus was putting maximum value on the Helper. And this brought me back full circle to my own statement to my friend Tay that I could "get along quite well" without the Holy Spirit. On the contrary, I found that according to the New Testament if we are without the Spirit, then we are without:

Joy
The awareness of God's love for us
The conviction of who Christ is
The ability to communicate the gospel in a life-changing way
The conviction of sin
Guidance
Healing
An intercessor with the Father
The gifts of the Spirit
The fruits of the Spirit
The pledge (or inner proof) of eternal life

For anyone who has the least desire to be a Christian, this seems like an extensive list of blessings to forego. Even from my incomplete examination, it was obvious that Jesus saw the presence of the Helper as the one gift encompassing all other gifts.

Having learned this much, my next question was "How does one go about receiving the Holy Spirit?" From the stories in the Acts, telling how different men received Him, it is obvious that there are many ways and no set techniques. Thus the outline I culled from Scripture at that time cannot be taken as final or rigid:

1. We have to be convinced that the Scriptures teach the indwelling of Christ in our bodies through the Holy Spirit, and we have to want His Presence for ourselves.
2. We have to go to Christ and ask for the gift.
3. We then reckon that the Spirit has taken possession of our bodies and is dwelling in us.
4. We receive proof of this, what some have called "the manifestation" of the Spirit.
5. We keep His Presence through obedience to the inner Voice.

Next I proceeded to ask for the Holy Spirit for myself. Nothing dramatic happened to me—no rushing wind or ecstasy or "speaking in tongues" as happened to the disciples at Pentecost. To this day I have experienced only a modicum of all that there is to know about the Helper. This is still a growing point for me, where further adventure awaits. But the little I have already learned about the Comforter I am eager to share, because it is exactly at this point that Christianity has become for me most practical and most provocative.

My first discovery was that there is nothing ethereal, no trace of the sanctimonious humbug that most people expect to find in the Holy Spirit. Nor is there any saccharine sentimentality. Quite the contrary; there is a down-to-earth quality of personality about the Holy Spirit so marked that I still would not believe it had I not experienced it.

The Spirit delights in mediating Christ to us in the everydayness of life. For instance: About two years after Peter Marshall had his first heart attack, one morning I was plagued by the insistent thought that I should learn to drive the family car. I mentioned the idea to my husband. He was not wildly enthusiastic; he knew that two drivers for one car could result in complications.

Over a matter of months the idea kept coming back, so persistently that I concluded that this was the Helper insisting. Finally Peter agreed to my taking driving lessons.

At the time of Peter's sudden death, I had been driving just long enough to have confidence to carry on. But if I had had to learn during the period of emotional turmoil immediately following his death, I might never have attempted it. Later on I realized that being able to drive also had significance in helping me towards the independence necessary to begin my new life.

The effect this sort of loving concern has on one is indescribable. To me this seems proof, as only the Comforter can give it to us, that God exists, and that He cares about us. It is one way that we can know, finally and forever, that we are loved and that this love can be expressed in simple, everyday ways straight from the unselfish heart of God.

Thus I discovered that no detail of life is too small for the Helper's concern. For years I had been hearing Christians discuss the question "Have we any right to bother God with the small details of daily life?"

Those who thought not would argue, "After all, it would be a low grade of Christian who would treat God as if He were a celestial bellhop created to serve our petty needs. Besides, since God has given us common sense, He expects us to use it for these small matters."

Certainly we should be wary of any interpretation of religion so self-centered that it continually seeks, "What can my faith do for me today? "We should have a healthy fear of making our God too small. They are right who see Him as the God of history with far-flung designs for man's destiny.

Yet the fact remains that Jesus added for us another dimension to the nature of His Father. "By all means you *should* bother the Father with details," Jesus seems to say in so many places in the gospels. He was constantly "bothering the Father" with the practicalities of life—with people's health problems, with securing the money for Peter's temple tax, with supper for a crowd of hungry listeners, with the wine running out at a wedding reception.

And after Jesus' resurrection, what then? Would men then have to revert to the God of the Old Testament—high and lifted-up, majestic, remote? No, the heavenly plan was that the Spirit would go on showing us this intimate side of the omnipotent God exactly as Jesus had. For in all ways the Spirit reflects Jesus.

Jesus cared about the everyday needs of men; so does the Spirit. Jesus stirred men's hearts, turned casual inquirers into passionate believers. Just so, the Spirit will recharge our emotions today. Sometimes I think this is the most vital work of the Spirit in the twentieth century. It has been said of our civilization that it deadens emotion. For millions of people in our thing-surfeited Western world, life has become tasteless. Nothing is as much fun as we thought it would be. Creative thought and work wither, since there are not emotional springs to nourish it. Strength and romance go out of love.

Society assumes a tepid state in which it admires detached neutrality, shows mild contempt for strong feelings. We are suspicious of anyone who becomes agitated about a principle or an issue.

This kind of apathy places our nation itself in jeopardy. Upon his retirement as Chief of Naval Operations in July 1961, Admiral Arleigh A. Burke sounded a note of warning: "I wonder if the American people have such strong convictions as they used to? We don't seem to see the necessity of living by our convictions and dying for them, if need be. I am concerned about comfortable living in relation to the people's determination to stand firm for what America believes."

If part of our problem today be lack of great passions, intense beliefs, then how is the Holy Spirit an answer? Because of His power to revive man's emotional life. For in the first century or the twentieth, people have never been able to confront Jesus Christ face to face and remain coolly impassive. Something about Him kindles either a total devotion or provokes men to violent opposition. And Jesus Himself seems always to have preferred antagonism to apathy. For apathy is the symptom of a sick and dying spirit.

Strong emotions surge through the gospels. Virile men did not leave their businesses and their homes to follow Christ without intense convictions. Men did not risk persecution and death out of lukewarmness. Those who were healed, who had sight restored, their children given back to them, could not be phlegmatic about it. The exuberance of the men who experienced the Spirit at Pentecost was such that they were accused of being drunk with new wine. Emotion beyond embarrassment, beyond caring what other people thought, towards the release of bound person-alities—all this is there for anyone to read.

I have watched the same process today in those whom the Holy Spirit touches. Feelings are sensitized. Life takes on relish. Joys are heightened. Here is the way one woman described her encounter with the Spirit:

> . . . I saw no new thing, but I saw all the usual things in a miraculous new light. I saw for the first time how wildly beautiful and joyous, beyond any words of mine to describe, is the whole of life. Every human being . . . every sparrow that flew, every branch tossing in the wind, was caught up in and was a part of the whole mad ecstasy of loveliness, of joy, of importance, of intoxication of life. . . .[11]

In the experience of everyone to whom I have talked about the Spirit, the word *joy* stands out. In the rebirth of our emotional selves this seems to be the essential missing ingredient which the Holy Spirit supplies.

I have written earlier in this book of the joy of childhood. For me it was in the fragrance of mint and honeysuckle, the feel of bare feet on moss, ice-cold apples, the magnificent fury of a thunderstorm, the far horizons of blue Appalachians. And all my life I have felt that this early joy was trying to teach me something, that it was not just a sentiment restricted to childhood. It seemed to reveal something fundamental and basic about the nature of the universe itself.

Surely I was right; surely this is the way things are in God's world! But only now do I see how God intends for us to know this. It is the Holy Spirit who is to open our eyes to the joy which undergirds the universe.

It was the Holy Spirit who opened Marianne Brown's eyes. Mrs. Brown is the wife of the Presbyterian minister in the small town of Parkesburg, Pennsylvania, mother of five children and mistress of an old-fashioned rambling eleven-room manse. The details of her story come directly from her.

Six years ago, if you had asked Marianne Brown what was the most basic truth about life, the last thing she would have answered would have been "joy!" She might have said "duty" or even, if she had been feeling brutally honest, "exhaustion."

Like many another minister's wife, Mrs. Brown was trapped in a maelstrom of activity—church meetings, the presidency of the women's organization, constant entertaining, a neighborhood kindergarten, supervising the area recreation program. She had a merciless conscience that drove her and a concern about other people's opinions that made her unable to say *no* to any request. Like most ministers' wives, she was not able to afford any household help.

Her one escape from exhaustion was to be ill at frequent intervals and go to bed for rest. This was not too difficult to manage, because the constantly overtired woman was an easy target for assorted viruses and disorders. Furthermore she had been born with a congenital heart defect, diagnosed by the doctors as mitral stenosis.

Marianne would lie in bed and brood. Why was her vitality so low? Why did black moods descend so often, periods of retreating within herself? Sometimes she would go for days, speaking grudgingly even to her family. She introduced every other thought with the words, "The trouble is—" It was indicative of her joyless outlook on life.

"Looking back now," she told me, "it seems to me that all my life had been a search for the joy that had been denied me. I remember once seeing a ragged child standing at the great wrought-iron gates of an estate, his hands clasping the bars. His eyes were glued wistfully on the winding walks among the great trees, the sweep of lawn in which he might have run and tumbled, the flower-beds, even a brook where a small boy might have gone wading and fishing . . .

"Well, I was like that little boy, hungrily staring at vistas of joy that seemed forever closed to me. That is, until six years ago."

Then six years ago a new life began for Marianne—quietly enough. A neighbor dropped in one morning. Over a cup of coffee at the breakfast table, the harassed minister's wife poured out her troubles. The friend admitted that she had no answers for Marianne but suggested that they pray together.

They did. There was nothing unusual or dramatic about the prayer. Yet it seemed to relieve the pressures, so they prayed together again. Then, one by one, other friends joined them. Eventually there was a small group of husbands and wives who met in each other's homes each Saturday evening.

A family crisis overtook the Browns soon afterward. Their high-school-age daughter suffered a nervous breakdown. The group that met in prayer gave them important support through the crisis. And once again prayer brought startling results.

Their daughter's early recovery filled the Browns with gratitude to God and to the friends who had shouldered their problems with them. On a certain Saturday night, as the meeting was being closed with a circle of prayer, Marianne found herself slipping to her knees as deep feelings of thanksgiving to God for His nearness and goodness bubbled up and spilled over into words, words that came and kept coming in a torrent.

Then suddenly—to Marianne Brown in Parkesburg, Pennsylvania in 1955—the Holy Spirit came. She had done no studying or thinking about the Comforter, indeed, was scarcely aware of Him at all. Let Marianne tell it:

> *God's Spirit took over and seemed to immerse my whole being—body, mind, and spirit. The Spirit came like tidal waves of "joy unspeakable and full of glory" and inundated me. Torrents of God's love swept over me for what seemed only a few minutes but lasted a long time. More than once I wondered if my human body could bear the ecstasy, and I both begged God to stop and feared that He would!*
>
> *That night my emotions found perfect expression. I know now that my emotions had been starved. I had been only half-living, because I had been only half-feeling.*
>
> *In those minutes God revealed more to me than I had ever learned in books . . . I knew that for the remainder of my life Jesus Himself would be my first love. In Him every desire I had ever had was fulfilled. And I knew that such communion with God is His will for every human being!*

Marianne's friends, even her husband, were stunned at what they were witnessing. The Reverend Mr. Brown had preached about Pentecost, talked about the Holy Spirit, sometimes in knowing theological tones. But witnessing Him in action—that was something else again! He and most of those present had always been wary of emotionalism in religion. We Presbyterians usually are! With the erudite John Calvin of Geneva and starchy John Knox of Edinburgh as the fathers of our church, this is only natural. And the educated clergy upon which the Presbyterian church has always insisted, usually puts inordinate emphasis on the mind, little emphasis on the emotions.

So it was a confused and wondering group that at a late hour reluctantly told one another good night and went back to their respective homes. Though they were not yet ready to admit it to each other, already something had happened to each of them through Marianne's experience: they too wanted the Holy Spirit and joy!

In the weeks that followed their wish was granted. It was like a fire that had descended on Marianne and then leaped from person to person, including her minister husband! As the fire spread, the group was welded together in a way none of them had ever known before.

There was no difficulty now in sharing with one another thoughts, joys, fears, hopes, disappointments, problems, triumphs. They lived in each other's lives, not just spiritually, but in practical fashion too. They were discovering *Koinonia*, the fellowship of the Holy Spirit that the first-century infant church had experienced following Pentecost. Eventually the one group grew into a series of them throughout the local church community.

As for Marianne herself, "Six years have passed since then," she told me. "I have not spent one day of them in bed. I find myself able, without fatigue, to care for my big house and the needs of my family, still without outside help. And there is more entertaining than ever. Our home is open house to friends from all over the world.

"The guidance of the Helper about my daily tasks is quite specific. He has enabled me to say a sure 'No' to what He does not want me to do. For what He directs me to undertake, there is an unfailing supply of vitality. Sometimes I have taught as many as five Bible classes a week."

Marianne Brown no longer searches for joy. She bubbles over with it. Her voice lilts with it. Life itself is joy.

It is the same exuberant joy that we experience as children. Christ said: "Except ye become as little children, ye shall not enter into the kingdom of heaven."[12] It is the Spirit saying *yea* to man's *can I*?

At the beginning of the book, I referred to the point, so often made now, that the only hope for our world is a change in human nature itself. Is it possible that the rising tide of interest in the Spirit all across the United States today is evidence that the Helper is undertaking this task?

One day last year two friends and I spent part of an afternoon in the apartment of Dr. Henry Pitney Van Dusen, President of Union

Theological Seminary, discussing this very possibility. Dr. Van Dusen's book on the Holy Spirit, *Spirit, Son, and Father*, reflects his own increasing emphasis on the Spirit as the most effective agent in human life.

The conversation turned to what each of us there that afternoon had at one time discovered: that the Spirit repeatedly brings us back to Jesus' emphasis—that real faith is no otherworldy affair. I know that again and again in recent years He has plucked me out of the clouds of theoretical Christianity back to earth where I belonged.

For when we allow the Spirit to guide us He will concern Himself with how we use our time and spend our money; with honesty and moral integrity and Christlike quality of character; with what is happening to our children; with the health of our relationship with other people and with our God. And, if our need is severe enough, the Holy Spirit will turn our lives upside down.

For man's chief problem is still man. The search that begins at the point of our need—the longing for Something More—in the end brings us back full circle to the inner man. With the threat of thermonuclear war hanging over us, civilization's problem is still unredeemed individuals. No summit meeting is held, no international conference convened but that our quandary is dramatized for us.

How, then, can human nature change? Men have demonstrated that they cannot change themselves. Nor can men change other men. We have seen that education does not necessarily achieve it, nor legislation, nor raising incomes, nor plying them with all the gadgets that money can buy. That brings us to the crown of the Holy Spirit's work among men. Only Christ can change human nature, and it is the Holy Spirit that makes Christ available to needy mankind.

That is what happened to Saul of Tarsus, to Augustine, to Ignatius Loyola, to St. Francis of Assisi, and to thousands through the centuries. It is still happening to men and women in our day.

How drastically and profoundly the Holy Spirit can turn a man's character upside down was demonstrated in the case of Starr Daily.

It was the year 1924. In a courtroom in the Midwest, the judge's voice was grave as he looked down at the prisoner standing before him. "I am about to sentence you to a major prison for the third time. I know you are sick. And I know that more punishment is not the remedy. But your record leaves me powerless."

And so "hopeless criminal" was society's judgment of Starr Daily. The verdict seemed justified. At sixteen Starr's only ambition had been to build a reputation as a dangerous man. He dreamed of the time when the police would refer to him with a shudder.

He achieved his aim by becoming the leader of a gang of safecrackers. There was no safe he could not open, no time lock he could not take apart. But finally liquor made him careless, and he was caught.

There followed fourteen years of penal farms, chain gangs, and two extended penitentiary sentences. Through all that time Starr's father never lost hope that his son might be redeemed from his life of crime. His best efforts failed. He lived to see his Starr re-enter prison for the third time. Starr never saw his father after that. The broken-hearted man died with a prayer for his son on his lips.

In prison Starr made two futile attempts to escape. Then he evolved a plan to instigate a prison riot. The deputy warden was to be seized and used as a shield and hostage. A stoolpigeon betrayed the plan, and Starr was sentenced to the dungeon.

Most strong men could not survive "the hole" for more than fifteen days. American prisons thirty-five years ago could be grim and brutal places. It was winter, and the walls of the dank cell seeped moisture. At six every morning, the prisoner would be given a piece of bread and a cup of water. Then he would be left hanging in handcuffs for twelve hours. At six in the evening, he would be let down for the night and given another piece of bread and another cup of water.

Starr survived fifteen days of this. By the last day in the cuffs, he could no longer stand on feet black with congealed blood. That morning "the Bull"—the keeper of the hole—had to lift the almost-unconscious man into the cuffs.

For weeks after that, the prisoner was allowed to lie on the icy stone floor—emaciated, unspeakably filthy, near death. He lost track of time. Mired in the lowest hell imaginable, only hate was keeping him alive— hate for the Bull, hate for the deputy warden who had vowed that he would force Starr to crawl to him like a dog, begging mercy.

Then there came a moment when the man on the floor was too weak to hate. Through that momentary opening crept a strange new thought:

All of my life I have been a dynamo of energy. What might have happened if I had used that energy for something good?

Then the thought faded. *It's too late now; I'm dying.* There followed a half-waking, half-sleeping state of unconsciousness: moments of delirium, times of awareness.

This was followed by disconnected dreams, like mists floating across the brain. Time was no more. The prisoner was aware no longer of the frozen stone floor, of his filth, or of anyone who came or went.

Finally, the dreams began to take on meaning, to become rational in form and sequence. Suddenly Starr seemed to be in a garden. He knew that he had been in this same garden before—many times in childhood. It was in a shoe-shaped valley surrounded by gentle hills. At one end of the garden a great white-gray rock jutted out. Then Jesus Christ, the Man whom he had been trying to avoid all his life, was coming toward him. Now He stood face to face with Starr, looking deep into his eyes as if penetrating to the bottom of his soul. Love of a quality that he had never before felt was drawing the hate out of his heart, like extracting poison from an infected wound.

With a strange clarity, one part of Starr's mind thought *I am submerged in Reality, I'll never be the same again, now and through all eternity.*

There followed another dream in which all the people Starr had ever injured passed before his eyes. One by one, he poured out his love to them.

Then all who had injured him appeared, and on them too he bestowed the love needed to restore and to heal. The love flowed from beyond him, poured through him in a torrent of caring and ecstatic gratitude.

When the prisoner returned to consciousness, the cell did not look the same. Its grim grayness was gone. For him it was illuminated with a warm light. His feelings too were different. The prison environment no longer had the power to give him pain, only joy.

The next thing Starr knew, the door opened and the Bull said in a tone of voice Starr had never before heard him use, "Are you hungry? I could steal a sandwich from the kitchen and bring it to you."

The prisoner stared in amazement. But he was even more startled at his own reply, "No, don't do that. Don't risk your neck by breaking a rule for me."

It was the Bull's turn to be astonished. He went off wonderingly, came back with the doctor, and Starr was carried to the prison hospital. Through a swift and surprising series of events, prison doors swung open for Starr Daily in March 1930, five years ahead of the time set for his release.

Was his experience on the cell floor a hallucination? No, not unless we would call what happened to Saul of Tarsus a hallucination. The proof was the change in the man. He who had been declared incorrigible by penologists, was from that moment cured of all criminal tendencies.

Peter Marshall loved the man that Starr Daily became and delighted in telling his story from the pulpit of the New York Avenue Presbyterian Church in Washington. In 1954, when I was in Hollywood for script conferences on *A Man Called Peter,* I drove out to the Daily's home in Van Nuys, California, for an overnight visit with Starr and his wife Marie.

A tall spare man, graying now, Starr's face bears the lines of the long hard years. But flashes of dry humor, spoken in a Midwestern drawl, light up the face.

From this man who had only a sixth-grade education have come eight books. He has lectured all over the nation. His knowledge of the criminal mind has contributed to valuable rethinking of prison techniques. He has personally been the Holy Spirit's vehicle for the reclamation of scores of criminals.

In speaking to me recently about the experience that changed his life, Starr Daily said, "The Holy Spirit came to me through the glorified Christ. He did not give me the gifts of the Spirit, rather the fruits of the spirit to be worked out in a day-to-day discipline. Perhaps that was necessary in my case, so that the fruits could be integrated with the drastic character changes necessary. Anyway, you remember that St. Paul said that this was "the most excellent way."

Can we change human nature? No, but the Holy Spirit can. His all-encompassing love is Jesus' love for us, the extension of Jesus' life and power in our day. The Helper takes our needs as His own. Our dangers He enters into with us. Our perplexities He illumines. Our joyousness, He sanctifies.

The Spirit was with John Sherrill that day when he entered into Life by saying *Yes* to Christ. He was with Stuart Luhan that night when the Winecoff Hotel caught on fire.

The Counselor helped my friend Beverley through the crisis with her boy, Kenneth. He enabled Raymond Thomas to dream of a better life than Radical Hill could bring him. He is with Betty Elliot and her small daughter, Valerie, in the South American jungle. And even now He is with Karen Emmott out in Oklahoma City—Karen of the piquant face, who still hopes to live her life in "the old natural normal way."

Do without Him? How could any of us who have embarked on the pilgrimage that is Christianity do without Him? For we who long for something more, for strength and hope and wisdom beyond our selves, discover to our joy that as the Comforter reveals Christ to us, in Him we have our heart's desire.

Fifteen
Afterglow

IT WAS THE afternoon of May first. I sat at the typewriter in my basement office. Through the picture window, I could see the first faint traces
of green on the sweep of trees down the hill. Spring had come late to
New York state this year.

Suddenly the telephone rang shrilly. Mother's voice leaped at me
over the wires from Evergreen Farm in Virginia. Her voice sounded
strange, I thought.

"Catherine, I have bad news," she said. Then there was a long pause.
"Dad's gone—"

"Dad is gone—?"

She rushed breathlessly on. "Dr. Oliver just came to tell me—"

"How? When?"

"About fifteen minutes ago. Dad left the house, saying he was going
up to the store for the mail, that he'd be back right away. He never came
back."

"You mean—?"

"He was sitting on a wooden chair in the store, talking and joking
with Mr. Janney and some other men. All at once he gave two faint
sighs—and that was it."

I sat staring at my typewriter, trying to take this in.

501

"Dr. Oliver tells me that when he got there, Dad was still sitting in the chair, his legs crossed, his hands on his lap. His head was bowed a little. There was a peaceful, happy expression on his face—"

"Oh, Mother—darling—" Desperately I tried to collect my thoughts. "It will be forty minutes or so before I can tell Len. He's on his way home from the New York office now. He will know about plane schedules to Washington. I'll get there just as soon as I can."

"Catherine, will you telephone Peter John at Yale—?"

"You know I will. Immediately."

As it turned out, Peter was in glee club rehearsal, where the group was working on numbers for the concert tour of South America scheduled for the summer. He did not get the news about his grandfather until early that evening.

How suddenly death interrupts life!

Yet two nights later, as the family gathered in the living room at Evergreen, it was not so much grief that we felt, but gratitude. In seventy-six years, Dad had lived a rich, full life. Forty-six active years in the ministry, nearly five wonderful years on the farm.

He had lived to give his blessing to Leonard LeSourd and me by performing our wedding ceremony on November 14, 1959, in the little Presbyterian Church in Leesburg, Virginia. Though he had shared the service with Len's father and with Dr. Norman Vincent Peale, it was he who had insisted on pronouncing the solemn words that launched us on our new life: "By the authority vested in me as a minister of the Church of Christ. . . ."

A lifetime dream had been fulfilled the preceding summer in a trip to Europe to see the Passion Play. And at Eastertime, as if to round out his last year, every member of Dad's large family had been gathered around him, including the three new grandchildren—Jeffrey, Chester, and Linda LeSourd.

Then there had been the Golden Wedding Anniversary celebration. Just a year ago, the old farmhouse had glowed and shone and overflowed with friends, some of whom had driven long distances to share Mother's and Father's joy. Exactly a year later on this third of May, Mother had memories that blessed and burned. On this, the evening of their fifty-first anniversary, Mother could not bear the thought of leaving at the impersonal funeral parlor the earthly form that Dad had cast off. That was why the casket was close by now in the farmhouse where our family had gathered.

"But how wonderful it was," Mother said, "that John had all this last year."

We spoke of our gratitude too for the gracious small providences of the last hours. How hard it would have been for Mother if she had been alone with Dad at the end. And what if heart failure had occurred at the wheel of his car on the way to the store? He had been spared invalidism too. How he would have hated giving up his projects! To the end, he was busy with them. We began enumerating them . . .

Only three days before he had finished building a wagon bed so sturdy that we wondered if the farm tractor could haul it.

Then, with as much delight as a small boy with a first wagon, he had painted it bright, shiny red. On the day of his death, he had been wondering about how many baby chickens to buy this year; how many new strawberry plants to set; how soon he and Earl Cook, our helper on the farm, could start work on the second terrace by the chicken house. Then of course, the base for the sundial had to be built—

My brother-in-law, Harlow Hoskins, said at that point, "But I thought Dad was planning on using the stump of the bee tree as a base for the sundial—"

"You mean," and there was a certain supercilious note in Peter John's voice, "the stump of that tree that Mother made forever famous with her deathless prose."

"Make fun of it, if you will, young man," his grandmother retorted. "Believe it or not, lots of visitors have wanted to see the stump of that locust tree."

"I can give you some new material, Catherine," my brother Bob added teasingly. "This happened when I was a little boy. Did you know about the Christmas that Pop was standing at the top of a ladder, trying to plug strings of outdoor Christmas lights into the socket on the porch ceiling? His hand slipped and he stuck his thumb in the socket. He let out a roar, almost leaped off the ladder, and out came a word that was hardly—um—ministerial. Then he looked down at me sitting on the porch floor, staring up at him with my mouth hanging open.

" 'Just forget I said that, son,' he said in a gruff voice."

Bob chuckled. "What Pop didn't know was that suddenly I felt a new and close bond with him. We men had shared something rather special."

A childish shriek in the hall pierced our conversation. Mary, my sister-in-law, and Em both rushed for their respective children, who had been playing tag on the stairs. Voices in the hall quieted down immediately, and we resumed our conversation. But a few minutes later, seven-year-old Mary Margaret crept into the room.

"Bobby is sitting on the top step and won't play any more and won't come down," she reported in her soft voice.

"Never mind, Mary," Mother said. "I'll take care of this."

Then we heard her voice. "Bobby, you misunderstood. Your mother wasn't shushing you because she thought you were being disrespectful of your grandfather. Why, Grandfather wouldn't want you children to be sad and long-faced. He's happy, and he wants you to be happy too. Besides, he loved having you children around him. You know that—"

"Oh, thank you, Grandmother," we heard Bobby say. She started to speak but then her voice trailed off, smothered in a little boy's hug.

Peter John shook his head wonderingly. "And on the night before the funeral. What a woman!"

"I suppose my children come by their exuberance naturally," Bob grinned. "Remember the lard-can story, Em?"

"Remember it! How could I forget it?"

Then they both started talking at once.

I looked up at Peter Marshall's portrait. It was easy to imagine what he would be saying at that moment, "Same old family.... Haven't changed a bit!"

Peter John observed, "We need Grandfather's booming voice to referee."

"All right," Em conceded. "I'll pass. You tell it, Bob."

"Well, Father was always immaculately dressed before he went into the pulpit of a Sunday morning. If possible he liked to wear a flower in his buttonhole. On this particular Sunday morning, he was wearing a freshly pressed white suit and white shoes—the only pair of white ones he owned. Just before leaving for the church, he headed for the back garden where he knew some Ragged Robins were in bloom.

"What he didn't know was that Em and I had booby-trapped the garden. We had begged empty lard cans from Mother—big ones—fifteen-pound tins. Then we'd sunk the cans in the earth, filled them with water, and neatly laid twigs and tufts of grass across the top to camouflage them."

"It was a dirty trick," Em muttered.

"Anyway, Father walked right into one of the traps set in the middle of the garden path. Em and I heard him bellow like a wounded bull and we ducked for hiding places. But he was in a fine fury and promptly rooted us out. One of his pant legs was wet halfway up and, of course, his shoe was sopping. I'm afraid Em and I didn't further his spiritual state that Sunday."

My sister Em picked up the conversation. "I was lying awake last night, remembering a lot of things too. Len, you've never heard this one. . . ."

Then she related an incident from Father's West Virginia pastorate. One day he had been seeking out a newcomer in town who worked in the Round House at the Baltimore and Ohio railroad yards. When Father finally located the man, he found him repairing an engine.

"Sorry, I can't shake hands with you, Preacher," the man said, holding up hands black with coal dust and engine grease.

Impulsively, my father stooped over and rubbed his hands in the soot that lay an inch thick on the floor. "Now there's no difference between us," he said. "You see, sir, I *want* to shake your hand."

"That man," Em added, "was father's friend for life."

"I can believe that story," Len said. "I've never known a man who loved people so much—all kinds of people. In Europe last summer, while Catherine and her mother would be looking at monuments or museums or paintings, Dad would be carrying on lively conversations with a bell-hop, a guard, a policeman, or assorted shopkeepers."

Len was right about Father's love for people. How wholeheartedly people responded was dramatized for us by this incident, among many. Frank Scott and others from Dad's Eastern Shore Church drove all night to get to the funeral. Mr. Scott is a farmer and a man of few words. "I loved Mr. Wood," he said simply as he gripped my hand. "I had to come."

The funeral service was anything but somber. David Crawford, the minister, had told me earlier, "Your father and I had a fine relationship. In fact, so good that he could tease me almost constantly. I couldn't possibly be long-faced in any service for him. If you don't mind, I'd like to make this a model of what I long for every funeral service to be."

So there was congregational singing. We sang Martin Luther's triumphant hymn

> A mighty fortress is our God,
> A bulwark never failing. . . .

I looked round and saw Earl Cook standing in the back of the church, cap in hand, his dusky face glowing, singing more lustily than any of us.

Mr. Crawford stood in front of the almost-full church. His head was lifted high, a look of exaltation on his face. He had picked passages of Scripture with the same ringing note in them. One sentence from the 121st Psalm leaped out at me:

> The Lord shall preserve thy going out and thy
> coming in from this time forth, and even for
> evermore.

Not a member of our family could escape the feeling that for Dad the Lord had fulfilled that promise exactly. Sitting there in the little church, my thoughts went back to the final afternoon of his life . . .

"I'm going out for the mail," he had said. "I'll be right back."

The love of God had tenderly overshadowed him as he went. The end must not come at the little single-land bridge abutment. No—not there. Nor at the sharp bend in the road by the Quaker Meeting House. No, he must have friends near, like Mr. Janney who owns the store— Mr. Janney, so much a part of the tiny community, the great-great-great-grandson of Hannah Janney. Why, as father was driving to the store, he passed the spot where Hannah is buried. . . . I like to remember Hannah. About the time another Quaker family was building Evergreen, she had been busy having twelve children. But she still had time to be the leader of the Meeting and the arbiter for the community to the end of her ninety-three years. . . . Yes, somehow it was fitting that it was Mr. Janney who had been with Dad at the end. . . .

So if the Lord had preserved Dad's going out in that minute way, we were sure that He had preserved his coming in to his new life as well.

That was why we could not be gloomy during the fifty-mile ride to the cemetery.

The procession traveled over the new George Washington Memorial parkway where the first glimpse of Washington is the spires of Georgetown. . . . Across the Memorial Bridge where the gold Italian statues glitter in the spring sunlight . . . Circle the Lincoln Memorial and let the eyes rest on its white symmetry. Surely the most beautiful building in Washington. . . . The cherry trees around the Tidal Basin are fading now.

Down Constitution Avenue—so familiar, so familiar. How many times I have traveled it. And on into the Maryland countryside to Fort Lincoln Cemetery . . . Peter Marshall had preached so many sunrise Easter services there. Now father will lie close to him. . . .

On the day after the funeral, Mother and I were going through Father's desk. From one drawer, I pulled out a letter that I recognized. It was a love letter I had spontaneously dashed off to Dad several months before.

"I'm surprised that he kept it," I commented.

"He read it over and over," Mother said. "You'll never know how much it meant to him."

I had forgotten what I said. Curiously I opened it:

I knew you were not feeling well when I told you goodbye at the airport. I've been thinking about you ever since then. This is being written on an impulse. Sometimes it's good to follow these spot impulses, speak what's in the heart. . . .

You and Mother gave me the most gorgeous childhood any little girl ever had, because you gave me so much of yourself. Remember all the things you built for me? That set of doll furniture . . . The little cupboard with the glass doors . . . And the dresser with its swinging mirror and the tiny glass knobs. I can see it yet.

Then there was the house in the cherry tree you made for me. And the croquet court with lights strung overhead. These were the myriad ways you entered so deeply into the lives of us children.

But of course, the greatest thing that you and Mother did for us was to bequeath us the sure knowledge of the love and goodness of God abroad in the world.

*Am I getting too sentimental? What I really want to say is, you're very
dear to me. . . .*

Slowly I returned the letter to its envelope and put it back in the
drawer. I was glad that I had followed my heart and written it.

Then I picked up Dad's final bank statement. I could scarcely believe what I was seeing. His balance was sixty-five cents.

It is true that you can't take it with you. But who ever heard of
anyone coming out *that* even at the end of life?

How typical of Dad! He never did have any money. The salaries of
preachers in small towns are notoriously small. Yet always he had been
supplied with every need—even to a college education for each of his
children and Evergreen Farm for his retirement. His sixty-five-cent statement somehow seemed right.

Father's life had taught me the one thing that really matters—
human relationships. The bonds that unite families and friends are not
forged for a little while, they are for eternity. They stretch across every
boundary of space and time. They twine and intertwine from one generation to another, weave and interweave, priceless beyond measure.
They are something to be cherished, to be fought for, to be kept intact
at all cost. People—with their fears and their foibles and their dreams.
People—with their struggles toward faith, with the pain and the exaltation of their pilgrimage. People—with personalities that live on and on,
growing, learning, loving, lending helping hands to others. *People*—that
is what life is all about.

Mother broke in on my soaring thoughts. Her mind was darting
ahead in several directions: "Probably the baby calf will be born in a few
days. . . . Oh, and Catherine, we must let Mrs. Ten Wolde in the Netherlands and Ray in Vienna know, as soon as possible, about Dad's death. . . .
Oh, and I've been thinking. There are some fine young people down at
the orphanage in the Valley of Virginia. You know, it might mean a lot
to one of those high school boys to live and work on the farm this
summer—"

In her eyes I saw the promise of the future.

Notes

Chapter 1: *Something More*
1. *Life* (November 28, 1960), p. 101.
2. The material that follows is from a speech made by Major William Meyer, Army Medical Corps, in San Francisco in 1958. This material has now been declassified by the Department of Defense.
3. Russell W. Davenport, *The Dignity of Man* (New York: Harper & Brothers, 1955), p. 25.

Chapter 2: *The Unselfishness of God*
1. Deuteronomy 33:27
2. Taken from Romans 8:35–39
3. Romans 8:28
4. This and what follows is detailed beginning on page 219 of Hannah W. Smith's *My Spiritual Autobiography, Or How I Discovered the Unselfishness of God* (New York: Fleming H. Revell Company, 1903).
5. Psalm 145:9
6. John 6:38 (Moffatt)
7. John 14:9 (Moffatt)
8. Luke 15:11–32
9. Matthew 7:9–11 (Moffatt)
10. Cairns, D. S., *The Faith That Rebels* (New York: R. R. Smith, Inc., 1930), pp. 211–213.
11. II Timothy 1:12 (Moffatt)

Chapter 3: *How to Enter In*
1. Luke 6:46
2. Matthew 12:43–45 (Moffatt)

Chapter 4: *The Secret of the Will*
1. Revelation 3:20

2. This and the quotes that follow are from Oursler's *Why I Know There Is a God* (New York: Doubleday & Company, 1950), pp. 17–20.
3. Philippians 2:13

Chapter 5: *Dare to Trust God*
1. Luke 7:50
2. Matthew 9:29
3. Mark 9:23
4. Matthew 21:22 (Moffatt)
5. Psalm 34:8
6. John 16:24 (Moffatt)
7. Matthew 7:11 (Moffatt)
8. Matthew 6:33
9. Psalm 81:10
10. Luke 12:33 (Moffatt)
11. James 2:17 (Moffatt)
12. I John 5:10 (Moffatt)

Chapter 6: *The Prayer of Relinquishment*
1. I Corinthians 1:25 (Moffatt)
2. Matthew 27:11–24; John 19:9–12
3. J. B. Phillips, *The Gospels Translated into Modern English* (New York: The Macmillan Company, 1942), p. 104.

Chapter 7: *Forgive Us Our Sins . . .*
1. John 1:9
2. John 6:37
3. Isaiah 1:18
4. Psalm 86:5
5. John 15:3
6. I John 5:19, 3:19 (Moffatt)
7. C. G. Jung, *Modern Man in Search of a Soul* (New York: Harcourt, Brace & Co., 1933), pp. 39, 40.
8. From Peter Marshall's sermon "Letters in the Sand," *A Man Called Peter* (New York: McGraw-Hill Book Company, Inc., 1951), p. 321.

Chapter 8: . . . *As We Forgive Those Who Sin Against Us*
1. Matthew 6:14, 15
2. Matthew 5:23,24
3. Ephesians 4:32
4. Matthew 6:15

Chapter 9: *How to Find God's Guidance*
1. Proverbs 3:6
2. John 10:3,6
3. James 1:5
4. John 16:13
5. Hannah Whitall Smith, *My Spiritual Autobiography*, pp. 70–72.
6. Romans 8:14 (Moffatt)

Chapter 10: *The Power of Helplessness*
1. Psalm 4:1 (Moffatt)
2. Romans 8:28
3. Fritz Künkel and Roy E. Dickerson, *How Character Develops* (New York: Charles Scribner's Sons, 1947), pp. 131–32.
4. John 15:5 (Moffatt)
5. *The Interpreter's Bible*, Vol. 8., p. 715.
6. John 6:44 (Moffatt)
7. John 6:15–16
8. Ephesians 2:8,9
9. John 5:30
10. A. B. Simpson, *The Gospel of Healing* (Harrisburg, Pa: Christian Publishers, 1915), p. 169.
11. Genesis 45:5,8
12. Genesis 50:20
13. Matthew 16:52 (Moffatt)
14. John 19:11 (Moffatt)
15. John 10:17,18

Chapter 11: *The Prayer That Makes Dreams Come True*
1. Glenn Clark's *I Will Lift Up Mine Eyes* (New York: Harper & Bros., 1937).

2. Mark 10:47,51 (Moffatt)

Chapter 12: *Ego-Slaying*
1. Mark 8:35
2. C. S. Lewis, *Beyond Personality* (New York: The Macmillan Company, 1947), p. 40.
3. Romans 6:1–11
4. Künkel and Dickerson, *How Character Develops*, pp. 105, 114
5. Colossians 3:3 (Moffatt)
6. Luke 9:23
7. Hebrews 12:6,7,11 (Moffatt)

Chapter 13: *The Gospel of Healing*
1. Luke 4:39
2. Luke 4:18
3. Luke 5:12; Mark 9:23,24
4. Luke 9:11 (Moffatt)
5. Matthew 5:10
6. Matthew 16:1–4
7. Luke 6:8–10
8. Luke 13:10–13
9. Luke 7:11–16
10. Luke 8:27–35
11. Luke 10:1–16
12. Luke 10:18
13. Luke 10:21,22
14. Mark 16:15,18
15. Hebrews 13:8 (Moffatt)
16. Matthew 28:20
17. John 5:6 (Moffatt)
18. Mark 11:4 (Moffatt)
19. Luke 19:9
20. Luke 13:12 (Moffatt)
21. Matthew 18:19 (Moffatt)
22. Another daughter of Dr. Bell, Ruth, is Mrs. Billy Graham
23. Matthew 13:58

Chapter 14: *Journey into Joy*
1. John 1:14
2. John 7:39,16:14
3. John 14:12
4. John 16:12,13
5. Galatians 2:20
6. I Corinthians 6:19
7. John 16:13–15
8. John 14:17; I Corinthians 2:14
9. John 1:33; Luke 11:13; John 14:16
10. Luke 24:49; Acts 1:4, 5,8
11. Margaret Prescott Montague, "Twenty Minutes of Reality," *Atlantic Monthly* (November 1916).
12. Matthew 18:3

Index